Popular representations of development and p
us, and scholars need to understand these alte
to enrich their own discipline-based analysis a
excellent volume suggests some ways in whic
gains and the pitfalls of engagement. It is a th
important issue in development studies.

Ravi Kanbur, Cornell University, USA

This book is for a worthy cause, that of going beyond the currently popular
quantitative and experimental approach to economic development, to look
into wider, often more insightful, humanistic forms of representation of the
development process. It shows how representations in literature, films,
television, and internet may capture the complexity and nuances of the social
processes involved in development in ways not considered in the standard
approach.

Pranab Bardhan, University of California, Berkeley, USA

This wonderfully engaging and thought-provoking collection provides many
lessons about representation and power for researchers and students alike. It will
prove to be an invaluable teaching resource and will become a benchmark for
much future research.

Cathy McIlwaine, University of London, UK

An important milestone in development studies which shows how literature,
film and other discourses need to be part of the mix when we try to understand
how other people live.

Giles Foden, author of The Last King of Scotland *and* Turbulence

An essential analysis of the world of international development… and essential
reading for rock stars everywhere.

Richard Bean, author of The God Botherers *and* One Man, Two Guvnors

Popular Representations of Development

Although the academic study of development is well established, as is its policy implementation, less considered are the broader, more popular understandings of development that often shape agendas and priorities, particularly in representative democracies.

Through its accessible and provocative chapters, *Popular Representations of Development* introduces the idea that while the issue of 'development' – defined broadly as problems of poverty and social deprivation, and the various agencies and processes seeking to address these – is normally one that is discussed by social scientists and policymakers, it also has a wider 'popular' dimension. Development is something that can be understood through studying literature, films, and other non-conventional forms of representation. It is also a public issue, one that has historically been associated with musical movements such as Live Aid and increasingly features in newer media such as blogs and social networking. The book connects the effort to build a more holistic understanding of development issues with an exploration of the diverse public sphere in which popular engagement with development takes place.

This book gives students of development studies, media studies, and geography as well as students in the humanities engaging with global development issues a variety of perspectives from different disciplines to open up this new field for discussion.

David Lewis is Professor of Social Policy and Development at the London School of Economics & Political Science (LSE), UK.

Dennis Rodgers is Professor of Urban Social and Political Research at the University of Glasgow, UK.

Michael Woolcock is Lead Social Development Specialist with the World Bank's Development Research Group in Washington, DC, and Lecturer in Public Policy at the Harvard Kennedy School, Harvard University, USA.

Rethinking Development

Popular Representations of Development
Insights from novels, films, television and social media
Edited by David Lewis, Dennis Rodgers and Michael Woolcock

Popular Representations of Development

Insights from novels, films, television and social media

**Edited by
David Lewis,
Dennis Rodgers and
Michael Woolcock**

Routledge
Taylor & Francis Group

LONDON AND NEW YORK

First published 2014
by Routledge
2 Park Square, Milton Park, Abingdon, Oxon OX14 4RN

Simultaneously published in the USA and Canada
by Routledge
711 Third Avenue, New York, NY 10017

Routledge is an imprint of the Taylor & Francis Group, an informa business

British Library Cataloguing in Publication Data
A catalogue record for this book is available from the British Library

Library of Congress Cataloging-in-Publication Data
Popular representations of development : insights from novels, films,
television and social media / [edited by] David Lewis, Dennis Rodgers,
Michael Woolcock.
   pages cm
Includes bibliographical references and index.
1. Economic development. 2. Popular culture. 3. Mass media. I. Lewis,
David, 1960- editor of compilation. II. Rodgers, Dennis, editor of
compilation. III. Woolcock, Michael J. V., 1964- editor of compilation.
HD75.P67 2013
338.9–dc23   2013009466

ISBN13: 978-0-415-82280-0 (hbk)
ISBN13: 978-0-415-82281-7 (pbk)
ISBN13: 978-0-203-55324-4 (ebk)

Typeset in Times New Roman
by Cenveo Publisher Services

Printed and bound in Great Britain by
CPI Group (UK) Ltd, Croydon, CR0 4YY

Contents

Figures and tables

Figures

Tables

Contributors

Veronica Davidov is Assistant Professor of Anthropology at Leiden University College. She is an environmental anthropologist interested in human–nature relations, the transformation of nature into natural resources, and discourses and practices of sustainable development. She has done long-term fieldwork in Ecuador, and is now also working on a project in Northern Russia.

Tobias Denskus is a Senior Lecturer in Communication for Development at Malmö University in Sweden. His research on social media, peace-building, and organisational ethnography has been published in a variety of academic journals. He blogs at www.aidnography.de.

Daniel E. Esser is Assistant Professor of International Development in American University's School of International Service and a former international civil servant in the United Nations system. His research has been published in *World Development*, *Urban Studies*, the *Journal of Modern African Studies*, *Third World Quarterly*, *Ethics and International Affairs*, *Environment and Urbanization*, *Critical Planning* and in the *Journal of Business Ethics*, among others. He blogs at http://danielesser.org.

John Harriss is Professor of International Studies at Simon Fraser University, and a former Director of the University's School for International Studies, as also – in an earlier avatar – of the Development Studies Institute at the London School of Economics. He started his teaching career in the School of Development Studies at the University of East Anglia in the 1970s. His research and most of his writing have to do with the society, politics and political economy of India.

Uma Kothari is Professor of Migration and Postcolonial Studies in the School of Environment and Development and Associate Director of the Brooks World Poverty Institute, University of Manchester. Her research interests include development history and theory; colonial and postcolonial analyses; and migration, culture and identity. Her publications include *Participation: The New Tyranny?* (Zed, 2001, co-edited with Bill Cooke) and *A Radical History of Development Studies: Individuals, Institutions and Ideologies* (Zed, 2005).

David Lewis is Professor of Social Policy and Development at the London School of Economics and Political Science. A social anthropologist by training, he teaches and researches the theory and practice of international development. He is the author of several books including *Non-Governmental Organisations and Development* (Routledge, 2009, with Nazneen Kanji) and *Bangladesh: Politics, Economy and Civil Society* (Cambridge University Press, 2012). A selection of his publications can be found at http://personal.lse.ac.uk/lewisd/.

Cheryl Lousley is Assistant Professor of English and Interdisciplinary Studies at Lakehead University, Orillia Campus, Ontario. Her research has been published in *Environmental Education Research*, *Interdisciplinary Studies in Literature and Environment*, *Canadian Literature*, *Environmental Philosophy*, *Canadian Poetry*, *Essays on Canadian Writing*, and elsewhere.

Ryann Manning is a PhD student in organisational behaviour at Harvard University. Her current research focuses on public-sector professionals in developing countries. She previously worked in international development, is a founding Director of the Welbodi Partnership and was once an intermittent blogger.

Simon Parker is Senior Lecturer in Politics and Co-Director of the Centre for Urban Research (CURB) at the University of York. His research interests chiefly centre on urban studies and urban theory, socio-spatial informatics, the politics of asylum and immigration, and comparative European politics (with particular reference to Italy). He is the author of *Urban Theory and the Urban Experience: Encountering the City* (Routledge, 2004), and *Cities, Politics and Power* (Routledge, 2011).

Dennis Rodgers is Professor of Urban Social and Political Research at the University of Glasgow. A social anthropologist by training, his research focuses on urban development issues, including conflict and violence, local politics, and the political economy of planning in Nicaragua, Argentina and India (Bihar). His recent publications include the edited volumes *Latin American Urban Development into the 21st Century* (Palgrave, 2012, with Jo Beall and Ravi Kanbur) and *Global Gangs* (University of Minnesota Press, 2014, with Jennifer Hazen).

Martin Scott is a Lecturer in Media and International Development at the University of East Anglia. His research explores the relationship between media and development, with a particular focus on media representations of the Global South. He is the author of a number of journal articles and industry reports on this subject as well as a co-author of *From Entertainment to Citizenship* (Manchester University Press, 2013).

Esha Shah is Assistant Professor in the Faculty of Arts and Social Sciences, Maastricht University. She is an environmental engineer by training and a social anthropologist and historian by choice and self-learning. She is currently developing her research interests on the way in which emotions and affects shape rationality and normativity, including scientific knowledge.

Michael Woolcock is Lead Social Development Specialist in the World Bank's Development Research Group, and Lecturer in Public Policy at Harvard University's Kennedy School of Government. He has written extensively on the institutional aspects of development, with a particular focus on understanding the social and legal dimensions of organisational change, and on assessing the efficacy of complex development interventions. An Australian national, he has a PhD in sociology from Brown University.

Acknowledgements

This volume has had a long gestation, partly due to the fact that our project of seriously exploring popular representations of development has had to deal with many obstacles over the years, both intellectual and practical, and has also undergone several different iterations. We have however been strongly supported and have received warm encouragements from a great number of people, including Tony Addison, Monica Ali, Stephen Biggs, Dan Brockington, Giles Foden, Sean Fox, Paola Grenier, Scott Guggenheim, John Harriss, Lorenza de Icaza, Craig Johnson, Gareth A. Jones, Naila Kabeer, Jenny Kuper, Peter Lanjouw, Vijayendra Rao, Sue Redgrave, Gerry and Janine Rodgers, Mitu Sengupta, Xavier de Souza Briggs, Imogen Wall, the 2002–03 and 2003–04 LSE Development Studies Institute MSc student cohorts, and 2010–11 and 2011–12 students enrolled in the University of Manchester MSc course "Poverty and Poverty Reduction in Context".

—The Editors

Part I

Introduction

1 Introduction

Popular representations of development

David Lewis, Dennis Rodgers and Michael Woolcock

Development is one of the dominant organising ideas of our time, and there are of, course, many ways to approach it. Most people – whether development professionals or ordinary members of the public – learn about development through predominantly economics-focused research studies and policy documents, or from sometimes informative but often unhelpfully simplified news reports. The humanistic side tends to receive less attention, as does the proliferation of different representations of development beyond academic texts and forums. Yet, as John Durham Peters (1997: 79) has observed:

> Part of what it means to live in a modern society is to depend on representations of that society. Modern men and women see proximate fragments with their own eyes and global totalities through the diverse media of social description.

Taking our initial cue from a once well-known but now largely forgotten book called *Sociology through Literature* by Lewis Coser (1963, revised and reissued in 1972), this volume aims to broaden our understandings of development by explicitly promoting a move to include sources beyond the conventional.

Development is an increasingly wide-ranging system of ideas and institutions that take shape in diverse and complex ways. Although the academic study of development is well established, as is also its policy implementation, less considered are the broader, more popular understandings of development that often shape agendas and priorities, particularly in representative democracies. These are arguably critical to comprehend if we are to understand development better, and more importantly, if we are to realise the goals of development more effectively. Partly for this reason, in 2008 we made a case in an article entitled "The Fiction of Development" – published in *The Journal of Development Studies*, and included in abridged form in this volume – that novels ought to be seen as potentially valuable sources of information about the development process, and their renderings of it taken seriously. We were writing not as scholars of literature but as development researchers who were becoming aware of the far wider forms of representation of development issues that could be drawn upon in debate and discussion.

This book extends this initial exploration of these themes by continuing, but also going beyond, the world of fiction to consider other forms of representation and media that intersect with the worlds of development.[1] We also deploy the idea of representation along both of the lines implied by its two different but nevertheless interconnected meanings. On the one hand, representation can be taken to refer to the way that art, literature and media are transformative, not so much mirroring reality but instead 'representing' it according to conscious or unconscious conventions. On the other, the word *representation* takes us into political territory and revisits older, but still relevant, debates about representative and participatory democracy. When we engage with the issue of public representations of development, the importance of recognising power relations within the public spaces in which representations are constructed and projected, or silenced and ignored, is a central theme.[2]

We were, of course, not doing anything new by seeking to bring the study of literature into social science research or indeed into public policy debates in our previously published article. This was ground that had been usefully explored previously by Coser (1963: 3), who contended that

> Fiction is not a substitute for systematically accumulated, certified knowledge. But it provides the social scientist with a wealth of sociologically relevant material ... The creative imagination of the literary artist often has achieved insights into social processes which have remained unexplored in social science.

More recently, Martha Nussbaum's book *Poetic Justice: The Literary Imagination and Public Life* (1997) mounted a solid defence of the arts, and the novel in particular, as helping to develop what she calls the "sympathetic imagination". She suggested that a realist novel with social themes such as Charles Dickens' *Hard Times* has useful social effects (see also chapter 3 by John Harriss). Nussbaum (1997: xviii–xix) argues this on the basis of her attempt to develop

> a vivid conception of public reasoning that is humanistic and not pseudoscientific, to show how a certain type of narrative literature expresses and develops such a conception, and to show some of the benefits this conception might have to offer in the public sphere.

The novel is a form that recognises the importance and diversity of individuals, and Nussbaum sees this as informing a particular conception of public reasoning, and as fostering the sympathetic imagination – the capacity to recognise the inner lives of others – as a social effect.[3] Nussbaum's work aims to contribute to the critique of what she sees as the dominant culture within public policy of utilitarian rational-choice models that are biased towards quantitative analyses of the public good. This dominant culture, she argues, operates in undesirable ways within public policy worlds and tends to generate depersonalised, reductive public policies. At the same time, our aim in our initial article was also to build upon the established tradition of the humanistic method within the social sciences, whose proponents have long argued the need to correct tendencies among researchers to prioritise a narrow search for objective truth that increasingly ignores "the concrete historical yet human experiences out of which societies are invariably composed" (Plummer, 1983: 5). This tradition stands in contrast to positivist social science that prioritises quantification and the search for generalisable laws over gaining a fuller and more holistic understanding of the lived realities of people's lives. As Nussbaum (1997) argues, such models are limited by their reliance on principles of aggregation and maximising, which tend to assume a qualitative sameness among individuals' preferences and their desires that is acutely at odds with the real world.

Forms of representation of social reality, of course, reflect wider social and economic changes. Peters (1997: 78) shows how the emergence in the eighteenth century of two new – but very different – forms of narrative in the shape of the novel and the science of statistics was strongly linked to the rise of a middle-class reading public and the establishment of rationalised bureaucratic administrative systems:

> The novel and statistics are each a narrative mode answering the problem of how to display a cross section of a quantitative complexity. One uses narrative, one uses aggregation. Both enact – and depend on – a new apprehension of space and time: the possibility of envisioning spatially dispersed events at a single moment in time ... The polarity of narrative and data marks the twin limits of modern social description, with many hybrid forms between. Academic battles between number crunchers and tale-spinners are only a local variant on this larger theme.

In the world of development, we suggest that a corrective towards humanistic approaches may be particularly relevant at the present time. Over the past decade, many development agencies and researchers have increasingly considered the definition and scope of knowledge about development to be based on rather narrow orthodoxies of 'results-based management' approaches on the one hand, and, on the other, to the supposedly definitive logic of once and for all proving 'what works', generally via standardised methodologies such as randomised controlled trials. Certainly, there has been a palpable shift away from interest in issues of substance and process towards preoccupations with management, mechanisms and the measurement of aid, as is perhaps best embodied in the Millennium Development Goals (MDGs) and the aid effectiveness agenda that emerged after a landmark Organisation for Economic Cooperation and Development (OECD) meeting in Paris in 2005.

Although there have been various efforts over the years to broaden the range of knowledge and representation, such as the World Bank's "Voices of the Poor" initiative that was undertaken over a decade ago (see Narayan et al., 1999), these seem to have lost popularity among mainstream donor agencies in recent years. One exception is the Swedish International Development Agency's (Sida's) Health and Education Reality Check project that started in Bangladesh in 2006.[4]

For five years, this project has attempted to listen to and document the voices and experiences of people living in poverty using an approach based on annual residential household visits by specially trained field researchers. This work seeks to 'humanise', using a methodology that emphasises face-to-face two-way communication, the information that policymakers use to plan and evaluate the two large multi-donor sector-wide reform programmes operating across that country.[5] However, this remains a rare exception. Even *PLA Notes*, the practitioner journal that for many years served as a repository for unconventional thinking and practice around alternative development approaches,[6] is finding it increasingly difficult to secure the comparatively small amount of funding it needs to maintain publication.

Indeed, the new proponents of evidence-based development policy – for example, Banerjee and Duflo (2011: 16) in their influential book *Poor Economics* – tend to make their case for a new positivism in development research in a confident and unambiguous manner that brooks little argument:

> The studies we use have in common a high level of scientific rigor, openness to accepting the verdict of the data, and focus on specific concrete questions of relevance to the lives of the poor.[7]

Yet, as Woolcock (2009) has argued, the appeal of what have increasingly become seen as 'gold standard' methodologies for acquiring knowledge do not relieve us of the need to engage with context and process by means of as wide a range as possible of qualitative, quantitative and historical social science tools. Within the approach we take in this book, we favour a more open and diverse view of what constitutes credible evidence akin to that advanced by Jennifer Greene (2009), whose work, in contrast to some current trends, recognises multiple voices, history and complexity and who prefers to see evidence more modestly in terms of "inkling" rather than "proof".

There is also a further dimension to exploring popular representations of development that we touched on in our earlier article: the reach of sources of information such as novels compared to academic texts and policy papers. There are few sources of information about poverty that have reached as wide an audience as Rohinton Mistry's novel *A Fine Balance*, for example, which has sold over a quarter of a million copies and counting, compared to less than 20,000 for a classic academic study of the phenomenon such as Janice Perlman's *The Myth of Marginality*, first published in 1976, for example. This aspect of more popular representations alone justifies taking an interest in them; as Joseph Stalin once put it, "quantity has a quality of its own".[8]

Building on the debate generated by our earlier article around literary sources, and following the logic of exploring further the diverse media now engaging with development issues, we decided to broaden our interest to other popular representations of development by commissioning researchers to contribute to an edited collection on this theme. Coser drew much of the material in his book from nineteenth and twentieth century literature,[9] but today the locations and sources of public knowledge relating to development and social change have diversified enormously to include film, television and the Internet. The aim of this volume is thus both to reveal the extent of alternative sources of information about development issues, as well as to explore the ways in which development, as a key idea of our times, is discussed beyond more conventional academic and policy texts. Diversity of representation is therefore a key theme among the contributions included here. At the same time, the book also explores the various ways in which particular development themes have been taken up in non-academic and non-policy contexts, and considers the potential impact and influence that such non-conventional, more popular representations of development may have, both positive and negative.

Representation and the growth of modern media

A discussion of issues of popular representation in any field necessarily leads us to consider the growth of the media, its generation, and exchange of meaning through the institutions of the mass media. The work of Jurgen Habermas – and in particular his book *The Structural Transformation of the Public Sphere* (1962) – provides an important initial reference point for our exploration. In this book, he elaborated his concept of the public sphere, analysing the rise of mass media by documenting the emergence during the eighteenth century of what he terms "publicity" as a new form of political organisation, associated with changes in the way modern states seek to build their legitimacy. In particular, Habermas argued that the state no longer governs through the production of forms of staged display that used to underline the feudal king's power (such as the spectacle of processions and public executions), but instead now tries to secure its legitimacy by making its deliberations visible to the public (the generation of legitimacy through the reason of public opinion).

Yet Habermas also recognises that this process of change is complex and remains incomplete. The public sphere all too easily becomes "re-feudalised" by market and state. For example, the mass media may continue to keep citizens "in awe" rather than provide them with accurate information, so that informed, rational discussion remains elusive and often illusory within the public sphere. Television, for example, is normally characterised by the tension between its role in informing citizens through news reporting, documentary, or drama, and its presentation of powerful advertising messages that are designed to sell commodities to consumers. These effects may also be seen in the representation of development issues, such as disaster or conflict reporting – part of what Lilie Chouliaraki (2006) has characterised as the "the spectatorship of suffering".

The impact of technological change on the organisation and projection of knowledge is a theme that also underpins several of the contributions to this volume. Here we also find resonances with the work of Manuel Castells (2000), whose concept of the "network society" is informed by the idea that technological change has in recent decades helped to move capitalism into a new stage of "informational capitalism" after its stagnation during the 1970s. He shows how a new immediacy of constantly circulating financial, technical and cultural information helps to shape economic relations, politics and organisational structures – and peoples' lives – in new and unpredictable ways, and where crises now arrive regularly and unexpectedly. New forms of work associated with these changes rely on flexibility, connectedness and alertness to opportunity, while to succeed, organisations of all kinds increasingly access new capabilities in the form of media-friendliness, Internet skills and global networking. In the world of development, these trends can be seen in the increasing efforts by international NGOs to boost their communications departments and by donors such as the World Bank's experimentation with alternative media (see chapter 4 by Davidov).

The field of "informational development" is clearly an area that increasingly demands more attention from researchers. At the same time, however, concern with the ways in which development issues are represented in the media is a long-standing issue, particularly with regard to the way that people who live in poverty are portrayed. In a recent study of the visual language of British NGOs, Dogra (2012: 3) explores the way that fund-raising imagery and messaging often construct ways of seeing that ultimately reinforce colonial stereotypes and depoliticised and ahistorical understandings of poverty despite a surface level that may claim to project counter-hegemonic messages:

> NGOs' messages project many colonial discourses even as they ironically erase the period of our connected history and its legacies that continue to shape existing global economic structures, power relations and the current state of poverty and prosperity across various regions.

In the flurry of mixed messages that she identifies from studying the range of public images used by a set of leading UK development NGOs in the media over a period of 12 months, Dogra's analysis finds a set of "mainly one way projections" (Dogra, 2012: 119) in which the voices of people who live in poverty, and those of the "majority world" more generally, remain largely submerged and unheard. For example, a recent campaign for the NGO Water Is Life run by marketing firm DDB – a leading US advertising company set up in 1949 by Bill Bernbach, Ned Doyle and Maxwell Dane – presents citizens of Haiti reading out and responding to tweets on the semi-ironic popular Twitter feed #firstworldproblems. The feed carries the tag line "Living in the first world can be so hard. Sometimes people just don't understand how difficult our life can be ...." One campaign video simply shows a laptop with the sentence "Slow Internet is the worst thing that can happen to you" while the camera slowly pans back to reveal a medical worker in an impoverished Port-au-Prince clinic where the huge scale of suffering is immediately apparent. The worker says "Slow Internet is not the worst thing that can happen to you". There is a simple eloquence to the way this further subversion of an ironic discourse communicates and underlines the obvious point that many of the problems facing wealthy citizens of the globe pale into insignificance against the scale of deprivation endured by many Haitians.[10]

The structure of the book

The 12 chapters that follow are organised into five sections: literature and fiction, television, film, history and technology. In Part II (following this introduction), we begin by reprising in abridged form our earlier paper on fiction and development. This chapter is followed by a contribution by John Harriss that reflects upon his recent efforts to incorporate fiction in the teaching of development studies, drawing on three novels: *Hard Times*, *Half of a Yellow Sun* and *The Quiet American*. Notable here was his interest in situating works of fiction alongside key academic texts, such as Karl Polanyi's *The Great Transformation* and Benedict Anderson's *Imagined Communities*. He shows how the analyses of social scientists and of historians are complemented by the work of creative writers, and documents the ways that the use of fiction served to deepen student interest in academic and policy texts by adding meaning to them. Finding that the novels he taught with served to humanise development knowledge, he suggests that such an approach helped to bring home "the significance for people of ideas and events and social trends", and helped students "to understand the experience of others".

Chapter 4 moves the discussion to a different type of literature: the Japanese manga comic book, which emerged in its modern form in the 1950s. Shifting the discussion from the classroom to the contemporary world of development agencies, Veronica Davidov's contribution analyses the *1 World Manga* series, a World Bank initiative to improve development education with narratives that loosely follow the MDGs. While manga comic books are not a new form, their use within a mainstream development agency such as the World Bank is highly innovative. However, despite its accessibility, Davidov's work suggests that this form of representation is limited by the way it structures the narrative of the protagonist's quests through sequential, compartmentalised encounters with the global issues being targeted. The books consequently generate a pedagogical metanarrative of 'development' that engages proximal and situational, rather than structural, causes of inequality and disenfranchisement that impede the characters' human development.

Part III moves the discussion of development representation to the world of popular mainstream television. Martin Scott's chapter is concerned with the ways that popular television programmes such as *The World's Strictest Parents* provide new opportunities for Western audiences to engage and respond emotionally to individuals from the global South. He begins by considering the different academic literatures on the "public faces of development" alongside that concerned with "public media and morality" and argues that both literatures need to engage more fully with the rise and current popularity of "factual entertainment" within the world of television. He demonstrates this by applying a modified version of Lilie Chouliaraki's "analytics of mediation" approach. This is followed by Simon Parker's contribution, which moves us from the global South to the inner cities of the United States. This chapter is concerned with *The Wire*, the widely acclaimed HBO TV series that was created by former crime reporter David Simon and ex-police officer Ed Burns, and which set out to explore aspects of a city that "America left behind". Parker builds on analyses of the "the social science of fiction" linked to this and other recent television dramas to show how *The Wire* makes visible important aspects of urban poverty as the state withdraws and capital disinvests from abandoned post-industrial urban spaces.

Part IV considers representations of development within the world of film. In a follow-up to "The Fiction of Development", chapter 7 explores the ways that movies provide different kinds of insights into development issues. Briefly exploring examples mainly, but not exclusively, drawn from commercial feature films, we identify ways in which the underlying logic of cinema as a representational medium both facilitates and constrains the projection, and consequently the understanding, of development issues. We also comment on how Western cinema since the 1980s can be very much analysed as reflecting changing attitudes to and knowledge about the "developing world". Esha Shah's contribution that follows (chapter 8) is concerned with narratives of poverty within Indian popular cinema. Shah shows how popular Hindi-language cinema can be seen as playing the role of a laboratory in its capacity for sensing and "intuiting" key aspects of Indian contemporary life within popular culture since Independence. The analysis is situated within a critique of mainstream development literature that tends to understand poverty in limited terms merely as a lack – of health, well-being, or income – with an emphasis on economic rationalities related to acquisition, allocation, or distribution of resources. The analysis of cinematic representations, argues Shah, shifts the analytical ground towards understanding poverty as an affect rather than simply as an effect. It becomes possible then to consider the changing "inter-subjective experience of poverty" in terms of less visible themes such as loss of self, bad luck, social dignity, disgrace and fear of pauperisation. In this way, she argues, popular cinema frames a new form of politics that is only rarely considered within mainstream development literature.

We turn to history in Part V. In chapter 9, Uma Kothari discusses how ideas about civility, modernity and progress, foundational to development discourse and practice to this day, are similar to those once deployed in popular visual representations of the British Empire. She analyses the British Government's Empire Marketing Board poster campaign that ran between 1926 and 1933, which aimed to demonstrate the humanitarianism upon which the Empire had supposedly been built. Kothari identifies continuities between past and present in such representations, where we find post-independence tourist products still actively marketing idyllic, deserted, exotic and isolated islands; she also draws parallels with important contemporary visual campaigns, such as the one associated with the promotion of fair trade. This is followed by Cheryl Lousley's contribution (chapter 10) that moves our discussion towards more recent history in the form of the July 1985 Live Aid music events, which took place in the United Kingdom and the United States as part of the West's response to the Ethiopian famine. Live Aid pioneered the modern practice of media-led fund-raising events for global poverty based on popular music concerts,[11] and Lousley analyses the longevity of this strategy within the popular imagination. She argues that continuing representations of this event in the form of memorabilia, as well as further events such as Live 8, should not only be read as representations of Africa and Africans, but also as an aspect of a Western "culture of sentimentality" in development. This culture uses mass media images of the "famine child" to facilitate a feeling of global connectedness, produced partly in the spheres of global communications media, celebrity, pop music and consumerism. Lousley draws on Alex de Waal's (1997) idea of the "humanitarian international" to argue that tracing the intersections between the circulation of affects and the circulation of capital is critical to understanding the political economy of a public media event such as Live Aid.

The final section, Part VI, moves from the argument that we need to broaden our sources of knowledge about development to examine recent claims that new information technology and social media may open up new ways of 'doing' development, or at least help create new forms of engagement with development by ordinary citizens. In chapter 11, Tobias Denskus and Daniel Esser take us into the rapidly expanding world of social media by analysing the blogs and tweets that related to a specific high-profile event in the recent international development policy calendar: the three-day Millennium Development Goals Summit held at the United Nations in New York in September 2010. A detailed analysis of these data reveals that far from opening up new space for critical or alternative commentary or ideas, it appeared that the content within this social media was mainly reproducing mainstream development discourse and practice. Finally, Ryan Manning's chapter 12 focuses on representations of development within the 'blogosphere'. This contribution perhaps provides a more optimistic view, arguing that online blogs constitute a form of the Habermasian 'public sphere', even though it is at present a public space that remains heavily dominated by elites. Following this final section, we offer some concluding thoughts outlining a preliminary agenda for future research.

Concluding reflections

In putting together this book, our aim is to try to frame and open up popular representation as an important new field of study that has to date been largely neglected by those engaged in research on international development. We ourselves write from the perspective of development studies, and we do not claim to bring the specialist knowledge to the subject that those more versed in media studies, literary theory, or postcolonial studies can bring to this topic (although some of our contributors are able to do so). However, we very much hope that this collection will draw closer attention to the field, and that it will stimulate new work across these boundaries and disciplines.

What can be learnt from the different contributions on popular representations of development offered in this volume? In the first instance, following on from our earlier article (Lewis, Rodgers and Woolcock, 2008), we believe that this volume reiterates the fact that development knowledge – or more specifically, what counts as serious or legitimate knowledge about development – has often been too narrowly represented within academic and policy discussions.

The papers here serve to counteract, or at least broaden, what feels like an increasing narrowing at the present juncture. Secondly, this collection highlights how if we look beyond conventional academic studies and policy reports – for example to films, posters, or fiction – then we may learn something new. For example, we may find forms of knowledge and representation that humanise development processes, or historicise our perspective in illuminating ways. Documents such as films or novels can also help us to make sense of the past in ways that may still inform the present.

At the same time, however, the rapid evolution of new information technology means that there are increasingly new and diverse areas of public (and private) space where popular representations of development take place – from blogs and social networking, to reality television and film. This may have implications both for the ways that development ideas are understood more widely in both Western and non-Western societies, as well as for the ways people participate in, and try to influence or critique, mainstream development processes and their understandings in the public sphere. Technology plays a role in transforming representation in both senses of the word raised by Williams (1976). Certainly, such an approach can throw new light on the ways established wisdoms and categories in development may be breaking down. For example, relationships between 'developers' and 'developed' have always been problematic and regularly contested, but new technologies may offer new spaces for representing and perhaps challenging these.

In a related manner, another theme that emerges from some papers is a critique of narrow (Western) development professionalism and expertise, and an implicit call for actively incorporating other voices and other forms of knowledge into the deliberative spaces wherein key development ideas, evidence, policy and practice are adjudicated. Popular representations of development are often more inclusive, being less imbued with exclusionary jargon, elitism and theoretical posturing. New media may also be more democratic in nature, yet questions of access, both technological and skills-wise, remain critical and problematic. Just as simplistic binaries between developed and developing, or North and South, are rapidly breaking down in the real world at the macro level – as a result of the ongoing financial crisis, or the rise of large middle-income countries such as Brazil and Indonesia, for example – perhaps we will continue to see more examples of challenges to traditionally unequal power relations within the public spheres of popular representation and knowledge. At the same time, we cannot be naïve about the inequalities that exist and the contestations taking place within this public sphere, as development knowledge becomes a commodity that is increasingly bought and sold by marketing firms.[12]

Finally, public representation has implications for how we conceive of development studies as a field of research and teaching – and reminds us of the wider options that are available in terms of both legitimate objects of, and techniques for, analysis. As Kregg Hetherington (2012: 143) has pointed out, development knowledge "is the name given to an appropriate (i.e., predictable) relationship between signal and response within a systematic totality" that is "tightly tied to a dream of certainty, order and efficiency". As such, it is "quite the opposite of the radical democratic uncertainty made possible by giving citizens access to documents and allowing them to contest the government, or each other, on the basis of what they find there." Ultimately, the aim of this collection is to open up new avenues and provoke new ideas concerning both the nature of development studies and also development itself. We explore some of these aspects in the Conclusion to this volume (chapter 13), but generally we hope that this book will serve to generate informed debate and exchange between as wide and as disparate a group of individuals related to and interested in development – which, after all, remains the only possible bottom line for a constructive and progressive development studies.

Notes

1 We take a broad view of development as a diverse concept, including the challenges of improving social justice, expanding human capabilities and reducing poverty, the international system of government non-governmental and intergovernmental institutions engaged in development intervention, and the broader trajectories of local and global capitalist transformation. At the same time, we do not see development as an idea restricted to the so-called Third World, as our inclusion of Simon Parker's work on representations of urban poverty and institutions in Baltimore attests.

2 Raymond Williams (1976: 225) offers a useful discussion of the "possible overlap between *representative* and *representation* in their political and artistic senses".

3 On this point, see also Hunt (2007), who argues that certain widely read novels in the mid-eighteenth century – such as Samuel Richardson's *Clarissa*, published in 1748 – embodied, consolidated, and actively promoted historically transformational shifts in attitudes towards slavery, judicial torture, and gender equality – in other words, the founding of universal notions of human rights – because of their powerful capacity to elicit sympathy from otherwise comfortable elites for the harrowing plight of the downtrodden.

4 For a short blog article describing the approach, see http://www.guardian.co.uk/global-development/poverty-matters/2011/mar/10/closing-gap-policymakers-people-bangladesh.

5 At the same time, one of the editors of this volume (Lewis) has been an adviser to this project, and reports that insights from the Reality Check initiative have been difficult to use within the current climate of thinking around aid impact and measurement agendas. For example, decision makers in government and donors are unused to forms of knowledge about development that do not fit easily in the familiar templates of statistical reporting, indicator logics, and large-scale sampling. For further details, see Lewis (2012), available at http://www.reality-check-approach.com.

6 PLA stands for Participatory Learning and Action. See http://www.iied.org/pla for the background on this journal and the approaches that underpin it.

7 One of the many ironies in these authors' self-proclaimed "radically new" approach to development is that it does not mention even once the strategies used by countries that have actually achieved truly radical – that is, historically unprecedented – rates of economic development in recent decades, such as Vietnam or Singapore, and it also ignores the fact that the use of randomised controlled trials, as a policy strategy and priority, played literally no role whatsoever in bringing these about. See Shaffer (2011) for a deft critique of randomized controlled trials in development more generally.

8 Stalin also famously contended that "novelists are forever trying to distance themselves from politics, but the novel itself closes in on politics. Novelists are so concerned with 'man's fate' that they tend to lose sight of their own fate. Therein lies their tragedy".

9 See also Edling and Rydgren (2011), who extend Coser's approach to understanding sociology to include not just literature but also philosophy and science.

10 See The Guardian's *Comment Is Free* site, www.guardian.uk/commentisfree for 9 October 2012 and the article by Emer O'Toole (accessed 1 November 2012), which considers the lively critical debate that emerged online about how far this campaign actually perpetuated or challenged stereotypes.

11 The Concert for Bangladesh organised by George Harrison and Ravi Shankar in New York City in November 1971 was probably the first example of this type of multimedia event (with a concert, a film, and records), but it was not until Live Aid over a decade later that the idea really became mainstream.

12 The recent incorporation of development knowledge by commercial publishing in the form of 'development blockbusters' is another example of this commodification (see Lewis, 2013).

References

Banerjee, A. V. and E. Duflo. (2011) Poor Economics: A Radical Rethinking of the Way to Fight Global Poverty. New York: Public Affairs.

Castells, M. (2000) The Rise of the Network Society. Oxford: Blackwell.

Chouliaraki , L. (2006) The Spectatorship of Suffering. London: Sage.

Coser, L. (1963) Sociology through Literature. Englewood Cliffs: Prentice-Hall.

de Waal, A. (1997) Famine Crimes: Politics and the Disaster Relief Industry in Africa. London and Bloomington: African Rights & the International African Institute in association with James Currey, Oxford & Indiana University Press.

Dogra, N. (2012) Representations of Global Poverty: Aid, Development and International NGOs. London: IB Taurus.

Edling, C. and J. Rydgren (eds.) (2011) Sociological Insights of Great Thinkers: Sociology through Literature, Philosophy and Science. Santa Barbara: Greenwood Publishing.

Greene, J. (2009) "Evidence and 'proof' and evidence as 'inkling'". In S. I. Donaldson, C. A. Christe, and M. M. Mark (eds.), *What Counts as Credible Evidence in Applied Research and Evaluation Practice?*. London: Sage, pp. 153–167.

Hetherington, K. (2012) "Promising information: Democracy, development, and the remapping of Latin America". *Economy and Society,* 41(2): 127–150.

Hunt, L. (2007) *Inventing Human Rights: A History*. New York: Norton.

Lewis, D. (2012) *Reality Check Reflection Report*. Dhaka, Bangladesh: Embassy of Sweden.

Lewis, D. (2013) "The Gift of Experience? The Rise of the Development Blockbuster Book." Unpublished seminar paper presented at The New Anthropology of the Gift, Department of Anthropology, University of Sussex and submitted to Forum of Anthropology.

Lewis, D., D. Rodgers, and M. Woolcock (2008) "The fiction of development: Literary representation as a source of authoritative knowledge". *Journal of Development Studies,* 44(2): 198–216.

Narayan, D., with R. Patel, K. Schafft, A. Rademacher, and S. Koch-Schulte (1999) *Can Anyone Hear Us? Voices from 47 Countries*. Washington DC: World Bank.

Nussbaum, M. (1997) *Poetic Justice: The Literary Imagination and Public Life*. Boston: Beacon Press.

Peters, J. D. (1997) "Seeing bifocally: Media, place, culture". In A. Gupta and J. Ferguson (eds.), *Culture, Power, Place: Explorations in Critical Anthropology*. Durham: Duke University Press, pp. 75–92.

Plummer, K. (1983) *Documents of Life: An Introduction to the Problems and Literature of the Humanistic Method*. London: Unwin Hyman.

Shaffer, P. (2011) "Against excessive rhetoric in impact assessment: Overstating the case for randomised controlled experiments". *Journal of Development Studies*, 47(11): 1619–1635.

Williams, R. (1976) *Keywords: A Vocabulary of Culture and Society*. London: Fontana.

Woolcock, M. (2009) "Toward a plurality of methods in project evaluation: A contextualized approach to understanding impact trajectories and efficacy". *Journal of Development Effectiveness*, 1(1): 1–14.

Part II
Literature and fiction

2 The fiction of development

Literary representation as a source of authoritative knowledge

David Lewis, Dennis Rodgers and Michael Woolcock[1]

Introduction: development and representation

"Development" is one of the key organizing concepts of the modern era. As such, ideas and images of development are inevitably represented in a wide variety of ways, whether within academia, the policy world, or the general public domain. To this extent, it can be contended that all forms of development knowledge can be – and historically have been – largely understood as a series of "stories". This is true not only in the pragmatic sense that to have an impact on public opinion, organisational strategy, or within academia, even the most elaborate equations and sophisticated data analyses need to be able to be expressed in everyday language (Denning, 2000), but also in the deeper philosophical sense that all knowledge claims are necessarily embedded in particular subjective understandings of how the world works, as was famously pointed out by Walter Benjamin (1989) in his classic essay "On the Program of the Coming Philosophy".

Benjamin not only contended that all knowledge of reality is unavoidably subjective but also that it is inevitably mediated by the representative forms that describe it, and that different modes of representation therefore impart different visions of the world. He was, of course, not the first to highlight this issue, which can be placed within a philosophical tradition going back in the West to the fourth century BCE and Plato's famous "Simile of the Cave", and even further in the East, to the sixth century BCE parable of the blind men and the elephant recorded in the Buddhist *Udana*. We take Benjamin (1989: 9–10) as our starting point, however, because he saw this concern as critical for the social sciences, arguing that the key challenge was the creation of "a concept of knowledge to which a concept of experience corresponds". Our purpose in this article is more modest: we seek merely to suggest that there may be a case for widening the scope of the development knowledge base that is conventionally considered to be "valid". In doing so, we aim to open up new ground within development studies for the further exploration of the value of different forms of development knowledge, and to this extent we acknowledge that this chapter inevitably seeks more to ask questions than to provide answers.

Our central contention concerns the potential contribution that works of literary fiction can make to development. It is important to note from the outset that our intention is not to make any relativist epistemological claims that literary forms of representation can substitute for academic or policy works in the study of development. Rather, we want to lay down a challenge to practitioners and academics within the field to include fictional representations of development issues within the scope of what they consider to be "proper" forms of development knowledge. The chapter begins by making some general remarks about the nature of knowledge, narrative authority and representational form, highlighting the common ground that exists between fiction and non-fiction. We then explore the contributions that modern popular fiction touching on development themes can potentially make to our understanding of development, and juxtapose these with more formal academic and applied approaches. A final section sets out an agenda for further debate, draws some preliminary conclusions, and proposes a list of works of fiction that we feel may be of interest to those who may have been persuaded of the importance of our endeavour.

Knowledge, authority and narrative form

There clearly exists within development studies a hierarchy of authority that determines what constitutes "valid" development knowledge. Although much of the sound and fury in today's development debates stems from what can be described as a "clash of epistemologies" – in which different understandings of the meanings and renderings of development come into contact with one another – in many ways, there exists a much deeper schism that affects the very nature of what is considered knowledge and what is not. This involves decisions about the acceptable form that development "stories" must take to be deemed serious. Even if in recent years there have been some attempts to broaden the development knowledge base beyond traditional academic monographs and policy manuals – including perhaps most notably the World Bank's "Voices of the Poor" initiative (Narayan *et al.*, 2000a, 2000b; and Narayan and Petesch, 2002), which explicitly sought to bring a story-telling methodology centre stage within the production of development knowledge – these remain overwhelmingly the standard representational form for the dissemination of development knowledge within the discipline. As such, they constitute the benchmark against which other forms of knowledge representation are measured within development studies – broadly construed as encompassing both the academic and practitioner worlds – and those that do not match up are generally discarded or ignored, including, in particular, literary forms of representation.

To a certain extent, this devaluing of narrative forms of knowledge mirrors a fundamental divide between literature and social science. As Barbara Czarniawska-Joerges (1992: 218) succinctly outlines – and simultaneously undermines – the separation derives from at least three factors:

> The first is that one is fiction and the other is non-fiction: the basis for telling the story is different. However, this is relative. There are many writers who use factual events for their novels and many social scientists who use

fictitious reality to illustrate their theses ... The second is that social scientists are obliged to be systematic, that is, to demonstrate a method, which is also relative. Writers often have a very systematic method ... The third is the presence or lack of aesthetic expression, and this is a difference that, following R.H. Brown ... I propose to abolish.

The historian Hayden White (1973) implicitly goes even further in dismissing this distinction in his famous study of the "historical imagination" when he contends that social science often tends to draw its authority from its perceived aesthetic value rather than the use of putatively "factual" data or "objective" theory. Focusing on nineteenth century European historical accounts, he shows how these were structured along similar lines to the realist novel, with their force and persuasion deriving principally from the deployment of similar rhetorical strategies to those found in the latter. According to White, this was because ultimately all interpretation is fundamentally rhetorical in nature; it is a process that occurs when there is uncertainty as to how to describe or explain a phenomenon, and consequently figurative rather than objective means of persuasion will inevitably be resorted to.

Seen in this way, the line between literature and the social sciences becomes a very fine one. This is also the case when storytelling is considered historically, as one of humankind's oldest methods of possessing information and representing reality. Certainly, as Michel Foucault (1984) pointed out, those texts that we today categorise as "literary fiction" – stories, poems, plays – were in fact once accepted as the primary media for the expression of essential truths about human dilemmas and understandings of the world, in the same way that in this day and age positivist scientific discourse is received as authoritative *pro forma*. Indeed, fiction is arguably to a large extent frequently about the very issues that at a basic level are the subject matter of development studies: the promises and perils of encounters between different peoples; the tragic mix of courage, desperation, humour and deprivation characterising the lives of the downtrodden; and the complex assortment of means, motives and opportunities surrounding efforts by outsiders to "help" them. From this perspective, one might even say – with apologies to William Shakespeare – that in many ways stories "are such stuff as [development studies] are made on".[2]

Furthermore, the role of literature has historically always been not only "to delight" but also "to teach", as was pointed out by the Roman poet Horace over 2000 years ago.[3] Sir Thomas More famously claimed that he was compelled to write his powerful political tract *Utopia* (1516) as "a fiction whereby the truth, as if smeared by honey, might a little more pleasantly slip into men's minds" (More, 1964: 251). This prescriptive ideal was perhaps most clearly expressed in late eighteenth century Britain during the debates around the so-called "republic of letters" that the Industrial Revolution and a concomitant concentration of an increasingly literate population into urban centres were seen to be creating (see Keen, 1999). Literature was considered politically charged within the context of Britain's changing social conditions, and a powerful vector for shaping of public values and morality, to the extent that the British anarchist William Godwin (1993 [1793]: 20) wrote:

> Few engines can be more powerful, and at the same time more salutary in their tendency, than literature. Without enquiring for the present into the cause of this phenomenon, it is sufficiently evident in fact, that the human mind is strongly infected with prejudice and mistake. The various opinions prevailing in different countries and among different classes of men upon the same subject, are almost innumerable... Now the effectual way for extirpating these prejudices and mistakes seems to be literature.

The power of literature to effectively convey complex ideas should not be surprising. Over 40 years ago, Lewis Coser published the first edition of his classic (but unfortunately now out-of-print) *Sociology through Literature*, an unprecedented introduction to sociology through an eclectic collection of literary fiction. Citing Henry James in the introduction to his volume, Coser (1972 [1963]: xv) argued that "there is no impression of life, no manner of seeing it and feeling it, to which the plan of the novelist may not offer a place". As such, writers of fiction "have provided their readers with an immense variety of richly textured commentaries on man's life in society, on his involvement with his fellow-men," to the extent that literature can constitute a key form of social evidence and testimony. Coser (1972 [1963]: xvi) was careful, however, not to suggest that literature could replace "systematically accumulated, certified knowledge". Rather, he saw them as complementing each other, but argued that "social scientists have but too often felt it is somewhat below their dignity to show an interest in literature". This "self-denying ordinance" was highly problematic according to Coser (1972 [1963]: xvi), who contended that

> there is an intensity of perception in the first-rate novelist when he describes a locale, a sequence of action, or a clash of characters which can hardly be matched by ... sociologists. ...The creative imagination of the literary artist often has achieved insights into social processes which have remained unexplored in social science.

From this perspective, an argument can be made that it might be useful to compare and contrast literary views on development with the ideas and perceptions of academic social science and the public policy world, in order to glean new insights and novel perspectives (so to speak). Certainly, the themes emanating from "development policy" documents – the official texts produced by multilateral development agencies, government planning offices and NGOs – can often be rather starkly contrasted with those of fictional writing on development. For example, in a stimulating study of the way in which the World Bank construes Egypt's development predicament, Timothy Mitchell (2002) underlines how official documents portray this as a function of demographic and geographic factors – too many people producing too little food because of not enough arable land – and how this has in turn given rise to a corresponding policy focus on agricultural and irrigation projects. However, literary authors such as the Nobel Prize winner Naguib Mahfouz, in his novels *Adrift on the Nile* (1993 [1966]) and *The Journey of Ibn Fattouma* (1993 [1983]), or Ahdad Soueif in her Booker Prize–nominated novel *The Map of Love* (1999), provide very different analyses, respectively pointing to factors including modernisation and the concomitant spread of anomie, religious fundamentalism and the colonial legacy as critical to explaining Egypt's contemporary predicament. The wider corpus of Mitchell's work (see 1991; 2000) strongly supports the notion that these are key factors to understanding the country's current development.

Similarly, the recent and influential World Bank (2000) report *Can Africa Claim the 21st Century?* – co-authored with several other development organisations, it should be noted – is another example of such disjuncture. It optimistically and proactively affirms that Africa's future depends on "determined leadership", "good governance", "sound policies", "improved infrastructure", "investments in people", "reduced conflict", "higher economic growth" and "reduced aid dependence". Although all of these factors are undoubtedly eminently sensible from an "orthodox" policy point of view, they ring like empty platitudes when held up against the insights of fictional accounts of Africa's developmental predicament such as Chinua Achebe's *Things Fall Apart* (1958) or J. G. Ballard's *The Day of Creation* (1987), for example. Achebe's novel details the lasting legacy of colonialism in Nigeria, including the conflicts generated around cultural practices, but it also traces the power struggles that traditionally run through tribal communities, showing these to also be a source of change and constant struggle. Ballard's *The Day of Creation* actually focuses directly on development practice insofar as the central character is a doctor – significantly named Dr. Mallory – running a WHO clinic in an unnamed underdeveloped, drought-plagued and poverty-ridden West African country caught in the midst of a civil war. As the novel unfolds, Mallory is confronted with the perversity of the processes and manifestations that he once saw as epitomising development, ultimately drawing conclusions about the futility of the process as conceived in Western terms.

The argument that we are making here is not that academic or policy approaches to development are necessarily wrong or flawed, nor is it that we think novelists should be put in charge of development ministries. Rather, our point is that the policy and academic literature of development often constructs development problems in a way that justify the response of the particular policies they advocate (Ferguson, 1990; Escobar, 1995; Mitchell, 2002), and that the way this literature is framed therefore makes a significant difference. This is, of course, an issue that can be said to go to the heart of the art of storytelling,[4] and indeed, Emery Roe (1991, 1994) argues that to a large extent policy documents such as those produced by the World Bank should be understood as "narratives" that frame what and how development problems are discussed by powerful actors, thereby validating the ubiquitous role of (and interventions by) professional "experts", and legitimising efforts to construe deeply complex historical and political issues as being most effectively – and most "rigorously" – addressed through technocratic means, for example, through the adoption of "tool kits", "better policies", "best practices" and "stronger institutions" as determined by "solid evidence" and "rational planning". Such documents inherently privilege certain forms of information, explanation and "evidence",[5] and in conjunction with the politically powerful places from whence they emanate – and the imperatives that Weberian organisations have for presenting problems and solutions in neat packages (Pritchett and Woolcock, 2004) – thereby according a particular status to certain forms of knowledge, authority and representation.

Obviously, as scholars–practitioners ourselves, we are acutely conscious of the constant need to frame complex development issues in ways that resonate with broad audiences – students, advocacy groups, politicians, bureaucrats – and that are plausibly "actionable" by front-line project staff. This inevitably often means accepting a certain amount of "blueprint development" that "tell[s] us at once that things happen 'like' the way they are described – after all narratives relate things causally – without, however, reflecting the fact that things happen … so uncertainly" (Roe, 1991: 296). At the same time, however, another way of putting this is that having a "good story" is essential if one wants to make a difference in the world (as most people in development surely do). Seen in this way, it can plausibly be contended that works of fiction, as original *bona fide* "stories", also potentially have much to contribute to the storehouse of knowledge on development processes, manifestations and responses. When one story is a more compelling means of articulating a situation than another, then development scholars and practitioners ought to perhaps think more positively about it, be it a novel, a poem, or a play rather than an academic monograph or policy report.

From this perspective, it can be contended that as the scholarly and policy communities continue to grapple in the beginning of this new millennium with ways to ameliorate their theories and strategies of development, turning to novelists, poets and playwrights for inspiration and ideas could plausibly be instructive. The next sections endeavour to take literary perspectives on development seriously, teasing out a number of themes and lessons from selected examples in order to demonstrate to those who primarily concern themselves with more formal – empirical, theoretical and applied – representations of development that alternative narratives may also be of potential interest.[6] The authors we have selected are those that, for different and sometimes idiosyncratic reasons, we feel have important things to say, regardless of their origins, and whose work illustrates the points that we wish to make. We do not claim to be either exhaustive or representative in our choices of literary works, which are dictated by our own personal readings, and hope that our partial coverage will stimulate others to propose their own shortlists of readings.

Moreover, although some of the works of fiction to which we make reference have been written by writers from the developing world, it is important to note that we are not attempting to construct a case for literature being a "voice from the developing world". This is an issue that Frederic Jameson (1986) considered in a classic essay on "Third-World Literature in the Era of Multinational Capitalism", where he proposed that all third world texts be read as "national allegories".

Jameson was subsequently widely accused of being patronising and Eurocentric (see, for example, Ahmad, 1987), although Imre Szeman (2001: 804) has recently suggested that "almost without exception, critics of Jameson's essay have wilfully misread it", thereby obscuring "a sophisticated attempt to make sense of the relationship of literature to politics in the decolonizing world". Although this latter issue is clearly relevant to our task at hand, our canvas is much narrower than that of Edward Said (1993: xiii), for example, who explores the world of narrative fiction in terms of its position "in the history and world of empire".[7] Along with Said, we very much recognise the fact that "the power to narrate, or to block other narratives from forming and emerging, is very important to culture and imperialism, and constitutes one of the main connections between them", but our focus is on literature in general as an alternative representational genre through which to understand development processes and phenomena.

The usefulness of literary perspectives on development

In her recent study of non-governmental organisation (NGO) issues in the Philippines, Thea Hilhorst (2003) begins by making a strikingly unfavourable comparison between mainstream academic writing on NGOs and the portrayal of the world of NGOs in a recent work of popular fiction. Hilhorst opens her monograph with a brief discussion of Helen Fielding's novel *Cause Celeb* (1994), a mainly light-hearted chronicle of the adventures of Rosie, a disenchanted London public relations manager who becomes involved in international humanitarian efforts to address famine in an African country.[8] Hilhorst's (2003: 1–2) point is that, perhaps unexpectedly, Fielding's novel presents a relatively nuanced picture of international development work and organisational life:

> In the novel, Rosie's NGO does what organizations do: it has a mission and clear objectives, staff with differentiated responsibilities, and it works with a budget for planned activities. Yet the novel also brings out how this NGO is shaped by actors in the organization and their surrounding networks. These people carry out activities according to their understanding of the situation and follow the whims of their personalities, motivated by various combinations of sacrifice, self-interest, vanity and compassion. It also places the humanitarian activities in their political context, both in the local situation of a country at war and in the politics of development bureaucracies and fundraising. Finally, the novel delightfully turns the refugees into real people— good *and* bad, loveable *and* pitiful—who actively endeavour to enrol NGO staff members and visitors to provide the necessary assistance.
>
> Fielding's novel is strikingly different from most of the scholarly literature on NGOs. Reading this literature, one is usually presented with a black-and-white picture in which managers play the lead roles, all other actors remain silent, and the organizations unfold their objectives in a participatory way. One wonders what these tidy organizations have to do with the other realities that reach us from developing countries, including social and political

movements, conflict and fundamentalism. And one keeps wondering what really happens inside the organizations and how this relates to the lives of the NGO staff, volunteers and beneficiaries.

Hilhorst goes on to ask the question: "Why would Helen Fielding succeed in giving this real-life account of an NGO where development scholars have failed, apart from the obvious reason that she brings her literary talent to this task?" The answer, she contends, is that development research on organisations in general and on NGOs in particular has paid too much attention to the formal organisational world and has assumed its boundaries, thereby ignoring the stories of the people who work in and with these organisations as well as the formal and informal relationships that link everyday practices across formal organisational boundaries. The nuanced portrayal of the NGO world in Fielding's novel contrasts strongly with this lack of imagination and depth, and illustrates well the point that informs our argument in this article, namely, that fictional accounts of development can sometimes reveal different sides to the experience of development and may sometimes even do a "better" job of conveying the complexities of development than research-based accounts.[9]

Akhil Gupta (2005) similarly demonstrates the power of fiction in a recent article where he draws on both academic and literary works in order to write about corruption in India, including in particular, the novel *Raag Darbari* by Shrilal Shukla (1992 [1968]). According to Gupta (2005: 20–21), this latter narrative is not only "one of the richest works of fiction about the postcolonial Indian state" but arguably "a work whose insights into politics and the state in rural India are without comparison". Indeed, Gupta goes on to claim that "it is hard for me to think of another novel or ethnography that gives a more clearly etched picture of the large villages and small tehsil towns". At the same time, however, it can be argued that Gupta (2005: 21) effectively treats *Raag Darbari* as quasi-formal ethnographic research when he claims that its sharp portrayal of social reality derives from the fact that Shukla

> served in the U.P. state provincial service, and then the Indian Administrative Service, being posted mainly around Lucknow. He could thus draw upon a lifetime of experience and observation in those settings that form the stage for the novel.

While this may well be the case, much of the force of the book clearly also derives from its literary qualities as a novel. *Raag Darbari* won one of India's most prestigious literary awards – the Sahitya Akademi Award – in 1970, and is widely considered to have taken the satirical genre to new heights within the context of Hindi-language post-Independence literature. The novel is a picaresque comedy that draws readers in through a series of interlinked stories that are in turn satirical, ironic and tragic, making witty use of vernacular wordplay and caricature, and providing rich, fine-grained descriptions of post-Independence rural small-town India. It furthermore ends on an unambiguous and in many ways prophetic message about the venality of local politics and the vice-like nature of poverty in the countryside that did much to change dominant perceptions of rural India at the time. In particular, the dramatic finale that suggests that migration is the only hope for the rural poor radically challenged prevalent romantic stereotypes of the Indian countryside being idyllic, harmonious and timeless in a way that many academic and policy texts on rural India pointedly failed to do during the 1950s and 1960s. As such, *Raag Darbari* arguably constitutes an example of literary fiction that can be considered "better" – albeit in hindsight – than much of the academic or policy-oriented research from this period as a result of its nuanced understanding and detailed depiction of key development issues.

One reason for *Raag Darbari*'s successful depiction of the nature of rural poverty in India is arguably also the fact that it was not written within the restrictive conventions of academic or policy writing. Beyond superficial issues such as the need for proper referencing, paying one's dues to predecessors, and so on, fictional writing can be said to enjoy a freedom of fabrication that allows it to present "ideal type" exemplifications of social phenomena in a way that empirically grounded academic literature sometimes cannot. The advantages are especially clear in relation to Rohinton Mistry's Booker Prize-nominated novel, *A Fine Balance* (1996), which is all the more germane to this discussion insofar as Mistry explicitly writes with the intention to do more than simply entertain, prefacing his work with a quotation from Balzac's *Le Père Goriot* that deliberately seeks to blur the boundary between "truth" and "fiction":

> Holding this book in your hand, sinking back in your soft armchair, you will say to yourself: perhaps it will not amuse me. And after you have read this story of great misfortunes you will no doubt dine well, blaming the author for your own insensitivity, accusing him of wild exaggeration and flights of fancy. But rest assured: this tragedy is not a fiction. All is true.

A Fine Balance is set primarily at the time of the 1975–1977 state of internal emergency in India, and traces the fortunes of four fictional characters as they try to survive communal tensions, rural to urban migration, downward socioeconomic mobility, the state violence of population control programs, and the fragile search for mutual support networks, productive activity, employment and informal social services in Bombay. It is a relentlessly downbeat novel that concerns itself with almost unbearable hardship and tragedy, but Mistry manages to entertain through the deployment of a style that borders on the ethnographic – a representational method that has only rarely been evident within the development studies mainstream – that invokes the essential "being there" quality that convinces a reader over and above "either a factual look or an air of conceptual elegance" (Geertz 1988: 4). The book is particularly carried by the powerfully drawn characters inhabiting this vividly described world, and *A Fine Balance* clearly has an edge over academic or policy texts as a result, as demonstrated by the fact that the novel has become a fixture on university reading lists for courses on subjects such as rural–urban migration, urbanisation and "livelihoods", over and above much of the extensive academic and policy scholarship that exists. This is, however, very obviously a function of the fact that Mistry's novel is a work of fiction, which meant that he had the freedom to carefully craft his characters in such a way as to reflect the dramatic social reality of impoverishment in India unhindered by the need to respect the inevitably limitations of – always imperfect and partial – empirical research.[10]

A Fine Balance's powerful narrative also allows it to transcend its difficult, even unattractive subject matter, and edge towards a universal appeal based on a kind of "humanism with politics". At least partly as a result of this, it has been taken up by a wide audience, selling over half a million copies in the United States alone by 2002, a much wider circulation than any academic or policy work on the same subject. This is clearly another way in which literary fiction can claim to often be "better" than academic or policy texts, as it is clear that they will generally reach far more people and may therefore be more influential than academic or policy works in shaping public knowledge and understanding of development issues, which is, of course, crucial in terms of building public support for development policies, insofar as this is rarely determined merely by their content.[11] Sometimes this is clearly the result of a specific conjunction of events. For example, the US invasion of Afghanistan and continuing War on Terror have obviously played a significant role in the success of Khaled Hosseini's extraordinarily popular novel *The Kite Runner* (2003), which has arguably done more to educate Western readers about the realities of daily life in Afghanistan (under the Taliban and thereafter) than any government media campaign, advocacy organisation report, or social science research.

The same is also true of another recent Booker Prize-nominated novel, *Brick Lane* by Monica Ali (2003). This rapidly became a fixture at the top of the UK bestseller lists following its publication, and led to its author joining the ranks of the prestigious "Granta New Young British Novelist" list. The novel chronicles the life of Nazneen, a Bangladeshi woman who is sent to Britain at age 18 to marry Chanu, a man twice her age. It provides a rich narrative of the joys and difficulties of her new life, magnificently situating it within wider descriptions of the Bangladeshi migrant community in London that traces its fears, tensions and aspirations. A particularly important element of the novel is the juxtaposition of Nazneen's life in London with that of her sister, Hasina, who has remained in Bangladesh. Through a series of letters, we see how Hasina's life becomes increasingly difficult after she leaves her violent husband, migrates from her village to Dhaka, falls afoul of prevailing gender norms, and loses her job in a garment factory when she is accused of behaving in a "lewd manner". The novel thus encompasses a wide range of themes centred on development and social change: the experience of migration to the UK, the politics of organising within migrant communities, inter-generational relationships, rural–urban migration, tensions around gender and culture, and the activities of charitable non-governmental organisations among destitute women workers in Dhaka. As the first book to enter the UK mainstream to feature the broad subject of Bangladesh and Bangladeshi people – which provides a substantial and increasingly visible immigrant community in the UK, and forms the location of one of Britain's largest aid programmes during the past 30 years – it is arguable that *Brick Lane* has contributed to wider public understandings of development in ways that no academic writing ever has.

There is also another reason why this novel is particularly relevant to our contention about the value of literary sources of knowledge about development. While it is reasonable to suppose that an author's reasons for writing a novel are bound up in a complex bundle of creative, personal and professional motivations, *Brick Lane* is at least partly inspired by recent academic research on Bangladeshi women. At the end of the book, the first acknowledgement is to the academic Naila Kabeer, "from whose study of Bangladeshi women garment workers in London and Dhaka (*The Power to Choose*) I drew inspiration" (Ali, 2003: 371).[12] Kabeer's (2000) book is a study of gender and labour markets within the context of the simultaneous growth of women's employment in the garment sectors of Dhaka and London. The book contrasts employment conditions for women among Bangladeshi communities in the UK, where women work as home-based machinists in an apparent throwback to a nineteenth century form of economic organisation, with those in Bangladesh, where women from the 1980s onwards have increasingly moved out of seclusion into wage employment within modern, large-scale, export-based garment factories. Ali first became aware of *The Power to Choose* while working at Verso Press, which published the book.[13] Here then is a novel that builds on academic research to construct a fictional narrative, responding no doubt to the powerful and evocative testimonies provided by the real women who speak through Kabeer's book. The Kabeer/Ali story is an example of an unusual relationship that developed between "fact" and "fiction" within a subject, and we argue that it is a useful one to consider. The purpose of this example is not to suggest that one "version" of the story of garment workers has more merits than another, but instead to show potential complementarities between two types of narrative, and to illustrate the ways in which the *form* through which knowledge is presented has important implications for its readership.

Conclusion: development through literature

Without falling into the trap of intellectual relativism, in which all "stories" are viewed as equal and thus none can claim to be superior, we have contended that relevant fictional forms of representation can be valuably set alongside other forms of knowledge about development such as policy reports or scholarly writing, as valid contributions to our understandings of development. In this way, literary accounts can be seen – alongside other forms – as an important, accessible and useful way of understanding values and ideas in society. Many of the fictional accounts of development-related issues that exist reveal different sides to the experience of development than more formal literature does, and may sometimes actually do a "better" job in conveying complex understandings of development in certain respects. While fiction may not always be "reliable" data in the sense of constituting a set of replicable or stable research findings, it may nevertheless be "valid" knowledge in that it may be seen "to reflect an external reality" (Elliot 2005: 22).

At the same time, storytelling as a narrative form and research method has long existed within the social sciences. It can come in the shape of case study material of individual experience or more broadly as ethnographic writing within anthropological texts, for example. While such narrative styles have long formed a part of the interdisciplinary field of development studies, they have rarely been part of the mainstream. The same is true at the level of policy, although individual narratives have found their way into policy discourses from time to time, as the "Voices of the Poor" case illustrates, or less recently, in the case of Ken Loach's *Cathy Come Home* television documentary, which influenced UK social policy debates about homelessness in the UK. Yet we must distinguish here between "stories" or "narratives" as a representational form of knowledge – a long-acknowledged research and presentation method in the social sciences (see Elliot 2005 for a good overview) – and "fiction" as a literary form that we argue can contribute usefully to development knowledge. While the World Bank's "Voices of the Poor" initiative offers stories as illustrations *within* a meta-narrative, a novel such as *A Fine Balance* provides a visceral, fine-grained account in which ordinary people *are* the narrative.

Works of fiction can thus offer a wide-ranging set of insights about development processes that are all too often either ignored or depersonalised within academic or policy accounts, without compromising either complexity, politics, or readability in the way that academic literature is often accused of doing. It is clear that literary works sometimes have a stronger Geertzian "being there" quality than certain academic and policy works, they may cover aspects of development that are often not made explicit in conventional academic accounts, or else they are written in a more engaging and accessible manner. Furthermore, partly for this latter reason, works of literary fiction often reach a much larger and diverse audience than academic texts and may therefore be more influential than academic work in shaping public knowledge and understanding of development issues. If more people get their ideas about development from fiction than from academic writing, then surely the fiction of development itself constitutes a potentially important site for the study of development knowledge.

The challenge is therefore to understand better the relationships between different accounts and forms of representation within development writing, as well as noting the multiplicity of voices and logics. In the UK at least, the interdisciplinary field of development studies has for the past decade and a half been struggling with two persistent dilemmas. The first is the "impasse" in development theory identified by David Booth (1985, 1993, 1994), while the second is the tension between theory and practice set out most vociferously by Michael Edwards (1989) in his accusation of the "irrelevance of development studies". We would like to add to this list the idea that there is perhaps also a crisis of representation in development research, which is highlighted by the power and success of the fictional accounts of development ideas and processes that we have drawn attention to in this chapter. In order to properly understand and communicate notions of development, it is perhaps necessary for us to develop forms of writing that can engage with the economic and political realities and human struggles and challenges of development in ways that go beyond the conventional academic and policy forms of development writing, and much may be learnt in this regard from fictional forms of representation.

Ultimately, as Anthony Giddens (1984: 285) has pointed out, "literary style is not irrelevant to the accuracy of social descriptions", because "the social sciences draw upon the same source of description (mutual knowledge) as novelists or others who write fictional accounts of social life". Indeed, this is something that is being increasing recognised in the opposite direction, with literature studies now beginning to borrow from formal development writing, as illustrated by the literary critic Olakunle George (2000) in a recent essay comparing Mahmood Mamdani's well-known political science monograph *Citizen and Subject* (1996) with the literary writings of Nobel laureate Wole Soyinka. Taking such efforts as an example, it is clear that a richer and "truer" perspective on the experience of development is most likely to be achieved by holding the insights and imperatives of literature, social science and policy-making in tension with each other, irrespective of which one is more "truthful". Ultimately, as Mario Vargas Llosa (1996: 320, 330) has pointed out, although it may well be that "novels lie", it is also the case that "men do not live by truth alone; they also need lies", and as such development studies can only benefit from broadening its sources of knowledge to include what we might term "the fiction of development". Indeed, it may even be an essential precondition to reviving the discipline of development studies; as George Eliot observed over 150 years ago:

> Appeals founded on generalizations and statistics require a sympathy ready-made, a moral sentiment already in activity; but a picture of human life such as a great artist can give, surprises even the trivial and the selfish into that attention to what is apart from themselves, which may be called the raw material of moral sentiment.[14]

Recommended reading list of literary fiction on *Development*

Note: All books are English-language or translations. Different and other language editions of these works may exist.

- Achebe, C. (1958) *Things Fall Apart*. London: Heinemann.
- Ali, M. (2003) *Brick Lane*. London: Doubleday.
- Amado, J. (1965 [1943]) *The Violent Land*. New York: Knopf.
- Ballard, J. G. (1994) *Rushing to Paradise*. London: HarperCollins.
- Ballard, J. G. (1987) *The Day of Creation*, London: Victor Gollancz.
- Borges, J. L. (2000 [1964]) *Labyrinths: Selected Short Stories and Other Writings*. London: Penguin Books.
- Boyd, W. (1982) *A Good Man in Africa*. London: Penguin.
- Boyd, W. (1991) *Brazzaville Beach*. London: Penguin.

- Brunner, J. (1968) *Stand on Zanzibar*. New York: Ballantine.
- Buck, P. S. (2004 [1931]) *The Good Earth*. New York: Simon & Schuster.
- Camus, A. (1994 [1948]) *The Plague*. New York: First Vintage International.
- Carpentier, A. (1989 [1957]) *The Kingdom of This World*. New York: Farrar, Straus & Giroux.
- Cohen, A. (1996 [1968]) *Belle du Seigneur: A Novel*. New York: Viking.
- Condé, M. (1996 [1984]) *Segu*. New York: Penguin.
- Conrad, J. (1990 [1902]) *Heart of Darkness*. New York: Dover Publications.
- Conrad, J. (1983 [1904]) *Nostromo*. London: Penguin.
- Darko, A. (1995) *Beyond the Horizon*. London: Heinemann.
- de Bernières, L. (1990) *The War of Don Emmanuel's Nether Parts*. London: Secker & Warburg.
- Desai, A. (2000) *Diamond Dust and Other Stories*. London: Chatto & Windus.
- Farrell, J. G. (1973) *The Siege of Krishnapur*. London: George Weidenfeld & Nicholson.
- Fielding, H. (1994) *Cause Celeb*. London: Picador.
- Forster, E. M. (2000 [1924]) *A Passage to India*. London: Penguin.
- Frisch, M. (1959 [1957]) *Homo Faber*. New York: Harcourt.
- Fuentes, C. (1989 [1987]) *Christopher Unborn*. New York: Farrar, Straus & Giroux.
- Galgut, D. (2004). *The Good Doctor*. London: Atlantic Books.
- Garcia Marquez, G. (1997 [1985]) *Love in the Time of Cholera*. New York: Knopf.
- Garcia Marquez, G. (1995 [1967]) *One Hundred Years of Solitude*. New York: Knopf.
- Genet, J. (1988 [1958]) *The Blacks: A Clown Show*. New York: Grove Press.
- Gordimer, N. (1978) *The Conservationist*. London: Penguin.
- Green, G. (1991 [1955]) *The Quiet American*. London: Penguin.
- Kadaré, I. (2005 [1981]) *The Palace of Dreams*. London: Harvill Press.
- Kingsolver, B. (1998) *The Poisonwood Bible*. New York: HarperCollins.
- Kipling, R. (1987 [1901]) *Kim*. London: Penguin.
- Kourouma, A. (1997 [1970]) *The Suns of Independence*. Teaneck: Holmes & Meier Publishers.
- Kourouma, A. (2001 [1998]) *Waiting for the Vote of the Wild Animals*. Charlottesville: University of Virginia Press.
- Kourouma, A. (2005 [2000]) *Allah Is Not Obliged*. London: Heinemann.
- Lahiri, J. (1999) *Interpreter of Maladies*. New York: Houghton Mifflin.
- Lapierre, D. (1985) *The City of Joy*. New York: Warner Books.
- Le Carré, J. (2000) *The Constant Gardener*. New York: Scribner.
- Maalouf, A. ([1983]) *The Crusades Through Arab Eyes*. London: Saqi Books.
- Mahfouz, N. (1993 [1966]) *Adrift on the Nile*. New York: Anchor Books.
- Mahjoub, J. (1989) *Navigation of a Rainmaker*. London: Heinemann.
- Mahjoub, J. (1994) *Wings of Dust*. London: Heinemann.
- Mistry, R. (1996) *A Fine Balance*. London: Faber and Faber.
- Molteno, M. (1992) *A Shield of Coolest Air*. London: Shola Books.

- Mwangi, M. (1976) *Going Down River Road*. London: Heinemann.
- Naipaul, V. S. (2001 [1961]) *A House for Mr. Biswas*. New York: First Vintage International.
- Narayan, R. K. (1993 [1976]) *The Painter of Signs*. London: Penguin.
- Neruda, P. (2003 [1947]) *Residence on Earth*. London: Souvenir Press.
- Neruda, P. (1993 [1950]) *Canto General*. Berkeley: University of California Press.
- Okri, B. ([1991]) *The Famished Road*. New York: Anchor Books
- Ondaatje, M. (2000) *Anil's Ghost*. London: Bloomsbury.
- Ousmane, S. (1972) *The Money Order*. London: Heinemann.
- Rush, N. (1992) *Mating*. New York: Vintage.
- Rushdie, S. (1981) *Midnight's Children*. London: Picador.
- Seth, V. (1993) *A Suitable Boy*. London: Phoenix.
- Sepulveda, L. (1993 [1989]) *The Old Man who read Love Stories*. New York: Harcourt.
- Shukla, S. (1992 [1968]) *Raag Darbari*. New Delhi: Penguin India.
- Soueif, A. (1999) *The Map of Love*. London: Bloomsbury.
- Soyinka, W. (1963) *A Dance of the Forests*. Oxford: Oxford University Press.
- Tweedie, J. (1987) *Internal Affairs*. London: Penguin.
- Vargas Llosa, M. (1975 [1969]) *Conversations in the Cathedral*. New York: Harper & Row.
- Walcott, D. (1990) *Omeros*. New York: Farrar, Straus & Giroux.
- wa Thiong'o, Ngugi, (1977) *Petals of Blood*. London: Penguin.
- wa Thiong'o, Ngugi, (1989) *Matigari*. London: Heinemann.
- Xingjian, G. (2000 [1990]) *Soul Mountain*. New York: HarperCollins.

Notes

1 This is an abridged version of the article "The Fiction of Development: Literary Representation as a Source of Authoritative Knowledge", *Journal of Development Studies*, Vol. 44, No. 2, pp. 198–216, 2008.
2 See Shakespeare's *The Tempest*, Act IV, scene 1, line 155.
3 Horace's (1959: 75) original expression was that literature – and more specifically poetry – should be both "sweet and useful". Its oft-cited formulation as "to teach and to delight" is generally attributed to the sixteenth century soldier-poet Sir Philip Sydney in his famous *Apology for Poetry* (2002 [1595]).
4 Indeed, as Mark Moore (1987: 80) astutely notes, the ideas that become dominant public ones frequently do so insofar as they "distinguish heroes from villains, and those who must act from those who need not. ...[T]o the extent that these distinctions fit with the aspirations of the parties so identified, the ideas will become powerful. If powerful people are made heroes and weaker ones villains, and if work is allocated to people who want it and away from people who do not, an idea has a greater chance of becoming powerful".
5 The same can also be said of some academic contributions – see for example Collier and Gunning (1999).
6 In some respects there are parallels between this chapter and Sherman (2001), who uses literary sources to document changing public attitudes toward the poor in turn of

the nineteenth century Britain. See also Herman (2001) on the rendering of the poor in nineteenth century Russian literature.

7 This is an issue that has been extensively taken up within the emergent field of "cultural studies", as part of its effort to achieve a synthesis of social science and literary studies. In particular, it aims to "dismantle the elitism of the distinction between high and popular culture within literary studies" (Schech and Haggis, 2000: 26), which in many ways we see as analogous to our interest in questioning the distinctions between different types of knowledge about development. Cultural studies as a discipline is however much broader and also concerned with the relationship between society and the production of texts.

8 Changing emphasis to a completely different subject matter, Fielding later went on to write the hugely popular and influential Bridget Jones "chick-lit" novels.

9 Many other scholars and practitioners have made similar use of literature to highlight an issue, although few explicit their logic for doing so as clearly as Hilhorst. Von Struensee (2004), for example, uses Nigerian writer Buchi Emecheta's novel *The Bride Price* (1976) as a means of introducing the subject of bride price in a recent overview paper on the domestic relations bill in Uganda. In a related manner, it is common for social scientists to preface their work with literary citations, implicitly because they are revealing of the issue being written about (and no doubt also because this tends to generate a certain aura of cultural sophistication).

10 For two examples of academic works that attempt to create a fictionalised "ideal type" of their object of study based on but not limited by the empirical reality of their underlying research, see Taussig (1996) and Hecht (2006), respectively on the nature of the state in Latin America and on the plight of street children in Brazil. Such works are extremely rare within the social sciences, however, and it is interesting to note that both of these originate from anthropology, perhaps the most empirical of social science disciplines.

11 Of course, it is important to note that the power of literary fiction as a widespread and significant source of popularised information to shape public opinion can also be appropriated to promote ideas and notion that could be construed as "anti-developmental". The controversy surrounding Michael Crichton's (2004) recent novel *State of Fear* and its message about the ambiguities of global warming is a case in point (see Crowley, 2006).

12 It is interesting to note that the novel also pokes fun at academic work. At one point, Nazneen's husband Chanu cites the London School of Economics "World Happiness Survey" to support his argument for returning to Bangladesh: "Research led by professors at the London School of Economics into links between personal spending power and perceived quality of life has found out that Bangladeshis are the happiest people in the world. And LSE is a very respectable establishment, comparable to Dhaka University or Open University." (Ali, 2003: 290). A further irony here is that despite this LSE study being cited from time to time in the press and on websites, we are unable to find any conclusive evidence that it ever existed.

13 Naila Kabeer, personal communication.

14 Cited in Gill (1970: 10).

References

Achebe, C. (1958) *Things Fall Apart*. London: Heinemann.

Ahmad, A. (1987) "Jameson's rhetoric of otherness and the 'National Allegory'". *Social Text*, 17: 3–25.

Ali, M. (2003) *Brick Lane*. London: Doubleday.

Ballard, J. G. (1987) *The Day of Creation*. London: Victor Gollancz.

Benjamin, W. (1989) "On the program of the coming philosophy". In G. Smith (ed.), *Benjamin: Philosophy, Aesthetics, History*. Chicago: University of Chicago Press.

Booth, D. (1985) "Marxism and development sociology: Interpreting the impasse". *World Development*, 13(7): 761–787.

Booth, D. (1993) "Development research: From impasse to a new agenda". In F. J. Schuurman (ed.), *Beyond the Impasse: New Directions in Development Theory*. London: Zed Books.

Booth, D. (1994) "How far beyond the impasse: A provisional summing up". In D. Booth (ed.), *Rethinking Social Development: Theory, Research and Practice*. London: Longman Publishing Group.

Collier, P., J. W. Gunning (1999) "Explaining African economic performance". *Journal of Economic Literature*, 37(March): 64–111.

Coser, L. (1972[1963]) *Sociology through Literature*. Englewood Cliffs: Prentice Hall.

Crichton, M. (2004) *State of Fear*. New York: Avon Books.

Crowley, M. (2006) "Jurassic President". *The New Republic,* 20 March.

Czarniawska-Joerges, B. (1992) *Exploring Complex Organizations: A Cultural Perspective*. Newbury Park: Sage.

Denning, S. (2000) *The Springboard: How Storytelling Ignites Action in Knowledge-Era Organizations*. Woburn: Butterworth-Heinemann.

Edwards, M. (1989) "The irrelevance of development studies". *Third World Quarterly*, 11(1): 116–135.

Elliot, J. (2005) *Using Narrative in Social Research: Qualitative and Quantitative Approaches*. London: Sage.

Emecheta, B. (1976) *The Bride Price*. London: Allison & Busby.

Escobar, A. (1995) *Encountering Development: The Making and Unmaking of the Third World*. Princeton: Princeton University Press.

Ferguson, J. (1990) *The Anti-Politics Machine: Development, Depoliticization and Bureaucratic Power in Lesotho*. Minneapolis: University of Minnesota Press.

Fielding, H. (1994) *Cause Celeb*. London: Picador.

Foucault, M. (1984) "What is an author?" In P. Rabinow (ed.), *The Foucault Reader*. New York: Pantheon.

Geertz, C. (1988) *Works and Lives: The Anthropologist as Author*. Stanford: Stanford University Press.

George, O. (2000) "African politics, African literatures: Thoughts on Mahmood Mamdani's *Citizen and Subject* and Wole Soyinka's *The Open Sore of a Continent*". *West Africa Review*, 2(1): 1–13.

Giddens, A. (1984) *The Constitution of Society: Outline of the Theory of Structuration*. Berkeley: University of California Press.

Gill, S. (1970) "Introduction". In E. Gaskell, *Mary Barton: A Tale of Manchester Life*. London: Penguin.

Godwin, W. (1993 [1793]) *Enquiry Concerning Political Justice and Its Influence on Modern Morals and Happiness*. Harmondsworth: Penguin.

Gupta, A. (2005) "Narratives of corruption: Anthropological and fictional accounts of the Indian state". *Ethnography*, 6(1): 5–34.

Hecht, T. (2006) *After Life: An Ethnographic Novel*. Durham: Duke University Press.

Herman, D. (2001) *Poverty of the Imagination: Nineteenth-Century Russian Literature about the Poor*. Evanston: Northwestern University Press.

Hilhorst, D. (2003) *The Real World of NGOs: Discourses, Diversity and Development*. London: Zed Books.

Horace. (1959) "The art of poetry". In *Satires and Epistles of Horace* (edited and translated by S.Palmer Bovie). Chicago: Chicago University Press.

Hosseini, K. (2003) *The Kite Runner*. New York: Riverhead Books.

Jameson, F. (1986) "Third-world literature in the era of multinational capitalism". *Social Text*, 15: 65–88.

Kabeer, N. (2000) *The Power To Choose: Bangladeshi Women and Labour Market Decisions in London and Dhaka*. London: Verso.

Keen, P. (1999) *The Crisis of Literature in the 1790s: Print Culture and the Public Sphere*. Cambridge: Cambridge University Press.

Mahfouz, N. (1993 [1966]) *Adrift on the Nile*. New York: Anchor Books.

Mahfouz, N. (1993 [1983]) *The Journey of Ibn Fattouma*. New York: Anchor Books.

Mamdani, M. (1996) *Citizen and Subject: Contemporary Africa and the Legacy of Late Colonialism*. Princeton: Princeton University Press.

Mistry, R. (1996) *A Fine Balance*. London: Faber and Faber.

Mitchell, T. (1991) *Colonising Egypt*. Berkeley: University of California Press.

Mitchell, T. (ed.) (2000) *Questions of Modernity*. Minneapolis: University of Minnesota Press.

Mitchell, T. (2002) *Rule of Experts: Egypt, Techno-Politics, Modernity*. Berkeley: University of California Press.

Moore, M. (1987) "What Sort of Ideas Become Public Ideas?" In R. Reich (ed.), *The Power of Public Ideas*. New York: Harper Business.

More, T. (Sir) (1964) "Letter to Peter Giles". In E.Surtz and J. H. Hexter (eds.), *The Complete Works of Sir Thomas More*, vol. 4. New Haven: Yale University Press.

Narayan, D., with R. Patel, K. Schafft, A. Rademacher, and S. Koch-Schulte (2000a) *Voices of the Poor: Can Anyone Hear Us?* New York: Oxford University Press.

Narayan, D., R. Chambers, M. Kaul Shah, and P. Petesch (2000b) *Voices of the Poor: Crying Out for Change*. New York: Oxford University Press.

Narayan, D., P. Petesch (2002) *Voices of the Poor: From Many Lands*. New York: Oxford University Press.

Pritchett, L., and M. Woolcock (2004) "Solutions when the solution is the problem: Arraying the disarray in development". *World Development*, 32(2): 191–212.

Roe, E. M. (1991) "Development narratives, or making the best of blueprint development". *World Development*, 19(4): 287–300.

Roe, E. M. (1994) *Narrative Policy Analysis*. Durham: Duke University Press.

Said, E.W. (1993) *Culture and Imperialism*. London: Chatto & Windus.

Schech, S. and J. Haggis (2000) *Culture and Development: A Critical Introduction*. Oxford: Blackwell.

Sherman, S. (2001) *Imaging Poverty: Quantification and the Decline of Paternalism*. Columbus: Ohio State University Press.

Shukla, S. (1992 [1968]) *Raag Darbari*. New Delhi: Penguin India.

Sidney, P. (Sir) (2002 [1595]) *An Apology for Poetry (or The Defence of Poesy)*. Manchester: Manchester University Press.

Soueif, A. (1999) *The Map of Love*. London: Bloomsbury.

Soyinka, W. (1996) *The Open Sore of a Continent: A Personal Narrative of the Nigerian Crisis*. Oxford: Oxford University Press.

Szeman, I. (2001) "Who's afraid of national allegory? Jameson, literary criticism, globalization". *South Atlantic Quarterly*, 100(3): 803–27.

Taussig, M. (1996) *The Magic of the State*. New York: Routledge.

Vargas Llosa, M. (1996) "The truth of lies". In *Making Waves: Essays*. London: Faber and Faber.

Von Struensee, V. (2004) "The Domestic Relations Bill in Uganda: Addressing Polygamy, Bride Price, Cohabitation, Marital Rape, and Female Genital Mutilation", paper downloaded from the Social Science Research Network (SSRN), http://ssrn.com/abstract =623501.

White, H. (1973) *Metahistory: The Historical Imagination in Nineteenth Century Europe.* Baltimore and London: John Hopkins University Press.

World Bank (2000) *Can Africa Claim the 21st Century?* Washington, DC: The World Bank.

3 Notes on teaching international studies with novels

Hard Times, Half of a Yellow Sun, and The Quiet American

John Harriss

> The creative imagination of the literary artist often has achieved insights into social processes which have remained unexplored in social science.
>
> Lewis Coser (1972: 3)

David Lewis, Dennis Rodgers and Michael Woolcock (2008: 199) have argued, in an article titled "The Fiction of Development", that "there may be a case for widening the scope of the development knowledge base conventionally considered to be 'valid'." They go on to discuss the importance, on the one hand, of narrative and of storytelling in social science and, on the other hand, the significance of 'fiction' as a means of exploring and of expressing fundamental truths about human experience and human understandings of the world. Theirs is a project that has parallels in some earlier work, such as in Philip Darby's book on *The Fiction of Imperialism: Reading between International Relations and Post-Colonialism* (1998), as well as, more importantly, Lewis Coser's *Sociology Through Literature* (1972), from which I have taken my opening epigraph. Indeed, Lewis and his co-authors explicitly refer to Coser's work, and their chapter explores the insights that fiction can offer in relation to various aspects of 'development'.

The aim of this chapter is to discuss an attempt over several years to put the arguments of "The Fiction of Development" into practice in undergraduate teaching, and in doing so to discuss the relevance of three novels written by very different novelists, from different periods. I hope to show here how the analyses of social scientists and of historians are complemented by the work of creative writers – and, at least in brief, what I believe my students gained from this. The aim is to straddle two ways of understanding the world, by bringing together different sorts of texts under one conceptual roof – in this case, that supplied by the idea of 'development'. Students are exposed to different ways of understanding the same historical experience, through approaches that both complement and diverge from each other.[1]

Core texts in international studies

This is the bland title of a course that I designed as part of the 'capstone' of the undergraduate major in International Studies at Simon Fraser University. But why study 'core texts'? What are 'core texts'? Of course, the only answer to the second of these questions is comparable with the answer to the question of what constitutes the 'great tradition' of English literature that is posed by F. R. Leavis's (1948) classic work of literary criticism. Leavis begins his book with the sentence "The great English novelists are Jane Austen, George Eliot, Henry James and Joseph Conrad ...". As he goes on to say, this is his critical judgement, which he then proceeds to defend vigorously. In much the same way, what may be considered 'core texts' in International Studies is a matter of judgement, and I am ready to defend mine. For present purposes, however, let me just say that my selection included Karl Polanyi's *The Great Transformation: The Political and Economic Origins of our Time* (2001 [1944/1957]); *Imagined Communities: The Origins and Spread of Nationalism* by Benedict Anderson (1983); and Odd Arne Westad's *The Global Cold War: Third World Interventions and the Making of Our Times* (2005).

Alongside these books by social scientists and historians, I took Charles Dickens' (1969) *Hard Times*, first published in 1854, which was read against *The Great Transformation*, as a study of the experience of nineteenth century industrialism and of the applications in society of utilitarianism – also discussed by Polanyi at some length; the Nigerian writer Chimamanda Ngozi Adichie's (2006) *Half of a Yellow Sun*, which as a novel about the Biafra war of the 1960s complemented *Imagined Communities*, as well as Westad's arguments about "identitarian politics"; and Graham Greene's (2004) *The Quiet American*, originally published in 1955, and set in Vietnam before the final defeat of the French – a novel about American interventionism in the context of the Cold War, which highlighted the contradictions of the youthful idealism of what Westad describes as the "the empire of liberty" that was sought to be established by the United States after 1945. The following sections explore how the second set of texts both complemented and diverged from the first in their representation of the above themes.

Hard Times[2]

Dickens is rather an obvious novelist to read in the context of studies of development, partly because – in the views of many critics – he took the English novel to new levels, in a time of rapid social change, and partly because he wrote with purpose, to make his readers think about what was going on in the society in which they lived (he is specifically referred to in this regard by Polanyi, for his campaigning against the Commission on the Poor Law, 2001: 102). Dickens was engaged with the meanings of modernity in the mid-nineteenth century, and though he is sometimes associated in the popular imagination with Mr Pickwick, the world of coaching inns and of "Olde England", he was actually fascinated by machines and especially by railways, about which he wrote quite a lot. In his mature work, including *Hard Times*, some of his writing is about the industrial society that he saw coming to be, and about which he held nuanced views. In this, he was like other nineteenth century writers who shared in Victorian doubts about 'progress'. In parts of his novels, and of his other writings, Dickens shows that he did not regret the passing of the old world of a primarily rural society – as did some of his contemporaries - and that he welcomed the possibilities of social change. In *Dombey and Son* (1848), for example, he describes a dismal scene unfolding before the eyes of Mr Dombey, looking out from the train on the approach to Birmingham, but he says that it is Dombey's own state of mind that leads him to see "ruin and a picture of decay, instead of hopeful change" (Dickens, 1848: 201).

Hard Times, on the other hand, written in the aftermath of Dickens' observations of a long lockout of workers in the northern English town of Preston, reflects nothing of this idea of "hopeful change". Though it is considered – as it was by Raymond Williams in *Culture and Society 1780–1950* (1958) – as being among the (generally unsuccessful) English "industrial novels" of the nineteenth century, *Hard Times* is not so much a report on conditions in an industrial town – disappointing some of its contemporary critics for this reason – as it is a critique of the culture of industrial capitalism. As the critic David Craig (1969: 14, 12) wrote, it is a "a source of insights into a specific phase in that long train of social experience which has brought us to where we are" – as a novel "about a kind of bondage to routine and calculation so integral to the culture of industrial societies". In its way, it is as much a moral critique of economic liberalism as is *The Great Transformation*.

The Preston that Dickens (1969: 65) saw in the early months of 1854 was probably not unlike the "Coketown" of his novel, or even cities in the emergent economies of our own day:

> It was a town of red brick, or of brick that would have been red if the smoke and ashes had allowed it … A town of machinery and tall chimneys, out of which interminable serpents of smoke trailed themselves for ever and ever and never got uncoiled. It had a black canal in it, and a river that ran purple with ill-smelling dye … It contained several large streets all very like one another, and many small streets still more like one another, inhabited by people equally like one another, who all went in and out at the same hours … to do the same work, and to whom every day was the same as yesterday and tomorrow...

The long descriptive passage from which these lines are taken brings out the theme of "routine and calculation" that Dickens, very much like Polanyi, saw as undermining our humanity. Later in the book Louisa, its tragic heroine, is described entering "one of the dwellings of the Coketown Hands":

> for the first time in her life, she was face to face with anything like individuality in connection with them … She knew them in crowds passing to and from their nests, like ants or beetles. But she knew from her reading infinitely more of the ways of toiling insects than of these toiling men and women. Something to be worked so much and paid so much, and there ended; something to be infallibly settled by laws of supply and demand … She had scarcely thought

more of separating them into units, than of separating the sea itself into its component drops ... (Dickens, 1969: 187)

Here the novelist conveys wonderfully well the meaning of what Polanyi describes as the necessary liberal fiction that labour – which really means 'people' – is simply a commodity. The description through the novel of the Coketown workers as 'Hands', reduced to minding machines, also anticipates some of Karl Marx's writing about the impact of capitalist industrialisation, and Harry Braverman's (1974) much more recent book on the effects of industrial organisation, which bears the subtitle "the degradation of work". The idea that "labour" under capitalism involves the alienation of human beings from their "species being" comes close to the central theme of *Hard Times,* which has to do with the inhumanity brought by utilitarian calculation. And Dickens' emphasis on the regulation of individual action – "people ... who all went in and out at the same hours ... and to whom every day was the same as yesterday and tomorrow" – anticipates E. P. Thompson's (1967) classic paper on "Time, Work-Discipline and Industrial Capitalism". In his essay about the novel, Craig (1969: 21) argues that "Dickens was never more surely in touch with rightful popular feeling than when, in this particular novel, he made rigid systematism ... his target rather than the more glaring sorts of material evil", before then going on to refer to a contemporary writer who said that the New Poor Law, the creation of Utilitarian philosophy, "did more to sour the hearts of the labouring population than did the privations consequent on all the actual poverty of the land".

The central character of *Hard Times*, Mr Thomas Gradgrind, Member of Parliament for Coketown, is introduced at the beginning of the novel in his schoolroom, and described as:

A man of realities. A man of fact and calculations ... With a rule and a pair of scales, and the multiplication tables always in his pocket, sir, ready to weigh and measure any parcel of human nature, and tell you exactly what it comes to. It is a mere question of figures, a case of simple arithmetic ... (Dickens, 1969: 48)

Gradgrind is Dickens' satirical portrait of the Utilitarian, an exponent of the philosophy associated above all with Bentham and Mill, discussed by Polanyi in his chapters on the birth of the liberal creed – and responsible, as Polanyi (2001: 147) saw it, for the contradiction of economic liberalism, as when he argues that "the introduction of free markets, far from doing away with the need for control, regulation, and intervention, enormously increased their range".

Certainly, *Hard Times*, throughout, conveys a strong sense of "lives clamped under a grid" (Craig 1969: 17). The opening chapters of the novel effectively link the experience of education in the mid-nineteenth century with the regulation of industrial society.[3] They juxtapose the cold rigidity of the schoolroom in which nothing is to be taught but facts – a child's knowledge of a horse from experience is, for example, worth nothing beside the capacity to rattle off an almost ludicrously abstract definition – with the warmth and humanity of circus people and the joy that they express through their performance. Essentially, for the book, they exemplify freedom from life "clamped under a grid". Gradgrind, on his way home from the school spies "a number of children … congregated in a number of stealthy attitudes, striving to peep in at the hidden glories [of the circus]", and is appalled to find his own children Louisa and Tom, among them: "his own metallurgical Louisa peeping with all her might through a hole in a deal board and his own mathematical Thomas abasing himself on the ground to catch but a hoof of the graceful Tyrolean flower-act!" (Dickens, 1969: 56).

The central narrative of the novel is about the tragedies of Louisa and Tom, the development and the expression of whose humanity is stunted by their upbringing and their education. But Gradgrind, the Utilitarian, is not a bad man. He means very well indeed and shows kindness in taking into his home one of the circus girls who has, it seems, been abandoned. He is at last devastated by the fate of his own children. Louisa finally returns home in despair and collapses in his arms: "And he laid her down … and saw the pride of his heart and the triumph of his system, lying, an insensible heap, at his feet" (Dickens, 1969: 242). As Leavis (1948: 269) says in his essay on the novel, which brings it into his canon of the "Great Tradition" of English literature, "the confutation of Utilitarianism by life is conducted with great subtlety".

But there are great weaknesses in the book, too, and it has been described as an implausible melodrama. The most serious weakness of all concerns Dickens' treatment of the industrial worker, as an object of pity, through the figure of Stephen Blackpool, who is represented as the cowed victim of events and as having little effective agency in his own life. The workers of Coketown, too, are shown as being easily manipulated by the union leader Slackbridge. Trade unionism is represented as an error – in a negative way that is surprising given Dickens' own observations in his report "On Strike", published in the periodical *Household Words* in February 1854, of how the Preston workers maintained their resilience, their solidarity and their dignity through 23 weeks of their lockout. Dickens here betrays a thoroughly middle-class sensibility, and though *Hard Times* was described by at least one of his contemporaries as 'socialist', the novel suggests no project of social change resulting from the collective organisation of workers, or from political reform. Dickens seems to hope for the restoration of 'harmony' in society, and the way out of what Stephen Blackpool refers to frequently in the book as the "muddle" of industrial life is through individual goodness and restraint; "It is, rather, individual persons against the System", as Raymond Williams (1958: 106) put it. Certainly, there is no sense whatsoever in *Hard Times*, of the 'double movement' that Polanyi saw as being inherent in the nineteenth century attempt to make a reality of the utopian idea of the self-regulating market in industrial society, as it is met by the resistance of people to their own treatment as commodities, and to the commodification of land (the environment), and eventually by the opposition of states, driven to defend business and accumulation from the effects of the treatment of money as a commodity through the gold standard.

Half of a Yellow Sun[4]

If *Hard Times* is about the cultural experience of early industrialism and of the attempt to establish the self-regulating market economy, Chimamanda Ngozi Adichie's novel *Half of a Yellow Sun* is about the experience of life in an African colony in the immediate aftermath of colonialism, and then in the context of state failure and civil war. As a reviewer wrote for the *New York Times*, it "takes us inside ordinary lives laid waste by the all too ordinary unravelling of nation states" (Nixon, 2006). The title of the book is a reference to the emblem of Biafra during the attempted secession from Nigeria of the Igbos in the south-east of the country between 1967 and 1970. Both of Adichie's grandfathers died as refugees in Biafra, and she writes that "I grew up in the shadow of Biafra … writing *Half of a Yellow Sun* has been my re-imagining of something I did not experience [she was born eight years after the end of the Nigerian civil war] but whose legacy I carry". She goes on to say that she wanted to "engage with my history in order to make sense of my present",[5] and she has spoken on another occasion of how her book has helped some people in Nigeria, at least, to break the general silence about the war in their country (Adichie, 2008). Though it is factually accurate – apart from a few minor details – the book is not at all a fictional history of the Biafran war. As Adichie (2008) put it in an interview: "Maybe *Half of a Yellow Sun* is a war book, but I wanted the war to be secondary. I wanted to write about the characters and the way they are changed by the war". The mostly very positive critical reception that her book has received is a tribute to the extent that she succeeded in this. As John Marx (2008: 597) wrote in a commentary, Adichie "portrays life during wartime as both intensely violent and remarkably ordinary".

The central characters in the novel are twin sisters – though they are very different both in looks and in personality – Olanna and Kainene, the privately educated daughters of Chief Ozobia, who is described as owning "half of Lagos" (Adichie, 2006: 59) and a member of Nigeria's ruling elite – depicted early in the book as corrupt and self-seeking. Olanna, recently returned from completing a master's degree in England, disappoints her parents by choosing to go to live with her lover, Odenigbo, a lecturer in mathematics in the University of Nigeria at Nsukka, and to teach sociology. Her sister, the enigmatic, independent Kainene, manages some of "Daddy's businesses" – "she has always had an excellent eye for business", her father says (Adichie, 2006: 31) – and becomes the lover of Richard, an Englishman who has come to Nigeria to write about Nigerian bronzes, but who is a diffident man, uncertain of himself and, as we see, seeking somewhere to belong. These four, together with Ugwu, a village boy who arrives in the first chapter to become Odenigbo's house-boy are the central characters of the novel, and the chapters are written in turn from the perspectives of Ugwu, Olanna and Richard. To a significant extent, however, *Half of a Yellow Sun* is Ugwu's story, and it comes to the reader as no surprise to know from published interviews with her that he is Adichie's favourite among the characters she has created – and he is rather a remarkable creation.

Interspersed through the book there are short passages, printed in a different typeface, that are taken, apparently, from a book about the war, and that are all entitled "The Book: The World Was Silent When We Died". In part, this is a device for providing background information about the history of Nigeria and the context of the civil war. We wonder whose words they are, and many readers will presume that they are Richard's. At the very end of the novel, however, we learn that they are Ugwu's. They are a symbol, perhaps, of the significance of the war for Nigerians' understandings of themselves, apart from the 'outside' knowledge of the intellectuals (but see Marx, 2008: 614ff).

The action of the novel moves between the early and the late nineteen sixties and back again – between the world of the university at Nsukka and the kind of 'salon' that takes place in Odenigbo's bungalow (and which problematises the role of the intellectual in post-colonial society), Ugwu's village, Lagos, and northern Nigeria in the years immediately before the war, and the war itself. In her depiction of the world before the war, Adichie makes her readers witness to the everyday dramas of race, gender and status distinctions in the post-colonial society of Nigeria, and to the tensions between the 'traditional' society of Ugwu's village and that of 'modern' Nigeria. The war overturns them all. The stories of Odenigbo and Olanna, of Richard and Kainene, are stories of loyalty and betrayal that subtly echo and are echoed in the political events of the book. The tensions between Olanna and Kainene, and the question of forgiveness between them, are another echo of Nigeria's politics. Ugwu, too, at a vital moment in the course of the war, under great pressure, betrays himself.

From more or less the beginning of the novel, we are made aware of ethnic differences in Nigeria. Descriptions of Odenigbo's 'salon' in Nsukka focus attention on group distinctions. Ugwu notes, for example: "The loudest [of those who come to Odenigbo's house] was Miss Adebayo. She was not an Igbo woman: Ugwu could tell from her name, even if he had not once run into her and her housegirl at the market and heard them both speaking rapid, incomprehensible Yoruba" (Adichie, 2006: 19). In the discussions in his house, Odenigbo talks a good deal about Pan-Africanism. The ideas of race and nation are, he says, a product of colonialism, but he also tries to maintain that his identity as Igbo is primordial. To this, Professor Ezeka – a character based, Adichie (2008) tells us, on Colonel Ojukwu, who lead the breakaway Biafran state – retorts 'but you became aware that you were Igbo because of the white man. The pan-Igbo idea came only in the face of white domination. You must see that tribe as it is today is as colonial a product as nation and race" (Adichie, 2006: 20). Or, in other words, as an "imagined community", very much along the lines described by Benedict Anderson in his *Imagined Communities* (1983).

It is not only through these didactic statements that Adichie's novel evokes Anderson's arguments. *Imagined Communities*, especially in the later edition with its added chapters on "Census, Map, Museum" and on "Memory and Forgetting", as it treats "The Last Wave" of more recent colonial nationalism, emphasises the role of the colonial intelligentsia. Adichie takes her readers into that world in Nigeria. The characters who come together in Odenigbo's salon are there as a result of what Anderson (1983: 142) talks of as the "educational and administrative pilgrimages" occasioned by colonialism and as a result of which 'Nigeria' can be imagined at all. It is imagined essentially through the medium of the English language, the language of the salon. Anderson (1983: 122) takes the example of Ghana, arguing that "nothing suggests that Ghanaian nationalism is any less real ... because its national language is English rather than Ashanti", ultimately contending that "print-language is what invents nationalism, not a particular language per se". Adichie's evocation of the world of the intelligentsia at the end of the colonial period, however, makes us aware of the contradictions of colonial nationalism, and of the problem of language. We see this at first through Ugwu's eyes and his experience of listening to the debates in the living room, and through his reaction on his first meeting with Olanna: "He wished she would stumble in her Igbo; he had not expected English that perfect to sit beside equally perfect Igbo" (Adichie, 2006: 23). John Marx (2008: 613) says of the salon "by doubly marking discussants as expert and ethnic it distances them from the citizenry they might otherwise represent". In the end the intelligentsia are marginalised. They have failed to develop 'a common political language' – ideas and values that are shared through society as a whole – substantially because of the contradictions that are associated with their use of English.[6] This is the context of the rise of what Westad (2005: 400) refers to as "identitarianism" – the affirmation of "other identities outside the immediate discourses of modernity" – that had already become significant during the late colonial era.

Language differences are important markers of group distinctions in Nigeria. Ethnic differences are remarked upon, too, through crude stereotypes, by Richard's first lover in Lagos, Susan, of the British High Commission: "She told him the Hausa in the north were a dignified lot, the Igbo were surly and money-loving, and the Yoruba were rather jolly, even if they were first-rate lick-spittles" (Adichie, 2006: 55). Through Susan's role in the novel Adichie portrays the 'unseeing', still dismissive and frankly racist attitudes of the former colonialists – who played a contradictory role historically, in the civil war (while the British government upheld the fight of the Nigerian government against Biafran secession, British NGOs were in the forefront of efforts to provide humanitarian assistance to Biafra). Later, Susan describes the Igbo as having "it coming to them ... with their being so clannish and uppity and controlling the markets. Very Jewish, really. And to think that they are relatively uncivilised; one couldn't compare them with the Yoruba, for example, who have had contact with Europeans on the coast for years. I remember somebody telling me when I first came to be careful about hiring an Igbo houseboy because, before I knew it, he would own my house and the land it was built on" (Adichie, 2006: 154). She says this to Richard shortly after he had witnessed the brutal murder before his eyes of the young Igbo customs officer to whom he had just been speaking at Kano airport.

Early in the novel, Olanna has gone to Kano to visit her uncle and aunt and her cousin. On the way from the airport, she passes by the Igbo Union Grammar School, and recalls people having talked "about the northern schools not admitting Igbo children" (Adichie, 2006: 38). But with her relatives "she felt a sense that things were in order, the way they were meant to be … This was why she came to Kano: this lucid peace" (Adichie, 2006: 39). She meets her uncle's friend Abdulmalik, a Hausa man who sells leather slippers in the market, and who gives her a pair; and she renews her acquaintance with a former lover, the distinguished, handsome Mohammed. Her next visit to Kano is terrifying. She is with Mohammed when they become aware that a riot has broken out, and he determines to take her to the railway station. On the way they hear "slow Hausa words resonating. 'The Igbo must go. The infidels must go. The Igbo must go'" (Adichie, 2006: 147). Then they see the destruction of her uncle's compound and the murdered bodies of her aunt and uncle: "'We finished the whole family. It was Allah's will!' one of the men called out in Hausa. The man was familiar. It was Abdulmalik. He nudged a body on the ground with his foot, and Olanna noticed, then, how many bodies were lying there, like dolls made of cloth" (Adichie, 2006: 148). The mystery of when neighbours kill each other is evoked with great power. Adichie makes her readers aware of the wider politics that have brought about these terrible events in Kano, and those that follow them, but she does not attempt to explain *why* it is that the killings take place. She helps us, her readers, however, to reach an empathetic understanding of how it can be that such killing comes about.

Secession is declared. The initial euphoria is quickly crushed by defeat, and Ugwu, Olanna and Odenigbo have to flee Nsukka. We, as readers, then experience bombing raids, fighting and deaths and the progressive onset of hunger as Biafra is slowly crushed. The charismatic, forceful Odenigbo declines into depression; Olanna shows remarkable resilience. Kainene goes missing, and her fate remains unknown. Ugwu, aged by now just 13, is at last forced into joining the army, and is introduced to "the casual cruelty of [a] new world", from which there "grew a hard clot of fear inside him" (Adichie, 2006: 359). In these passages of the book, Adichie takes us into the world of a child soldier. Ugwu kills and earns the nickname "Target Destroyer"; shortly afterwards he is with others in a bar, and more or less made to drink himself silly with the local gin. He escapes outside for a while, but when he goes back in he finds the bar-girl being raped and is driven by the taunts of his fellows to rape her as well. "Finally he looked at the girl. She stared back at him with calm hate" (Adichie, 2006: 365). The rape haunts him and drives him to write. His "knowing by suffering" (Das, 2006: 75) makes him, in John Marx's (2008: 621) argument, an "uncredentialed expert of the war zone".

Another aspect of the novel that is significant in regard to development studies has to do with the role that Richard plays. Portrayed very sympathetically by Adichie, he is well meaning, but also ineffectual. He wants very much to identify with Biafra, yet he remains an outsider. The powerful passage in which he witnesses the murder of Igbo at Kano airport makes him seem almost like a voyeur of others' suffering. Through the character of Richard, Western readers may be led to reflect upon their own roles in other societies, and it is one of the ways in which Adichie's novel took my students from the "cool distance" of the work on state failure and civil war by historians and social scientists "to the inside of the maelstrom" (Sylvester, 2006: 75).

The Quiet American[7]

Christine Sylvester's remark above also applies to much of the writing of Graham Greene, who certainly has a claim to having been one of the greatest English novelists of the twentieth century, and who was also a journalist and at one point an intelligence agent. *The Quiet American,* which drew on his experience as a war correspondent in Indochina in the early 1950s, though it is constructed and reads like a thriller, is an emphatically political novel – and came to be seen as having anticipated the disaster of American involvement in Vietnam. It is a searing critique of American interventionism in the Cold War – to be read very profitably alongside Westad's more analytical account in *The Global Cold War,* from the intervention against Mossadeq in Iran in 1953 and Arbenz in Guatemala in 1954,[8] to "Charlie Wilson's War" in Afghanistan in the 1980s (this was the title of a movie, released in 2007, about the role of Texas Congressman Charlie Wilson in setting up covert operations against the Soviet Union in Afghanistan).

Westad explains the reluctance of the United States to support the efforts of the Europeans to retain control of their Asian empires in the aftermath of the Second World War. The United States was drawn into supporting the French in southeast Asia only because the French were struggling against communism, and Greene evokes the tensions in the relationship between France and the United States in a description of a press conference addressed by a French officer. There are tense moments when the officer is driven to refer to supplies promised by the United States not arriving, but then says that his statement is not to be printed:

> Perhaps the American newspapers would say "Oh, the French are always complaining, always begging". And in Paris the Communists would accuse "The French are spilling their blood for America and America will not even send a second-hand helicopter". It does no good. At the end of it we should still have no helicopters, and the enemy would still be there, fifty miles from Hanoi. (Greene, 2004: 57)

At the same time, the two principal characters of the novel are Thomas Fowler, an English journalist who is approaching middle age, and an old hand in Asia, who pretends to somewhat world-weary detachment; and Alden Pyle, the quiet American, whom Fowler had first seen

> coming across the square towards the bar of the Continental: an unmistakably young and unused face flung at us like a dart. With his gangly legs and his crew-cut and his wide campus gaze he seemed incapable of harm … Perhaps only ten days ago he had been walking back across the Common in Boston, his arms full of the books he had been reading in advance on the Far East and the problems of China. (Greene, 2004: 9-10).

The extent to which the two are 'representatives of their nations' is at once apparent. The two become rivals for the affections of a Vietnamese woman,

Phuong, who has some fascination for the West – she is described as "looking at the pictures in an old *Paris-Match*. Like the French she has a passion for the Royal Family" (Greene, 1955: 93) – and who seems detached but, it appears, is easily moulded to their wills by the two men. She, evidently, is an allegorical representation of Vietnam. Pyle has come to Saigon ostensibly to join the staff of the American Economic Mission, but we learn eventually that he is with the CIA (though it is referred to in the book as the 'OSS' – the Office of Strategic Services, which was the precursor of the CIA).

Fowler says "Pyle was very earnest and I ... suffered from his lectures on the Far East, which he had known for as many months as I had years. Democracy was another subject of his – he had pronounced and aggravating views on what the United States was doing for the world" (Greene, 2004: 4). Later we come to know that "Pyle came out here full of York Harding's idea" – Harding being "a superior sort of journalist" (Greene, 2004: 160), who has written books with such titles as *The Advance of China*, *The Challenge to Democracy* and *The Role of the West*, and who is the author of the idea of a Third Force that will be capable both of ending colonial rule and of defeating the communists. It becomes clear that Pyle, behind the cover of his role in the Economic Mission, is working to put the idea of the Third Force into practice, through working with General Thé, "the dissident Chief of Staff who had recently declared his intention of fighting both the French and the Vietminh" (Greene, 2004: 76). The notion of a 'Third Force' corresponds with Westad's analysis of the American search for appropriate allies in Asia in the 1950s. Initially ready to support "radical Third World nationalism of the nativist kind" (Westad 2005: 119), like that represented by Sukarno's party in Indonesia, the United States soon started to intervene against even very moderate regimes, fearing that they smacked of communism, and began to support groups comparable with the fictitious General Thé's. One of Westad's (2005: 119) central arguments is that "Washington willfully reduced its potential for real alliances with popular nationalist movements. It was this self-inflicted isolation from associations of the more syncretic kind that forced the US to intervene repeatedly in the Third World".

Fowler and Pyle find themselves stranded through the night in a watchtower, surrounded by the Vietminh, on the way back into Saigon from General Thé's headquarters, and this becomes the moment for the confrontation of their different world views – though the conversation is dictated by Fowler. He says to Pyle of the frightened Vietnamese soldiers: "Do you think they know they are fighting for Democracy? ... You and your like are trying to make a war with the help of people who just aren't interested", and he sweeps aside Pyle's protestations that "they don't want Communism", suggesting that "the political commissar" is the only one likely to treat the ordinary peasant as a man, rather than as a "unit in the global strategy" (Greene, 2004: 86-89). Fowler protests that he is not 'engaged', while arguing forcefully against imperialist meddling in the affairs of others. Later, after General Thé's forces, with Pyle's assistance, have exploded bombs in the city, killing innocent people, it seems that the American is indeed ready to treat people as "units in a global strategy". He is shocked at finding blood on his shoe, but he says distractedly, "I must get them cleaned before I see the Minister"

(Greene, 2004: 161). Though Fowler is willing to concede that Pyle did not quite know what he was saying – "He was seeing a real war for the first time" – he retorts angrily that "You've got the Third Force and National Democracy all over your right shoe" (Greene, 2004: 162). Then, as Pyle goes off muttering about how General Thé must have been deceived by the Communists, Fowler remarks "he was impregnably armoured by his good intentions and his ignorance" (Greene, 2004: 163). This is a comment that must have struck some readers of the book in the course of the last decade as being a remarkably appropriate commentary, applying as well to American (and British) action in Iraq and Afghanistan as to Indochina in the 1950s.

Conclusion

What is gained by bringing together different ways of understanding the ideas and the events and actions that have shaped the social world as we know it – the more or less detached analyses of historians and social scientists on the one hand, and works of fiction on the other? At the very least, according to the responses I've had from my students, reading the novelists' explorations of such themes as those of the implications of Utilitarianism, or the politics of ethnicity, or the impact of great power interventions during the Cold War, has served to bring these problems alive for them. Reading the novels has often helped to excite their interest in the texts, because it has brought home to them the significance for people of ideas and events and social trends that are analysed, often dispassionately, by the historians and social scientists. The novels have helped them to understand and to empathise with the experience of others, and in this way to appreciate the human significance of the arguments of the social scientists and made their reading of the texts more meaningful. A common reaction that I've heard from students is that reading the novels has made it possible for them to relate as human beings to the experiences of others, coming from different backgrounds and at different points in history, as well as leading them to reflect upon their own experience. One has written to me, for example, about how reading *Hard Times* led him to think about the significance of technology in relation to social change – "for me, at least, as a student I was led to reflect upon the multitude of technological changes occurring around us now, and their implications" – while reading *The Quiet American*, he said, had helped him to appreciate what it meant to have been a young American in Indochina in the context of the Cold War.

So what is the value, to continue with this example, of reading Graham Greene on American intervention in Asia alongside the work of a historian such as Odd Arne Westad? In this particular case, I think that it is partly because Greene helps us to understand the way of thinking that led to what proved to be disastrous mistakes – following from what Westad (2005: 119) speaks of as the United States' "self-inflicted isolation". It is very important for the novel that Pyle is so well intentioned. He is a decent man – while Fowler really is not, as he himself recognises. But as Westad (2005: 404) concludes: "Seen from a Third World perspective, the results of America's interventions are truly dismal. Instead of being a force for good – which they were no doubt intended to be [as support for General Thé was believed to be by Pyle] – these incursions have devastated many societies and left them more vulnerable to further disasters of their own making". Of course, Graham Greene did not 'predict' the American war in Vietnam, but readers at the time – in the mid-1950s – stood to gain insights into the minds of those who were just beginning to set the United States onto the dangerous path of intervention. For all that Greene was seen, quite reasonably, as anti-American,[9] I think it can be argued that he actually shows sympathy for the American position, through Fowler's response to Pyle and his recognition of Pyle's values.

At the very least, fiction is an aid to the kind of empathetic understanding that makes for the best history writing – and, for the student mentioned above, is a means to understanding "what it was like, to have been that sort of a person, at that time". In a similar way, as I argued earlier, though Adichie does not offer her readers a scientific analysis of ethnic conflict, my students clearly gained a better understanding of what it means to live in a society that has been taken over by "identitarian politics". And a novel such as *Hard Times* is in many ways an historical document that teaches us how the events and ideas of Dickens' time were interpreted in the imagination of a creative writer (and it is through creative writing that we can hope to understand changing sensibilities in societies, exactly as Anderson argues in *Imagined Communities*). *Hard Times* is a part of the cultural experience of what Polanyi refers to as the utopian idea of the self-regulating market. At times, too, creative writers help to push out the frontier of enquiry, as I think that Adichie does with her exploration of the role of the intelligentsia in post-colonial society.

Ultimately, as George Eliot once wrote, "appeals founded on generalisations and statistics require a sympathy ready-made, a moral sentiment already in activity; but a picture of human life such as a great artist can give, surprises even the trivial and the selfish into that attention to what is apart from themselves, which may be called the raw material of moral sentiment" (quoted in Lewis, Rodgers and Woolcock, 2008: 210). This sums up very well the reactions of many of my students to their reading of the novels that I have described here. They are certainly not young people who are "trivial and selfish" – most are drawn to the field because of their often idealistic interest in what is going on in the world, and their drive to have some positive impact upon it. But many have written for me about the ways in which the novels have enhanced their understanding of "how social processes affect people's lives", and drawn their "attention to what is apart from themselves". The portrayals of the social impact of early industrialism, of colonialism, of ethnic conflict, and of the impact of war on the lives of the characters in the three novels discussed here do indeed extend readers' moral sensibilities, and in doing so, bring greater meaning to the study of social science.

Notes

1 I owe this last formulation to Neera Chandhoke.
2 Page references are given to the Penguin English Library edition, first published in 1969, listed in the bibliography.

3 An old but interesting source on Dickens' treatment of education and of political economy in *Hard Times* is Robin Gilmour's essay on "The Gradgrind School: Political Economy in the Classroom", *Victorian Studies*, 11:2 (December 1967), pp. 207–24.

4 Page references are given to the Harper paperback edition of 2007, listed in the bibliography.

5 See http://www.halfofayellowsun.com/ (accessed 21 July 2011).

6 I am influenced here by Sudipta Kaviraj's (1991) arguments about the mutual incomprehension of elite and masses in India.

7 Page references are given to the first edition of the novel, published by Heinemann in 1955, listed in the bibliography.

8 The American intervention against the social democratic government of Jacobo Arbenz in 1954 is the subject of a magnificent, recently rediscovered painting of Diego Rivera's, with the ironic title 'Glorious Victory', which I have used in lectures to introduce Westad's themes.

9 Certainly, *The Quiet American* angered many American readers at the time for what was seen as Greene's one-sided representation of what America was doing. The reviewer for the *New York Times,* for example, wrote that "if much of the description of Indochina at war is written with Greene's great technical skill and imagination, his caricatures of American types are often as crude and trite as those of Jean Paul Sartre. He is not ashamed as an artist to content himself with the picture of America made so familiar by French neutralism; the picture of a civilisation composed exclusively of chewing gum, napalm bombs, deodorants, Congressional witch-hunts, celery wrapped in cellophane, and a naive belief in one's own superior virtue". (Davis, 1956). Davis' argument that Greene employs his "characters less as individuals than as representatives of their nations or political factions" does an injustice, however, to the complexity of the narrator, Fowler, through whom Greene explores broader themes relating here especially to the idea of commitment – that, in fact, run through much of his work (see Thomson, 2009).

References

Adichie, C. N. (2006) *Half of a Yellow Sun*. London: Harper.

Adichie, C. N. (2008) "Interview". *Bookforum*, December–January 2008, available online at: http://www.bookforum.com/inprint/014_04/1403 (accessed 5 February 2013).

Anderson, B. (1983) *Imagined Communities: Reflections on the Origins and Spread of Nationalism*. London: Verso.

Braverman, H. (1974) *Labor and Monopoly Capital: The Degradation of Work in the Twentieth Century*. New York: Monthly Review Press.

Coser, L. (1972 [1963]) *Sociology through Literature*. Englewood Cliffs: Prentice Hall.

Darby, P. (1998) *The Fiction of Imperialism: Reading between International Relations and Post-Colonialism*. London: Continuum.

Das, V. (2006) *Life and Words: Violence and the Descent into the Ordinary*. Berkeley: University of California Press.

Davis, R. G. (1956) *"Review of The Quiet American"*. *New York Times,* March 11.

Dickens, C. (1969 [1854]) *Hard Times*. Harmondsworth: Penguin.

Dickens, C, (1848) *Dombey and Son*. London: Bradbury and Evans.

Craig, D. (1969) "Introduction". In C. Dickens, *Hard Times*. Harmondsworth: Penguin.

Greene, G. (2004 [1955]) *The Quiet American*. London: Vintage.

Kaviraj, S. (1991) "On state, society and discourse in India". In J. Manor (ed.), *Rethinking Third World Politics*. Harlow: Longman.

Leavis, F. R. (1948) *The Great Tradition*. Harmondsworth: Penguin.

Lewis, D., D. Rodgers, and M. Woolcock (2008) "The fiction of development: Literary representation as a source of authoritative knowledge". *Journal of Development Studies*, 44(2): 198–216.

Marx, J. (2008) "Failed-state fiction". *Contemporary Literature*, 49(4): 597–633.

Nixon, R. (2006) *"Review of Half of a Yellow Sun"*. *New York Times,* October 1.

Polanyi, K. (2001 [1944/1957/]) *The Great Transformation: The Political and Economic Origins of our Times*. Boston: Beacon Press.

Sylvester, C. (2006) "Bare life as a development/post-colonial problematic". *The Geographical Journal*, 172(1): 66–77.

Thomson, B. (2009) *Graham Greene and the Politics of Popular Fiction and Film*. London: Palgrave Macmillan.

Thompson, E. P. (1967) "Time, work discipline and industrial capitalism". *Past and Present*, 38 (December): 56–97.

Westad, O. A. (2005) *The Global Cold War: Third World Interventions and the Making of Our Times*. Cambridge: Cambridge University Press.

Williams, R. (1958) *Culture and Society 1780–1950*. Harmondsworth: Penguin.

4 Considering 'pedagogical' fictions and metanarratives of development

1 World Manga[1]

Veronica Davidov

Introduction

In 2007, Viz Media and the World Bank teamed up to produce a faux-manga series entitled *1 World Manga*. The series, framed and structured as a homage to the bona fide manga series, feature a protagonist named Rei who wants to be a martial artist and is aided by his spirit guide (who can transform into any animal) on a series of quests called 'passages'. Each passage tackles a 'development' issue (poverty, HIV/AIDS, global warming, child soldiers, girls' education, and corruption), many of which resonate with the Millennium Development Goals. In this article, I analyze the framework and the structure of the protagonist's quests, and argue that the series generates a pedagogical metanarrative of 'development' that engages behavioral and situational, rather than ontological and structural causes of inequality and disenfranchisement that impede the characters' human development. I argue that this 'pedagogical' metaframework, informed by a rhetoric of universal humanism, is explicitly linked to what I discuss as the normative development discourse, which is centered around recognizable, fixed sets of circumstances, actors, and outcomes.

While many texts can be described as 'pedagogical' in one way or another, in this case awareness-raising was an explicit and intentional part of the production and circulation design of *1 World Manga*, as, according to Patricia Kayaman at World Bank Publishing group, who came up with the idea for the project, the series was conceived and designed "to inform youth about these issues in the developing world ... [The series was] geared towards a developed country to get [youth there] interested, and to get them to appreciate what was happening in the other parts of the world".[2] Each 'passage' is accompanied by educational materials that direct the readers to 'find out more', offer the readers the opportunity to self-test their newly gained knowledge with quizzes and 'did you know?' bullet-point charts, and feature sections that direct the readers how to 'teach others' about the issues in question (so, the HIV/AIDS 'passage' is followed by a guide entitled 'Teach Others to Protect Themselves').

1 World Manga: *the context of production*

Manga is the Japanese comic book art that is exported to many other countries, and informs various hybrid art forms. *Manga* itself is a Japanese word that means

Figure 4.1 A typical manga character.
Source: "Manga boy" by Zabiamdeve, purchased from the image bank Dreamstime.com.

comics in general; however, the term is widely used outside of Japan to specifically refer to Japanese comics (Oóhagan, 2007: 247). Some canonical manga series that have achieved immense popularity outside Japan include *Sailor Moon* and *Dragon Ball*, two offerings that Juüngst (2007: 250) argues shaped the general idea of manga for a general audience. Manga is a highly 'globalized' genre – as Oóhagan (2007: 242) writes, "Examples of the influence of manga and anime range from Hollywood films such as *The Matrix* and *Kill Bill* to a UK publisher's recent launch of a Manga Shakespeare series, turning Romeo and Juliet into a contemporary story set in Japan with Japanese characters depicted in a distinctive manga style". The distinctive style mentioned refers to a broad, easily recognizable visual conventions associated with anime, where characters are generally depicted with big hair and large eyes (Figure 4.1), although within that framework, different manga artists have distinct and unique techniques.

1 World Manga exemplifies what Oóhagan (ibid.) refers to as "the so-called Amerimanga and Euromanga, i.e., the adoption of manga form by comic artists in the US and Europe". Still, as a project, it is less a manga-qua-manga series, or even an artistic hybrid/homage, and more an attempt by an institution to capitalize on a popular visual form that has already been established as a 'global' export. Of course, issues of 'authenticity' in cultural production are complex, but in my interviews with the creators, they themselves referred to the series as 'faux manga', and the stories reference the frame and the visual style of manga, while being paired with content that is, first and foremost, explicitly educational (departing from conventional manga in that sense as well).

To better understand the context and process of creation of the series, I interviewed its creators: Patricia Katayama, Acquisitions Editor at the World Bank, and Annette Roman, Editor at Viz Media. Patricia had come up with the idea for *1 World Manga*, and Annette authored the stories themselves. Patricia told me that one of the main reasons was the fact that the then World Bank president emphasized youth outreach: "In 2005 talking about it, the President of the World Bank, Wolfensohn, was promoting youth outreach, initiatives to interest youth... in the appreciation of development issues, we thought we need some things in our publication line to help with youth outreach ... we mainly reach out to policymakers and researchers, we publish about 180 titles a year, most are very academic publications. So we discussed that, we got support from the unit, and external relations ... we couldn't just do it because it was a fun idea, it had to fit with the objectives of the institution, and since reaching out to youth was one of the issues considered important at the time, the timing was right". The harmony between the vision of development and the World Bank positions was an explicit part of the production process: "We would propose a few themes [to Annette], she would come up with storyline, then the Bank... our office had to approve the topic ... There had to be something important for development ... and the relevant unit within the bank, they would set the content, and make sure that the facts and the messages were in line with the bank's research on the issue ..."

The process of the production, as it was described to me, was designed to ensure that the messages and the framework of the series were consistent with the vision and the position of the World Bank. The creative process was described by both Patricia and Annette thus: Annette was provided with case studies from around the world that she would integrate into a plot. Patricia explained, "I would get some of the Bank material on the topic, send it to Annette, and she would create a proposed storyline. I would run it by whoever was the designated head communications officer for that subject or topic. The World Bank is divided into networks and issue areas, and some issue areas are owned by a number of units, like the human development network within the bank. We always made sure we had unit's clearance, it was a red-flagging exercise ..."

Fiction and/in development

Theorizing the relationship between development and fiction is a fruitful, if a somewhat uncommon endeavor. Beyond the seminal article by Lewis, Rodgers, and Woolcock (2008) exploring the multifaceted ways in which works of fiction can offer insights about development processes, it is a somewhat esoteric and under-theorized subject, possibly owing to the disciplinary chasm between scholars who tend to study fiction, and development studies scholars. Of course, there are ways to bridge that chasm, including discourse analysis, which I will rely on in this article, and, certainly, literature on the subject does exist. Even without explicitly engaging with representations of development in fiction, scholars make connections between the semiotics of fiction and the narratives of development. In his piece on the globalization/science fiction intertext (which uses 1950s science fiction, specifically Asimov's *Foundation* series as the basis for its argument), Weldes (2001: 662) correctly notes that "it is these broad intertextual knowledges – the culture's 'image bank', including, for instance, standard narratives and conventional tropes from science fiction – that 'pre-orient' readers and allow them to make meanings, in this case about globalisation, in some ways rather than others". Weldes (ibid.) then concludes that "the liberal globalisation discourse is science fiction, as both discourses – that of globalisation and of 1950s utopian science fiction ... provide an optimistic vision of a globalised, or indeed galactic, future that rests upon a liberal, market-oriented, techno-utopian individualism". This argument about the discourse of globalization can be convincingly mapped over onto discourses of development, resonating with Klak and Myers' (1997: 133) analysis of the discursive tactics of neoliberal development in small developing countries: "The typical advertising package combines three themes: neoliberal and contextual depiction (pledges of subsidies, an open economy, and cheap and unorganized labour; tropical paradise and friendly natives), science fiction (dreams of high technology, telecommunications, and informatics), and strategic omission (exclusion of strife, resistance, hardship, and societal degradation)".

It is hard to delineate what, exactly, is 'fiction' in the context of 'development' and of the issues faced by people in 'developing' countries. There is no discrete genre of 'development' fiction, although many novels use development issues either as a plot point in a mystery (like John Le Carre's 2002 *The Constant Gardener*, a thriller that revolves around illegal experiments by a pharmaceutical company in Kenya), or that use development as a backdrop to *bildunsgroman* narratives about privileged Westerners discovering themselves (like Benjamin Kunkel's 2005 novel *Indecision*).

It could be argued that the medium where fictions (or at least meta-fictions) of 'development' circulate most prominently today is the flourishing industry of youth-oriented 'reality shows' such as *Trippin'* and *Exiled* (that would have to be classified as 'enhanced reality' at the very least, if not fiction) that are build around semiotics of radical alterity of 'exotic' peoples in developing countries, but that also double as lightly pedagogical development awareness platforms with associated websites, where issues implicitly referenced but never discussed on air are explicated. The development awareness platforms in such contexts are almost always embedded within a discourse that Catherine Lutz and Jane Collins (1993: 60) characterized (when writing about *The National Geographic*) as "classical humanism, with its romance of universalism, drawing readers' attention through its portrayal of difference, and then showing that under the colorful dress and the skin, as it were, we are all more or less the same". Such universalist humanism is an easy and convenient framework for development-issues-driven plots, not to mention a pedagogically friendly one. One recent example of this synergy is James Cameron's hit film *Avatar*. The film generated discussions and debates among scholars, especially anthropologists, about whether it was truly radical in its rejection of 'development' as colonialism, or whether it merely reproduced the discourse of 'bad development' versus the 'noble savage', with the latter being a marketable trope in 'good' sustainable development. *Avatar* is grounded quite literally in such universalist humanism, as its protagonist, the paraplegic soldier Jake Sully, becomes physically transformed into an indigenous Na'vi leader, who defends 'his' land and people against a violent, greedy mining corporation. In addition to its commercial success, the film inspired a variety of Web-based peda-gogic material, including The Global Avatar ED Project, "designed to facilitate the use of the film *Avatar* as part of a global citizenship curriculum ... [for] under-graduate college students or senior high school students",[3] Avatar Film Discussion Guide and CST produced by Education for Justice and available in their Economic Justice and Development section,[4] and Avatar with Kids: A Discussion Guide.[5]

Such universalist humanism is also present in the design and the structure of *1 World Manga*. As Patricia explained about the setting of the series: "We deliber-ately kept it vague – one requirement of the series was that we would not be spe-cific with the countries ... that would be problematic – we did not want people to think that we were making specific statements about specific countries ... Some of the names were foreign-sounding, but nothing too specific that could pinpoint a specific country ... maybe the region, but not the country". Indeed, some pages feature Rei finding himself in a city where business signs on busy streets are writ-ten in Asian ideograms, some of the characters he encounters have tattoos that seem inspired by both Melanesian and Polynesian designs, the name of his would-be-paramour in "First Love" is Somalee, which simultaneously evokes the coun-try name 'Somalia and the female name Sonali, of Sanskrit origin, and widely used in India. As Patricia elaborated: "We wanted to keep a vague feeling of 'somewhere in Africa' or 'somewhere in southeast Asia' or 'somewhere in the subcontinent' or 'somewhere in Eastern Europe'... we didn't want anyone reading into this more than we were intending to do, which was just to inculcate some interest in these issue areas, and encourage the kids to learn more and study more, so we put some references into the back to other sources of information... but we didn't want any specific countries associated with the stories". The process of creating the series also ensured this bricolage approach consistent with universal-ist humanism: "We gave Annette case studies, she took bits and pieces from dif-ferent case studies from different countries".

I argue that when 'universal humanism' figures as the meta-framework for plot and character development, it produces a closed discourse that obfuscates other meta-frameworks that would encourage critical engagement with the narratives, even (or perhaps especially) when the narratives are composed of archetypal tropes of the normative development discourse. Any of the stories in *1 World Manga* on their own merits could be analyzed in terms of other meta-frameworks – structuralist theory of development, or dependency theory, or any other kind of macro-systemic framework that engages with political economy and the social consequences of global inequalities. But the implicit yet ubiquitous universalist humanism informing Rei's adventures promotes the literal interpretation of the 'passage' narratives, and, in synergy with the plot arcs that focus on choices of individual actors, promotes a proximate, rather than ontological approach to the challenges faced by the *1 World Manga* characters.

What about 'Development'?

Although the word *development* is not an explicit part of *1 World Manga*, the narrative and the pedagogical lens employed in these series pivots, first and foremost, around 'development' as an aspirational, desirable trajectory. In his now-classic text on development in Lesotho, James Ferguson (1990: xiv) wrote: "Development institutions generate their own form of discourse, and this discourse simultaneously constructs Lesotho as a particular kind of object of knowledge, and creates a structure of knowledge around that object. Interventions are then organized on the basis of this structure of knowledge ..." While Ferguson's observations drew on a particular ethno-historical example, they have broader applicability. The development discourse he analyzes constructs its subjects (be they developing nations, failed states, communities, or 'civil society') as intervention sites that can be known, analyzed, and acted upon, through and within a very specific framework of meaning-making based around standardized assessments and desirable outcomes.

Furthermore, Ferguson (ibid.) wrote: "If 'development' is today from time to time challenged, it is still almost always challenged in the name of 'real development'. Like 'goodness' itself, 'development' in our time is a value so firmly entrenched that it seems almost impossible to question it, or to refer it to any standard beyond its own". Building on this observation by Ferguson, I will refer to what is in *1 World Manga* as 'normative development discourse' – a discourse that can and ought to be interrogated through looking at representations of development in fiction, or even through an analysis of development as fiction. Both of these approaches may help illuminate the meta-narratives that belie and shape the normative development discourse, opening it up for interrogation in a way that is radically different from the false juxtaposition of a critiqued notion of 'development' with a 'real' development that Ferguson notes.

It is not my intention to critique a publication geared towards youth for a lack of a nuanced and multifaceted perspective on development. However, at the same time, something that is so 'distilled' allows for an excellent analysis of what the normative development discourse is – and what kinds of narratives and tropes are deployed with the explicit goal of introducing audiences to the issues of global challenges and development 'hot topics' for the first time. The fixed narrative that clearly attributes virtue and blame, and links causes and effects to individual actors, does not stem from any limitations of the medium per se (a young adult manga-like comic book); certainly, alternative – and arguably much more radical – interpretations of development exist in equally 'simple' formats (the *There You Go* pamphlet by Oren Ginzburg, distributed through Survival International, comes to mind).[6] Lewis, Rodgers, and Woolcock (2008: 207) wrote that "works of literary fiction often reach a much larger and diverse audience than academic texts and may therefore be more influential than academic work in shaping public knowledge and understanding of development issues. If more people get their ideas about development from fiction than from academic writing, then surely the fiction of development itself constitutes a potentially important site for the study of development knowledge". Their argument is especially relevant for a portrait of development in a pedagogical framework that is quite possibly formative for its audiences.

In the next section, I am going to draw on three of the passages to explore how the normative development discourses are used in *1 World Manga*, and the sort of pedagogical space they engender. Like any pedagogical space, the one created by *1 World Manga* is strategically constructed and characterized by its own architecture of inclusion and exclusion: of the relevant frameworks and facts that are illuminated, and the obfuscated or marginalized factors or nuances.

Rei's quests: the normative approach to AIDS, toxic dumping, and corruption

First love

My first example is "Passage 2: HIV/AIDS – First Love". In this passage, Rei finds himself in an unnamed Asian city; in a discotheque he meets a waitress called Somalee, who invites him to stay with her. At her house, he discovers that Somalee's mother is dying from AIDS, which, Somalee reveals, she contracted because Somalee's father was unfaithful to her. "You get it from sleeping with someone! From sex! Or sharing needles", explains Somalee to Rei. Condoms are prominently featured and promoted throughout the passage – at the beginning of the narrative, Rei innocently mistakes them for unusual party balloons, but by the end he understands the importance of using them, although he and Sonalee still abstain from sex as she wants to wait for the man she will marry, so that she can be faithful to him.

The representation of HIV/AIDS as a 'development' issue here strongly resonates with O'Manique's (2004: 9) argument that the discursive and political field of HIV/AIDS has been dominated by the biomedical approach and the behavioral approach, "a narrow public health lens that focuses on individual sexual behavior". The two, according to her, have shaped both the body of knowledge around the disease, and dictated the interventions into its spread. Various scholars have critiqued the behavioral emphasis for obfuscating structural inequalities that range from lack of access to appropriate pharmaceuticals to the fact that factors such as malaria and malnourishment increase HIV/AIDS susceptibility. Stillwaggon (2006) shows in detail how the same conditions that amplify the likelihood of other infectious diseases and parasites contribute to the spread of HIV/AIDS in poor populations. Others concur: "Programs to prevent HIV transmission are unlikely to succeed unless they address the underlying causes of its spread ... HIV prevention must be based on scientific evidence regarding cofactor conditions, not, as they currently are, on unproven assumptions about the primacy of behavioral factors" (Gillespie, 2006: 29) – these cofactor conditions include poor nutrition/absence of food security, schistosomiasis, and malaria, among others. All of these exacerbate susceptibility to HIV transmission, and the vulnerability to developing full-blown AIDS, and all of these are factors structurally rooted in what Stillwaggon (2006) calls "the ecology of poverty", or what Farmer (2005: 222) calls "pathogenic effects" of inequality rather than 'bad' decisions by individuals.

It is especially interesting that 'folk knowledge' about AIDS in developing countries – this is especially true of African countries (Nauta, 2010) – often attributes high rates of transmission to physical vulnerabilities that result from 'exotic' sexual practices such as female circumcision, while overlooking *virtually identical physical vulnerabilities* can stem from the parasitic disease schistosomiasis,[7] which affects over 200 million people in 74 countries, and which has been exacerbated by water 'development' projects, especially dam construction (Sharp, 2003). So, 'savage' cultural practices that theoretically can be constructed as 'choices' are foregrounded as causes of HIV/AIDS, more so than parasitic co-factors inescapable in areas that are either impoverished, or 'developed' in specific ways (or both), even when genital lesions are the results of both possibilities. Scholars point out that development literature on HIV/AIDS, which is predominantly concentrated on African, especially sub-Saharan countries, is rooted in a historical tendency to study the sexuality of the colonial subject, eventually turned development subject, as "different from our own... described as wild, animal-like, exotic, irrational and immoral" (Gausset, 2001: 510). This "exotic and exceptional sexuality" (Stillwaggon, 2006: 142) is perceived to consist of polygamy, adultery, wife exchange, female circumcision, dry sex practices, etc. The over-emphasis on 'exotic' sexual practices further legitimates the behavioral approach to HIV/AIDS, wherein contracting the disease is connected to poor choices made by people who live in a culture that has historically sanctioned such choices, but who, thanks to health-focused development programs and interventions, ought to know better by now.

Behavioral emphases, especially on monogamy and fidelity, have also been heavily criticized for their neoliberal approach to health that resonates with the 'radical individualism' of discourses of neoliberalism (Marchand and Runyan, 2000) and downplays complex socio-historical factors that make fidelity challenging on a systemic level, as "sexual behaviour is understood as autonomous from other social forces and relations" (O'Manique, 2004: 46). In one in-depth ethnohistorical analysis of HIV/AIDS in urban East Africa (Kenya and Tanzania), Silberschmidt (2001) creates a compelling and complex portrait of a culture where colonialism transformed traditional notions of masculinity, altering traditional division of labor in the household, and bringing with it Euro-American notions of patriarchy, wherein masculinity was both associated with aggressive affect, and linked to economic performance (in the context of wage work). She documents the way in which the drop in the income-earning capacity in the region due to economic turbulences produced systematic unemployment and poverty, which reinforced male violence and aggression, and led to a crisis in the male identity, especially since the men's former prestige-giving activities such as tribal warfare and tending to cattle camps had disappeared, as development discourses and programs focused almost primarily on female empowerment. Silberschmidt argues that, as compensation, men focus on the pursuit of sexual conquests for the purpose of affirming their masculinity, regardless of health consequences. In more contemporary linkages, various other studies have documented a direct correlation between an increase in HIV/AIDS and the appearance of resource extraction-driven forms of development in regions (Pegg, 2006; Kojucharov, 2007; Kimmerling, 2007). The 'first love' passage draws exclusively on the ahistorical, behavioral paradigm of HIV/AIDS (and its standard attendant intervention discourse, commonly known as 'the ABC: Abstain, Be Faithful, and use Condoms'), teaching its readers a specific and strategic narrative of how HIV/AIDS is spread in the developing world, and who is vulnerable.

The lagoon of the vanishing fish

"Passage 3: Global Warming – The Lagoon of the Vanishing Fish" finds Rei solving an environmental crime. The story culminates with the identification of the perpetrator of ongoing toxic dumping in a region that seems like a hybrid of Melanesia and Micronesia – 'a truck from the Zinglam Factory with the logo painted over'. It is explained that "Zinglam Corp has been expelled from three countries for their flagrant disregard of pollution regulations" and that they are infamous for illegal maneuvers, and for covering their tracks: "It is impossible to manufacture products so cheaply without producing massive toxic by-products – but inspectors can never find a trace of them in the waste pipes ..." At the climactic moment, the characters exchange the following expository dialogue:

"They built a manufacturing plant here because the authorities don't have the resources to enforce the island's environmental protection laws ..."
"Looks like they are dumping something ... those barrels must be leaking hazardous waste into the lagoon ... that's what killing and driving off fish!"

The vanishing fish is determined to be caused by illegal toxic dumping, and this form of pollution is pedagogically linked to global warming. The responsibility for halting global warming is placed on authorities: "This is a job for presidents, prime ministers, and kings, too, we need leadership in a global scale. This battle requires treaties and laws and regulations ..." Then, the educational resources section that follows this particular passage advocates the use of controversial biofuels, along with wind and solar energy in the 'what we can do' coda. Thus, in this passage, the framework of how development trajectories intersect with environmental issues features a private-sector villain that commits clearly illegal acts anonymously and cleverly enough to fool inspectors. Environmental protection laws are explained to be in place, but they cannot be enforced because of lack of resources. Global partnership on the highest level is expected to help.

There are a number of issues that this normative discourse obfuscates. Even leaving aside the links between the types of deregulation associated with standard protocols of neoliberal economic development (articulated in and enforced through structural adjustment programs) and the presence of transnational companies attracted by weaker environmental and labor regulations in developing nations, and the larger issues of global inequalities and ecological debt involved in the framing of global warming as a 'global problem', the story of the toxic dumping itself is obfuscatory in its normativity. What is marginalized in the *1 World Manga* narrative of toxic dumping? First and foremost, the long-standing practice wherein developing countries are used for dumping toxic waste produced not by specific corporations operating, in flagrant disregard of established laws, on those countries' territories, but by operators from industrialized countries who export their toxic waste to these countries, in a process that has been called 'toxic colonialism' – a process that, in a sense, has been normalized through a variety of measures and treaties designed to regulate it. In 1989, the Basel Convention on the Transboundary Movements of Hazardous Wastes and Their Disposal was signed, theoretically in order to protect the interests of the vulnerable developing countries, but its consequences have been complex and far from successful. Some scholars, such as Andrews (2009), in fact, argue that the Basel Convention provides a basic legal framework within which international trade of hazardous waste can take place. Although in 1994 a coalition of developing countries and environmental NGOs lobbied to completely ban trade in toxic waste between developed and developing countries, the subsequent ban was not a part of the convention itself, but, rather, became an amendment, which as of today has still not been ratified by three-quarters of the parties to the convention, which would make it binding. The ban has not been ratified both by the major exporters of toxic waste (such as the United States and Japan) but also by the major importers of hazardous materials, such as India and Pakistan.

The narrative of a private company illicitly dumping its own waste in order to maximize profit from its cheaply made goods is, in and of itself, certainly not untrue, but it is a villain that can be fought and sanctioned within the framework of an existing eco-social contract, where environmental infractions may occur, but a good governance framework can help manage it. What it obfuscates is the status quo, where existing global inequalities have made the import of hazardous materials a 'relative comparative advantage' niche for developing countries, and the fact that the very convention designed to stop the practice of toxic dumping as an environmental crime has essentially legitimated the practice of industrialized countries outsourcing waste disposal and the environmental and public health risks associated with it by providing a framework of a mutually beneficial economic transaction, putatively based on informed consent. Although the well-publicized toxic dumping, such as the 2006 Cote d'Ivoire toxic waste dump of over 500 tons, was illegal and was found to be at least partially the fault of corrupt officials (Fagbohun, 2007), an equally, if not more, common scenario is the sort of free-market arrangement in which less industrialized countries are offered significant sums of money for accepting hazardous materials – significant for the impoverished countries, that is. In one legendary example, the African nation of Guinea-Bissau "in the 1980s received an offer of $600 million [several times that nation's annual gross national product] from a coalition of US and European private companies to accept toxic waste" (Friman and Richard, 1999: 173). But such 'large' figures would be several magnitudes larger in developed countries. Numerous developing countries, especially in Africa (including Benin, Congo-Brazzaville, Equatorial Guinea, Mozambique, and others) have regularly imported hazardous waste (industrial, pharmaceutical, e-waste) at a cost that could be as low as $40 per ton, while disposal of hazardous waste can cost upward of $2000 in Western countries.

Again, it is understandable that this is not the nature of a challenge Rei finds himself in – what sort of quest-appropriate conclusion could be found in a situation where toxic dumping would turn out to be the result of the unnamed country with a large national debt opting to accept a large cash payment in exchange for receiving such hazardous materials? But realistically, it is a likely scenario; as Pratt (2011: 591) points out, "Many of these countries face large debts and require hard currency to service these debts and boost their economies... Hazardous waste disposal contracts that promise large amounts of foreign currency are hard to refuse...When a large, cash-on-delivery payment is presented, these costs are often overlooked for the short-term gain". And, if we continue considering the pedagogical aspect of the narrative, we can see that the lessons being transmitted here are about illegal activities possible in the absence of strong regulation, rather than an existing framework of 'mutual consent' that is fundamentally rooted in poverty and inequality.

Broken trust

Passage 6, titled "Corruption: Broken Trust", follows Rei teaming up with an aspiring investigative journalist to investigate a bridge collapse. It turns out that the bridge was cheaply made, and was not in compliance with safety standards. In the course of their investigation, Rei and his sidekick uncover the procurement documents that indicate that the highest bid on the bridge contract was accepted. The paper trail leads to the Public Works Commissioner, who turns out to have been involved in bribery and nepotism. The story is implicitly informed by the idea that transparency is the key to both preventing and fighting corruption; and the infrastructure of 'transparency' is shown to be heavily reliant both on literacy and the cultural knowledge of bureaucratic tools of governance such as 'citizen surveys', graphs of 'community corruption' and 'freedom of information acts'. The passage's framing and portrayal of 'corruption' resonates with Krastev's (2002: 101) assessment of the normative anti-corruption discourse: "Corruption is conceptualized as an institutional issue and not as a cultural or even political phenomenon... Corruption is constructed as a measurable phenomenon ... [and] decontextualized for the purpose of fighting it ... The mainstream anti-corruption discourse is not interested in the contextual nature of corruption... [and] the policy preoccupation of the recent anti-corruption studies narrows the territory of what is perceived as useful knowledge on corruption". In other words, corruption is, in a sense, depoliticized (Krastev, 2004), and only linked to poverty in a very linear sense – as Weszkalnys (2011: 355), in agreement with Krastev, puts it, "Whereas corruption was once seen as a result of poverty, beginning in the 1990s the Washington Consensus became that corrupt countries are poor".

The issue is not that corrupt officials as the proximate causes for shoddy construction and an ensuing tragedy are factually incorrect; it is the fact that the discourse around 'corruption', from its focus on the choices and actions by individual actors rather than the sociopolitical field, to the casual stigmatization of nepotism, which is so frequently the subject of a cultural gap in settings where 'modern' forms of governance are applied to kin-based societies, brings to mind the concept of 'virtualism'. Carrier and Miller (1998) define it as an attempt to make the real world conform to an abstract model of itself. The concept has since been theorized and applied by other scholars as a critique of the paradigm in economics that abstracted "human decision-making from its complex social context and [built] models of the world and its workings that cannot take the full range or complexity of people's daily social activities, practices, and lives into account" (West and Brockington, 2006: 609). And a pedagogical framework, such as the one conveyed in 'Broken Trust', actively participates in producing and defining the limits of what Krastev (2002) describes as 'useful' knowledge on corruption – given that the pedagogical aspect is geared toward young adults, this knowledge may very well be formative, or foundational. Learning about 'development' issues is inherently a foundational learning process – the narratives highlight global challenges and problems faced by people in developing nations, but they also shape the readers' perspectives of how one learns about development, what kinds of questions one asks when encountering 'development' issues, and what range of answers (or outcomes) one can expect.

Pedagogical and ethnographic fictions: discussion and conclusion

Of course, there is not a single, monolithic reading of *1 World Manga*. For one, its existence, in and of itself, generates questions analogous to the aforementioned debate about *Avatar*: Does *Avatar* teach mainstream audiences about the crimes of resource colonialism, or does it fetishize the idea of the ecologically noble savage, which is fraught with issues of limited legitimacy and environmental dispossession for indigenous people? Is it ultimately beneficial to familiarize young readers with vulnerabilities facing people in developing countries, or is it harmful to do it in a way that reproduces narratives of development that promote neoliberal individualist approach rooted in ethnocentric universalist humanism, rather than an ontological, systemic analysis of how global inequalities are produced and sustained? And even those questions engage with just one aspect of the series – they are questions about the books' existence as pedagogical tools for young adults in the West (or the Global North).

Circulation beyond the west

But even though *1 World Manga* is a 'Western' product, it obviously circulates in spaces of cultural production beyond 'the West'. Both within the World Bank itself and beyond, the series found international distribution. As Patricia explained: "We had a lot of internal interest in it, we did get a good number for some of our units in the Bank who wanted to use it for youth outreach in developing countries ... The other thing is, we have a lot of translations, we are allowed to license translations, because Viz did not do it..." Although for policy reasons no one I interviewed was able to disclose exact sales figures, the series obviously enjoyed wide distribution, as they were translated into French, Spanish, Vietnamese, Chinese, Korean, Arabic, and Indonesian languages. One example of global circulation of the series came from Egypt; after Arabic rights to the series were licensed to Nahdet Misr, a publisher in Egypt, two passages ("Global Warming" and "Child Soldiers") were selected by the Egyptian Ministry of Education for distribution in Egyptian schools. As a result of this decision, the original print of 4000 copies each was augmented by an additional print of 8000 copies each for dissemination to schoolchildren.[8]

After being licensed by independent publishers in Indonesia, South Korea, Vietnam, etc., the series circulated in 'developing' markets as an adventure story no longer formally affiliated with or distributed through World Bank publications or institutions. Although it is beyond the scope of this chapter to do a reception study of the series' circulation after being licensed by local, non-Western publishing houses, it would be naive to assume that it forced readers into one, hegemonic reading wherever it circulated – it is far more likely that it became incorporated into local systems of meaning-making and knowledge practices. One small glimpse of that appears as a part of the blurbs on the back cover of the comprehensive volume, where all six passages are published under one cover: "I really like Passage 1. Ayeesha starts down here [in abject poverty], but at the end she is raised up!" reads the cover quoting Nicholous Kori, a 17-year old AMREF filmmaker (who is also described as a 'former street kid').[9] In my interview with Annette, I asked her about this blurb; she explained that during a presentation of *1 World Manga* at a conference in Italy, she and the Viz team met a group of young filmmakers from Nairobi, who were very enthusiastic about the series, and gave very positive feedback to Viz, because, as they explained, each passage had a 'happy ending' and the overall message of the book was optimistic.

While for an academic Western reader such as myself the story of Ayeesha, a woman who escapes poverty by joining a microfinance women's cooperative, may seem to promote the normative development discourse at the expense of obfuscating the larger structural context of poverty and inequality, I recognize Nicholous Kori's reading as a common and highly meaningful one in 'development' contexts. In my own fieldwork in indigenous Amazonian villages, often debating the merits of becoming involved with various sustainable development and educational NGOs, the circulation of positive stories was important emic currency. Although 'development' jargon such as 'empowerment' or 'capacity-building' was used in villages in very different ways than it would be in policy documents, the terms themselves were frequently articulated, and appropriated into the emic discourses of development. In other words, they were ways of talking about hopes and desirable outcomes from affiliations with international NGOs and aid organizations.

This appreciation of 'happy endings' in development narratives is a part of a larger phenomenon. In many cultural contexts, in developing countries, notions of 'globalization', 'development', or even 'modernity' become meaningful and powerful cultural categories. 'Development' and the attendant concepts of 'empowerment', 'capacity building', and 'transparency' may (and do) become both discursive loci for asserting sovereignty for the states, as they leverage their public image as 'more' or 'less' developed in negotiating relationships with other states, and with international financial institutions, and ways of performing 'modernity' for its citizens – often in places where 'being modern' is a status symbol of sorts. Furthermore, as concepts and narratives of 'development' become emic, other forms of fictions emerge around development, just as in the past fictions – of history as sorcery, as Taussig (1984) described it – emerged around colonialism, in the form of 'cargo cults' in Melanesia (Kaplan, 1995; Jebens, 2004), Hauka possession cults in West Africa (Rouch, 1955), and lore of white vampires in colonial ambulances in Tanganyika and Kampala (White, 2000). Many contemporary 'fictions' around 'development' comprise versions of the phenomenon highlighted by anthropologists: the emergence or intensification of cultural fantasies of dark sorcery and occult as a response to new capitalist forms and practices that are brought by a certain type of economic development programs (Comaroff and Comaroff, 1999; Lindquist, 2006; Smith, 2008). Parallel to those 'dark' fictions there also 'resistance' fictions, such as the rumors and stories of development workers being repeatedly foiled in their quest for the mythological, nonexistent mineral 'red mercury' in the hills of Kenya (Onneweer, 2010). There are 'aspirational' fictions – folk mythologies about desirable outcomes where somewhere, for someone, interactions with NGOs or aid workers or foreign companies met local expectations. Such fictions or imaginaries of 'development' delivering on its promises may in some cases serve as motivators to become involved in 'development' projects in the first place, and in other cases result in performative 'imitations' of behaviors and lifestyle markers associated with 'development' or capitalism (Rollason, 2011). It is easy to imagine that, outside the West, *1 World Manga* can become a part of a much more broad and fluid semiotic space where different forms of 'fictions' of development circulate. Depending on the context, *1 World Manga* can simultaneously be an instance of pedagogical intention and emic reception.

Concealments and revelations

What simultaneously differentiates and links such pedagogical fiction of development and the emic fictions that emerge around and through development (even when both categories may describe the same text) is the discourse of normativity, that in the cauldrons of cross-cultural and transnational encounters becomes transformed into emic forms of meaning-making. In both cases, the fictions signify something about the framework of their production, and the values they communicate – they both obfuscate and reveal, and they are both about producing and communicating certain forms of knowledge that are true, even if they are not literal or intentional. The normative development discourse pertaining to HIV/AIDS may be fictional and 'flat' in its emphasis on the primacy of behavioral factors in transmission – but it also inadvertently reflects certain truths about the design, structure, and funding of HIV/AIDS intervention programs in developing countries. The frequently paranoid folk beliefs and myths about HIV/AIDS origins and vaccination programs in developing countries may be fictional on the literal level, but they reveal symbolic and powerful truths about the ways in which pharmaceutical practices in the developing world are often steeped in systemic global inequalities and neocolonial ideologies. Every official, normative discourse of 'development', whether it is articulated in a policy document or fictionalized, has an emic, ethnographically thick discursive counterpart, the truth or cultural logic of which may be encoded in a form of fiction, myth, or rumor. Whether one looks at the discourses of development in fiction, or discourses of and around development as fiction, one must consider what these fictions reveal or conceal on a meta-narrative level, even as they may become fluid and transformed through circulation.

What does *1 World Manga* conceal and reveal? On the one hand, it is designed to foster a particular kind of "developmentality", at a life stage when it is cosmological more than instrumentalist, but which, as the series' Western readers age, may be parlayed for some into preferences around travel, behaviors as tourists, choices about what kinds of charities, volunteer programs, or NGOs should be supported, and maybe even internship and career choices. On the other hand, perhaps, as an integrated, accessible synthesis and embodiment of the World Bank's prevailing view of development, it may lay groundwork for eventual critical reflection more readily than working papers, reports, and academic publications on specific topics or geographic areas that remain largely esoteric to nonspecialists. Even as it conceals that its message is not as neutral and self-evident as it appears, it distills the World Bank perspective into a text that, by the virtue of being a constructed narrative of Rei's adventures in the literal sense, may invite questions about the constructed narrative about development in a broader sense. In other words, its existence as a piece of fiction genre-wise may serve as an inadvertent meta-pragmatic gateway toward reflecting on the extent to which it may be a fiction of ideology as well.

Notes

1 This chapter was originally published as an article in the *Journal of Development Studies*, 2013, 49(3): 398–411.
2 Here (and henceforth): from an interview with Patricia Katayama, 15 July 2011.
3 See https://sites.google.com/site/globalavataredproject1pandora (retrieved on 14 July 2011).
4 See http://www.educationforjustice.org/resources/avatar-film-discussion-guide-and-cst (retrieved on 14 July 2011); CST stands for Catholic Social Teaching.
5 See http://www.parentingsquad.com/avatar-with-kids-a-discussion-guide (retrieved on 14 July 2011).
6 See http://www.survivalinternational.org/thereyougo (retrieved on 14 July 2011).
7 As Marble and Key (1995) noted, schistosomiasis causes genital lesions in females, often located inside the vulva and the vagina, that bleed both spontaneously and from contact, including sexual contact, allowing the HIV virus to access the bloodstream directly.
8 Personal communication with Annette Roman, 06 July 2011.

9 AMREF stands for "African Medical and Research Foundation" and the children Annette met were a part of the Dagoretti Child In Need project, which is described on
the AMREF website: "A group of former street children turned filmmakers from the
Dagoretti slum in Nairobi have produced a television news feature highlighting the daily
struggles of people living with HIV in poor settings and the leadership initiatives taken
by members of those communities in dealing with the epidemic". http://www.amref.org/
news.former-street-children-show-the-way-in-fight-against-hiv/ retrieved on 07 July
2011.

References

Andrews, A. (2009) "Beyond the ban—can the Basel convention adequately safeguard the
    interests of the World's Poor in the International Trade of Hazardous Waste?". *Law,
    Environment, and Development,* 5(2): 167–183.
Carrier, J., and D. Miller (1998) *Virtualism: A New Political Economy.* Cambridge: Berg.
Comaroff, J., and J. Comaroff (1999) "Occult economies and the violence of abstraction".
    American Ethnologist, 26(3): 279–301.
Fagbohun, O. (2007) "The regulation of transboundary shipments of hazardous waste:
    A case study of the dumping of toxic waste in Abidjan, Cote d'Ivoire". *Hong Kong Law
    Journal,* 37(3): 831–841.
Farmer, P. (2005) *Pathologies of Power: Health, Human Rights, and the New War on the
    Poor.* Berkeley: University of California Press.
Ferguson, J. (1990) *The Anti-Politics Machine: "Development", Depolitization and
    Bureaucratic Power in Lesotho.* Cambridge: Cambridge University Press.
Friman, H., and P. Richard (1999) *The Illicit Global Economy and State Power.* Maryland:
    Rowman & Littlefield.
Gausset, Q. (2001) "AIDS and cultural practices in Africa: The case of the Tonga
    (Zambia)". *Social Science and Medicine,* 52(4): 509–518.
Gillespie, S. (2006) "Aids, poverty, and hunger: Overview". In S. Gillespie (ed.), *AIDS,
    Poverty, and Hunger: Challenges and Responses (Highlights of the International Con-
    ference on HIV/AIDS and Food and Nutrition Security, Durban, South Africa, April
    14–16, 2005).* Washington, D.C.: International Food Policy Research Institute.
Jebens, H. (2004) *Cargo, Cult and Culture Critique.* Honolulu: University of Hawaii Press.
Juüngst, H. (2007) "Manga in Germany—from translation to simulacrum". *Perspectives,*
    14(4): 248–259.
Kaplan, M. (1995) *Neither Cargo Nor Cult: Ritual Politics and Colonial Imagination in
    Fiji.* Durham: Duke University Press.
Kimmerling, J. (2007) "Transnational operations, bi-national injustice: ChevronTexaco
    and indigenous Huaorani and Kichwa in the Amazon rainforest in Ecuador". *American
    Indian Law Review,* 31(2): 445–508.
Klak, T., and G. Myers (1997) "The discursive tactics of neoliberal development in small
    Third World Countries". *Geoforum,* 28(2): 133–149.
Kojucharov, N. (2007) "Poverty, petroleum, and policy intervention: Lessons from the
    Chad-Cameroon pipeline". *Review of African Political Economy,* 34(113): 477–496.
Krastev, I. (2002) "A moral economy of anti-corruption sentiments in Eastern Europe". In
    Y.Elkana, I.Krastev, E.Macamo, S. Randeria (eds.), *Unraveling Ties—From Social
    Cohesion to New Practices of Connectedness.* Frankfurt/Main: Campus Verlag.
Krastev, I. (2004) *Shifting Obsessions: Three Essays on the Politics of Anticorruption.*
    Budapest and New York: Central European University Press.

Kunkel, B. (2005) *Indecision*. New York: Random House.

Le Carre, J. (2002) *The Constant Gardener*. New York: Scribner.

Rouch, J. (1955) *Les Maitres Fous* [DVD]. France: Les Films de la Pléiade.

Lewis, D., D. Rodgers, and M. Woolcock (2008) "The fiction of development: Literary representation as a source of authoritative knowledge". *Journal of Development Studies,* 44(2): 198–216.

Lindquist, G. (2006) *Conjuring Hope: Magic and Healing in Contemporary Russia*. New York–Oxford: Berghahn.

Lutz, C., and J. Collins (1993) *Reading National Geographic*. Chicago: University of Chicago Press.

Marble, M., and K. Key (1995) "Clinical facets of a disease neglected too long". *AIDS Weekly Plus,* 7 August: 16–19.

Marchard, M., and A. Runyan (2000) *Gender and Global Restructuring*. London: Routledge.

Nauta, W. (2010) "Saving depraved Africans in the age of neoliberalism: How the fight against HIV/AIDS has cast the victims". *Journal of Developing Societies,* 26(3): 355–385.

Oóhagan, M. (2007) "Manga, anime and video games: Globalizing Japanese cultural production". *Perspectives,* 14(4): 242–247.

O'Manique, C. (2004) "Global Neoliberalism and AIDS Policy: International Responses to Sub-Saharan Africa's AIDS Pandemic". *Studies in Political Economy,* 73(Spring/ Summer): 47–68.

Onneweer, M. (2010) "The Elusive Resources of Kitui, Postscripts of a Colonial Crisis", paper presented at the European Association for Social Anthropology Annual Conference, University of Maynooth, Maynooth, Ireland.

Pegg, S. (2006) "Can policy intervention beat the resource curse? Evidence from the Chad-Cameroon pipeline project". *African Affairs,* 105(418): 1–25.

Pratt, L. (2011) "Decreasing dirty dumping? A reevaluation of toxic waste colonialism and the global management of transboundary hazardous waste". *William and Mary Environmental Law and Policy Review,* 35(2): 581–623.

Rollason, W. (2011) "My boss: Insincerity, capitalism and development in PNG". *Etnofoor,* 22(1): 103–117.

Sharp, D. (2003) "Dam medicine", *The Lancet,* 362: 184.

Silberschmidt, M. (2001) "Disempowerment of men in rural and urban East Africa: implications for male identity and sexual behaviour". *World Development,* 29(4): 657–669.

Smith, J. (2008) *Bewitching Development: Witchcraft and the Reinvention of Development in Neoliberal Kenya*. Chicago: University of Chicago Press.

Stillwaggon, E. (2006) *AIDS and the Ecology of Poverty*. New York: Oxford University Press.

Taussig, M. (1984) "History as Sorcery". *Representations,* 7(Summer): 87–109.

Weldes, J. (2001) "Globalisation as science fiction". *Millennium—Journal of International Studies,* 30(3): 647–668.

West, P., and D. Brockington (2006) "An anthropological perspective on some unexpected consequences of protected areas". *Conservation Biology,* 20(3): 609–616.

Weszkalnys, G.. (2011) "Cursed resources, or articulations of economic theory in the Gulf of Guinea". *Economy and Society,* 40(3): 345–372.

White, L. (2000) *Speaking with Vampires: Rumor and History in Colonial Africa*. Los Angeles: University of California Press.

Part III
Media and television

5 More news is bad news

Why studies of 'the public faces
of development' and 'media and
morality' should be concerned with
reality TV programmes

Martin Scott

> Whilst the public faces [of development] ... are a significant element of the
> politics of development, there has been relatively little systematic research in
> this area, nor has there been an attempt to begin to consolidate what work has
> already been done ... Much of the academic and practitioner research in this
> area has been fragmented and remains unconnected, often due to different
> disciplinary bases.
>
> Smith and Yanacopulos (2004a: 658–660).

Introduction

If the study of popular representations of development is to fully establish itself
as part of mainstream development research then, as Matt Smith and Helen
Yanacopulos make clear above, there is much work to be done. In particular, they
highlight the need to connect and consolidate existing work within different disciplines regarding media coverage of development and the Global South. This
chapter begins by drawing together conversations taking place simultaneously in
media studies and development studies about this subject by outlining their shared
concerns for global relations of power and media influence on public perceptions.
Despite often adopting different terminology and conceptual frameworks, both
sets of literature share the premise that media representations of the Global South
have 'real-world' consequences.

It is particularly striking that neither of these bodies of literature has, until now,
focused its attention on more popular, entertainment-based, representations of the
Global South. Instead, each chooses to focus on 'peak moments' of media coverage during disasters (Robertson, 2010). This 'blind spot' stems at least partly
from the (mistaken) belief that when the Global South appears in the Western
media, it is almost always in the news and in the context of suffering. This focus
on peak moments is also partly the result of a political science approach that
understands the media largely as an informational resource "with the potential, or

not, for producing 'well-informed citizens'" (Robertson, 2010: 106). While television may indeed play an important informational role, it also contributes to the *affective* dimension of mediated experience. As Roger Silverstone (2006: 19) argued, the representational work of the media "is not confined to that undertaken in the news or current affairs, where claims for truth and trust and literalness are most obviously articulated ... [it] extends to the play of narrative and performance across all the genres". Indeed, in her empirical research into public talk about the television coverage of overseas disasters, Maria Kyriakidou (2008: 288) finds that "discourses relating to distant humanitarian disasters are bound to popular fiction rather than recourse to rational argument and deliberation".

This chapter seeks to begin to amend for this failure to focus on popular representations of development and the Global South by discussing the BBC reality-television programme *The World's Strictest Parents*. It draws on the results of a recent textual analysis of the programme using a modified version of Lilie Chouliaraki's (2006) 'analytics of mediation'.[1] This is combined with analysis of the results of a study of audience responses to this and other international programmes on UK television. Both sets of results suggest that there is something particular about the format of some reality-television style programmes set in 'other' countries, which means that they actively lend themselves to providing proximate, emotional and egalitarian mediated experiences of humanised distant others. I conclude that for those seeking to identify representational practices that disrupt conventional hierarchies of place and human life, reality-TV programmes may provide a valuable source of material. More broadly, I contend that the struggle to bring recognition to the study of representations of development should not lead us to focus only on the serious, the sensible, and the suffering. If we agree that such representations matter at least partly for their ability to regulate popular public perceptions, then ought not the popular be at the heart of our concerns?

Consolidating conversations

In development studies, work that attempts to engage with debates about how the Global South appears in the media are usually framed in terms of "the public faces of development" (Smith and Yanacopulos, 2004b). Such work regularly adopts the language of "representations" (Wright, 2004) and "portrayals" (Poland, 2004) of development and developing countries and the effects that these have on "understandings of the South and of North–South relations" (Cameron and Haanstra, 2008: 1477). There have been a small number of individual articles in development studies journals or specific special journal issues, most notably *The Public Faces of Development* (Smith and Yanacopulos, 2004b). In the UK, this language is also adopted within policy research commissioned and published by the Department for International Development (DFID, 2000) and various NGOs (VSO, 2001; Smith *et al.*, 2006; Scott, 2008; Harding, 2009).

In media studies, the same conversations have been taking place under the banner of "media and morality" (Tester, 1994; Silverstone, 2006; Chouliaraki, 2006). These have drawn on the language of "mediation" (Thompson, 1995), "distant others" (Silverstone, 2006), "the politics of pity" (Boltanski, 1999) and "cosmopolitanism" (Beck, 2006). Work in this area has been described as representing a "dramatic moral–ethical 'turn' in media studies" (Ong, 2009: 449) – away from being "morally cretinous ... facile and useless ... about nothing other than [itself]" (Tester, 1994: 3–10), and towards a media studies that has a concern for morality at its heart. Morality, in this context, is understood as "the judgement and elucidation of thought and action that is oriented towards the other, that defines our relationship to her or him in sameness and in otherness, and through which our own claims to be moral, human beings are defined" (Silverstone, 2006: 7).

Such differences in terminology reflect subtle but important conceptual differences between these two literatures. In the media studies literature, for example, the concept of 'mediation' is generally preferred to 'representations'. It is argued that the latter term fails to capture the complex ways in which the media are implicated in the relationship between audiences and distant others and that it lacks the analytical edge to allow a full understanding of the power of the media to enact audiences' encounters with distant others (Cottle, 2006: 9). Taking account of the *constitutive* role of the media in establishing audiences' experiences of distant others requires a much broader analytical and theoretical approach such as that provided by the concept of mediation. Mediation is defined as a "dialectical and institutionally and technologically driven phenomenon" (Silverstone, 2006: 189) that involves both "overcoming distance in communication" (Tomlinson, 1999: 154) and the process of "passing through the medium" (Tomlinson, 1999: 155).

Similarly, the media studies literature increasingly refers to 'distant others' rather than to specific groups of people or particular parts of the world. Terminology such as 'developing countries' assume that there are fixed, 'knowable' parts of the world that the media somehow distort through their representations. By contrast, the term 'distant others' refers to persons who are constructed as being both geographical, socially/culturally and morally distant from spectators and who "only appear to us within the media" (Silverstone, 2006: 109). Thus, the term makes clearer the role of the media in constructing or reinforcing the boundaries between *imagined* communities of belonging.

Notwithstanding the significance of the differences between concepts such as 'mediation' and 'representation', both literatures are united by their common understandings of why media coverage of the Global South matters. Firstly, there is a shared concern for the ways in which such media coverage is implicated in public perceptions of development and the Global South and how this in turn has real-world consequences. Such concerns include how mediated public perceptions impact, or not, upon levels of charitable donations (Moeller, 1999; Brown and Minty, 2006), support for international NGOs (Vestergaard, 2008), public policy (VSO, 2001), ethical consumerism (Wright, 2004), the formation of a global civil society (Smith and Yanacopulos, 2004a), or a cosmopolitan public (Beck, 2006). Whether these public perceptions are understood in terms of "mediated experiences" (Thompson, 1995), involving dimensions of proximity, agency and options for emotion and action (Chouliaraki, 2006), or variously as "attitudes", "perceptions", "understandings" and levels of "engagement" (DFID, 2000), the general premise of the concern is the same.

Secondly, there is a shared concern for the ways in which the manner of the appearance of the Global South in the media reinforces (or otherwise) global power relations between the North and South – which is another "significant element of the politics of development" (Smith and Yanacopulos, 2004a: 659). As regards contributions that explicitly address development studies, Smith and Yanacopulos (2004a), for example, claim that it is through the construction of the "public faces" of development in the North that relationships between individuals and communities in the North and South are produced, and that this in turn sustains prevailing global political and economic power relations. Similarly, the premise of John Cameron and Anna Haanstra's (2008: 1476) work on the increasing tendency of Northern NGOs to portray development as "sexy" is that such practices have "important implications for power relations between the populations of North and South". Such studies tend to draw on the ideas of Edward Said (1979), Stuart Hall (1992) and Arturo Escobar (1995) to provide the foundation of such concerns.

Equally, in media studies accounts, the manner of the appearance of distant others in the media is understood to be important for the ways in which this contributes to reinforcing global power relations through the reproduction of hierarchies of place and of human life and the normalisation of inequalities (Pieterse, 1995: 234). One of Chouliaraki's (2006: 7) aims, for example, is to explore further the ways in which hierarchies of place and of human life are reproduced in the news narratives of television coverage of distant suffering or "how a more egalitarian representation of the other can take place in these narratives". Despite their use of different terminologies, studies of the "public faces" of development and "media and morality" are both interested in the influence of the media on public perceptions of development and on global relations of power.

My intention in drawing attention to the shared concerns of what has often been rather separate, self-referential sets of literature is to identify a basis upon which we can begin to consolidate what work has already been done. In particular, there is a rich body of theoretical work, referred to mostly in media studies, which can help to enrich future research in this area (see Boltanski, 1999; Silverstone, 2006). Before discussing the work of Lilie Chouliaraki (2006) in more detail as one example of this, I wish to draw attention to another commonality between these two sets of literature: their lack of attention to the role of less serious, entertainment-based television programming.

More news is bad news

For those writing under the banner of "media and morality", the focus has been almost entirely directed at distant *suffering* in television *news* coverage. Alexa Robertson (2010) describes this as a concentration on "peak moments" of television coverage of trauma, including suffering, disasters, conflict and tragedy. Indeed, one of the overarching questions of the call for papers for a recent conference on mediated cosmopolitanism was, "Can other popular media texts, besides news, also contribute to cosmopolitanism, or is this debate only limited to hard news and their representation of distant suffering?"[2] Qualitative studies of how distant others are mediated in contexts outside of 'peak moments' of television coverage are very rare.

Among those concerned with the "public faces" of development, although there is an understandable emphasis on examining the nature of humanitarian campaign material (Cameron and Haanstra, 2008; Dogra, 2012), we also find a focus on other forms of media including television news coverage (DFID, 2000), newspapers (Scott, 2009a) and radio (Poland, 2004). Indeed, in this volume alone, the focus ranges from literature and film to social media and manga. Aside from two other chapters in this book, however, a lack of focus on more popular, entertainment-based television programming is also evident.

This lack of focus is problematic for three reasons. Firstly, despite common assumptions, the Global South *does* regularly appear in factual television coverage outside of news, humanitarian communications and 'serious factual' documentaries. In both 2007 and 2010, nearly half of all international non-news factual programming on UK television was not in the form of conventional documentaries (Scott, 2011). In 2010, this included 75 hours of "factual entertainment" programming (22%) and 62 hours of "hobbies and leisure" (18%). "Factual entertainment" refers to popular factual material, including reality shows and docu-soaps. The sub-genre of "hobbies and leisure" includes gardening, home, DIY, travel and cookery programmes (Ofcom, 2010).

Secondly, there is evidence to suggest that many audiences actively avoid conventional documentaries and peak moments of news coverage of the Global South because they have come to associate such programming with emotional pressure and "difficult viewing" (Scott, 2009b). It is often claimed that international programming in the form of "factual entertainment" and "hobbies and leisure" receives larger audiences than equivalent 'serious factual' programming (Smith *et al.*, 2006: 9), although audience data to support such claims is not publicly available. As Phil Harding (2009: 31) put it, "when done well ... [these programmes] do a very good job on the mainstream channels in reaching audiences who do not want to sit through heavier fare".

Finally, and perhaps most importantly, those (few) authors who have considered this issue have suggested ways in which such television genres may actively help to destabilise taken-for-granted theories about development and "forms of representation that belittle the agency of those deemed in need of 'development'" (Yanacopulos and Mohan, 2006: 20). For example, in their discussion of the BBC1 television series *African School*, first broadcast in 2005, Helen Yanacopulos and Giles Mohan (2006: 20) suggest that a 'docu-drama' style of programming helps to challenge partial representations of the Global South by "bring[ing] out stories from real lives. In presenting the stories and 'characters', they are named, the viewer is told details about them, and they are then allowed to speak about themselves." In doing so, such formats might also help to "acknowledge the connections in a world of difference" (Yanacopulos and Mohan, 2006: 20) by pointing out the similarities between 'us' and 'them' and thus normalising the lives of faraway others. Finally, Yanacopulos and Mohan (2006: 21) highlight the importance of looking beyond the serious: "Humour plays a big part in the series – which gives it balance – and this is sometimes extremely important in dealing with some ... difficult issues".

In summary, there are a number of reasons for taking seriously less serious forms of television content in studies of "media and morality" and the "public faces" of development. In the remainder of this chapter, the value of expanding our focus in this direction is explored by analysing a particular example of 'factual entertainment' programming from the perspective of its content and reception.

Capturing mediation

In the UK, one of the most frequently broadcast programmes about distant others in the sub-genre of 'factual entertainment' programming is *The World's Strictest Parents* (Scott 2011). This reality television series, originally broadcast in the UK in 2008, follows pairs of 'unruly' British teenagers who are sent abroad to live with 'strict' families in other countries. The premise of the 60-minute programme is that the experience will lead the teenagers to change their 'unruly' behaviour. There have so far been four series of *The World's Strictest Parents* broadcast in the UK and episodes receive relatively large audiences (an average initial audience of 400,000 in series 3). *The World's Strictest Parents* has been particularly successful at generating relatively large audiences through 'nonlinear' or 'time-shifted' viewing. For some episodes, the numbers of requests on the catch-up service – BBC iPlayer – has actually exceeded the size of the initial 'linear' audience (Scott, 2011). Localised versions have also been produced and broadcast in countries including Australia (three series), Germany (three series), the USA (two series), Denmark (two series) and Poland (one series).

The episode chosen for analysis was broadcast on BBC3 on Monday 9 February 2009, between 8 pm and 9 pm and involved two British teenagers being sent to live with a family in Jamaica. This particular episode was chosen because it falls within the same time period of the audience study discussed below. The framework used to analyse this text is Chouliaraki's (2006) "analytics of mediation", which "takes its point of departure in the ethical norms embedded in reports on suffering and seeks to problematise the meaning-making procedures through which these norms acquire systematicity and legitimacy in and through television" (Vestergaard, 2008: 476). In doing so, it seeks to allow the analyst to establish both the character of mediated experience of distant suffering that the text offers to audiences and the ways in which hierarchies of place and of human life are reproduced, or otherwise. Given the complexity of Chouliaraki's approach, particularly for those not accustomed to the language of media and morality, I shall summarise the five key stages in the development of her approach.

Firstly, Chouliaraki (2006: 32) shows how previous studies of media and morality are characterised by an adherence to one of two contrasting "optimistic" and "pessimistic" narratives. Either the process of "passing through the medium" (Tomlinson, 1999: 154) of television enhances the capacity of the medium to "overcome distance" (Tomlinson, 1999: 154) between audiences and distant others, leading to a sense of proximity and immediacy (see Szerszynski and Toogood, 2000), or it necessarily disrupts the quality of audiences' mediated experiences of distant others (see Moeller, 1999). Secondly, Chouliaraki argues that rather than making such *a priori* assumptions about the capacity of mediation to produce particular kinds of mediated experience, the question of how distant others are mediated by television should be answered empirically by analysing how these either/or arguments are seemingly resolved within individual texts.

Thirdly, in order to examine empirically how the either/or understandings of mediation are temporarily resolved, Chouliaraki identifies three contradictions that exist between the competing narratives. The first of these "paradoxes of mediation" is the "paradox of technology", which is described as the competing thoughts that technology both distorts the authenticity of suffering, which leads to indifference, and that it connects the sufferer with the audience and therefore leads to a sense of immediacy. The second "paradox of mediation" is the "paradox of distance", which can be found in the competing ideas that mediation situates audiences 'too far' from suffering, leading to depersonalisation and indifference, and at the same time, that it brings audiences close to suffering, leading to intimacy and connection. The third such contradiction is the "paradox of in/action" in which mediation is understood as situating audiences both as inactive onlookers to the scene of suffering and as active, involved actors (Chouliaraki, 2006: 37–46).

Fourthly, Chouliaraki incorporates understandings of mediation as a process involving both "immediacy" and "hypermediacy". The former is understood by Bolter and Grusin (2000: 272) as the dimension of mediation allowing audiences to recognise that the experiences we have when consuming media are brought about through the presence of a medium. Immediacy is defined by Bolter and Grusin (2000: 272) as "a style of visual representation whose goal is to make the viewer forget the presence of the medium and believe that he [or she] is in the presence of the objects of representation". These two concepts help both to preserve a concern for mediation as "passing through the medium" and as "overcoming distance" when investigating each of these three dimensions of mediation. They also help to provide clear guidance as to the precise questions we should be asking of media texts if we are to investigate how they direct audiences in relation to distant others.

Fifthly, in order to analyse mediation in terms of both immediacy and hypermediacy, Chouliaraki proposes two levels of analysis. The first is a multi-modal analysis that is concerned with how meaning making takes place on the television screen. The second level of analysis is critical discourse analysis (CDA), or the study of technology as being embedded within power relations. Combining multi-modal analysis and CDA provides an overall account of how the text seemingly positions audiences vis-à-vis distant suffering, which "takes into account the embeddedness of media texts both in technological artefacts and in social relationships" (Chouliaraki, 2006: 153). Table 5.1 summarises the principal questions to be asked of media texts in order to investigate how the three paradoxes of mediation are seemingly resolved.

Table 5.1 A summary of the principal questions to be asked in applying the analytics of mediation

Paradox to be resolved	Level of analysis	Mediation as hypermediacy	Mediation as immediacy
Paradox of technology	Multi-modal analysis	What forms of realism are established by the process of passing through the medium?	How does the mode of presentation and verbal–visual correspondence contribute to establishing the overall semiotic effect of the text?
Paradox of distance	Critical discourse analysis	How does the process of passing through the medium regulate space-time relationships between spectators and distant others?	What are the spatiotemporal characteristics of the particular emotional and practical realities which the spectator is being presented with by the text?
Paradox of in/action	Critical discourse analysis	To what extent are distant others humanised through the process of passing through the medium?	What universal value of how to respond towards distant others, if any, is articulated by the orchestration of the benefactor and persecutor figures?

As with most theoretical literature in the field of media and morality, the analytics of mediation was developed in order to examine distant suffering in specific news texts, within the framework of the "politics of pity" (Boltanski, 1999). Yet my concern here is with a reality TV programme involving distant others who are not suffering. Despite this apparent incompatibility, I maintain that this approach remains relevant here because relationships of pity do persist in this programme, albeit in an unconventional form. Specifically, my analysis demonstrates that this programme reverses the traditional choreography of suffering found in the news by casting UK parents as sufferers (of the symbolic violence of their 'out-of-control' children), the teenagers as perpetrators (of such violence) and distant others as benefactors (alleviating the suffering of UK parents). Consequently, pity and gratitude are at the heart of this programme, even if they flow in unexpected directions.

It is also worth noting that if distant others are not suffering, it is not a "paradox of in/action" that is set up between the competing narratives (since no action is required), but a "paradox of humanity" in which television either constructs distant others as being like 'us', sharing a common humanity, or as something other than human because they are "disembodied and disindividulated" (Tester, 2001: 6) or simply a property of the screen. Thus, we should not consider the extent to which distant others are humanised only as a means of determining the audience's sense of agency in relation to them, as Chouliaraki (2006: 88) suggests, but as an important dimension of audiences' mediated experiences of distant others in itself.

A final point worth making about this approach is that, although Chouliaraki's analytics of mediation is regarded by many in media studies as a "groundbreaking" (Ong 2009: 450) approach to understanding and investigating empirically the mediation of distant suffering (see also Vestergaard, 2008; Robertson, 2010), the in-built assumptions about how audiences will react to different media texts remain empirically untested. As Simon Cottle (2009: 137) argues, "different 'regimes of pity' may or may not register and resonate with actual audiences ... When audiences do respond to calls for compassion embedded into news packages and visuals of human suffering they may be doing so in differentiated and quite distinct ways." Indeed, Chouliaraki (2006: 3) readily accepts that her approach is "neither about news production ... nor news interpretation ... [it] is [solely] about the news text that reaches our living room'."

In order to address this issue, a textual analysis of *The World's Strictest Parents* is combined with an examination of public talk and written comment about this particular text. This talk and comment is taken from a wider audience study conducted in 2009 alongside the market research company, TWResearch (see Scott, 2009b). In this research, we followed Nick Couldry, Sonia Livingstone and Tim Markham (2007) in combining two phases of interviews/focus groups with a (two-month) diary study in an attempt to move participants beyond the often 'contrived' nature of talk in one-off focus groups. By including two different phases of focus groups, having two methods for capturing participants' mediated experiences of distant others, and by involving participants in the research process over an extended period of time, we aimed to generate more genuine accounts of participants' mediated experiences of distant others. The study initially involved 108 participants across a range of ethnicities, levels of education, ages, length of residence in UK, viewing habits and interest in the Global South. Forty-six of those participants also took part in the diary study and the second phase of focus groups. In total, 33 different focus groups were conducted over the two phases, generating around 26 hours of talk, while the diary study generated 290 responses.

Textual analysis of *The World's Strictest Parents*

Resolving the paradox of distance: considering multi-modality

The episode of *The World's Strictest Parents* under analysis follows two 17-year-old British teenagers, Charlotte and Sam, who are sent to live with a Jamaican family, the Roses, for one week. The video footage consists largely of various incidents taking place in and around the home of the Jamaican family and the participants' diary pieces to camera in which they express their thoughts and feelings in relation to other actors and the behaviour of the teenagers. This is interspersed with narration and commentary on events. Rather than presenting a purely 'factual' and objective account of reality, as many conventional documentaries, news programmes and humanitarian communications seek to do, the "mode of presentation" (Chouliaraki, 2006: 74) of this reality-style programme purports to document dramatic and entertaining events that take place when 'ordinary people' are placed in abnormal situations. As such, I regard the "mode of presentation" as informing a "categorical realism", or a reality of emotions (Chouliaraki, 2006: 75), because the strongest appeal is to a reality evoked by strong feelings rather than facts.

The dominance of categorical realism is confirmed by a number of dimensions of the verbal, the visual and their correspondence, or the second key dimension of "passing through the medium" (Chouliaraki, 2006: 76). With regards to the meta-narrative, both teenagers appear to go through dramatic personal transformations within the course of the programme, from being "beyond [their] parent's control" to "finding a new way of life", as Sam explains: "Coming here has made every-thing different. I ain't complaining no more. I ain't got nothing to complain about. I'm just gonna basically not be such a little whining twat". Audiences are encour-aged to feel for and identify with the British teenagers as they go through this emotional journey through the many personal details and testimonies given about the teenagers, often told by the teenagers directly to the camera. Sam, for exam-ple, speaks frequently about how his father recently "buggered off" and the impact this has had on him emotionally and spiritually. Sam tells of how he now refuses to step inside a church or use the word 'dad' since his father left home.

Audiences are also encouraged to feel for and identify with distant others in the programme, principally the different members of the Jamaican host family who are placed in the role of benefactor. In particular, Sharon, the mother, is shown in a variety of contexts, dancing, disciplining, listening and talking to the teenagers and expressing varyingly affection, pride, hope and disappointment towards them. In one scene in which Charlotte has just read a letter from her mother, Sharon is shown embracing Charlotte and saying, "I'm so proud of you, are you proud of yourself?"

Despite the dominance of "categorical realism", there is also evidence of "ideological realism", or a reality of our deep-seated certainties and beliefs about the way the world is or should be (see Chouliaraki, 2006: 75). Ideological realism is produced through an appeal to a sense of justice, which in this case takes the form of explicit appeals by the British parents for their 'unruly' British teenagers to be better behaved and more respectful of them: "She just walks all over me. She's got no respect for me; none whatsoever ... I really hope I've got a new Charlotte back" (Charlotte's mother). As is evident from this quotation, the prin-cipal persecutor figures evoked in such claims for justice are the British teenagers. They are described as being not only "beyond their parent's control" but actively persecuting their parents: "She'll shout and be aggressive, she'll slam doors, she'll try to overpower me and I think she knows she can. She just walks all over me ... Its tiring, its draining – a complete battle that I'm not winning" (Charlotte's mother). Similarly, this sense of ideological realism reinforces the role of the Rose family, and the 'old-fashioned' parenting techniques to which they adhere, as the benefactor figure because it is they who challenge the teenager and protect the 'victims' (the British parents).

As a result of the centrality of appeals to the emotional reality of events in *The World's Strictest Parents*, it could be argued that the main responses audiences are invited to adopt are ones associated with "philanthropy" (Chouliaraki, 2006: 83), or feelings of tender-heartedness towards both the sufferer (the UK parents) and the benefactor (the Jamaican family) who comforts the sufferers' pain (Boltanski, 1999: 115). We may even hypothesise, in line with Harding (2009) and Smith *et al.* (2006), that because of their tendency to sensationalise events and focus on dramatic and entertaining scenes, such reality TV style programmes actively lend themselves to the preferencing of emotional responses to distant others. Such a preference for appeals to a 'reality of emotions' over a 'reality of facts' can be found in similar programmes such as *Holiday Hijack* and *Can Fat Teens Hunt?* Such emotional responses to distant others – rather than responses in the form of indifference or reflective contemplation, for example – are significant because an emotional appeal can, for some audiences who might otherwise be disinterested in development issues, provide a way of engaging with such issues. As is concluded from the audience research conducted for the VSO report, *Live Aid Legacy* (2001: 3), a lack of emotional connection "generates emotional distance, which generates disinterest … [Whereas] programmes that don't just educate, but [which] create emotional points of connection … [can] trigger the desire for greater knowledge and understanding [about development and developing countries]".

Resolving the paradox of distance: considering space-time

In Jamaica, events are shown to take place in numerous, real, private and public spaces, including every room of the Roses' home, a number of different rooms in the local secondary school (Denby High), the local church, a farm, Sangter International airport and a number of streets around these specific locations. The narrator renders these spaces specific by giving details of their names and precise locations and through the time the audience spends in each scene of action, helping to construct them as unique places. These spaces are also shown as populated by individualised people, such as "nineteen year old Malachi Johnson [who] lives in Portland Cottage in the Southern Hurricane belt". The Rose family parents, Sharon and Dave, arrange a meeting between Sam and Malachi, "which they hope will be a wakeup call for Sam ... [because] his father also walked out on him and they think Sam could learn from his example". During the meeting Malachi is individualised further by the details of his personal life and through meeting his family and seeing his home. Each of the members of the Rose family is also individualised through the frequent occasions in which they speak about their lives and interact with the British teenagers.

In relation to time, the life-worlds of distant others are less multiple and complex as they are situated largely within the week of the teenager's stay. Most references to time by the narrator are given in relation to the British teenagers, for example, "It's day four. The teens are halfway through their experience in Jamaica". However, there are several occasions in which a wider historical context is invoked. For example, Malachi Johnson explains his present circumstances through past occasions, such as the loss of his job, a hurricane, his dad leaving and challenges to his Christian faith, and also speaks about how this was likely to affect his future. Such factors are further expanded upon by other actors, who discuss the long-term causes of Malachi's personal circumstances. As a result, this programme often presents conditions of poverty within a "logic of causality" (Chouliaraki, 2006: 99), or as being a product of longer-term consequences and more subtle contexts.

These various properties of space-time signal a significant degree of spatio-temporal complexity, which invites audiences to consider distant others as proximate. This is important because if audiences consider distant others to be close, then they are more likely to care about them and potentially take action on their behalf (when called upon). Furthermore, the "logic of causality" in *The World's Strictest Parents* stands in direct contrast to many representations of poverty in humanitarian communications, for example, in which the structures and processes that sustain poverty in the Global South are obscured, and causality is presented as being dictated by the immediate context (Dogra, 2012). Such decontextualised representations are problematic because they deflect attention away from the need for deeper structural change and ultimately leave audiences with a severely limited understanding of the causes of poverty. In *The World's Strictest Parents*, such reductive accounts of poverty are not only avoided but often replaced with more complex accounts.

Resolving the paradox of distance: considering mobility

The space and time inhabited by distant others is also rendered complex and proximate by the strong sense of *mobility* apparent in the text, or connections between the life-worlds of audiences and distant others. This mobility is evident in the meta-narrative of the programme in which two British teenagers travel to Jamaica to live with a local family and experience life in Jamaica and then return home to the UK. It is also evident in the visual montage through frequent juxtapositions between footage of the UK and footage of family life and attitudes towards parenting in Jamaica. For example, just before going to school in Jamaica for the first time, Charlotte talks directly to the camera about her lack of achievement in education in the UK. This is combined with a montage of short video-clips of Charlotte at her school in the UK and a testimony from her mother about her attitude towards education. The narrative then returns to Jamaica in which the visual depiction of iconic shots of Jamaican schoolchildren is accompanied by the following voiceover: "In Jamaica, education is truly a means for a better life .... Education is a means of escaping the rural hardship". Sharon then explains, "In Jamaica, you go to school to do well and be successful". This verbal and visual juxtaposition serves to contrast Charlotte's attitude towards schooling with attitudes towards schooling in Jamaica. It is typical of the ways in which the audience is invited to draw connections between the two countries, or the mobility of the text.

Mobility is also evident on numerous occasions when actors explicitly compare life in Jamaica with life in the UK. As the father of the Rose family says, "Kids in England and America live a life of paradise, they need to come to Jamaica. This Jamaica can be a hellhole at times ... Things in England are put on a silver platter". Such mobility is a feature of many reality-TV programmes set in other countries on UK television. For example, programmes such as *Who Do You Think You Are?*, *Last Man Standing* and *Millionaire's Mission* all involve following the experiences of one or more UK citizens as they travel to 'other' countries, either to compete in sport, discover their genealogy, or to apply their entrepreneurial skills. Although following the experiences of a Westerner in a foreign country does not necessarily mean that a text appeals to a sense of mobility, in many occasions it will.

A strong degree of mobility is significant because it further reduces the moral distance between audiences and distant others and challenges the notion that 'they' are too far away from 'us' to be worth paying attention to. In particular, mobility is often considered a key constituent of a cosmopolitan disposition, which is itself necessary for the formation of a global civil society. As Szerszynski and Urry (2006: 117–118) argue, a sense of mobility provided by television can

> create an awareness of interdependence, encouraging the development of a notion of 'panhumanity', combining a universalistic conception of human rights with a cosmopolitan awareness of difference ... Illustrations of such panhumanity include ... the giving to distant (unknown) others of money, time, objects, software and information or political support (through mega-events like Live Aid and Live 8[3], local events or the Internet).

Resolving the paradox of in/humanity: considering the agency of distant others

Distant others in *The World's Strictest Parents* are frequently afforded what Chouliaraki (2006: 88) describes as "sovereign agency", or the power to respond to the persecutor's actions, assume the role of benefactor, and act upon their condition sufficient to be qualified as human beings. For example, Malachi Johnson, is afforded considerably agency over his life and the condition of his family when the narrator tells the audience of how, "by contrast to Sam, he has shouldered responsibility for his whole family despite facing extraordinary adversity ... He gave up his education to get a job to provide for his seven siblings after his father left". Moreover, the mother and father of the Rose family, the head teacher of the local school and even the 7-year-old daughter in the family are each shown exerting agency over the British teenagers and, in some cases, over British parents. For example, in two adjacent scenes, the head teacher of the school the teenagers attend in Jamaica not only convinces Charlotte to complete an exam after she had initially refused to work, but also subsequently talks to her about her problems and, in Charlotte's own words, teaches her "'something about herself".

The mother of the Rose family adopts a similar role on a number of occasions. For example, when Sam adopts the role of persecutor by refusing to attend church and arguing with Sharon, the mother exerts her own authority over him by saying "no, no, no, you don't tell me what to do" and sending the 17-year-old to bed early. The narrator's commentary on this incident implies that even Sam's parents in the UK do not have sufficient authority to make him do this: "Back home, after an argument, Sam would normally storm off. Instead he's sent to bed early". Sharon is even shown to have power over the British parents. This is evident both in the meta-narrative, in which the teenagers are sent to live with the Rose family in order to learn things their parents in Britain could not teach them, but also on a number of occasions when the narrator or the mother speak about what parents in the UK can learn from Jamaican parents. In the quotation below, for example, Sharon's use of the phrase "too privileged" implies that British parents spoil their children, and her reference to the need for discipline implies that her 'relentlessly strict' approach would be more appropriate: "These kids need discipline. It's not about them, it's about the parents, it's too much. [They're] too privileged".

Affording distant others sovereign agency by constructing them as able to improve the condition of UK citizens is a feature of many recent UK reality-TV programmes set in the Global South, such as *Tribal Wives*, *Last Man Standing* and *Meet the Natives*. In each of these programmes, the conventional roles of distant others and audiences as victim and benefactor respectively are entirely reversed. The affordance of sovereign agency to a range of distant others is significant because it renders them "thoroughly humanised and historical beings" (Chouliaraki, 2006: 159) and challenges the widely held belief, reinforced by most humanitarian communications, that "benevolent donors in the North are the primary source of solutions for the 'problems' of the South" (Cameron and Haanstra, 2008: 1478). This is significant because it also challenges the "strong cultural grounding in the North for paternalistic, charity-based and frequently neo-colonial development practices and projects" (Cameron and Haanstra, 2008: 1478). The specific idea that 'we' might have something to learn from 'them' is particularly challenging to the construction of others in the South as helpless victims and those in the North as superior and benevolent (VSO, 2001: 3).

Audiences of *The World's Strictest Parents*

A perhaps surprising amount of evidence emerged from discussions among the focus group and diary study participants about this particular episode of *The World's Strictest Parents* to suggest that these audiences did indeed regularly adopt the responses vis-à-vis distant others that have been identified above. The references to "joy", "laughter" and crying in the quotation below, for example, were symptomatic of the frequent emotional responses to *The World's Strictest Parents* and support the suggestion that this text invites emotional, tender responses in relation to distant others: "I found quite a lot of joy and laughter ... [in] *The World's Strictest Parents*, although that did make me cry" (London 2B). Furthermore, participants' talk and comment about *The World's Strictest Parents* also mirrored these readings above of the way in which role of the persecutor, benefactor and victim were occupied. In the first quotation below, UK teenagers are constructed as the persecutors (though not of distant others); in the second quotation, parents and teachers in the UK are constructed as victims; and in the third and fourth quotations respectively, distant others occupy the role of benefactor in relation to both UK teenagers and even to audience members themselves:

- "It really made me embarrassed about the kids in our country. They are so spoiled. They've got no respect for no-one or nothing" (Diary 28).

- "It showed me how much is taken away from the parent or teacher in this country, how we are not allowed to discipline them" (London 2A).
- "It was clear that in the boy's case, he lacked a father figure and learnt a lot from the father of the house" (Diary 39).
- "They are very respectful, unlike over in this country. I loved watching every minute of it because it gave me an idea on how to cope with my own children" (Diary 4).

These comments also allude to the sense of mobility frequently found in participants' talk. This was especially the case in the diary entries, although more comments focussed on comparisons rather than connections between places, as the following diary extract illustrates:

> The programme pointed out the contrast between the family structure from which teenagers came in UK and what they experienced in a Jamaican family ... Jamaica: discipline, clear boundaries, consequences following good or bad behaviour, routine, hard work, active help for the disadvantaged in society, respect for others, obedience. UK: freedom without duties, lack of respect for parents, no experience of hard work, no active awareness of how badly off other people may be (i.e., the disabled, etc.) over concern with their own selfish needs (Diary 41).

One participant even commented upon how this mobility was made possible by the text, suggesting that the British teenagers in the programme "are representing us, even though they're kids, so it's a little bit like how it would be if we went there" (Norwich 2B).

It is interesting to note that while participants often drew connections between the space-time of their lives and the lives of distant others in the programme, they still maintained a clear sense of difference between 'them' and 'us'. At no point in their expressions of mobility were distant others brought so close as to challenge the sense of 'otherness' – that 'they' might be the same as 'us'. As one participant put it, "very, very different, aren't they?" (Norwich 1I). Despite evidence of mobility in the way a number of participants talked about *The World's Strictest Parents,* there were also a number of participants who rejected the thought that it might connect them in some way to the life-worlds of distant others. This rejection appeared to stem largely from existing attitudes towards the sub-genre of reality-television style programming. Participants variously claimed that this and other reality-TV programmes were "hammed up" (London 2A), "not true to life" (London 2A), or "staged for entertainment purposes" (Norwich 2B) and in so doing rejected the thought that they could allow them to reflect upon their own connections to distant others.

Some responses also had strong parallels with what Irene Bruna Seu (2010) describes as a 'shoot the messenger' form of denial in which audiences combine a questioning of the integrity and trustworthiness of the 'messenger' with a justification for unresponsiveness: "They go out of their way to find the most unruly kids to meet the strictest parents" (London 2A). Indeed, by preferring a 'reality of emotions' over a 'reality of facts' such reality-TV programmes may have an active tendency to feed such strategies of denial. Those participants who did not adopt this perspective spoke and wrote about distant others in the programme almost always as complex, fully humanised individuals, just as was suggested in the textual analysis. This was apparent in the thought that 'we' might have something to learn from 'them', evident in a number of the quotations above, but also in references to various forms of agency and to their apparent moral values:

- "I saw how poor country's parents would inspire their children to participate in building up domestic and self reliance skills whilst maintaining discipline at school and home" (Diary 24).
- "They have pride in the things they do and make good use of what they have" (Diary 12).

In fact, the 'humanisation' of distant others was a feature of most talk and comment about other episodes of *The World's Strictest Parents* and reality-TV programmes in general: "I liked *Last Man Standing*. It came across that everyone in the world is making the best of what they've got" (London 2A).

In summary, aside from those who rejected the authenticity of the programme, almost all respondents provided evidence of emotional, proximate and mobile encounters with humanised distant others in their talk and comment about this text. This general character of responses to *The World's Strictest Parents* was particularly apparent when compared with responses to news coverage of distant others, which was generally characterised by indifference, distance and dehumanisation. As one participant said in a conversation about distant suffering on television news, "I don't think a lot of people let it get to them do they because it's so far away and you tend to distance yourself from it. I do anyway" (Norwich 1G). The same was also true for a significant majority of responses to NGO communications. In fact, it was only really in talk and comment about "factual entertainment" and "hobbies and leisure" programmes (and some conventional documentaries, particularly those involving celebrities) that evidence of mobility and humanisation was found.

Conclusion

In applying Chouliaraki's analytics of mediation to an episode of the *World's Strictest Parents*, I have provided evidence to suggest that this particular programme offers audiences emotional responses to proximate and humanised distant others in a way that 'peak moments' of television coverage often do not. Drawing on the results of a series of focus groups and a diary study, I have also argued that such responses are largely borne out in talk and comment about this text, notwithstanding some important exceptions. Although this is only an exploratory study, it nevertheless indicates that popular entertainment television programming, outside of news, conventional documentaries and humanitarian communications, does at least have the capacity to evoke relatively intense mediated experiences of distant others. We may even hypothesise that there is something particular about the format of some reality-television style programmes set in 'other' countries which means that they actively lend themselves to providing more intense mediated experience of distant others than 'peak moments' of television coverage. In particular, focussing on Westerners' experiences of foreign countries, the lives of 'ordinary' people in these countries who often act as benefactors, and their appeals to a reality of emotions appears to afford such programmes greater capacity for providing more mobile, proximate and emotional mediated experiences of humanised distant others. In doing so, such texts can challenge conventional hierarchies of place and human life and provide rare examples of "a more egalitarian representation of the other" (Chouliaraki 2006: 7).

Given this analysis, I hope to have begun to articulate the value of expanding the focus of studies of the "public faces" of development and "media and morality" to include encounters with distant others in more popular, entertainment-based television genres. This discussion also has implications for those (public service) broadcasters with an interest in or commitment to providing audiences with engaging international content. It suggests that their efforts to fulfil such commitments should extend beyond the genres of news and 'serious factual' documentaries. The BBC, for example, has a public service commitment to "bring the world to the UK", or more specifically to "broaden UK audiences' experience of and exposure to different cultures from around the world" (BBC Trust, 2006: 2). This has traditionally been interpreted only in terms of news and current affairs content. Recently, however, the BBC has discussed amending this global purpose to include explicit reference to a much wider range of genres, in particular referring to the BBC's obligation to "making people in the UK aware of international issues and of the different cultures and viewpoints of people living outside the UK through news and current affairs *and other outputs such as drama, comedy, documentaries, educational output and sports coverage*" [emphasis added].[4] Given the discussion in this chapter, I would argue that this proposal is most welcome and one that other broadcasters around the world should strongly consider following.

Notes

1 I wish to thank Lilie Chouliaraki for her very helpful comments on an earlier draft of this chapter.
2 See http://thecommunicationspace.com/forum/topics/cfp-cosmopolitanism-media-and (accessed 7 February 2013). The conference on *Cosmopolitanism, Media and Global Crisis* was held at Kingston University, London, on 4 June 2011 (see http://fass.kingston.ac.uk/activities/item.php?updatenum=1418, accessed 7 February 2013).
3 See chapter 10 (by Lousley) for a discussion of Live Aid and Live 8.
4 See the debate on OpenDemocracy.net at http://www.opendemocracy.net/ourkingdom/campaign-for-press-and-broadcasting-freedom/bbc-strategy-review-campaign-for-press-and-br (accessed 7 February 2013).

References

BBC Trust (2006) *BBC Public Purpose Remit: Bringing the UK to the World and the World to the UK.* London: BBC.

Beck, U. (2006) *The Cosmopolitan Vision*. Cambridge: Polity Press.

Boltanski, L. (1999) *Distant Suffering: Morality, Media and Politics*. Cambridge: Cambridge University Press.

Bolter, J. D., and R. Grusin (2000) *Remediation: Understanding New Media*. New York: MIT Press.

Brown, P. H., and J. Minty (2006) "Media Coverage and Charitable Giving after the 2004 Tsunami". William Davidson Institute Working Paper No. 855, University of Michigan.

Cameron, J., and A. Haanstra (2008) "Development made sexy: How it happened and what it means". *Third World Quarterly*, 29(8): 1475–1489.

Chouliaraki, L. (2006). *The Spectatorship of Suffering*. London: Sage.

Cottle, S. (2006). *Mediatized Conflict*. Maidenhead: Open University Press.

Cottle, S. (2009). *Global Crisis Reporting*. Maidenhead: Open University Press.

Couldry, N., S. Livingstone, and T. Markham (2007) *Media Consumption and Public Engagement: Beyond the Presumption of Attention*. Basingstoke: Palgrave MacMillan.

DFID (2000) *Viewing the World*. London: DFID.

Dogra, N. (2012) *Representations of Global Poverty: Aid, Development and International NGOs*. London: I. B. Tauris.

Escobar A. (1995) *Encountering Development: The Making and Unmaking of the Third World*. Princeton: Princeton University Press.

Hall, S. (1992) "The west and the rest: Discourse and power". In S. Hall and B. Gieben (eds.), *Formations of Modernity*. Cambridge: Polity Press, pp. 275–331.

Harding, P. (2009) "The Great Global Switch-Off: International Coverage in UK Public Service Broadcasting". Oxfam, Polis, and International Broadcasting Trust (IBT) report. Available at: http://www2.lse.ac.uk/media@lse/POLIS/Files/globalswitchoff.pdf (accessed 7 February 2013).

Kyriakidou, M. (2008) "Rethinking media events in the context of a global public sphere: Exploring the audience of global disasters in Greece". *Communications*, 33(3): 273–291.

Moeller, S. D. (1999) *Compassion Fatigue: How the Media sell Disease, Famine, War, and Death*. New York: Routledge.

Ofcom (2010) Public Service Broadcasting: Report 2010 Annexes. London, UK Office of Communications. Available at: http://stakeholders.ofcom.org.uk/binaries/broadcast/reviews-investigations/psb-review/psb2010/appendix.pdf (accessed 7 February 2013).

Ong, J. C. (2009) "The cosmopolitan continuum: Locating cosmopolitanism in media and cultural studies". *Media, Culture and Society,* 31(3): 449–466.

Pieterse, J. N. (1995) *White on Black: Images of Africa and Blacks in Western Popular Culture*. New Haven: Yale University Press.

Poland, K. (2004) "Development moments: Radio's public face of development". *Journal of International Development*, 16(5): 705–715.

Robertson, A. (2010) *Mediated Cosmopolitanism: The World of Television News*. Cambridge: Polity Press.

Said, E. W. (1979) *Orientalism*. New York: Vintage Books.

Seu, I. (2010) "Doing denial: Audience reaction to human rights appeals". *Discourse and Society*, 21(4) 438–457.

Scott, M. (2008) "Screening the World: How UK Broadcasters Portrayed the Wider World in 2007–8". London: IBT. Available at: http://www.ibt.org.uk/all_documents/research_reports/screening_the_%20world_June2008.pdf (accessed 7 February 2013).

Scott, M. (2009a) "Marginalized, negative or trivial? Coverage of Africa in the UK press". *Media, Culture and Society*, 31(4): 533–557.

Scott, M. (2009b) "The World in Focus: How UK Audiences Connect with the Wider World and the International Context of News in 2009". London: IBT & CBA. Available at: http://www.cba.org.uk/wp-content/uploads/2012/04/The-World-in-Focus.pdf (accessed 7 February 2013).

Scott, M. (2011) "Outside the Box: How UK broadcasters portrayed the wider world in 2010 and how international content can achieve greater impact with audiences". London: IBT. Available at: http://www.ibt.org.uk/all_documents/research_reports/ibt_OTB-090611finalLRv2.pdf (accessed 7 February 2013)

Silverstone, R. (2006) *Media and Morality: On the Rise of the Mediapolis*. London: Polity Press.

Smith, J., L. Edge, and V. Morris (2006) "Reflecting the Real World: How British TV portrayed developing countries in 2005". London: IBT. Available at: http://www.cba.org.uk/wp-content/uploads/2012/04/reflectingtherealworld.pdf (accessed 7 February 2013).

Smith, M., and H. Yanacopulos (2004a) "The public faces of development: An introduction". *Journal of International Development*, 16(5): 657–664.

Smith, M., and H. Yanacopulos (2004b) "The public faces of development". Special issue of the *Journal of International Development*, 16(5): 657–749.

Szerszynski, B., and M. Toogood (2000) "Global citizenship, the environment and the media". In B. Adam, S. Allan, and C. Carter (eds.), *Environmental Risks and the Media*. London: Routledge, pp. 218–228.

Szerszynski, B. and J. Urry (2002) "Cultures of cosmopolitanism". *The Sociological Review*, 50(4): 461–481.

Tester, K. (1994) *Media, Culture, and Morality*. London: Taylor & Francis.

Tester, K. (2001) *Compassion, Morality and the Media*. Maidenhead: Open University Press.

Thompson, J. (1995) *The Media and Modernity: A Social Theory of the Media*. Cambridge: Polity Press.

Tomlinson, J. (1999) *Globalization and Culture*. Chicago: University of Chicago Press.

Vestergaard, A. (2008) "Humanitarian branding and the media: The case of Amnesty International". *Journal of Language and Politics*, 7(3): 471–493.

VSO (2001) *Live Aid Legacy: The Developing World through British Eyes—A Research Report*. London: VSO (Voluntary Service Overseas). Available at: http://www.eldis.org/vfile/upload/1/document/0708/DOC1830.pdf (accessed 7 February 2013).

Wright, C. (2004) "Consuming lives, consuming landscapes: Interpreting advertisements for cafedirect coffees". *Journal of International Development*, 16(5): 665–680.

Yanacopulos, H., and G. Mohan (2006) "Learning from African school". *Development Education Journal*, 12(2): 19–22.

6 "Hidden in plain sight"

Baltimore, *The Wire,* and the politics of under-development in urban America

Simon Parker

"There is a game of puzzles," [Dupin] resumed, "which is played upon a map. One party playing requires another to find a given word – the name of town, river, state or empire – any word, in short, upon the motley and perplexed surface of the chart. A novice in the game generally seeks to embarrass his opponents by giving them the most minutely lettered names; but the adept selects such words as stretch, in large characters, from one end of the chart to the other. These, like the over-largely lettered signs and placards of the street, escape observation by dint of being excessively obvious; and here the physical oversight is precisely analogous with the moral inapprehension by which the intellect suffers to pass unnoticed those considerations which are too obtrusively and too palpably self-evident."

Poe (2005 [1844]: 64)

Introduction

The epigraph above is from 'The Purloined Letter', a short story by the Baltimore essayist and poet Edgar Allan Poe. He wrote it in 1844 at a time when his hometown had become "the chief black metropolis of the nineteenth century" (Graham, 1982: 252). In so far as Baltimore can be considered emblematic of the American black metropolis, it is also an urban archetype for the post-industrial city that "America left behind" (Parker, 2010; see also Moyers, 2011). At the same time, Baltimore also corresponds to Lacan's idea – exposed in relation to his reading of 'The Purloined Letter' – of the manifest being that which most eludes us, taken up by Gilles Deleuze in his famous essay 'How Do We Recognize Structuralism?', and where he posits that

> structuralism is not only inseparable from the works that it creates, but also from a practice in relation to the products that it interprets. Whether this practice is therapeutic or political, it designates a point of permanent revolution, or of permanent transfer.
>
> (Deleuze 2003: 190).

Though Deleuze's reflections on Lacan, structuralism and Poe predate the May 1968 events of Paris, there is a definite identification with an emerging revolutionary un/consciousness that was to find a resonance in many sites of urban contestation around the world at this time. The linking of anti-colonial and national liberation struggles in the southern hemisphere to anti-imperialist and civil rights movements in the cities of the Global North began to break down the political and cultural divisions that had separated subaltern movements in 'periphery' and 'core' regions of the globe. This was particularly apparent in relation to Baltimore. For two weeks following the assassination of Martin Luther King on 4 April 1968, large parts of central East Baltimore became the focus of violent social unrest. Reports of arson and looting prompted the Maryland governor Spiro Agnew to declare a state of emergency, and 6,000 National Guardsmen were sent into the city and given orders to fix bayonets in order to disperse the crowds defying the curfew. Angry, jubilant protesters were heard to chant "We've got the key to the city" and "We shall overcome".

Forty years after the riots, much of the former retail district in central East Baltimore remains an urban wasteland, the burnt-out stores and taverns were never rebuilt, and the stampede of the city's remaining white middle class for the safety of the suburbs was quickly followed by much of the business community. But it was the proximity of this insurgent black metropolis to the federal capital, Washington, DC, from which one of the most savage, intense and costly wars since the one that led to the Union's consolidation and triumph was being waged at the time – in Vietnam – that lent a special poignancy to the moral inapprehension of a Washington political consensus that suffered to pass unnoticed those considerations in its own backyard which were too obtrusively and too palpably self-evident. As Clay Risen (2008) writes:

> De facto segregation, workplace discrimination, police brutality and immense poverty were the inescapable realities of ghetto life, and they chafed against the postwar national rhetoric of consensus and progress. By the mid-1960s, ghettos around the country were tinderboxes, going off at the slightest provocation. And King's assassination was the greatest provocation possible.

Despite the late Gil Scott Heron's famous claim that "the revolution will not be televised",[1] the liberation struggles in Africa, Asia and Latin America became linked through the medium of television reportage with the streets of Detroit, Chicago, Los Angeles and Baltimore. Indeed, the Kerner Commission, which investigated the causes of the 1967 urban revolts across the United States, in fact explicitly acknowledged that the rallying cry of 'Black Power' had crossed the Atlantic and found fresh adherents on the streets of America's cities. The report concluded that "our nation is moving toward two societies, one black, one white – separate and unequal" (Parker, 2004: 91). But the "plainly hidden" explanation linking racial discrimination, lack of economic opportunity, and a sense of historic injustice as a highly combustible combination of causes was unacceptable to America's political elites and middle-class voters. Attempts at racial integration such as bussing and affirmative action met with great hostility among the majority white population, as did calls to tackle urban poverty through increased tax contributions. The result was a long period of Republican dominance in the White House and many state capitols across the United States, which eventually saw the Reagan administration dismantle virtually every aspect of Lyndon Johnson's earlier social reforms and the entrenchment and intensification of racial and economic segregation (Wilson, 1987; Massey and Denton, 1993).

As Greg Squires and Charis Kubrin (2006) write in the context of the contemporary United States:

> Place and race continue to be defining characteristics of the opportunity structure of metropolitan areas. … Dominant features of metropolitan development in the post-World War II years are sprawl, concentrated poverty and segregation (if not hypersegregation). Clearly, these are not separate, mutually exclusive patterns and processes. Rather, they are three critical underpinnings of the uneven development of place and privilege.

The affluent and predominantly white Washington, DC, suburb of Bethesda, Maryland, has one paediatrician for every 400 children, while the poor and predominantly black neighbourhoods in the District's southeast side have one paediatrician for every 3,700 children. And while the hospital admission rate for asthma in the state of New York is 1.8 per 1000, it is three times higher in the Mott Haven area of the South Bronx (Squires and Kubrin, 2006). These glaring levels of socio-spatial/racial inequality are captured in data that reveal that while African-Americans earn about 60 per cent of the income of the white population in the United States, their net wealth is around one-tenth that of whites (Squires and Kubrin, 2006) – a racialised socioeconomic disparity that is consistent with several developing societies in Latin America (Nopo *et al.*, 2004; McLucas, 2005; Villarreal, 2010).

Seen from this perspective, while agreeing with Lewis, Rodgers and Woolcock (2008: 201) that "fiction is arguably to a large extent frequently about the very issues that at a basic level are the subject matter of development studies: the promises and perils of encounters between different peoples; the tragic mix of courage, desperation, humour and deprivation characterising the lives of the downtrodden; and the complex assortment of means, motives and opportunities surrounding efforts by outsiders to 'help' them", it is important not to confine the potential of such artistic insights to the geographies of development traditionally associated with the Global South. As Herbert Marcuse (1978: 9–10, 72, cited in Catterall, 2011: 277, italics in original) wrote,

> Inasmuch as man and nature are constituted by an unfree society, their repressed and distorted potentialities can be represented only in an *estranging* form … The encounter with the truth of art happens in the estranging language and images which make perceptible, visible and audible that which is no longer, or not yet, perceived, said and heard in everyday life.

This is a universal process, and not one that is confined to the developing world. Certainly, as Jacques Lacan (1972: 40) wrote in his seminar on 'The Purloined Letter':

> It is the symbolic order which is constitutive for the subject by demonstrating in a story the decisive orientation which the subject receives from the itinerary of a signifier. It is that truth, let us note, which makes the very existence of fiction possible. And in that case, a fable is as appropriate as any other narrative for bringing it to light-at the risk of having the fable's coherence put to the test in the process. Aside from that reservation, a fictive tale even has the advantage of manifesting symbolic necessity more purely to the extent that we may believe its conception arbitrary.

The symbolic necessity of the arbitrary nature of social inequality and uneven geography can in fact often be more effectively communicated through the signifying medium of film and television than through conventional textual analysis. Take, for example, the ability to render and reveal the structures and relations through which the city's institutional and associational power is organised and to convey the micro-politics of these more "molar" power configurations – see Deleuze and Guattari (1987) – at the level of the human subject. This is a feat that has been achieved by very few writers. The fictionalised London of Charles Dickens and the Dublin of James Joyce's *Ulysses* are two of the most obvious exceptions (Clayton, 1995), insofar as they are fictions that draw from life and return to it a more intense "structure of feeling" (Williams, 1961) than that which can be perceived monadically or through ethnographic or documentary research. In the case of Baltimore, however, rather than any book, this is something that has perhaps best been achieved by the hit HBO TV series *The Wire*.

Playing out over 5 series and 60 episodes, *The Wire* engages with Baltimore – 'The City' – through a series of interlinked narratives that draw the viewer into a series of complex urban and institutional environments. In the first series, the focus is on 'the pit' – an open space surrounded by low-rise public housing in West Baltimore where the young lieutenants of the Avon Barksdale drug gang ply their trade – and 'the detail', a special undercover narcotics unit set up by the Baltimore Police Department to collect evidence in order to identify and prosecute the leading figures in a gang that some officers believe had been responsible for a large number of unsolved or unsuccessfully prosecuted homicides.

In the second series, the focus shifted to the city's docks, which has shed most of its employment as a result of containerisation and a lack of investment in the unloading and warehousing facilities necessary to compete with other ports. The docks nevertheless provide a relatively unguarded back door into the city for the lucrative global trade in human trafficking, contraband and narcotics. The third series, in a deliberate nod to Dutch experiments with drug legalisation, explores the consequences of an unofficial inner-city drug toleration zone ('Hamsterdam') and the severe political consequences that inevitably follow any attempt to decriminalise/demilitarise the war on drugs.

Series four follows the life of four young middle-school students as they come of age in a world that provides few opportunities or incentives to avoid the life of the street. The public school system, and the policy advisers who make comfortable livings from metricising and evaluating its shortcomings, provide the context for a broader critique of neoliberal divestment in public institutions. The destruction of social institutions and spaces that are generative of social solidarity provides the backdrop to a story line that blends hope with tragedy in unequal measure. The final series takes up this theme by following the declining fortunes of the city's main newspaper, *The Baltimore Sun*, against a plot involving an attempt by rogue detective Jimmy McNulty to fake a serial killer panic in a bizarre attempt to focus public attention on the 'plainly hidden' drug-related homicides that the Police Department refuses to investigate.

The narrative of *The Wire* requires what Atkinson and Beer (2010) refer to as an "andragogic" relationship with the audience in which the viewer is encouraged to make an intellectual as well as an emotional investment in order to bring coherence to the apparent chaos and random connections between institutions and characters than a more episodic reading permits. Certainly, for the many fans it is individual characters or even individual series that hold a particular and enduring fascination (Busfield and Owen, 2009). Contrary to the view of Baltimore's former mayors who objected to *The Wire*'s apparent claims to be an authentic portrayal of 'their' city (see Schmoke, 2008),[2] the motives of *The Wire*'s creator David Simon (2010) were always less parochial and more international in aspiring to create a TV show that was

> not about crime. Or punishment. Or the drug war. Or politics. Or race. Or education, labor relations or journalism. It was about The City. It is how we in the West live at the millennium, an urbanized species compacted together, sharing a common love, awe, and fear of what we have rendered not only in Baltimore or St. Louis or Chicago, but in Manchester or Amsterdam or Mexico City as well.

Simon's reference to the links between the Baltimore experience of urban deprivation and that of Manchester and Mexico City is a challenge to public policy and social science portrayals of ghettos as othered spaces that are nevertheless assimilable to an interiorised American narrative about the 'culture of poverty' and an elective belonging of criminality, worklessness, immorality and contempt for authority (Parker, 2010). To this extent, *The Wire* is arguably an important resource for students of development studies precisely because, in the manner of Poe's "game of puzzles", it seeks to connect the giant letters that spell 'U-N-D-E-R-D-E-V-E-L-O-P-M-E-N-T' across the continental divides that have so often bedevilled the study of comparative disadvantage and the buried histories of enforced subalternity. The next sections of this chapter explore how *The Wire* does this and what can be learnt from its particular presentation of Baltimore.

Baltimore: a Third World city in the First World?

As Immanuel Wallerstein (1974: 390) reminded us nearly four decades ago, "the only totalities that exist or have historically existed are mini-systems and world-systems, and in the nineteenth and twentieth centuries there has been only one world-system in existence, the capitalist world-economy". As one critic argues, part of the distorting effect of traditional development studies has not only been an over-focus on the analysis of nations and countries as opposed to cities and regions – and spaces within cities and regions, but also a reliance on often-mis-leading accounts of modern European history as a benchmark for comparison with 'Third World' development. A persistent belief in homogeneous 'core–periphery' geographies also tends to downplay the effects of uneven development within the same continent, between countries and in many cases within the same national territory (Halperin, 2007: 545).

An enduring problem for scholars of comparative urban deprivation in advanced economies is that the high levels of relative underdevelopment in the poorest neighbourhoods of Western cities are often masked by data that reflects the general well-being of the nation as whole. National indices such as the United Nations Development Programme's Human Development Index are problematic at the urban scale because they rely on aggregate national data such as life expectancy at birth, adult literacy and per capita income for which city-level data is often unavailable or incomplete (Moser *et al.*, 1996). But if the dualism so often associated with the study of development in the Global South is defined as "the presence of a modern economic sector that fails to transform the rest of society" (Halperin, 2007: 545), a strong case can be made for the inclusion of Baltimore as a dualist city-region during the course of its growth and development from the late eighteenth century onwards.

For the first century and a half of its existence, Baltimore's prosperity owed much to the export of tobacco, cotton and sugar, the production of which depended on the enslavement of large numbers of native Africans in the surrounding states of the American South. Despite the State of Maryland prohibiting the direct impor-tation of slaves in 1783, there is evidence of Baltimore's illicit complicity in the trade in the early part of the nineteenth century while slave ownership continued in the city right up until the civil war (Rawley and Behrendt, 2005: 350). Opportunities for unskilled employment and domestic service, however, attracted freed blacks and their descendants to Baltimore in such large numbers that according to one author, by 1860 there were 10 free blacks to every slave in the city (Phillips, 1997). But the work available to the city's poor black and migrant population was no less arduous and often no better rewarded than those who remained in bondage. Street cleaning, ditch-digging, woodcutting, stevedoring and – for women and children – rag-picking, seamstressing and domestic service were the reason that working-class Baltimoreans "lived poor", enjoying very little control over their own labour, and often facing long periods of unemployment and privation (Rockman, 2009: 2).

As the city grew more prosperous during the post-bellum era, racial intoler-ance and hostility to the emancipated black population on the part of the city's white inhabitants continued to promote discrimination and highly demarcated employment and residential patterns, which persist to this day. By the beginning of the 1970s, Baltimore's economic development went into reverse, and the city experienced a process of de-urbanisation and de-industrialisation. Between 1950 and 1970, Baltimore lost 46,000 manufacturing jobs (United Workers, 2011: 3). Bethlehem Steel, one of the city's largest companies, provided work for 30,000 employees in 1970. Thirty years later, only 5,000 were employed at the plant. Shipbuilding and repair alongside stevedoring all but disappeared. As David Harvey (2000: 148) describes, "[t]he geographical disparities in wealth and power increase to fashion a metropolitan world of chronically uneven geographical development". By 1995, only 8 per cent of Baltimore's jobs were in manufacturing compared to 34 per cent in 1950 (Levine, 2000: 137).

Despite the regeneration of Baltimore's harbour front in the 1980s and 1990s, which sought to replace the image of a declining port city with that of the 'Renaissance City' founded on tourism, sports and convention dollars, one of the city's former mayors proclaimed that Baltimore was "a Third World city in the First World" (Pietila, 1996 in Levine, 2000: 124). While 'Harborplace' and the 'Gold Coast' hotels, offices and condominiums represent the only Baltimore most visitors are likely to see, Levine points to two other versions of the city. On the one hand, "the 'Underclass City' of desolate neighbourhoods marked by social exclusion, high rates of crime and drug abuse, deepening ghetto poverty, and dilapidated or abandoned housing, where much of the city's predominantly black population lived". In 1990, over 100,000 Baltimoreans lived in census tracts where at least 40 per cent of the population was officially classed as poor—double the number in 1960 (Levine 2000: 138). On the other hand, a third Baltimore relates to the rapidly expanding white suburbs often outside the limits of the metropolitan city, often referred to as 'the County'.[3] By the 1990s, the per-capita income of the City of Baltimore was only 64.3 per cent of the surrounding suburbs (Levine 2000: 124), and despite some halting attempts at gentrification beyond the 'Renaissance City' water margin, the segregating effects of urban poverty continued to intensify during the 2000s.

It is not difficult to see why Baltimore's former mayor talks of the city as having Third World characteristics when one considers that an estimated 9 per cent of the city's population were thought to be addicted to illegal drugs and Baltimore's hospitals had the highest rate of admissions for drug-related emergencies of any city in the United States in the mid-1990s (Levine 2000: 124). In 2010, Baltimore also ranked 8th among the United States' most dangerous cities with an average of 1,455 violent crimes per 100,000 people.[4] In this year, there were 35 murders per 100,000 people, four times the national average. Seen from this perspective, there is no doubt that the residual city has become a place of abandonment and social and economic divestment. Time series data for Baltimore City schools reveals a dramatic decline in enrolment from just under 123,000 students in 1968–1970 to just under 62,000 in 2000. Segregation data for 1999–2000 found that 77 per cent of pupils were poor,[5] with African-American pupils in particular experiencing some of the highest isolation indices in the country, reflecting an increasing ethnic segregation between the predominantly black inner city and the homogeneously white suburbs.[6]

Kurt L. Schmoke, Baltimore's first black mayor (and the supposed model for Mayor Royce in *The Wire*),[7] sought to portray an altogether more regeneration friendly impression by promoting a 'carnival city' vision of Baltimore, through investing millions of dollars in tourist and entertainment led development in the downtown area, while the rest of the city experienced mounting 'social and economic distress'. However, as Marc Levine (2000: 134–35) points out, "there are serious questions regarding the social justice of the 'carnival city' strategy. Jobs have been created in the Inner Harbor but the quality of these jobs is dubious: they are not unionised, contain few fringe benefits or career ladders, are typically part-time, and pay about 60 per cent of the average city wage". The economic conditions in which many Baltimore workers have found themselves for the past 20 years are typical of the precarious, low-wage, non-unionised labour markets associated with rapidly urbanising cities in the Global South (Sassen and Holston, 1999), and it is perhaps not surprising that a survey conducted in the early 1990s found that 27 per cent of people using soup kitchens and other voluntary aided welfare services in Baltimore worked full-time (United Workers 2011: 20).

A recent report on working conditions in Baltimore highlighted that "workers who toil for long hours at the Inner Harbor are often hidden in plain sight. Yet, their stories are the only ones that can really tell us whether the jobs created by publicly supported development projects deliver a path out of poverty for local residents ... Inner Harbor restaurants pay servers $3.63 per hour. The servers are expected to make the rest of their wages in tips. If the total for the week falls below minimum wage, restaurants are supposed to pay the difference. Many do not." (United Workers, 2011: 11). This gentrified civic space, which is either out of bounds to the majority of the city's black population or only available through an exploitative service economy, is sensitively explored in Series Four of *The Wire* when former police lieutenant-turned-social worker 'Bunny' Colvin takes a group of his school students to a smart harbour-front restaurant as a reward for winning a model-building competition. The young black students feel awkward, alienated and out of place, and their mentor feels remorse at assuming that invisible boundaries are any easier to traverse than the more visible social, cultural and economic barriers of the street (Parker, 2010: 551). In this, as in many other scenes in *The Wire*, it is the power of the hidden, the submerged and the unspoken – rhetorical devices that cannot be rendered through the insistent, declarative intrusion of the text – that endows the best televisual drama with its qualities of empathy and authenticity.

Understanding Baltimore's uneven geography through televisual drama

Leonie Sandercock (1998: 37) refers to cities as "being full of stories in time, some sedimented and catalogued; others spoorlike, vestigial and dispersed.... Their identities, modes, forms, categories and types recombine in the gray matter of streets. City narratives are, as a result, both evident and enigmatic. Knowing them is always experimental." A similar perspective is offered by Lewis, Rodgers and Woolcock (2008: 199) when they write that "ideas and images of development are inevitably represented in a wide variety of ways, whether within academia, the policy world or the general public domain. To this extent, it can be contended that all forms of development knowledge can be – and historically have been – largely understood as a series of 'stories'." Our perception and knowledge of cities – even those in which we may live and work – is more often reliant on the stories that others tell us than on our first-hand experience. The complex, ineffable character of metropolitan life could only be fully communicated, according to Walter Benjamin (1999: 249), through the poetical reconstruction of the "ruined present" of the city in the work of writers such as Charles Baudelaire or artists such as Paul Klee. Similarly, one can argue that it is up to contemporary poets, lyricists, writers and film makers to creatively reconstruct the exploded fragments of history that would otherwise "pass unnoticed".

The literature on the 'universal' characteristics of cities in the developing world/Global South often refers to states of 'lack': insufficient water, food, sanitation, transportation, education, health care, employment, housing, law and order, combined with a general absence of political and human rights. While for many observers the megacity has become a synonym for the megaslum (Roy, 2011), which is defined in terms of 'excess': surplus population and labour, unsustainable pressures on the urban environment and infrastructure, extreme beliefs and ideologies (especially those identified with violence and intolerance), excessive consumption and anti-social behaviour. The fictional portrayal of these "maximum cities" (Mehta, 2005) has changed little since Rudyard Kipling brought the genre of slum *noir* to a mass readership with the publication of *City of Dreadful Night* in 1891 (Parker, 2004: 189).

Much of what Victorian writers such as Mayhew, Dickens, Hugo and Balzac observed in nineteenth century London and Paris finds echoes in both fictional and non-fictional portrayals of slum life in the contemporary megacity. Recurring negative themes include the high incidence of crime, which is often a consequence of the general absence of the state (apart from the operation of sporadic 'revanchist' policing); problems of alcohol and drug dependency, which in turn are linked to poor health and high levels of mortality; the exploitation and neglect of the vulnerable; the precarious nature of labour; and the endless competition for work. More positive images touch on what one might call 'the solidarities of the subaltern' including the sharing of clothes, food and lodgings; informal networking to secure work or an entrepreneurial opportunity; an often strongly rooted religiosity that offers hope and a narrative of salvation to the urban poor; and a distinct and often highly localised vernacular culture that provides a sense of belonging and social identity (see Simone, 2010).

Representations of urban dislocation, violence and poverty can often be more effectively communicated through the medium of film, television and video because even vividly written ethnographic accounts of groups and communities lack the affective immediacy and valency of televisual drama. This is especially true where the aim of the director of the Brazilian film *City of God/Cidade de Deus* is explicitly to "look like we were losing control, because, as time went on, alphabetically, the state was losing control of the area to the drug dealers, and that only leads to chaos" (Fernando Meirelles in Rohter, 2003: 5, cited in Chan and Vitali, 2010: 16). As a *Der Spiegel* report on Rio de Janeiro's drug gangs notes:

> The government is almost completely absent from most slums and police presence is rare. The drug gangs are often so well armed that only heavily armed special units dare to enter the favelas. Police officers, many in the drug dealers' pay, look the other way when the gangs go to war, uninterested in endangering their own illegal earnings from the cocaine trade. Corruption reaches right to the top ranks of law enforcement. The public prosecutor's office is currently investigating Rio's former police chief for taking bribes from the mafia (Jens Glüsing in Chan and Vitali, 2010: 26).

The intensity and frequency of violent crime and homicide may be higher in certain parts of Rio de Janeiro, Ciudad Juarez, Caracas, Johannesburg and other notoriously dangerous cities of the Global South, but the waste of human, natural and economic resources are generated from the same sources, and the structurations of power follow very similar contours in places such as Baltimore, and the 'meta narrative' of a beleaguered society within a society that is entirely cut off from what Jacques Rancière (2006) refers to as "police order" – or the order of governance – can arguably be discerned more clearly through a metonymic reading of films and television. From this perspective, *The Wire* clearly constitutes an equivalent to Meirelles's *City of God/Cidade de Deus* or José Padilha's *Bus 174* and *Elite Squad*. "By using precise geography", *The Wire* creates, not a true-to-life but "a fully conceptualized city" (Simon, 2000), in the mode of James Joyce's Dublin or Louis-Ferdinand Céline's Paris. The story developments "culled from actual casework" are intended to impress the viewer "as something so clearly real that the traditional conceits of police melodrama are seen as such". This does not mean that every character, case and historical event has to be authentically re-assembled and filmed, but rather the creative reconstruction of Baltimore with all its chiaroscuro elements needs to be authentic in terms of its narrative intent. Often this required filming more 'typical' drug corners and vacant lots from East Baltimore for the scenes that were apparently set in the West (Dechter, 2006), or using dramatic license to edit out the *longeurs* of pounding the beat or the more sober off-duty fraternisation of the Baltimore Police Department (Moskos 2008).

Nearly all of the action in *The Wire* is set in the City of Baltimore or its environs, which extend to the county jail, although one episode involves a road trip to Philadelphia as part of a training exercise orchestrated by gang leader Stringer Bell. A rare exception occurs in series 5 when *The Wire's* anti-hero Omar Little, after a daring and successful heist involving a shipment of heroin that he successfully sells back to its intended customer (Proposition Joe), moves into self-imposed exile with his lover Renaldo in San Juan, Puerto Rico. Omar's idyllic retirement to a conventional 'Third World' city provides a powerful and ironic contrast to the violent and brutal metropolis he has left behind. When Omar decides to return to Baltimore to avenge his uncle's murder, the viewer is once more transported back to the fatal geographies and unregulated violence of the American ghetto.

This sense of a tightly confined and contained urban habitus is fundamental to our appreciation of what, following David Harvey (2001), we might refer to as the "spatial fix" of surplus labour, which under the conditions of a globalised and politically unaccountable capitalism is forced to exploit and often eliminate itself in a macabre 'play within a play' imitation of more scalar geopolitical hegemonies. As in life, these shadow geographies are only glimpsed in *The Wire* through the fleeting presence of a major league drug importer, when the prospect of a political scalp presents itself to the FBI, or when jobs need to be shed in the interest of 'revitalisation' and 'corporate restructuring' in the Baltimore docks or on the *Baltimore Sun*. Or as Toscano and Kinkle (2009) argue, "rather than thinking it as a successful mapping of the uneven urban development of capitalist accumulation and its social effects, *The Wire* could be seen as dramatising the struggles of any critical or political 'will to know' in the current ideological and institutional dispensation".

Following the money

David Harvey (1985) reminds us that the story of urbanisation is also the story of capitalist development. However, this process is far from linear and unidirectional. It is marked by periods of stagnation and decline that continue to produce new contours of uneven geographical development. Cities on the way up sometimes pass cities on the way down. But what all contemporary cities share, as Georg Simmel (1950) noted, is an existential reliance on the making and spending of money, and the relations surrounding these are inherently complicated. A good deal of *The Wire*'s achievement is its ability to explore the parallel institutions, actors and networks of power that comprise the so-called legitimate economy and the criminal underworld through a series of compelling storylines that evince an easy distinction between the two. The introductory 'pitch' to the pilot script of *The Wire* defines the show as "in the strictest sense, a police procedural set in the drug culture of an American rust-belt city, a cops-and-players story that exists within the same vernacular as other television fare". But through the medium of the police procedural, the creators aimed to produce "far more than a cop show" by breaking new television ground in dealing "with the human condition, the nature of the American city... the national culture ... and even the American experiment" (Simon, 2000).

The setting is an "Eastern rust-belt city, majority black but with white ethnic elements still clinging to certain quadrants as well as the power structure. An incumbent black mayor and police commissioner signal the arrival of the city's black voting block, but other bureaucrats – deputy commissioners, prosecutors, and many line officers and firefighters remain white". The population are "poor, uneducated, and struggling with a huge heroin and cocaine problem", and the city is one in which "unlike the new Metropolises of the West. We are in a remnant of

Old America as it struggles to make itself into part of the new" (Simon, 2000). In microcosm, David Simon is painting a picture of the ethnicised power hierarchies that are all too familiar within the uneven geographies of the Global South, where powerful white corporate, military and diplomatic elites enjoy close and often corrupt relations with their native counterparts who remain aloof and detached from the desperate lives that many of their countries' poorest citizens are forced to endure (see Sachs, 2011).

Unusually for a police procedural, there is no denouement or cliff-hanger at the end of each episode, outside of the opening and closing titles the soundtrack is diegetic, most of the shooting was intended to be done on location on the streets and bars of Baltimore using 16 mm film and hand-held cameras rather than in the studio – although 35 mm cameras were mostly used – while many of the actors are non-professionals with backgrounds as police, ex-criminals, reporters and school students. The 'hyper-realism' thus generated is based on the dramatic principle that nothing should happen on the screen that hasn't in some fashion happened on the streets. The quasi-documentary technique that David Simon refers to as "stealing life" – see Talbot (2007); also Penfold-Mounce *et al.* (2011) – is inspired by some of the great contemporary and classical dramatists. As Simon (2000) writes in the pilot pitch:

> In the first story arc, the episodes begin with what would seem to be the straightforward pursuit of a violent drug crew … But within a brief span of time the officers who undertake the pursuit are forced to acknowledge truths about their department, their role, the drug-war and the city as a whole. In the end, the cost to all sides begins to suggest not so much the dogged police pursuit of the bad guys, but rather a Greek tragedy. At the end of thirteen episodes the reward for the viewer … is not the simple gratification of hearing handcuffs click. Instead, the conclusion is something that Euripides or O'Neill might recognize: an America at every level at war with itself.

Thus, the opening scenes of the first episode feature a back street dice game that ends in murder when the unfortunately named 'Snot Boogie' steals the cash from the pot once too often. The insistence by one of the potential witnesses to the shooting, that despite previous wrongdoing, everyone should be given a second chance – "This is America man …" – defines the nature of the 'game' in inner-city Baltimore as one in which opportunity and risk are existential features of a world where the state and justice, just as in the anarchic *favelas* of Meirelles and Lund's *City of God*, are almost entirely absent. Similarly, when a shipping container full of dead young women is discovered at the beginning of the second series, with the exception of rogue detective Jimmy McNulty, the police authorities are keener to disavow responsibility for the anonymous victims than to bring the perpetrators to justice. On the one hand, the use of the port as a conduit for sex trafficking provides a fictional reminder of Baltimore's historically ambiguous relationship to the nineteenth century slave trade and the re-purposing of once flourishing industrial geographies as 'grey spaces' for informal and illicit economic activities

(Yiftachel, 2009). On the other hand, as David Harvey (2000: 148) points out, "containerization of port operations and automated ship loading have reduced employment on the docks to a shadow of its former importance", and as long-shoreman union boss Frank Sabotka more prosaically puts it in *The Wire*, "You know what the trouble is, Brucey? We used to make shit in this country, build shit. Now we just put our hand in the next guy's pocket".

To this extent, when veteran detective Lester Freamon announces, "When you follow drugs, you get drug addicts and drug dealers. But you start to follow the money, and you don't know where the fuck it's gonna take you", we are arguably invited, like Dupin's Prefect in Poe's *Purloined Letter*, to confront the plainly hidden features of the Baltimore drug trade. This is a radically different notion of justice from the public-relations-oriented corner busting of Commander Rawls or the clandestine drug kingpin hunting of maverick detective Jimmy McNulty. Freamon's objective, on the other hand, is simply to identify the money trail and thereby show how the web of corruption links Baltimore's multi-million dollar waterfront hotels, offices and condos to the 11-year-old kids selling rocks on the abandoned corners of West Baltimore. His disillusion with Baltimore's public institutions is shared by retired Police Lieutenant 'Bunny' Colvin, who, having tried and failed to establish a truce in Baltimore's war on drugs by creating an Amsterdam style drug toleration zone, finds similar levels of institutional cynicism and genuflection to neoliberal authority in the school and probation services (Bryant and Pollock, 2010).

According to dependency theory, the use of public funds to attract private capital investment, which more often than not fails to yield jobs or growth, is characteristic of the underdeveloped economies of the Global South (Cockcroft *et al.*, 1972; Amin and Pearce, 1978; Halperin, 2007). However, the increasing use of public subsidies to retain or attract wealthy corporations, the encouragement of predatory lending to predominantly minority ethnic sub-prime mortgage customers, and the resort to revanchist policing and state-orchestrated gentrification as a mechanism for making the central city safe for bourgeois accumulation is as much a feature of the shrinking metropolitan cities of the United States and the neoliberal economies of the Global North as the majority urban world of the Global South (Smith, 1996; Wyly *et al.*, 2006).

The final series of *The Wire* shifts the institutional focus of the drama to the newsroom of the fictional *Baltimore Sun* and explores the symbiotic and often corrupt relationship between politicians, the press and the police. As they contemplate the reasons for the dismantling of their murder investigation, detectives Freamon, McNulty and Moreland lament the un-newsworthiness of the dozens of young, black males who have fallen victim to 'misdemeanour homicides'. Contrasting the wall-to-wall media coverage of a young middle-class white girl from the suburbs who had been reported as missing, Bunk Moreland reminds McNulty, "this ain't Aruba bitch". In other words, race and place are interpolated through the lens of a media industry whose exclusive concern with the lives of 'citizens' ensures that the urban outcasts of the American Dream remain as firmly peripheral to its national story as the sweatshop workers of Mexico's *maquiladoras*, the 'illegal' Chinese *hukou* migrants who service America's voracious appetite for cheap consumer goods, or the nameless victims of the global drugs war in the devastated villages of Colombia, Afghanistan and Pakistan.

Conclusion: subaltern urbanism and *The Wire*

As David Simon (cited in Moyers, 2011) observes:

> America now jails more of its people than any country, including all totalitarian states. We pretend to a war against narcotics, but in truth, we are simply brutalizing and dehumanizing an urban underclass that we no longer need as a labor supply.

The increasing spatial concentration of poverty and disadvantage in the cities of the Global North and the negative economic, educational, health and welfare consequences for the populations who make up the "hyper ghetto" (Wacquant, 2008) increasingly calls into question the geographical confinement of what Ananya Roy (2011) refers to as "subaltern urbanism" to the megacities of the Global South. Urban marginalisation, segregation and inter-generationally maintained racial and ethnic disadvantage are not just an aberration in the history of the United States – they increasingly define the 'two Americas'.

During a round table discussion with some of America's leading conservative commentators, *The Wire's* creator David Simon insisted that

> For 35 years, you've systematically deindustrialized these cities. You've rendered them inhospitable to the working class, economically. You have marginalized a certain percentage of your population, most of them minority, and placed them in a situation where the only viable economic engine in their hypersegregated neighborhoods is the drug trade. Then you've alienated them further by fighting this draconian war in their neighborhoods, and not being able to distinguish between friend or foe and between that which is truly dangerous or that which is just illegal. And you want to sit across the table from me and say "What's the solution?" and get it in a paragraph? The solution is to undo the last 35 years, brick by brick. How long is that going to take? I don't know, but until you start it's only going to get worse (Walker, 2004).

During the same exchange, Simon describes his ambition at the beginning of *The Wire* as remarkably modest:

> *The Wire* will have an effect on the way a certain number of thoughtful people look at the drug war. It will not have the slightest effect on the way the nation as a whole does business. Nor is that my intent in doing the show. My intent is to tell a good story that matters to myself and the other writers – to tell the best story we can about what it feels like to live in the American city.

The eminent Harvard sociologist, William Julius Wilson, was rather more flattering about *The Wire*'s exploration of urban sociological themes, declaring Simon and Burns' achievement to be "truly exceptional", and going on to add:

> I do not hesitate to say that it has done more to enhance our understandings of the challenges of urban life and urban inequality than any other media event or scholarly publication, including studies by social scientists... *The Wire* develops morally complex characters on each side of the law, and with its scrupulous exploration of the inner workings of various institutions, including drug-dealing gangs, the police, politicians, unions, public schools, and the print media, viewers become aware that individuals' decisions and behaviour are often shaped by – and indeed limited by – social, political, and economic forces beyond their control. (cited in Penfold-Mounce *et al.*, 2011: 152).

In this respect, *The Wire* as a work of 'social science-fiction' is no different – if a good deal more honest – than many books and articles written on Third World poverty. To return in conclusion to Rancière's (1998: 29) definition of political activity (whether fictional or not), this

> is whatever shifts a body from the place assigned to it or changes a place's destination. It makes visible what had no business being seen, and makes heard a discourse where once there was only place for noise; it makes understood as discourse what was once only heard as noise.

Seen from this perspective, while we can make no assumptions about the new ways of seeing and hearing that may be occasioned by fictions of development, we can at least hope that by opening up the discourses of the subaltern to different publics, a willingness to engage with troubling and difficult social challenges may extend itself beyond the immediate scope of aesthetic consumption.

Notes

1 See http://www.youtube.com/watch?v=rGaRtqrlGy8 (accessed 7 February 2013).
2 See also the comments of former mayor Sheila Dixon at the preview gala of the fifth and final series of *The Wire* (http://www.youtube.com/watch?v=JmKUvgodphA), in which any real association between the TV series and Baltimore politics and society is vigorously denied.
3 Although there are in fact two counties that surround the City of Baltimore: Baltimore County and Anne Arundel County.
4 Violent crime includes murder and non-negligent manslaughter, forcible rape, robbery and aggravated assault (see http://www.businessinsider.com/most-dangerous-cities-2011-5#8-baltimore-md-18 (accessed 7 February 2013).
5 Defined as eligible for free or reduced price school meals, which requires a household income of less than $32,000 a year for a family of four.
6 The isolation index is the percentage of same-group population in the elementary schools where the average member of a racial/ethnic group attends. It has a lower parameter of zero (for a very small group that is quite dispersed) to 100 (meaning that

group members are entirely isolated from other groups). This index is affected by the size of the group – it is almost inevitably smaller for smaller groups, and it is likely to rise over time if the group increases in size (see http://www.s4.brown.edu/schoolsegregation/schoolsegdatapage/codes/schoolseg.asp, accessed 31 July 2012).

7 Kurt Schmoke makes a guest appearance as a Health Commissioner in episodes 11 and 12 of the third series of *The Wire*.

References

Amin, S., B. Pearce (1978) *Accumulation on a World Scale: A Critique of the Theory of Underdevelopment*. Hassocks: Harvester Press.

Atkinson, R., and D. Beer (2010) "The ivorine tower in the city: Engaging urban studies after The Wire". *City*, 14(5): 529–544.

Benjamin, W. (1999) *Illuminations*. London: Pimlico.

Bryant, A., and G. Pollock (2010) "Where do Bunnys come from? From Hamsterdam to hubris". *City*, 14(6): 709–729.

Busfield, S., and P. Owen (2009) *The Wire re-up: The Guardian Guide to the Greatest TV Show Ever Made*. London: Guardian Books.

Catterall, B. (2011) "Is it all coming together? Thoughts on urban studies and the present crisis: (22) Mediations, entrapment and counterrevolution". *City*, 15(2): 276–284.

Chan, F. and V. Vitali (2010) "Revisiting the 'realism' of the cosmetics of hunger: Cidade de Deus and Ônibus 174". *New Cinemas: Journal of Contemporary Film*, 8(1): 15–30.

Clayton, J. (1995) "Londublin: Dickens' London in Joyce's Dublin". *NOVEL: A Forum on Fiction*, 28(3): 327–342.

Cockcroft, J. D., A. G. Frank, and D. L. Johnson (1972) *Dependence and Underdevelopment: Latin America's Political Economy*. New York: Anchor Books.

Dechter, G. (2006) "Wish You Weren't Here: A Guided Tour Of *The Wire*'s East Baltimore". *City Paper,* 24 May. Available at: http://www2.citypaper.com/bob/story.asp?id=11846 (accessed 7 February 2013).

Deleuze, G. (2003) *Desert Islands and Other Texts (1953–1974)*. New York: Semiotexte.

Deleuze, G. and F. Guattari (1987) *A Thousand Plateaus: Capitalism and Schizophrenia*. Minneapolis: University of Minnesota Press.

Graham, L. (1982) *Baltimore, The Nineteenth Century Black Capital*. Washington, DC: University Press of America.

Halperin, S. (2007) "Re-envisioning global development: Conceptual and methodological issues". *Globalizations*, 4(4): 543–558.

Harvey, D. (1985) *Consciousness and the Urban Experience*. Oxford: Blackwell.

Harvey, D. (2000) *Spaces of Hope*. Edinburgh: Edinburgh University Press.

Harvey, D. (2001) "Globalization and the 'spatial fix'". *Geographische Revue*, 2, 23–30.

Lacan, J. (1972), "Seminar on 'The Purloined Letter'". *Yale French Studies*, 48: 38–72.

Levine, M. V. (2000) "'A third-world city in the first world': Social exclusion, racial inequality, and sustainable development in Baltimore". In M. Polèse and R. E. Stren (eds.), *The Social Sustainabilty of Cities: Diversity and the Management of Change*. Toronto: University of Toronto Press, pp. 123–156.

Lewis, D., D. Rodgers, and M. Woolcock (2008) "The fiction of development: Literary representation as a source of authoritative knowledge". *Journal of Development Studies*, 44(2): 198–216.

Marcuse, H. (1978) *The Aesthetic Dimension: Toward a Critique of Marxist Aesthetics*. Boston: Beacon Press.

Massey, D. S., and N. A. Denton (1993) *American Apartheid: Segregation and the Making of the Underclass*. Cambridge: Harvard University Press.

McLucas, K. L. (2005) "Race and inequality in Brazil: The Afro-Brazilian struggle in the racial democracy". *Identity Culture, Society, and Praxis*, 4(1): 85–90.

Mehta, S. (2005) *Maximum City: Bombay Lost and Found*. London: Review.

Moser, C., M. Gatehouse, and H. Garcia (1996) "Urban Poverty Research Sourcebook Module II: Indicators of Urban Poverty". Urban Management and Poverty Reduction Working Paper no. 5, Washington DC: UNDP/UNCHS (Habitat)/World Bank.

Moskos, P. (2008) *Cop in the Hood: My Year Policing Baltimore's Eastern District*. Princeton: Princeton University Press.

Moyers, B. (2011) "The Straight Dope, Bill Moyers interviews David Simon". *Guernica*, 1 April. Available at: http://www.guernicamag.com/interviews/2530/simon_4_1_11/ (accessed 7 February 2013).

Nopo, H., J. Saavedra, and M. Torero (2004) "Ethnicity and Earnings in Urban Peru". Middlebury College Economics Discussion Paper No. 04-05, Middlebury: Middlebury College.

Parker, S. (2004) *Urban Theory and the Urban Experience: Encountering the City*. London and New York: Routledge.

Parker, S. (2010) "From soft eyes to street lives: The Wire and jargons of authenticity". *City*, 14(5): 545–557.

Penfold-Mounce, R., D. Beer, and R. Burrows (2011) "The Wire as social science-fiction?". *Sociology*, 45(1): 152–167.

Phillips, C. (1997) *Freedom's Port: The African American Community of Baltimore, 1790–1860*. Chicago: University of Illinois Press.

Pietila, A. (1996) "A Third World City in the First World", *Baltimore Sun,* 16 February.

Poe, E. A. (2005 [1844]), "The Purloined Letter". In E. A. Poe, *The Best Short Stories of Edgar Allan Poe*, Stilwell: Digireads.com Publishing.

Rancière, J. (1998) *Disagreement: Politics and Philosophy*. Minneapolis: University of Minnesota Press.

Rancière, J., and G. Rockhill (2006) *The Politics of Aesthetics: The Distribution of the Sensible*. London: Continuum.

Rawley, J. A., and S. D. Behrendt (2005) *The Transatlantic Slave Trade: A History*. Lincoln: University of Nebraska Press.

Risen, C. (2008) 'The legacy of the 1968 riots', *The Guardian,* 4 April 2008.

Rockman, S. (2009) *Scraping By: Wage Labor, Slavery, and Survival in early Baltimore*. Baltimore: Johns Hopkins University Press.

Roy, A. (2011) "Slumdog Cities: Rethinking Subaltern Urbanism", *International Journal of Urban and Regional Research*, 35(2): 223–238.

Sachs, J. D. (2011) 'The Global Economy's Corporate Crime Wave'. *Project Syndicate,* 30 April. Available at http://www.project-syndicate.org/commentary/the-global-economy-s-corporate-crime-wave (accessed 25 November 2012).

Sandercock, L. (1998) *Making the Invisible Visible: A Multicultural Planning History*. Berkeley: University of California Press.

Sassen, S., and J. Holston (1999) "Whose City is It? Globalization and the Formation of New Claims'. In J. Holston (ed.) *Cities and Citizenship,* Durham: Duke University Press, pp. 177–194.

Schmoke, K. (2008) 'The Wire and the real Baltimore', *The Guardian* 'Comment is free' online commentary, 11 January. Available at: http://www.guardian.co.uk/commentisfree/2008/jan/11/thewireandtherealbaltimor (accessed 7 February 2013).

Simmel, G. (1950) "The Metropolis and Mental Life". In K. H. Wolff (ed.), *The Sociology of Georg Simmel.* Glencoe: Free Press, pp. 409–426.

Simon, D. (2000) 'The Wire: A Dramatic Series for HBO', mimeo. Available at: http://kottke.org.s3.amazonaws.com/the-wire/The_Wire_-_Bible.pdf (accessed 7 February 2013).

Simon, D. (2010) 'Quality trumps ad nauseam'. *The Sydney Morning Herald,* 9 January. Available at: http://www.smh.com.au/news/entertainment/tv--radio/simon-says/2010/01/09/1262453695066.html?page=fullpage#contentSwap1 (accessed 7 February 2013)

Simone, A. (2010) *City Life from Jakarta to Dakar: Movements at the Crossroads.* London: Routledge.

Smith, N. (1996) *The New Urban Frontier: Gentrification and the Revanchist City.* New York: Routledge.

Squires, G. D., and C. E. Kubrin (2006) 'Privileged Places. Race, Opportunity and Uneven Development in Urban America', *Shelterforce Online,* Fall. Available at: http://www.nhi.org/online/issues/147/privilegedplaces.html (accessed on 25 November 2012).

Talbot, M. (2007) 'Stealing Life. The Crusader Behind the Wire'. *The New Yorker,* 22 October. Available at http://www.newyorker.com/reporting/2007/10/22/071022fa_fact_talbot (accessed 25 November 2012).

Toscano, A., and J. Kinkle (2009) 'Baltimore as World and Representation: Cognitive Mapping and Capitalism in The Wire', *Dossier,* 8 April. Available at: http://dossierjournal.com/read/theory/baltimore-as-world-and-representation-cognitive-mapping-and-capitalism-in-the-wire/ (accessed on 25 November 2012).

United Workers (2011) 'Hidden in Plain Sight: Workers at Baltimore's Inner Harbor and the Struggle for Fair Development', Baltimore and New York: United Workers/NESRI.

Villarreal, A. (2010) "Stratification by Skin Color in Contemporary Mexico". *American Sociological Review,* 75(5): 652–678.

Wacquant, L. (2008) *Urban outcasts: A Comparative Sociology of Advanced Marginality.* Cambridge: Polity.

Walker, J. (2004) 'David Simon Says'. *Reason.com,* October. Available at: http://reason.com/archives/2004/10/01/david-simon-says (accessed 7 February 2013).

Wallerstein, I. (1974) "The Rise and Future Demise of the World Capitalist System: Concepts for Comparative Analysis". *Comparative Studies in Society and History,* 16(4): 387–415.

Williams, R. (1961) *The Long Revolution.* London: Chatto and Windus.

Wilson, W. J. (1987) *The Truly Disadvantaged: The Inner City, the Underclass, and Public Policy.* Chicago: University of Chicago Press.

Wyly, E., M. Atia, H. Foxcroft, D. J. Hamme, and K. Phillips-Watts (2006) "American home: Predatory mortgage capital and neighbourhood spaces of race and class exploitation in the United States". *Geografiska Annaler: Series B Human Geography,* 88(1): pp. 105–132.

Yiftachel, O. (2009) "Theoretical notes on 'Gray Cities': The coming of urban Apartheid?". *Planning Theory,* 8(1): 88–100.

Part IV

Film

7 The projection of development

Cinematic representation as an(other) source of authoritative knowledge?

David Lewis, Dennis Rodgers and Michael Woolcock[1]

Introduction

The wide-ranging and intrinsically public nature of development means that getting to grips with broader, more popular understandings of the concept is critical to improving the way development policies are conceived, debated, implemented and assessed. Partly for this reason, we made a case in an article entitled "The Fiction of Development" that novels ought to be considered potentially valuable sources of information about development, since they both supplement and challenge more familiar forms of academic or policy knowledge, and may also qualify or even overtly challenge mainstream thinking about knowledge authority (Lewis *et al.*, 2008; reproduced as chapter 2 of this volume). In that paper, we limited our discussion to literary fiction, but we recognised that other forms of fictional representation, such as films and plays, also constituted important communicative mediums for addressing key themes in development. Building on some of the insights of our earlier article – and as promised in one of its footnotes – this chapter extends our arguments to the interface between cinema and development.[2]

This chapter aims to introduce the subject of cinema and development as a potentially fruitful area for future research, and using some brief and selective examples, to draw out some preliminary insights. In recent years, for instance, relatively popular films such as *Blood Diamond* (2006) and *The Constant Gardener* (2005) have told stories that attempt both to entertain and to engage audiences with important global development issues. What is distinctive about how development issues are rendered in such films, as compared with scholarly publications and policy reports? We do not attempt to be comprehensive and – as was also the case in our previous paper on literature – make no claim to be drawing upon a "representative" body of films about development.[3] Rather, the chapter draws on a range of personally selected historical and contemporary examples, which include both Western and some developing country films, in order to explore the power and limitations of cinematographic representation as an(other) authoritative source of development knowledge.

Our focus is principally on drama rather than on documentary forms of film.[4] We write primarily from the perspective of development studies, and we do not engage in any depth with film theory in this chapter, but we hope that this exploratory work can help to stimulate such a conversation. We are also acutely conscious that our selection is drawn primarily from popular films that have been influential in the global North. We hope to encourage further work that can give due coverage to films from India, Nigeria, South Africa, South Korea and elsewhere, many of which explicitly address development issues. These clear limitations notwithstanding, for present purposes, we focus on three key issues, namely:

(i) The nature of film as a representational medium for development concerns.
(ii) Some of the potential pitfalls associated with film as a representational medium for certain specific development-related issues and contexts.
(iii) The way that cinema shapes, but also fundamentally reflects, popular conceptions of development in the West.

What we hope to show is that, similar to any form of representation, film brings both strengths and limitations to the ways that it conveys complex issues.[5] Although we argue that films can be a legitimate and potentially important medium for representation, both intrinsically and instrumentally, we also highlight issues and problems in the underlying nature of their particular representational power, as well as the inherent ambiguities associated with films as fundamentally contextualised forms of representation. Awareness of these strengths and limitations is especially important for teaching development, given the increasing incorporation of film into university classroom discussions and online debates.

Film and development

Few feature films have been concerned directly with agency-led development interventions or projects. One exception is Martin Campbell's feature film *Beyond Borders* (2003), which stars Angelina Jolie as an aid worker who abandons a comfortable socialite life in London to become an aid worker in Ethiopia, participating in events reminiscent of the Ethiopian famine of 1984–1985 and the international humanitarian relief effort that followed. It was marketed with the rather dismal tagline "In a place she didn't belong, among people she never knew, she found a way to make a difference". The film was neither a critical nor a box office success, but it did attempt to raise some important issues about the politics of aid along the way.

More common, however, are films that engage tangentially with a variety of broader development issues – war, conflict and violence, humanitarianism, commerce, poverty, politics and more – as part of their setting or plot. One trope that emerges very frequently, however, is contentious interaction between people from rich and poor countries. Indeed, the divide between rich and poor – or more precisely, between Westerners and "locals", as most of these films we discuss tell their stories from a Western point of view – is arguably *the* key concern in most films that can be categorised as "development films".

Recent films such as *Blood Diamond* (2006), *The Constant Gardener* (2005), *The Hurt Locker* (2008), or even *Casino Royale* (2006) and *Quantum of Solace* (2008), fall into this category.[6] At the same time, in addition to focusing on the divide between rich and poor and outsiders and locals, their narratives are soon complicated by additional storylines that centre on exposing and exploring the tensions *within* certain key groups – such as pharmaceutical companies, the military, the media, aid organisations, governments or citizen groups – on one or both sides of the divide. So while the initial focus may be a deadly conflict in a developing country – whether it be a "civil war", a humanitarian intervention, an outright invasion, or drugs-trade-related violence – the central drama concerns the deep moral ambiguities, personal misgivings and overt power struggles that the protagonists, whether as reluctant, accidental or noble heroes, find themselves navigating. Indeed, much of the narrative *animus* turns out to be driven by the crises, contradictions and greed among those (at least nominally) on their own side.

This kind of narrative arc, done carefully, bears repeating, and as a depiction of "reality" may improve on what passes today for news coverage of such events, where a two-minute (at best) loop provides viewers with estimates of body counts and property damage, and explains the carnage as an outcome of a contest between the two most proximate actors (see Chouliaraki, 2010). Despite being generally plagued by an audience-appealing imperative to juxtapose relatively clear fault lines of good and evil, the best films in this genre seek to complicate these categories. They suggest that the very fluidity and ambiguity of virtue and vice at any given time and place may itself be a factor driving human tragedy, even as it can also, occasionally, provide narrow windows of opportunity that the fortunate, the persistent, or the deftly strategic can exploit. In the acclaimed film *Hotel Rwanda* (2004), for example, one might initially think the distinctions between good and evil would be relatively clear and straightforward, but the film does a careful job of showing that there was plenty of blame to go around, the atrocities initiated, sustained and intensified by a complicated storm of local, national, regional and international factors.

If moral ambiguities are well-worn tropes in commercial films, much less so are themes seeking to convey how highly educated, mostly well-meaning people come to preside over vast technologies of decision making that, by privileging certain forms of knowledge-claiming over others, become complicit in perpetuating (sometimes intensifying) widespread human suffering. Beyond the world of familiar contests between good and evil people (doctors, drug lords) engaged in good and evil practices (saving lives, money laundering), there exists a more pervasive everyday reality in the international aid business, one in which billions of dollars must be mobilised and dispersed with a minimum of fuss in the service of "projects" that strive to meet objectives such as enhancing access to education, water, jobs and justice, among others. Countries and companies have a mixture of motives for engaging in such activities, the efficacy of which is (for the most part) inherently uncertain, and mediated via (even as it actively sustains) a complex political economy of domestic and international actors. How this pervasive uncertainty is resolved – and what imperatives it generates among constituent actors to sustain the system's legitimacy and validate one's contribution to it – is rarely the subject of cinematic attention.[7]

A second general theme often found in development films is "commerce", where confusion, prejudice, indifference and exploitation drive human suffering through the dynamics and imperatives of market exchange. Here, the central argument is not just that the powerless are shamelessly coerced or manipulated by the powerful, but that these differentials are compounded by, or even directly premised on, the qualitatively different ways in which various groups involved understand the transactions taking place. The introduction of money – an abstraction that is alien to many groups – as the basis of exchange erodes the integrity of social relations and sometimes alters entire cosmologies (Gauri et al., 2011). A classic film in this genre is *The Gods Must be Crazy* (1981), in which a Coca-Cola bottle, nonchalantly tossed from a passing aeroplane only to land at the foot of a perplexed San tribesman in rural Africa, becomes the fulcrum around which turn multiple confusions between colonisers and local populations.[8]

A more recent rendering of the deep ambiguities and contestation surrounding commercial exchange is *También la Lluvia (Even the Rain)* (2010). This is a film about a documentary about a movie depicting the brutal manner in which the (Christian) Spaniards, led by Christopher Columbus, conquered and then suppressed the ("heathen") indigenous populations of Santo Domingo in the sixteenth century. Making this film, however, are an ambitious but struggling young director and producer, whose careers turn on completing the project and making good on the considerable investments that have been ploughed into making the film; should it fail, they face professional and financial ruin. The film is being made, however, not in coastal, tropical Santo Domingo but mountainous, temperate Bolivia (because the local actors are much less costly) and against the backdrop, so everyone learns to their consternation, of an increasingly violent dispute in the area between the government and community groups over the privatisation of water, an actual event that took place in Cochabamba in 2000. "Even the rain", it seems, can be commoditised, bought and sold. Weaving his way into this contentious mix is Daniel, the film's lead indigenous actor but also high-profile critic of the government's policies, who for his efforts is repeatedly beaten and imprisoned, thereby jeopardizing the film's tight production schedule.

Even the Rain has many messages, but a central one is that while the characters and contexts may change, powerful people fuelled by appropriate combinations of ideas (progress, efficiency, aspiration), interests (money, fame, salvation) and material resources continue to wreak havoc on the less powerful. These tumultuous processes, however, are not just driven by those with money, connections and guns against noble, innocent villagers,[9] but are also grounded in orthogonal cosmological and epistemological understandings of the purpose(s) and mechanics of life. In a particularly powerful scene, an episode from the sixteenth century encounter is being re-enacted wherein a band of indigenous women and their children are chased into a river by Spanish soldiers and their attack dogs. The director, Sebastian, explains to the actors how, facing a certain and gruesome death, the women chose to drown their children, preferring the trauma of murdering their own flesh and blood over experiencing the even greater trauma of watching their innocent children be mercilessly butchered. In order to be faithful to the historical account, Sebastian informs the women actors, they should run into the river carrying their children, at which point filming would momentarily cease while the screaming children are replaced by dolls, and the women would then simulate the drowning of their actual children. "Don't worry, nothing will happen to your children – they won't even get wet", Sebastian reassures the mothers, "but we need you to do this because this is how it happened". Unable to even conceive of taking such actions, let alone willing to "act" it out for monetary gain, the indigenous cast members simply walk off the set, leaving unfinished a pivotal scene in Sebastian's steadily unravelling film.

The potential pitfalls of cinematic representation

The popularity of cinema as a form of entertainment is often assumed to derive at least in part from its specifically visual form, or put another way, from the power of the moving image to touch and influence viewers' minds in a manner unmatched by either the spoken or the written word. The visual element of a film's narrative "goes well beyond what can be expressed in words" (Suber, 2006: xxix–xxx). This power imbues films with the capacity to represent particular types of situations or events – such as, with regard to development, poverty, conflict, or a specific context – much more immediately and empathetically. But the representational power of a film with regard to development issues also lies in the extent to which the audience has prior knowledge of the contexts and events being depicted. Films that have explicitly sought to make developing contexts central to their content have only become popular in the West since the advent of mass tourism and travel. Although Western films set in the developing world go back a long way, prior to the 1990s these rarely made such contexts a central element, generally offering them as backdrops to a more universal story. Compare, for example, two Academy-Award-winning films set in India: *Gandhi* (1984), which clearly focused on a particular individual's political trajectory but offered little of wider Indian society and context; and *Slumdog Millionaire* (2009), which explicitly offered a grittier neo-realist depiction of contemporary Indian society.[10]

At least part of *Slumdog's* success was due to the reduction of global distance. Western audiences today are more familiar with Indian society than they were 25 years ago. From this perspective, we need to consider critically how films reflect specific development-related societal trends and issues. Indeed, one could even argue that it is misleading to view such popular films as authoritative repositories of knowledge.[11] Two films that centre on urban violence in Latin America highlight this issue particularly well. The first is *City of God* (2002), a Brazilian film directed by Fernando Meirelles, which was a surprise global hit and garnered a number of critics' prizes, as well as four Oscar nominations in 2004. The second is *La Yuma* (2010), the first full-length feature film to emerge from Nicaragua in over 20 years. Directed by the Nicaragua-based Frenchwoman Florence Jaugey, it has not been distributed as widely as *City of God* but has been extensively lauded in the media and at independent film festivals all over the world, and was Nicaragua's submission for the 2011 Best Foreign Film Oscar.

City of God was one of the first films to bring the critical development issue of Brazilian urban violence into the Western mainstream, and has without doubt helped put the subject on the public agenda. Such is the power of the film that it is frequently shown in North American and European university settings as a quasi-documentary, despite the fact that it makes no claims to being a veridical depiction of Brazilian urban violence. As Armstrong (2009: 85) has pointed out, "American and European reception of creative art from the developing world is usually framed by the assumption that it has a testimonial value and points to a collective condition", and it was in this way that a short excerpt was used (without forewarning) at an academic conference attended by one of us (Rodgers) in 2003 in order to introduce the general theme of the paper he was presenting on gang violence in Nicaragua.

The problem, however, is that the film is not a documentary. Although *City of God* draws on a semi-autobiographical novel of the same name published in 1997 by the Brazilian author Paulo Lins,[12] and its basic storyline plausibly depicts the evolution of organised gang violence in the *Cidade de Deus* suburb of Rio de Janeiro between the 1960s and the 1980s, the film is also riddled with stereotypes that both project and confirm certain critically flawed ideas about gangs and gang members, that have moreover long contributed to preventing sensible public action being taken to tackle gang violence all over the world.[13] For example, Little Zé, a central character who is presented as the driving force behind the growth of crime and violence in the *Cidade de Deus* suburb, comes across as a psychopath. This implicitly places the blame for his brutality on individual characteristics rather than the structural circumstances that the overwhelming majority of gang research has repeatedly highlighted ever since Frederick Thrasher's (1927) ground-breaking study of gangs in Chicago.[14]

This issue starkly highlights the potential pitfalls associated with seeing films as authoritative representational forms. More so than any academic or policy text, the credibility of a film derives squarely from its narrative structure, and cinematographic imperatives being what they are, facts frequently have to give way to dramatic effect.[15] This is also evident, though in a different way, with regards to *La Yuma*. This film tells the story of a young girl struggling to escape a life of poverty in the *barrios* of Managua through boxing. It chronicles her relationships with family, the local street gang (to which she belongs), as well as with a middle-class journalism university student. Issues such as domestic violence, abuse, gangs, inequality and class difference are all tackled in a way that offers an unusually realistic representation of the difficult nature of life in poor urban neighbourhoods, and part of the film's appeal clearly derives from its realism. At the same time, however, although much of what is depicted in *La Yuma* rings true, the overall effectiveness of the film is paradoxically based on significant simplifications of a complex reality, to the extent that they are actually extremely distorting.

Most blatantly, although the film is set at some point after 2006, it depicts gangs as they existed in the 1990s, ignoring the dramatic and messy consequences that the widespread emergence of crack cocaine in the early 2000s had in poor urban neighbourhoods in Nicaragua. Previously semi-ritualistic, vigilante-style gangs became more brutal and more predatory of their local communities as a result of both crack consumption and trafficking (see Rodgers, 2006), but depicting this would have no doubt confused the relatively straightforward overarching narrative of the film, which manages to remain appealing despite its dramatic subject matter by offering generally positive representations of unsavoury phenomena. Gang violence, for example, is portrayed almost comically, while depictions of other forms of everyday chronic brutality, such as domestic violence and abuse, are kept to a minimum, and generally implied rather than explicitly shown.

Similarly, inequality is tackled by bringing together the film's eponymous heroine with a university student from Nicaragua's very small – and not terribly significant, at least from a sociological point of view – middle class rather than juxtaposing her life with that of an individual emanating from the country's shockingly venal elite (see Rodgers, 2008). As such, the film can be said to offer an incomplete and indeed rather particular consideration of what is perhaps the most fundamental dynamic of contemporary Nicaraguan society. Although critical of the yawning gap between rich and poor, in representational terms it arguably misses its target, as the film's central protagonists all tend to correspond to exceptional rather than archetypal characters within Nicaraguan society.

At the same time, Jaugey obviously plays hard and fast with the fabric of social reality in order to bend it to the needs of crafting a clear and deeply empathic fictional narrative, and succeeds very well in this respect, for the film's storyline is both engrossing and empathy inducing. Its nature is, however, slightly off-putting for anybody who has a prior knowledge of Nicaragua – and more specifically of the country's poor urban neighbourhoods – owing to the underlying distortions. Seen from this perspective, it is perhaps unfortunate that the film is being actively promoted by the French film association as a means through which schools can teach youth about Nicaragua and Central America, although admittedly in explicit contrast to more commercial films that involve highly sensationalistic depictions of Central American gangs, such as Cary Fukunaga's widely acclaimed *Sin Nombre* (2009), for example.[16]

The power of film as a particular representational genre is clearly a double-edged sword. There is no doubt that films can convey a visceral sense of a given situation or issue more vividly than any academic text or policy report. For example, David Wheatley's film *The March* (1990), a serious and ultimately tragic satire about famine, humanitarianism and the West's relationship with the South, is a brilliant teaching tool to shock romantic students into realising that the primary imperatives guiding the development business are rarely idealistic. Although by no means a new point, it is one that is rarely discussed explicitly in academic – and even less policy – texts, and *The March* provides excellent dramatic insight into the issue. But this power is extremely seductive, and in the same way that the narrative sleights of anthropologists – "I've been there and you haven't" – and the mathematical mystification of econometricians enable them to authoritatively bulldoze over underlying deficiencies in their academic texts, it means that cinematic representations of issues and situations are often not challenged, especially when films are popularly acclaimed.[17] In this respect, *The March* sometimes verges on caricature. Many of the details that it offers – such as those concerning the workings of European Union, for example – are plainly wrong, but have been clearly modified in order to tighten the narrative structure of the film. But then, as Mark Twain (in)famously put it, one should "never let the facts get in the way of a good story", of course.

Films as popular representations of development

This final section discusses some of the ways that film has both represented and shaped ideas about the development encounter in the popular realm. Film, we argue, like literature, has played a role in the ways that public understandings of development have been historically constructed. This is, of course, a very large subject, and we choose to approach it selectively through a short case study of a sub-genre of films within a moment of Western cinema during the first half of the 1980s. From the work of Edward Said (1978) on "Orientalism" onwards, we have become aware of how the construction of the colonial "Other" is inherently tied to the construction of notions of selfhood within the colonising "Self". This idea continues to resonate with those wishing to understand how Westerners encounter and view the rest of the world, and films can clearly help us to understand how the framing of North/South relationships has evolved and changed, reinforcing or attempting to challenge dominant ideas and stereotypes among their audiences. Smith and Yanacopulos (2004: 660), for example, argue that the "public understanding of development" is a difficult area for study precisely because development itself is a contested subject, and "the fact that there are multiple public faces of development reflects a complex situation about which we have relatively little understanding". Film, we would argue, is a useful place to start in order to see such complexity in action.

We find it significant that during the early 1980s, a crop of left-of-centre yet mainstream popular action thrillers started appearing in cinemas. These all shared a common but arguably new set of anxieties about the changing relationship between the West and the "Third World", and took as their central narrative the idea of a Western citizen (normally a journalist) thrown into an unstable or threatening situation in the developing world.[18] Three notable examples of the genre include *Missing* (1982), set during the post-Pinochet coup period in Chile; *Under Fire* (1983), on the last days of the Somoza regime in Nicaragua; and *The Year of Living Dangerously* (1982), which takes place during the failed 1965 communist coup attempt in Indonesia against Sukarno.[19] The central Western character – respectively played by Jack Lemmon, Nick Nolte and Mel Gibson – initially has little interest in the situation around him, but is slowly forced by events to engage more fully and even to take sides in the struggle for justice within the conflict encountered.

Missing (1982) was directed by the Greek film maker Constantin Costa-Gavras, who shared a screenplay adaptation Oscar for the film, which was also awarded the Palme d'Or at the Cannes film festival in 1982. Katz (1994: 295) describes the film as "a piercing, factually-based drama about American-sanctioned political atrocities in post-Allende Chile". *Under Fire* (1983) was directed by the Canadian film-maker Roger Spottiswoode, who began his cine-matographic career as a film editor for Sam Peckinpah, the well-known director of classic Westerns such as *The Wild Bunch* (1971) and *Pat Garrett and Billy the Kid* (1973). The film tells the story of a US journalist who becomes drawn into helping the *Sandinista* revolutionaries in Nicaragua maintain their momentum for the final push of their struggle by taking a bogus picture of their fallen leader that makes him appear to be alive, thus denying the government both a propaganda victory and its final consignment of US weapons. Finally, Australian director Peter Weir's *The Year of Living Dangerously* (1982) follows an inexperienced Australian jour-nalist called Guy Hamilton as he becomes caught up in the turbulent politics of Indonesia in 1965, and has his indifference to his surroundings challenged.

All three films enjoyed significant popular and critical acclaim. In general terms, they can be seen to form a sub-genre of "Westerners lost and found in Third World conflicts". People are caught up within the local realities of global conflicts and forced to reassess their attitudes and their place in the world. As Hettne (2009: 84) writes in his overview of development thinking, "the 1970s was a decade of crisis and rethinking, paving the way for significant discursive change. The shift to a new development discourse, which was centred on the concept of globalisation, came around the year 1980". Although the end of the Cold War was still some years away, the seeds of a new reality were becoming increasingly evi-dent. Hettne, in particular, draws attention to a specific set of factors that contrib-uted to the new development paradigm of "globalism" at this time, including the rise of the New Right, a neo-liberal "counter revolution" in development econom-ics, the collapse of communism, and the rise of post-modernism. All three of the films touch directly on these issues, and in doing so both reveal aspects of this period of change, whether in terms of national level transformation in relation to global economic and political interests, or the level of the personal, through the narratives of individual actors caught up in events.

In *Missing*, for example, Charlie, the idealistic "anti-establishment" young American writer – naïve, but curious about the world about him – is living in Chile with his wife Beth. Travelling outside Santiago, Charlie is trapped by the coup, and the film retrospectively follows his efforts to get back safely through the maze of Chilean army check points and encounters with dubious US under-cover agents. We know that Charlie did not return, and is listed by the authorities as missing. Eyewitnesses report that he was arrested by the military, but the US embassy denies any knowledge of this and insists that he is more likely to be in hiding since he had supposedly been associating with radical students. The film then traces the efforts of Beth, and Ed Horman, his businessman father, who flies to Chile to uncover what actually happened. The setting of post-Allende Chile is an environment that first challenges, then traumatises and eventually transforms, Ed Horman. He begins the film as a conservative Christian Scientist with com-plete faith in the integrity of the US government, but his worldview is shaken when he finds out the truth about the extra-judicial killing of his "disappeared" son during the recent US-backed coup. The film exposes US involvement in the coup in support of companies operating in Chile's markets, and Ed Horman's narrative arc depicts the questioning by ordinary citizens of what is being done in their name in the Third World. Ed initially refuses to see the evidence of US complicity in the terrible events that have just taken place in Chile, but is eventually persuaded by the weight of evidence that Beth shows him, by the callous double-speak of officials who claim to be trying to help him, and eventually by the hundreds of bodies that he sees in the local morgue. At the end of the film, when Ed confronts the US Ambassador he is told: "If you hadn't been personally involved in this … unfortunate incident, you would be sitting at home complacent and more or less oblivious to all this".

Missing makes the personal political, but the neo-liberal ravages of Thatcherism and Reaganism during the 1980s – the part of the ideological foundations for which had been laid in Chile under the authoritarian Pinochet regime – highlight how such a distinction is ultimately spurious. Certainly, this is one of the messages contained in *Under Fire*, which explicitly shows how individual personal experience comes together with wider global issues. In this film, the central character, photographer Russell Price, has flitted from war zone to war zone until he finds himself taking pictures in Nicaragua just before the 1979 *Sandinista* revolution. Events, however, lead him to abandon his position of cynical detachment when he is forced to take sides, after witnessing what he eventually comes to see as a collision between heroic local struggles and malign global forces. The opening scene of the film takes place in Chad, where Price bumps into an American mercenary, Oates, who is used to changing sides regularly in local conflicts, and often does not even know if he is with the government or the rebels. The narrative then moves to Nicaragua, the next global trouble spot, where we meet boozy press man Alex and his journalist wife Claire, who are separating. When Russell is later taken to meet renowned guerrilla leader Rafael, Claire pointedly tells him that "the world is not divided into East and West any more, it is divided into North and South".

On the one hand, the Cold War period is spelled out through the idea of journalists and mercenaries moving from one war zone to another, indifferent either to the human suffering or the politics in which they are implicated. On the other hand, however, the film depicts a changing world order, in which the power play between East and West is becoming characterised by growing tensions between rich and poor areas of the world, a new geopolitical turning point. Its vision is intimately tied up in the individual personal epiphanies of the Western bystander characters in the film, but the film also reveals the indifference of global American power to poverty and social justice. When towards the end of the film Claire sees her husband Alex's filmed death at the hands of the military on a television screen at a hospital for a second time, she looks away in pain. A Nicaraguan medical staff person tells her: "50,000 Nicaraguans have died; now perhaps Americans will be outraged by what is happening here. Perhaps we should have killed an American journalist 50 years ago".[20]

The film also brings a strongly cinematic view of development because it attempts consciously to be a film about "seeing", and tries to "sync" the visual medium of film with some of its ideas. The power of the visual/representation is revealed through the main character, a photographer, whose pictures are central to both the storytelling and the structure of the film, and issues of representation are framed in moral and political terms. Russell says at one point to a radical Nicaraguan priest he meets in a police cell, "I don't take sides, I take pictures", and is told by the priest to "go home" if he can't do more. The film also relies on the power of Russell's photographs for much for its impact. We are often shown significant events through the roving, obsessive lens of his camera, with the action suddenly frozen in a still that turns from colour into black and white. This stylistic freeze frame technique recurs throughout the film, forcing us (and the characters) to look more closely at the details of poverty, injustice and violence, and perhaps at the same time revealing (and challenging?) the implicit exploitation within our gaze.[21] Here, the potential for connecting the study of development films more tightly with film theory, and what Narine (2010: 120) describes as "cinematic looking relations" becomes particularly apparent. The key themes of power, seeing and representation are, in fact, given centre stage in the central dramatic turning point in the film, where during the *Sandinistas'* final push Russell is asked to take sides and stage a photograph that makes the recently killed rebel leader appear to still be living, to prevent new US arms shipments to Somoza's regime. As a *guerrillero* puts it, "You're a great photographer, make him alive".

The Year of Living Dangerously similarly engages with relationships between the First and the Third Worlds. An important contrast with the other two films, however, is the different narrative point of view, insofar as the story of *The Year of Living Dangerously* is mainly told from the point of view of Billy Kwon, a Chinese-Australian photographer who has formed close relationships with local people and is highly sensitive to events going on all around. As in *Under Fire*, Western ways of seeing are both problematised and politicised within the film's narrative. We see Kwan's photographs being developed in the darkroom, and they help to reveal the human and political stories of poverty and underdevelopment that are lost on the other Westerners.[22] He adopts and tries to educate Hamilton, feeding him contacts and telling him "you have got to listen harder". Hamilton becomes more sensitive to his surroundings, meets and falls in love with Gill, who works at the British Embassy, and he begins filing hard-hitting news stories about what is going on, including a passionate report on the Lombok famine.

The film's main narrative turning point occurs when Hamilton is presented with an ethical challenge in the form of information that an arms shipment from China has arrived that will make a Communist uprising possible, but unlike Russell in *Under Fire*, he fails the test. He decides to turn the information into a good story that will further his career, but instead of remaining discreet as his source had requested, he asks questions and puts others in danger. For Billy, this is nothing less than a betrayal, and he rebukes him: "You have abused your position as a journalist … I made you see things; I made you feel something about what you write". Hamilton's inability to fully alter his worldview, beyond a superficial concern that serves his career, can be read as a metaphor for the indif-ference and collusion of the West in Third World poverty. One way this is expressed is through Hamilton's relationship with his loyal driver and Communist sympathiser Kumar, whose life becomes threatened after the ensuing PKI upris-ing fails. "Tell me", Kumar asks him, "Am I a stupid man? … Why should I live like a poor man my whole life when stupid people in your country live well?" When Hamilton says that this is a "good question", but that he has no answer, Kumar replies, "So why do you condemn those in my country who try to do some-thing about it? … Mister Billy Kwon was right. Westerners do not have answers anymore". The world, and the West's position within it, has changed within a shifting global order, but only a few are yet able to see it.

These films both reflected but also arguably contributed to shaping several important strands of changing development thinking during the 1980s. The onset of globalisation, in which the distance between individual Western lives and the "masses" of the developing world suddenly seemed to become shorter, is clearly reflected in all three, for example. The complacency of Western citizens about poverty and oppression is highlighted.[23] *Missing* and *Under Fire* explicitly ques-tion Cold War assumptions about the West propping up authoritarian regimes irrespective of the human consequences of this policy, and arguably herald the rebirth of an ethically and human-rights-driven approach to development (see Little, 2003), in stark contrast to the technocratic vision that predominated during the 1960s and 1970s. Another issue that emerges clearly from all three films is the growing distrust of the state, and, in particular, of what the Western state tells its citizens about the wider world – a critical view of the state that was already begin-ning to feed into the new neoliberal orthodoxy. It is difficult to separate cause and effect here, of course, but the popularity of this particular genre suggests that it captured something of an epochal *zeitgeist*, both reflecting and most likely influ-encing people's hopes, fears and assumptions. Although *The Year of Living Dangerously* is set in the 1960s, and *Missing* and *Under Fire* in the 1970s, the concerns of these films are fully those of the mid-1980s.

Conclusion

In this chapter, we have tried to open up a range of themes within the "projection of development" in order to promote further engagement with the idea of film as an important but as yet under-studied medium for development knowledge. We began our exploration with a discussion of the nature of film as a representational medium for development concerns, and noted the ways that a number of films have explored key themes within the landscape of global inequalities and power relationships. For example, films have shown a particular capacity for exploring a range of disjunctures[24] between policymakers and the impact of their decisions upon people, the neglect of history and context by decision makers doomed to repeat their mistakes, and the dynamics and morality of market exchange between rich and poor groups. And as *Even the Rain* shows us, we can even draw a potentially useful analogy between the production of a film and a development intervention. It is no accident that a film is normally described as a "project", and is a venture that requires the top-down directed organisation of a mixed group of insiders and outsiders into meaningful action and outcomes. When they were asked to act out scenes that they found objectionable, the indigenous cast members of the film portrayed in *Even the Rain* simply walked off the set, just as community members may exit development projects that fail to meet their needs and resist policy decisions over which they have little say. There is therefore a fairly straightforward argument that can be made concerning the power of films as additional and legitimate forms of development knowledge, both because film is a popular medium, and because films are documents with a capacity for dealing with certain types of complexity and offering distinctive insights.

Yet there are also potential pitfalls and limitations that are apparent within this brief review. As both *La Yuma* and *The March* show us, powerful visual storytelling all too easily comes at the cost of factual detail and historical accuracy, raising the question of whether the gains made by the medium of film within one area of the representation of development knowledge may all too easily become weakened or even invalidated by the losses within another. There is also a constant and often unhealthy tension between the emphasis on individual actors and their moral and political dilemmas and the wider structural and societal factors that conditions the social settings in which these stories are told. And while films that focus on Westerners engaging with their own consciences, dilemmas, and contradictory feelings towards global conflict and inequality doubtless provide instructive insights that can feed usefully into public understanding of development issues and may even (at best) contribute to awareness raising and even politicisation, there is often a high cost paid in terms of the relative lack of local voices.

In short, many of the films we have discussed here raise important problems that will need further elaboration than the brief treatment we have been able to provide: including the over-reliance on particular narrative imperatives, the seductiveness of film as a medium, the personalising of politics, the selectivity of issues that are focused upon, the inability to address structural complexity, and the tendency for trivialisation of serious issues within star actor vehicles. Despite this double-edged sword, the way cinema plays a role in shaping and reflecting popular perceptions of global development issues in the West cannot easily be ignored. Films set at particular historical junctures such as *La Yuma* may, as we have seen, display jarring anachronisms, but the film itself is of its time and speaks to its own present. Similarly, *The Year of Living Dangerously* says as much about the growing awareness of a moment of globalisation in the 1980s as it does about Sukarno's Indonesia in 1965.

As we attempted in our earlier chapter in relation to the development novel, we have tried to argue in this chapter that there are important opportunities for a closer engagement with film as a medium for discussing the ideas and processes of development. If it sometimes feels that the boundaries of acceptable development knowledge are being significantly narrowed by the current emphasis on quantification (e.g., the formal measurement of "impact", "effectiveness" and "results", the heightened attention to randomised controlled trials), it is instructive to recognise the value of films as an archive of popular ideas about the vicissitudes of development, as reflections of the prevailing societal *zeitgeist*, and last but not least, as powerful teaching tools for bringing alive and humanising important, if inherently vexing, global issues.

Suggested films on development issues

The following list represents a personal and idiosyncratic selection of films that we hope will constitute a starting point rather than an endpoint for anybody interested in exploring the cinematographic representation of development. With the exception of a couple discussed in this chapter, we have limited ourselves to English-language films.

- *Apocalypto* (2006)
- *Avatar* (2009)
- *Bamako* (2006)
- *Beyond Borders* (2003)
- *Black Robe* (1991)
- *Blood Diamond* (2006)
- *Cannibal Tours* (1989)
- *Casino Royale* (2006)
- *Circle of Deceit* (1981)
- *City of God* (2002)
- *Critical Assignment* (The Guinness film, 2003)
- *Dirty Pretty Things* (2002)
- *Entre Nos* (2009)
- *Even the Rain (También la lluvia)* (2010)
- *Gandhi* (1984)
- *Gangs of New York* (2002)
- *Gangster's Paradise: Jerusalema* (2008)
- *Hotel Rwanda* (2004)
- *In the Loop* (2009)
- *Johnny Mad Dog* (2008)
- *Journey to Banana Land* (1950)
- *Jungle Drums of Africa* (1953)
- *La Yuma* (2010)
- *Men with Guns* (1997)
- *Missing* (1982)
- *Salaam Bombay* (1988)
- *Salmon Fishing in Yemen* (2011)
- *Salvador* (1983)
- *Sin Nombre* (2009)
- *Slumdog Millionaire* (2009)
- *Tears of the Sun* (2003)

- *The Beach* (2000)
- *The Constant Gardener* (2005)
- *The Day after Tomorrow* (2004)
- *The Fog of War* (2003)
- *The Gods Must be Crazy* (1981)
- *The Hurt Locker* (2008)
- *The Killing Fields* (1984)
- *The Last King of Scotland* (2006)
- *The March* (1990)
- *The Mission* (1986)
- *The Motorcycle Diaries* (2004)
- *The Painted Veil* (2006)
- *The Year of Living Dangerously* (1982)
- *Tsotsi* (2005)
- *Turistas* (2006)
- *Under Fire* (1983)
- *Viva Zapata* (1952)
- *Volunteers* (1985)
- *White Material* (2009)

Notes

1 This chapter is an abridged version of an article previously published in the *Journal of Development Studies*.

2 Some of the books discussed in our original article, such as Graham Greene's *The Quiet American* or Monica Ali's *Brick Lane*, have been made into films. While it might be worthwhile to compare themes across different media, we mainly focus here on a fresh selection of development-related films.

3 For example, Zaniello (2007) summarises over 200 films on globalisation. While Zaniello's stance is one of explicit critique, our focus here is on the distinctive contribution that films bring to development debates.

4 Although our main focus is on dramas, many of the points that we raise are clearly also applicable to documentaries, even if there also exist numerous differences between films and documentaries (see Eitzen, 1995, for further critical discussion).

5 We acknowledge that considering the nature of the audiences for which these films are produced is also an important issue, although for reasons of space we have chosen not to focus on this particular topic in any depth. Many of the films that we discuss in this chapter have been made specifically for Western audiences – even if they also circulate globally – and that this conditions their general tenor, which tends to be critical but overall offers a non-radical perspective on "development". At the same time, to a large extent, this is very much an organic process, and we would not want to suggest that the contemporary "development film" business is (necessarily) a propaganda machine in the way that the Colonial Film Unit, which produced instructional films for African subjects of the British Empire, for example, was in the past.

6 Many of the popular (Western) films on development are adaptations of books. We are unable to say whether this is the result of a wider trend within the film industry to reduce risk by filming books (and making remakes) or whether it reflects a distinctive point about development film making.

7 While the narrative demands of a "development drama" structurally lend themselves to a portrait of development focused on individuals rather than structures, this may not be

the "fault" of any particular film but an inherent issue affecting the genre as a whole. We are grateful to Veronica Davidov for pointing this out to us.

8   The film was also criticised at the time for itself reinforcing racial and cultural stereotypes.

9   One of few representational missteps in *Even the Rain* is the overly noble and internally unified manner in which indigenous populations are portrayed. A more realistic account would surely depict the deep divisions within such communities, and the further unhappiness that flows from capitulation – whether driven by reasonable or selfish motives – by indigenous elites to external commercial or political pressures.

10   The extent to which *Slumdog Millionaire* is realistic is open to question (Sengupta 2010). Furthermore, Mira Nair's *Salaam Bombay* (1988) offered a much grittier depiction of urban deprivation to Western audiences a full two decades earlier.

11   One could argue of course that the veracity of cinematic representation is not the point. The popularity of the medium may still serve to promote a concern for development issues more widely than is generally the case with academic or policy outputs, irrespective of whether the film is "right" or "wrong".

12   Although Paulo Lins grew up in the *Cidade de Deus* suburb, his writing drew much more on his experiences as research assistant for Alba Zaluar, one of Brazil's foremost anthropologists (personal communication with Dennis Rodgers, 19 October 2009). It is also important to note that there are major differences between the book and the film.

13   More generally, as Bülent Diken (2005: 311–312) points out, the film also represents the *favela* (slum) in a particular way, based on "the logic of oppositional differences between normality and perversion, law and despotism, mind and body, reason and desire. Through a power–knowledge nexus, the … *favela* is frozen in stereotypes. … In other words, the *favela* is constituted as a fantasy space that both conditions and escapes the 'social'. Fantasies create objects of desire, but they create these objects as being out of reach".

14   In a related manner, the scene in the film where a street child is made to choose and kill one of his peers, an act that is depicted as presenting him with an extreme moral dilemma, may lack plausibility. Much research on street children has highlighted how they are generally bound to other street children by rather weak and often very temporary ties that mean they often betray each other with little thought or remorse (Herrera et al., 2007; Wolseth, 2009).

15   Armstrong (2009: 92), for example, notes that *City of God* mixes an "MTV style" with "neo-realist technique", and that it is very much this eclectic cinematographic style that enables the film to live up to Frederic Jameson's (1992: 1) famous aphorism that "the visual is essentially pornographic, which is to say that it has its end in rapt, mindless fascination".

16   See http://www.cinelangues.com/wp-content/uploads/Dossier_La%20yuma.pdf [accessed 10 June 2011].

17   This issue is not just limited to film, but also applies more generally.

18   An alternative type of film about Western citizens in danger in the "Third World" has emerged during the last decade, perhaps reflecting new anxieties about the exploitative relationships between the West and "the Rest". For example, the 2006 film *Turistas* (also known as *Paradise Lost*) portrays a group of Western tourists who are kidnapped in order to have their organs harvested. The physician who performs the operations explicitly frames his actions in developmental terms, explaining to his victims that "rich gringos" exploit Brazil and have done so for years, but that by harvesting their organs and sending them to urban hospitals to give to poor Brazilians, "it is time to give back".

19   Other films in this mini-genre include Volker Schlondorff's *Circle of Deceit* (1981) about a disillusioned West German man in a barren marriage who goes to work as a war correspondent in Beirut, and Oliver Stone's *Salvador* (1986), about a US journalist who leaves behind his problems to drive to El Salvador.

20   The broader point being made here relates to the relationship between authority and one's position within development contexts writ large. The value of being a white

Westerner is presented as offering a comparative advantage in drawing attention to a specific issue. It is interesting, however, to note that more recent films, such as *The Last King of Scotland* (2006), make a similar point somewhat differently, insofar as the film ends with a Ugandan doctor sacrificing himself to save a Scottish doctor's life so that the Scottish doctor can tell the world about the brutality of the Idi Amin regime, explicitly saying that because he is white, people will listen and they will believe him.

21 Such themes are, of course, reflective of the post-modern concerns with representational issues that were beginning to gain influence within anthropology, development studies, and other fields of the social sciences during the 1980s.

22 The role of the figure of "the photographer", who recurs in *City of God*, *Under Fire* and this film, is a central device in development films that requires a more detailed analysis than can be provided here, bringing an apparently neutral gaze that enhances the proximity of the viewer. We are grateful to an anonymous referee for this point.

23 These films perhaps prefigure what Narine (2010: 120) analyses as the way Western film viewers are made to feel implicated in "the promulgation of the global traumas our leaders have been impotent to prevent".

24 See Lewis and Mosse (2006) for a discussion of "order and disjuncture" in development.

References

Armstrong, P. (2009) "Essaying the real: Brazil's cinematic *retomada* and the new commonwealth". *Journal of Iberian and Latin American Studies*, 15(2): 85–105.

Chouliaraki, L. (2010) "Ordinary witnessing in post-television news: Towards a new moral imagination". *Critical Discourse Studies*, 7(4): 305–319.

Diken, B. (2005) "City of god". *City*, 9(3): 307–320.

Eitzen, D. (1995) "When is a documentary?: Documentary as a mode of reception". *Cinema Journal*, 35(1): 81–102.

Gauri, V., M. Woolcock, D. Desai (2011) *Intersubjective Meaning and Collective Action in 'Fragile' Societies: Theory, Evidence and Policy Implications*. World Bank Policy Research Working Paper no. 5707, Washington, DC: The World Bank.

Herrera, E., G. A. Jones, and S. T. de Benitez (2007) "Tears, trauma and suicide: Everyday violence among street youth in Puebla, Mexico". *Bulletin of Latin American Research*, 26(4): 462–479.

Hettne, B. (2009) *Thinking About Development*, London: Zed Books.

Jameson, F. (1992) *Signatures of the Visible*. New York: Routledge, Chapman and Hall.

Katz, E. (1994) *The Macmillan International Film Encyclopaedia*, 2nd edition. London: Macmillan.

Lewis, D., and D. Mosse (2006) "Encountering order and disjuncture: Contemporary anthropological perspectives on the organisation of development". *Oxford Development Studies*, 34(1): 1–13.

Lewis, D., D. Rodgers, and M. Woolcock (2008) "The fiction of development: Literary representation as a source of authoritative knowledge". *Journal of Development Studies*, 44(2): 198–216.

Little, D. (2003) *The Paradox of Wealth and Poverty: Mapping the Ethical Dilemmas of Global Development*. Boulder: Westview Press.

Narine, N. (2010) "Global trauma and narrative cinema". *Theory, Culture and Society*, 27(4): 119–145.

Rodgers, D. (2006) "Living in the shadow of death: Gangs, violence, and social order in urban Nicaragua, 1996–2002". *Journal of Latin American Studies*, 38(2): 267–92.

Rodgers, D. (2008) "A symptom called Managua". *New Left Review*, 49: 103–120.

Said, E. (1978) *Orientalism*. Harmondsworth: Penguin.

Sengupta, M. (2010) "A million dollar exit from the anarchic slum-world: Slumdog Millionaire's hollow idioms of social justice". *Third World Quarterly*, 31(4): 599–616.

Smith, M., and H. Yanacopulos (2004) "The public faces of development: An introduction". *Journal of International Development*, 16(5): 657–664.

Suber, H. (2006) *The Power of Film*. Studio City: Michael Wiese.

Thrasher, F. (1927) *The Gang: A Study of 1,313 Gangs in Chicago*. Chicago: University of Chicago Press.

Wolseth, J. (2009) "Good times and bad blood: Violence, solidarity, and social organization on Dominican streets". In G. A. Jones and D. Rodgers (eds.), *Youth Violence in Latin America: Gangs and Juvenile Justice in Perspective*. New York: Palgrave, pp. 63–82.

Zaniello, T. (2007) *The Cinema of Globalization: A Guide to Films about the New Economic Order*. Ithaca: Cornell University Press.

8 Affective histories

Imagining poverty in popular Indian cinema

Esha Shah

Development theories routinely conceptualize poverty in rational, abstract, and cognitive terms as an effect or cause of one or the other form of "lack" – for instance, lack of health, income, resources, well-being, education, or capabilities. Such theories overwhelmingly emphasize economic rationales, whereby a freely choosing individual becomes the vehicle for the acquisition, allocation, or distribution of resources and capabilities. As such, they foreclose the possibility of getting to grips with the subjective dramas of multiple actors populating "poverty situations", and they also widely employ mechanical, spatial, and hydraulic metaphors – up/down, below/above, centre/periphery, inside/outside, and inclusion/ exclusion – to quantify or qualify the phenomena of poverty, which is therefore largely described negatively – the meaning of poverty implies below, down, periphery, outside, and exclusion. These cognitive theories arguably reflect the epistemology of the researching subject rather than the researched subject, and construct poverty as an abstract measure of some sort of lack signifying a negative status rather than seeing the phenomenon in relational terms, as an inter-subjective experience.

This chapter looks at the affective narratives of poverty in Indian popular cinema in Hindi. It maps the way in which the "poverty situations", as inter-subjective dramas, have been depicted in popular culture since independence. The emphasis here is on mapping the shift in the affective mood and, correspondingly, the underlying norms and values delineated in these dramas. Mapping this shift in the representation of poverty as an inter-subjective aspect of affect is the means by which the chapter aims to offer an alternative explanation of the way in which poverty situations are embedded, on the one hand, in the psychic structures of public morality, and on the other, in the social and cultural institutions of the time.

Poverty as affects

Poverty is an intensely debated topic in India. Estimating poverty trends – the extent to which poverty has declined in general and especially since the liberalization as a result of increasing economic growth – has been a controversial topic (Sundaram and Suresh, 2003; Deaton, 2004; Dreze and Sen, 2008; Deaton and

Dreze, 2002). The debate is heavily polarized: the current times, for example, are described by the proponents of economic growth as a period of unprecedented improvement, whereas opponents see widespread impoverishment. Some statisticians conclude that merely 15 per cent of the population lives under the poverty line, whereas pessimistic estimates put the figure as high as 35 per cent. Methodologically, these debates, irrespective of the viewpoint, focus largely on counting "headcount ratios", poverty indexes, or poverty-gap indexes. For instance, after exhaustively consulting National Sample Survey data, Deaton and Dreze (2002) conclude that during 1993–1994 and 1999–2000 there was a sustained poverty decline, from 36 per cent to 26 per cent, in most states in India. However, they argue that although poverty in the absolute sense has declined, there has been a marked increase in inequality – which is measured here in terms of the disparities in per capita expenditure, cereal consumption, and other indications such as rates of literacy, nutrition, and crime.

These debates represent the epistemology of the researching subject – that is, the researcher – and have a kind of muting quality about the life situations of poor people – the researched subject. They consider poor people as merely a population group ascending or descending the ladder of poverty by the sheer force of methodological magic. More so, poverty in these debates is not only a measure but overwhelmingly a material measure. The aspirations of poor people, their personal journeys, their perceptions of the deprivation they suffer, their social relations, and the way in which other people's actions and perceptions *affect* them (Gialdino, 2006: 474–475) rarely find expression in these debates. When the epistemology of the researching subject sees poor people as objects of professional judgment, research, and policy, they fail to register what it means to be poor or what it is like to live in a world of inequality.

Consider, for example, this remark by Amartya Sen: "With rising inequality half of India will come to look and live like California and the other half like sub-Saharan Africa" (Interview in *India Today*, 20 February 2006). In Sen's remark, poverty as a manifestation of inequality is still material, but it is described by a vast, almost unbridgeable *affective* distance. This distance cannot be comprehended as a variable of purely material measure. Similarly, Krishna and Pieterse (2008: 221) describe this aspect of inequality in the metaphor of dual economy – dollar economy and rupee economy: "Images of dollar-based lifestyle are still physically unavailable – except a blurry and intermittent black and white television signal". Others argue similarly. "They sell newspapers they will never read, sew clothes they cannot wear, polish cars they will never own and construct buildings where they will never live" are the moving and powerful words of Eduardo Galeano talking about the service people in Latin American cities (cited in Guha, 2007: 702). These descriptions of poverty treat poor people as feeling and aspiring subjects. Failing to represent poor people as subjects, the policy-oriented debates on poverty fail to explain the rising distance between rural and urban India and the wider climate of rural alienation commonly expressed in the dystopian utterances such as "we are like the living dead", "we are stuck here", "nothing can possibly change", and "nothing can possibly be done" (see Mohanty, 2005). The policy debates also fail to explain farmers' suicides – a quarter million farmers committing suicide over a period of a decade and a half – which, I argue elsewhere, relate to the experience of humiliation caused by the rising feelings of rural alienation (Shah, 2012).

I argue that poverty as affect and as a subjective relationship to the other can help go beyond the methodological turf war toward explaining poverty as a life situation. Affects here are not purely feelings or emotions, but as William Reddy (2001: 16) describes, "affect can be understood as a deeply ingrained, overlearned habit" that goes beyond a Cartesian dualism of reason against feelings. Expressed in symbols and images, affects impart supra-individual and inter-subjective meaning to the historical present and their relationship with life experiences. Explaining the shared affective atmosphere can explain the collective importance of the substantive values upon which the aesthetic judgment of the good life is based, when at the same time, affects as intersubjective dramas denote the index of relations of power (Berlant, 2008: 846–848). Affects thus collapse the difference between justice and ethics. The affective turn in history, as some scholars argue, is a mode of analysis that moves us away from the dialectic of structure and agency (Berlant, 2008: 846) towards conjectures, emotions, daily life, and individual experiences (Lash, 2000). This chapter considers affects as a kind of intelligence about history; it regards affects as a locale, "as [an] exemplary laboratory for sensing and intuiting contemporary life" (Berlant, 2008: 845, 846).

I have taken a series of popular films made in Bombay since independence as an exemplary laboratory to map the historical shift in the depiction of poverty in the popular imagination. The films here serve a role of fantasy that articulates an absence of one or the other form of utopia. In Lacan's work, fantasy narratives structure social practices by providing a convincing explanation of the lack of "total enjoyment" (*jouissance*).[1] This lack is articulated in terms of an absence of one or the other form of utopia – a lack of, for instance, the good life, a just society, or material prosperity. In its construction of the lack expressed as an absence of a socio-political or material utopia, the fantasy narratives foster solidarity of affective communities (Glynos and Stavrakakis, 2008; Stavrakakis, 1999: 5 & 99–100). Contrary to the popular belief that cinema in general and more acutely Bombay cinema breeds an escapist tendency — in fact, fantasy and utopia projected in Bombay cinema are regularly posed as inverse to reality (Dyer 1993, Dwyer 2000) — this essay considers fantasy as a necessary vehicle to organise reality in a coherent whole (Zizek, 1987). Cinematic fantasy therefore is neither a flight away from reality in the form of escapism, idealism, and illusion nor an entirely subjective experience. This chapter explores how fantasy narratives in popular Bombay cinema are linked to affects of poverty and how these affects link subjectivity with socio-political reality. The emphasis in this chapter therefore is on delineating the content, context, and organization of fantasy of Bombay cinema in explaining poverty as affects.

Poverty in Bombay cinema

Popular cinema in India plays a highly influential role in shaping the politics of public culture and public morality. It is not only considered the world's largest film industry, but on an average day, it releases two and a half feature films that are watched by 15 million people in over 13,000 cinema halls. Below, I aim to map the historical shift in the affective narratives of poverty in *mise-en-scène* and narrative styles, structures, and content of a group of chosen films from three distinct phases in the history of popular cinema in Hindi, which arguably also roughly reflect the distinct socio-economic and political eras in Indian history. These phases are as follows:

1.   The 1950s to the late 1960s, when the agrarian theme toward building a community – village and nation – dominated. This is when the conflicts between rural and urban, and rich and poor were popularly depicted in ways that morally privileged the rural and poor.
2.   The 1970s and 1980s, in which began a powerful trend centered on the urban and on the personalized individual turning against the self or social order in which poverty was depicted as an experience of not only violence, but also humiliation, loss, indignity, and shame.
3.   The early 1990s onward, the post-liberalization period, during which the agrarian and the rural significantly disappeared from popular cinematic representations and were replaced by two contradictory trends: one of them, termed the Bollywoodization of Indian popular cinema, which depicted the grandiose urban lifestyles of the Anglo-American diaspora (Vasudevan, 2008; Prasad, 2003; Rajadhyaksha, 2003), and the other, which portrayed the crime-ridden, rotting underbelly of urban India (Mazumdar, 2007). In such depictions, the fantasy of the glitter of urban modernity and its "dark" shadow have been resolutely separated in the distinct cinematic frames, which denote the absence of any direct social and cultural intercourse between the rich and poor.

I argue here that the paradigmatic shift in depictions of poverty of popular cinema thus denotes a journey from the discussions on "possible nations" to the emergence of "two nations" mutually alienated in affective terms with disastrous effects that might even provide an explanation for numerous incidents of farmers' suicides in the last decade and a half.

1950s: dignity of labor

The decade of the 1950s soon after independence was a crucial period in Indian history during which possible nations were being imagined and debated. Two films produced in 1957—*Mother India* and *Naya Daur* – depict two such foundational imaginaries of possible nations. *Mother India*, in particular, is a cinematographic reinvention of the most powerful myth of Nehruvian socialism – the myth that the nation's progress and modernization will alleviate the harsh living conditions of the toiling masses. *Mother India*, directed by Mehboob Khan, is one of the most popular classics and also the most revered film in Indian film history. In the iconic story of Radha – a peasant woman – the film epitomizes the struggles of India's hard-working agrarian population; *Naya Daur*, on the other hand, is a challenge to the idea of high industrialization and domination of machines. It depicts the Gandhian ideal – self-sufficient, village-based industries with low technology and the trusteeship role played by the wealthy. Where *Mother India* projects the limitation of human efforts in a continuous tug-of-war with nature and establishes the importance of mechanization in building communities (at both the national and village level), *Naya Daur* depicts instead the limits of mechanization and its impact on rural employment and social relations. Despite these paradigmatic differences between the utopian ideals that both films uphold, they share a common representation of the toiling rural people as courageous, hard-working, and morally and ethically upright.

Mother India opens with a close-up of the deeply wrinkled face of a woman, Radha. She is holding in her hand a lump of earth that she brings close to her forehead in a gesture of reverence. In a long shot, she is shown squatting in a field freshly ploughed by a heavy-duty tractor now driving behind her. When she lifts her eyes from the tilled earth, we are shown in a brief moment a glimpse of the technological progress – some enormous machines working in fields, high-tension wires, electric poles, motorized roads, a dam under construction, a canal-full of flowing water, a crane cleaning canal, and a bridge under construction. Completing this brief tour, we arrive in a prosperous and flourishing village in which Radha is living. A group of men arrive in a jeep, position themselves in front of ailing and old Radha, declare to her how water and electricity have arrived in her village – someone is tuning a radio in the background – and ask her to inaugurate a new canal. She first steadfastly refuses to accept the invitation, but yields to her son's insistence. At the dam site, she again refuses to be garlanded, but coyly accepts all the honor bestowed upon her. With the fragrance of the garland, her memories of her wedding day is invoked, and in the next three hours we are shown how Radha, then young, dreamy, and newly wed, arrives in the village and how she goes through a life of hardship and suffering, how she bears these vicissitudes with stoic strength and a high sense of moral integrity.

The film shows how she loses her husband to misfortune, how she struggles to retain the ownership of her piece of land, how she single-handedly raises two sons against all odds, resists the sexual advances of the moneylender, survives a terrible flood and famine, and finally how she kills her own teenage son – whom she loves the most – because he breaks the moral code of the village community. Enmeshed with her existential struggles are the socio-political and natural realities – the moneylender usurping most of what is produced in her fields against a small sum of money borrowed at one point, the limitations of the bare-handed human labor, and the unpredictability of nature. Thus, Radha's personal and existential trials, tribulations, and deprivations are related to a socio-political utopia – the lack of high-technology-aided progress. *Mother India* is the epic saga of an iconic Indian (peasant) woman and her sufferings, sacrifices, and strength. In Radha's story, Mehboob Khan constructs a trinity of India's national icons – woman, peasant, and progress – historically contingent at that moment (Schulze, 2002). In the cinematic imagination of *Mother India*, the suffering but strong and self-sacrificing Indian peasant woman is at the center of the fantasy of Nehruvian-style socialism and progress.

Radha's past is constructed in the background of the depiction of the progress at the beginning of the film. But this past is neither deplored nor denounced; rather, this past is a cherished memory. This is reflected in Radha's character. All through the film, she stands tall against all odds. She refuses to accept pity and charity. It is Lala – the moneylender (*baniya*) – who is shown to be knee-soft, bent from the waist, looking dwarf-like in comparison to Radha's formidable moral strength. His heartless greed for money is punctuated by the moments in which Radha is shown throwing her gold bangles on his face towards the payment of interest, the way in which she refuses to accept his offer to feed her family after she loses her husband, and the way in which she makes her starving child spit the food Lala offers soon after the terrible flood and famine. In *Mother India*, a never-compromising, self-sacrificing, hard working, and morally upright peasant woman is the icon of the invented tradition of the Indian nation and public morality.

In this high-intensity melodrama of Mehboob Khan, Radha's trials and tribulations generate an affective atmosphere of sympathy but no pity; in Radha's story there is injustice, but no humiliation; there is pain in the relentless series of unfortunate events inflicted upon her life, but there is no shame in Radha's experiences. Radha is deprived and struggling, but not needy and marginal. In material poverty, Radha radiates the spiritual, ethical, and moral richness. In this melodramatic fiction, Radha's personalized experiences are recalibrated as a public morality that takes pride in the dignity of labor and celebrates the rural, the agrarian, and the earthen. In my interpretation, the affective investment in the film is towards building the legitimacy for the utopia of progress in the process of nation building but not at the cost of dishonoring or disgracing what it transforms. In fact, in terms of melodramatic representation, Radha's personality emerges as a vehicle for the continuity of a certain public morality of dignity and integrity of labor in the face of the impending arrival of high-technology modernity.

One can usefully contrast these images of popular fiction with other forms of imaginaries of poverty employed especially by policymakers during the same period. In a way, *Mother India* anticipated the advent of the green revolution, which was introduced in India in 1966/1967. But there is no sense of dignity of labor and veneration for the courage and hard work of the rural people in the imaginaries mobilized toward the legitimization of the green revolution. For instance, Chidambaram Subramaniam, the agricultural minister in Indian government between 1964 and 1967, who is believed to be the political architect of the green revolution in India, narrates an incident in his memoirs in which he gives a passionate speech in parliament that was meant to make a strong appeal to the MPs to consent to the introduction of the green revolution. In his speech, he quotes from an article by two Harvard economists, William and Paul Paddock, entitled "Famine 1975! America's Decision: Who Will Survive?". The Paddocks predicted that in the decade of the 1970s, millions would die of starvation in developing countries. They divided developing countries into three categories of "battlefield" according to the philosophy of triage. In the battlefield, there are the "slightly wounded", who receive a little attention and return to normal; the "more seriously wounded", who receive medical and surgical treatment; and those whose injuries are so grave that they are generally not attended to and left to die. The Paddocks put India in the third category, described it as an incurable case that cannot be helped out. "India … is the bellwether that shows the path, which the others, like the sheep going to the slaughter, are following. The hungry nation that today refuses to heed India's history will be condemned to relive it" (Subramaniam, 1979: 10).

The images of famine and millions of faceless and nameless people dying of hunger were popular among policymakers even before the twentieth century. For instance, in the midst of the famine of 1876–1877, a poem ten pages long was written as a pamphlet to elicit money and sympathy from England. A few lines are quoted by Darren Zook (2000: 116):

> Hunger – a deadly canker – only tears
> His bowels starved: and pain inflames his soul …
> This famished peasant oft attempts to stand …
> We cry—relieve us.
> Do grant
> This boon. For the aid from thee we anxious pant.

This sort of representation of a hunger that is supposed to have been experienced by the known subject but that is articulated by the researching (knowing) subject is antithetical to the affective intensities of Radha's character. Radha never describes herself as helpless and needy. The stern determination with which she insists that her starving toddler son spit out the food offered by the moneylender stands in stark contrast to the incurably hungry, dying, and begging, and pleading subject represented by the knowing subject – in Subramaniam's story and in the above poem written by the charity organizations in the 1880s.

1970s: poverty as humiliation and fear of pauperization

The affective mood of the representation of poverty in the cinema of 1950s shifted in the 1970s. This was a crucial period in Indian politics. The romantic ideas of progress and nation building of the 1950s and 1960s had given way to multiple challenges to the authority of Indian state (Kothari, 1990: 120). Unemployment and inflation were on the rise. In the face of increasing opposition, the then prime minister, Indira Gandhi, declared Emergency between 1975 and 1977 and suspended the constitutionally granted political and civil liberties. During this period, the nature of Indian cities was also radically transformed. A large influx of populations from the rural into urban areas created an underbelly of official cities.

The Bombay film industry was also acutely influenced by these wide-ranging political changes. Madhav Prasad discusses in detail how these changes launched a serious challenge to the aesthetic and material organization of Bombay cinema, which responded with what Prasad refers to as "populist aesthetics of mobilization". The popular cinema regrouped around a figure of mobilization – the charismatic star persona of Amitabh Bachchan (Prasad, 1998: 24). This new trend within popular Bombay cinema centered on the image of Amitabh Bachchan, which depicted an individual's struggles in the shifting landscape of urban geography and in the process became a popular subject. The new phenomenon of the angry young man, antihero, or proletariat hero – a deprived, exploited, and exiled individual turning against the self and the social order – and the link between the cinematic emergence of this phenomenon and the wider social and political transformations during this period, are widely debated in Indian film studies (Prasad, 1998; Vasudevan, 2010; Mazumdar, 2007; Lal, 1999). These scholars discuss Amitabh Bachchan films through a number of analytic registers: how these films tend to perpetuate and reproduce the dominant ideology (Kazmi, 1999: 143), how they produce a consensus effect (Prasad, 1998: 23), how narratives of anger and revenge reproduce urban subjectivity in unintended cities (Mazumdar, 2007: 1–31), and how they signify paradigm shifts in cinematic iconography (Vasudevan, 2010: 306–312).

Having taken note of these analytic registers, we can now unpack the affects of humiliation and shame as a precursor to anger and rage and their relationship with the images of poverty in the cult film *Deewar*, an epic about the conflict between the state and its other – law-abiding, contractual society and the criminal obverse (Prasad, 1998: 145). This conflict is played out as a rift between two brothers, Ravi (a police inspector played by Shashi Kapoor) and Vijay (a dockworker turned smuggler played by Amitabh Bachchan). The brothers share a common childhood of deprivation and poverty. Despite the common past, the elder brother Vijay is forced to share a larger burden of the "humiliation" that follows their father's disappearance. Their father led a strike of coal mine workers. He was blackmailed by the owners of the coal mines into sabotaging the interest of his fellow workers. Not able to bear the shame of being described as a traitor, he runs away into a life of obscurity. The mother now bears the burden of raising two young children. She migrates to Bombay, works as a construction laborer, and makes a home on the pavement (called "footpath" in the film) under a bridge. The child Vijay supports her by working as a shoeshine boy and with the help of their combined income the younger brother Ravi is sent to school. Ravi shines in his studies, grows into an exemplary citizen, and after a few futile attempts to find a job trains as a police inspector. The adult Vijay on the other hand becomes a dockworker and defends his fellow workers against the gangsters who extort part of their weekly income. Impressed by his courage, the rival gangster invites him to join his gang, where he quickly becomes the second in command. The film climaxes into a heroic conflict between the two brothers – one a guardian of the state law and the other a criminal. Some critics describe the film as deeply dystopian (Mazumdar, 2007: 6), because after his girlfriend is killed by the rival gangster, Vijay goes on a murdering spree and eventually gets killed by his brother Ravi.

Deewar is described as a tale of urban poverty and despair. Especially, what Mazumdar calls the "inner exile" of Vijay and his estrangement from family, law, and city are associated with the childhood experiences of homelessness and deprivation – which are in turn grounded in the affects of humiliation and shame (Mazumdar, 2007: 14). Vijay bears the double burden of humiliation: after his leader-father runs away to obscurity, the disappointed union workers tattoo Vijay's right arm with *mera baap chor hai* (my father is a thief). He is condemned to bear the scar of his father's alleged unethical behavior.

However, I want to focus here on the sense of humiliation spawned by the experiences of living on a pavement and the fact that the mother had to work as a laborer at a construction site. The film portrays Vijay's side of the story, which highlights the "pathos" and the "pain" of a mother forced to earn a living as a construction worker. The music, the *mise-en-scène* of the construction site, the way she is shown lifting a heavy load on her head and walking with difficulty – are meant to generate pity for her situation. In the next scene, she is shown on her corner of the pavement which she has made her home – two children sleeping on her lap when she is sitting wide awake, pained and worrying. This life in the city for her is clearly a degeneration of her earlier life, in which she was a home-maker, mistress of a small but well-organized home, married to a husband who was well regarded in the community, and with two children who were studying in a school. The family was not particularly wealthy but apparently ate well – on a normal evening she had made *kheer* (a sweet with coconut, rice, sugar, and milk) for her children. The humiliation of her situation is caused not entirely by the fact that she is on the pavement, but by the fact that she does not belong "there". The melodrama constructs a subjectivity that is at once personalized and public – the storyline addresses the public and demands pity for her fall from paradise, and in this fall the height of her personal misfortune is the fact that she now has to work as a menial laborer.

Ashis Nandy (1999: 2) argues that "the popular cinema is the slum's point of view of Indian politics and society". Nandy thinks that the popular cinema depicts the sensibilities and hopes and aspirations of India's lower middle class. Perhaps. But in my opinion this argument would apply to the films of the 1970s and 1980s but not of the 1990s. The definition of middle class in Nandy's argument is more political-cultural than economic or social. For Nandy, this is the class that lives with the hopes of breaking into the upper echelons of society on the one hand and on the other lives with the fear of slipping into a slum or never getting out of it. The psychological existence of this class is at the margins of two utopias – one of them is located in the future in the form of a dream of a modern urban life and the other in the past in the form of a fantasy of a rural, peasant paradise (Nandy, 1999: 5).

The affect of humiliation, however, has to be understood as a relationship that is realized only when both humiliator and humiliated understand and accept their relative position, says Nandy (2011). Humiliation is a form of human relation that can never be a one-way exchange (Nandy, 2011: 42). To assume that the subjectivity of Vijay in *Deewar* is driven by the affects of shame and humiliation, which are in turn produced entirely on the site of – on the roadside pavement of – urban modernity would be a mistake. The affect of humiliation and shame experienced by the character of Amitabh Bachchan in *Deewar* is produced on the interface of the fear of pauperization and the dream of material prosperity. In my reading, the fear of pauperization finds its expression not only in the humiliation triggered by the fact that the family had to make the pavement their home, but also in the actualization of the wider cultural stigma attached to physical labor. What is degrading about destitution is its association with manual labor – to be reduced to work as a manual laborer is a form of pauperization that would mean the worst fear coming true. Thus, my claim is that in invoking and living through the dread of pauperization actualized as a form of menial labor, the sense of humiliation is acknowledged and accepted by the humiliated.

The affect of fear of pauperization has a long history in Indian culture; it is "deeply ingrained" in the collective psyche and memory in Indian society. The extent to which the individual has to succumb to manual labour is an index of pauperization. This stigma not only has a long history, but most importantly, it is an expression of social power. The ideologies of social hierarchies that attach a stigma to the performance of manual labor have for long been producing strong emotions. These emotions produce a sense of humiliation and shame and could have profound effect on the life chances.

A real-life historical example of this comes from the colonial period. In south India, the British administration commonly divided the peasantry into two categories: *ryots* (landed farmers) and *coolies* (landless laborers). Whether or not such crude categorizations adequately represented the complex local agrarian system, the relational hierarchy of this division became "deeply ingrained" in the social psyche. David Arnold (1984) explains how during the 1876–1878 famine in the Madras presidency, when all but the wealthiest were suffering, the ryots considered it degrading to take up laboring work on public relief schemes. So strong was the antipathy of the ryots for coolie work that even at the height of the famine, in the words of the Collector, the ryots would consider it disgraceful to perform earthwork even to keep alive. Similarly, Vasavi (1996) discusses the partial acceptance of famine relief work in north Karnataka during a number of incidents of food scarcity and famine in the late nineteenth and early twentieth centuries. The stigma attached to manual labor was one of the reasons the ryots refused food for work.

In a myriad different ways, this stigma is depicted in many other Amitabh Bachchan films produced in the 1970s and 1980s. In *Trishul*, the mother of Amitabh Bachchan's character (also named Vijay, as in *Deewar*) is deserted by her ambitious lover when she is pregnant. She raises her son Vijay to adulthood by "working hard". Similar to the *mise-en-scène* of *Deewar*, this film also shows the pathos and pain of a single woman struggling with a heavy load in a stone quarry. The song that is played in the background is again intended to produce pity (and anger) among the audience about her situation. In the film, she demands that her son, when he grows up, repay the price of her milk by taking revenge on his father. The intensity of her misfortunate in the film is displayed in the form of her hard work in the rugged environment of sand, dust, and stones.

The films made by the trinity of Yash Chopra as director, Salim–Javed as script writer, and Amitabh Bachchan as main character have recurring tales of past paradises reduced to misfortunes of hard physical work. In the film *Kaala Patthar*, the character of Amitabh Bachchan (named once again Vijay) is a disgraced navy captain – he was named a coward and jeered by friends, family, and society for abandoning a ship with several passengers – now living a life of anonymity as a coal mine worker. In *Deewar*, *Trishul*, and *Kaala Patthar*, Vijay's brooding self and daredevil heroism has as its reference point the misfortune of a fall from the place of a good life. The audience is made to understand that the dangers he faces in his heroic acts are nothing compared to the hardships he (and his mother) suffer in a life of misfortune (and hard work). The iconography of the rugged and brooding characterization of Amitabh Bachchan in *Trishul*, *Deewar*, and *Kala Patthar* is complete with the use of the same "working-class" attire in these films – a denim shirt and a white or khaki trouser.

This stigma and its powerful impact are intimately rooted in the historically bounded cultural imagination of the self and other, glued by the ideologies of hierarchies. Implied in this stigma is a long history of imagining the lives of the laboring classes – those who work with stones, sand, mud, dust, and earth – as worthless, lesser, and lower lives. In the elitist imagination, a life reduced to working with stone, mud, sand, and earth is a life wasted. It is the contention of this chapter that attributing the affects of humiliation and shame as experienced by the character of Amitabh Bachchan in *Deewar* (and also in *Trishul* and *Kaala Patthar*) purely to the political economy of destitution caused by the shifting geography of urban space overlooks the ways in which the life processes of individuals are linked to what Anthony Giddens called the *longue durée* of institutions. The affective responses of the character of Amitabh Bachchan, his rage and anger rooted in the experiences of destitution and humiliation, are sedimented histories of the cultural experiences survived in the form of supra-individual *durée* – a continuous flow – of the social institutions of hierarchy stretched over a long period of time. Behind the experiences of humiliation and shame are therefore not only the violence of "unintended cities", but also a long history of social imagination of dispossession and violence inscribed in the collective memory that produces powerful emotions and aesthetic-reflexive judgments about what could be considered as a worthwhile social life.

In the current social and political context, the fear of pauperization rooted in the *longue durée* of the ideologies of hierarchy is closely intertwined with the wider issue of rural alienation. What is particularly significant is the way metaphors of worthlessness are associated with agricultural work. A 90-year-old Lambani woman who worked as an unattached agricultural laborer for most of her life described her life as "a life wasted making dust, sifting mud, and breaking stones". I have discussed this in detail elsewhere with reference to the incidents of farmers' suicides in India (Shah, 2012). Not so uncommonly, the practice of agriculture itself is stigmatized as a worthless enterprise, as a lowly profession, for lesser people, lacking respectability – an affect of pauperization.

Working with mud, stones, and bricks is not only lowly, but it is also not 'futuristic'. Gupta (2005: 751) puts it this way: "Town is not coming to country, as much as the country is reaching out to town, leaving behind a host of untidy debris". Refusing to work with mud, stones, earth, and sand could even be interpreted as an act of seeking dignity and worth. In the suicide-prone Vidarbha region in Maharashtra, many young villagers increasingly prefer to work with the nearby chemical industries where the working conditions are dangerous and unhealthy. These industry-employed youth not only earn less than what they could otherwise make from agriculture, but the wage labor does not produce an assured year-round employment. In other parts of India, the previously untouchable castes now not only identify themselves by respected names, for example, so-called lower caste members call themselves Adi-dharmis in Punjab and Adi-Karnataka in Karnataka, but they also forge a symbolic defiance toward their social superiors by refusing to perform any menial work for them (Gupta 2005).

Yet another side of this quest for dignity (and corresponding devaluation of menial labor) is the emergent dominant trend all over rural India to seek non-agricultural work even if it involves danger, unhealthy and filthy living conditions, lower income, and uncertainties in urban and peri-urban areas. Even when the "paupers" might have symbolically moved on and away from mud and stones, the meaning and social ideology of pauperization survives. These ideologies survive in the form of what is socially imagined, what is "deeply ingrained" as affects on collective imagination as lower and lesser. Performing menial tasks in mud, stones, and sand has become the symbolic equivalent of pauperization. In comparison with the urban counterpart, all aspects of agriculture are now a pauper's profession – worthless, which inspires scholars such as Dipankar Gupta (2005) to declare, "whither the Indian village".

1990s: fantasizing happiness

The question arises, however, as to why these images of pauperization dominated the films made in 1970s and 1980s when affects associated with pauperization have a long history. My claim is that the reorganized Bombay cinema around the star persona of Amitabh Bachchan in the 1970s projected the dialectic between the fear of pauperization and the dream of prosperity. Amitabh Bachchan's screen persona of this period is widely hailed as an angry young man overcome by the emotions of rage and revenge. But whom and how exactly is he revenging? Eventually in the film, the conflict and trauma generated by the experiences of destitution are resolved by generating an image of the possible future of material prosperity. As soon as Vijay acquires the position of a second in command in the rival smuggler gang, *Deewar* quickly moves on to the images of luxury and comfort. Not only has Vijay quickly changed into the attire of a "suited-booted" man, the kind that he despised as a young shoe-shine boy, but he now moves into the upper echelons of society. In the background of his movements, the images of luxurious five star hotels, swimming pools, high-end restaurants, corridors glittering with dazzling lights, and expensive cars unfold.

The imaginaries of destitution – a home on the pavement, the mother working at the construction site – are now counterposed with the images of wealth. After Vijay successfully completes an assignment, his boss leads him to a display of bundles of currency notes, which are presented to him as his share of the loot. He buys an expensive house, which he shows to his mother in all its splendor (the audience consuming all these images of prosperity). He also purchases the high-rise building for the construction of which his mother had "lifted bricks" years ago. My claim is that the affective investment in the images of the humiliation and shame caused by the destitution is a ploy, merely a reference point, to legitimize the unfolding of the fantasy space of material prosperity as the mainstay of these films. Below is what Subhash Ghai, one of India's most commercially successful directors, known as the "showman" of the industry, has to say about the Bombay cinema:

> Do not call it Bollywood …. We are not trying to copy Hollywood. We are making films for an audience of a billion people. Over 80% of these people don't have enough food in their bellies. Our country does not provide its people with pool halls, basketball courts and video parlours, so we make films for them that will let them forget their lives for 3 hours. We create total fantasy, not the polished reality that Hollywood portrays. Never forget that, never forget that we are making films that allow people to believe for 3 hours that they are not poor and hungry. (quoted in Vasudevan, 2008).

This statement is fascinating. It brilliantly describes the ideology of the Bombay film industry. It explains why the fantasies of aliens invading the planet or dinosaurs going berserk are not particularly popular fantasy subjects in Bombay film industry. Whether or not 80 per cent of the cinematic audience does not have enough food in their bellies is doubtful, whether or not the poor and hungry indeed need pure fantasies – pool halls, basketball courts, and video parlors – to forget their hungry stomachs for three hours is doubtful. Do poor people need Bombay cinema to forget about their poverty? I am sure this is more complicated than the pop sociology of Subhash Ghai. The fact is that it is Bombay cinema that needs the obverse of the agency of the poor and hungry to legitimize its existence both outside and inside the cinematic frame. The affective investment in the images of poverty in the films of 1970s, especially the representation of poverty as humiliation and shame, was an ideological necessity to legitimize the seeds of neoliberalism thus sown in public culture. The imaginative construction of the dehumanizing images of poverty provided the foundation upon which well-organized, fantasy narratives of the material abundance and the desire for such materiality were generated in the films in the 1970s.

This construction of fantasy became increasingly aggressive in the 1990s. At the core of *Deewar* and *Trishul* is a moral conflict involving rich and poor. In fact, the utopia of the eventual acquisition of the riches by the hero is a means by which these conflicts are partly resolved. This resolution, however, is no happy resolution in *Deewar*, as Vijay is the personified carrier of these conflicts, and is eventually killed – this is how the conflict was ultimately resolved. In *Trishul*, it is the father, a similar protagonist at the core of the moral conflict, who dies. The production and consummation of desire for wealth here have no happy ending. In the films in the 1990s, such conflicts were no longer at the core of the cinematic imagination, however. Even the agents of such conflicts, the poor and the rural people, completely disappeared from the cinematic representation of a series of popular films made in the 1990s.

A number of critics refer to this trend as a Bollywoodization of Indian cinema. It is defined by the emergence of the global nation in which the non-resident Indians (i.e., the Indian diaspora) symbolically have a high-profile presence. This trend addresses the high-end migrant culture in the Anglo-American world in which the cinema itself plays a small but significant role in the entire commodity edifice of fashion, advertising, music, sitcoms, and dotcoms (Vasudevan, 2008; Rajadhyaksha, 2003). A series of blockbuster, highly popular among the diaspora were made from the 1990s onward that represent this trend. Such films include *Hum Aapke Hai Kaun* (1994), *Dilwale Dulhaniya Le Jayenge* (1995), *Dil To Pagal Hai* (1997), *Kuchch Kuchch Hota Hai* (1998), *Kal Ho Na Ho* (2003), *Kabhi Khushi Kabhi Gam* (2001), *Kabhi Alvida Na Kahena* (2006), and *Zindagi Na Milegi Dubara* (2011). Of these, the films *Hum Aapke Hai Kaun* (HAHK), and *Dilwale Dulhaniya Le Jayenge* (DDLJ) had such a seismic impact that they radically redefined the way films are watched in India. In the wake of the release of HAHK and DDLJ, a range of multiplex, small-size cinemas catering to largely middle-class and upper-middle-class – and family – audiences emerged in India in the early 1990s and forever transformed the practice of cinema-going in India.

Vasudevan (2008) discusses Bombay cinema's investment in family as a commodity form in the early 1990s. This was a watershed period in Indian politics. The Indian government accepted the terms of the IMF and adopted the neoliberal policies in 1991 by opening up to the international trade, deregulation and privatization. The newly available commodities mobilized a desire for narratives that expressed and drew upon the fascination for the aesthetic ornamentation and lustrous side of this commodification. However, unlike the trend in the 1970s, this new trend needed narratives that could robe the newly found desires with a coherent and happy drape. A range of fantasy family dramas produced during this period focused on the ritual of weddings and displayed the lifestyle of the highly rich in nauseating detail. Discussing HAHK, Bharucha (1995) names this fantasy drama as the utopia of happiness that is anchored by two pillars: family and wealth. A film such as HAHK could serve as a perfect example of Margaret Thatcher's famous neoliberal aphorism: "There is no such thing as society, there are individual men and women and their families". Beyond the decorated drapes of these filmy families, there is no society and hence no politics either.

Conclusion

Discussing Lacan and the political, Stavrakakis (1999: 100) thinks that utopia is generated by the surfacing of grave antagonism and dislocation in the social field. Utopias are the images of future communities in which these antagonisms and dislocations finally will be forever resolved. Lacan identified the utopian dream of a perfectly functioning society as a highly problematic area. The fantasy of attaining a perfectly harmonious world is sustained through the construction of some particularity that needs to be eliminated. Fantasy has thus on the one side a beatific and stabilizing side and on the other a horrific and profoundly destabilizing side. Most importantly, the beatific side cannot exist without its dependence on the production of the other (Žižek, 1997).

The cognitive theories on development and globalization that depend upon the binary of state/society and structure/agency in explaining the historical shift in poverty (as an abstract measure) fail to take into account the powerful impact the affective atmospheres have on constructing the subjectivity and on correspondingly shaping social and political reality. They also cannot explain the widespread dystopian utterances in rural India made in the background of a quarter million farmers committing suicide over a period of a decade and a half: "We are like the living dead", "We have been stuck here", "Nothing can possibly change", "How long should our lives be tied down to mud?" "Our lives are wasted making dust and sifting mud". This chapter has used popular Hindi films to sense and intuit contemporary culture and to show how the shifts in the way poverty situations are represented in the fantasy narratives of Bombay cinema hint at the historical change in public morality.

Bombay cinema is far more eclectic than the films discussed here; however, my aim has been to delineate the trends of affective intensities represented in popular films in Hindi and the way these trends signify a historical journey in public culture from one form of dominant affective atmosphere to the other. My claim is that the historical journey from projecting rural people as courageous, hard-working, and morally and ethically upright in the 1950s to the production of cinematic images of humiliation and shame associated with menial labor – a form of pauperization – in the films of 1970s to, finally, the cinematic exclusion of the rural and agrarian (as a form of poverty) from the highly influential trend of family films since the liberalization in 1990s signify an affective shift toward the devaluation of the rural, agrarian, and poor in the public morality. This trend is the other side of the beatific aspect of the fantasy narratives of the aesthetically decorated world of material prosperity. In the 1970s, the popular films of Amitabh Bachchan projected the moral conflict between these two sides – the two sides occupied the same cinematic canvas. But in the 1990s, the fantasy of the beatific side became a stabilizing form of cinematic representation that came into being by silencing the destabilizing side of the images of depravity. This shift is reflected in the wider forms of rural alienation, farmers' suicides being just one form of such alienation. As Žižek (1997: 117, 118) argues, "How to keep the minimum of distance from the fantasmatic frame that organized our enjoyment, how to suspend its efficiency … is perhaps the foremost political question".

Notes

1 In Lacanian psychoanalysis, *jouissance* is a pre-symbolic real enjoyment that is always posited as something lost, as a lost fullness – the part of ourselves that is sacrificed

when we enter the symbolic system of language and social relations. It refers to the desire for fullness that is ultimately impossible (see Stavrakakis, 1999: 41, 42).

References

Arnold, D. (1984) "Famine in peasant consciousness and peasant action: Madras 1876–78". In R. Guha (ed.), *Subaltern Studies 3*. Delhi: Oxford University Press.

Berlant, L. (2008) "Intuitionists: History and the affective event". *American Literary History*, 20(4): 845–860.

Bharucha, R. (1995) "Utopia in Bollywood: 'Hum Appke Hain Koun..!'". *Economic and Political Weekly*, 30(15): 801–804.

Deaton, A. (ed.). (2004) *The Great Indian Poverty Debate*. New Delhi: Macmillan.

Deaton, A., and J. Drèze (2002) "Poverty and inequality in India: A re-examination". *Economic and Political Weekly*, 37(36): 3729–3748.

Drèze, J., and A. Sen. (2008) *India: Development and Participation*. New Delhi: Oxford University Press.

Dwyer, R. (2000) *All You Want is Money, All You Need is Love: Sexuality and Romance in Modern India*. London: Casell.

Dyer, R. (1993) "Entertainment and Utopia". In S. During (ed.), *The Cultural Studies Reader*. London: Routledge, pp. 371–81.

Gialdino, I. V. D. (2006) "Identity, poverty situations and the epistemology of the known subject". *Sociology*, 40(3): 473–491.

Glynos, J., and Y. Stavrakakis (2008) "Lacan and Political Subjectivity: Fantasy and Enjoyment in Psychoanalysis and Political", paper presented at the 58th Political Science Association annual conference, Swansea, 1–3 April.

Guha, R. (2007) *India After Gandhi: The History of the World's Largest Democracy*. London: Pan Books.

Gupta, D. (2005) "Whither the Indian village: Culture and agriculture in rural India" *Economic and Political Weekly*, 40(8): 751–758.

Kazmi, F. (1999) "How angry is the angry young man? 'Rebellion' in conventional Hindi films". In A. Nandy (ed.), *The Secret Politics of Our Desire: Innocence, Culpability, and Indian Popular Cinema*. New Delhi: Zed Books.

Kothari, R. (1990) "Capitalism and the role of the state". In G. Shah (ed.), *Capitalism Development: Critical Chapters*. Bombay: Popular Prakashan.

Krishna, A., and J. N.. Pieterse (2008) "Hierarchical integration: The dollar economy and rupee economy". *Development and Change*, 39(2): 219–237.

Lal, V. (1999) "The impossibility of the outsider in the modern hindi film". In A. Nandy (ed.), *The Secret Politics of Our Desire: Innocence, Culpability, and Indian Popular Cinema*. New Delhi: Zed Books.

Lash, S. (2000) "Risk culture". In B. Adam, U. Beck, and J. V. Loon (eds.), *The Risk Society and Beyond: Critical Issues of Social Theory*. London: Sage.

Mazumdar, R. (2007) *Bombay Cinema: An Archive of the City*. New Delhi: Permanent Black.

Mohanty, B. B. (2005) "'We are like the living dead': Farmer suicides in Maharashtra, Western India". *The Journal of Peasant Studies*, 32(2): 243–276.

Nandy, A. (1999) "Indian popular cinema as slum's eye view of politics". In A. Nandy (ed.), *The Secret Politics of Our Desire: Innocence, Culpability, and Indian Popular Cinema*. New Delhi: Zed Books.

Nandy, A. (2011) "Humiliation: Politics and the cultural psychology of the limits of human degradation". In G. Guru (ed.), *Humiliation: Claims and Context*. New Delhi: Oxford University Press.

Prasad, M. (1998) *Ideology of the Hindi Film: A Historical Construction*. New Delhi: Oxford University Press.

Prasad, M. (2003) "The Thing Called Bollywood". *Seminar, 525*, available online at: http://www.india-seminar.com/2003/525/525%20madhava%20prasad.htm (accessed 5 February 2013).

Rajadhyaksha, A. (2003) "The bollywoodisation of Indian Cinema: Cultural nationalism in a Global Arena". *Inter-Asia Cultural Studies*, 4(1): 25–39.

Reddy, W. (2001) *The Navigation of Feelings: A Framework for the History of Emotions*. Cambridge: Cambridge University Press.

Schulze, B. (2002) "The cinematic 'Discovery of India': Mehboob's re-invention of the Nation in Mother India". *Social Scientist*, 30(9/10): 72–87.

Shah, E. (2012) "'A life wasted making dust': Affective histories of dearth, debt and farmers' suicides in India", *Journal of Peasant Studies*, 39(5): 1159–79.

Stavrakakis, Y. (1999) *Lacan and the Political*. London: Routledge.

Subramaniam, C. (1979) *The New Strategy in Indian Agriculture: The First Decade and After*. New Delhi: Vikas Publishing House.

Sundaram, K., and D. Suresh (2003) "Poverty in India in the 1990s: An analysis of changes in 15 major states". *Economic and Political Weekly*, 38(14): 1385–1393.

Vasavi, A. R. (1996) "The 'millet drought': Oral narratives and the cultural grounding of famine-relief in Bijapur". *South Indian Studies*, 2(July–December): 205–233.

Vasudevan, R. (2008) "The meanings of Bollywood". *Journal of Moving Images*, 7, available online at: http://www.jmionline.org/film_journal/jmi_07/article_08.php (accessed 5 February 2013).

Vasudevan, R. (2010) *The Melodramatic Public: Film Form and Spectatorship in Indian Cinema*. New Delhi: Permanent Black.

Žižek, S. (1997) *The Plague of Fantasies*. London: Verso.

Zook, D. (2000) "Famine in the landscape: Imagining hunger in South Asian History, 1860–1990". In A. Agrawal and K. Sivaramakrishnam (eds.), *Agrarian Environments: Resources, Representation, and Rule in India*. Durham: Duke University Press, pp. 107–131.

Part V

Public campaigns

9 Visual representations of development

The Empire Marketing Board poster campaign, 1926–1933

Uma Kothari

Introduction

The significance of visual representations of contemporary development in, for example, charity advertisements and media campaigns, is receiving increasing attention.[1] For instance, there has been much recent analysis of Fair Trade campaigning and the ideas of development represented through its advertising and marketing posters (see Goodman, 2010). However, the use of such popular images in campaigns is not wholly new but draws upon a historical legacy of popular and visual representations of development issues and concerns as well as of the relationship between consumption and development (Trentmann, 2007; see Figure 9.1 below). This chapter contributes to a historical analysis of the emergence and use of images of development in the past. More specifically, it examines how development issues were transmitted through popular visual representations of colonised people and places during the poster campaign of the Empire Marketing Board (EMB) from 1926 to 1933. This campaign, in which images and texts of the British Empire overseas were depicted in posters placed on public displays in cities around the UK, signifies one of the most systematic and paradigmatic examples of a public campaign in which posters were used to visually represent and advertise development issues and through which the ideas of progress and humanity that were embodied within them were conveyed.

Through historical analyses, it is possible to identify continuities of representations over time and how they have been adapted and reworked in the present. Indeed, an examination of the EMB poster campaign reveals how historical, and particularly colonial, tropes continue to pervade contemporary popular and public imaginaries of development. To understand how these are reproduced and modified in the present, studies of marketing, advertising, and branding development today have provided forceful examples. A particularly poignant comparison is made by Trentmann (2007) in his study of the relationship between the EMB and present-day Fair Trade campaigning for the ways in which they both address the interconnectedness of trade, consumerism, and development. He argues that the EMB campaign represented a precursor of care and reciprocity evident in the contemporary fair trade movement showing the genealogy of current norms and practices of ethical consumerism. Popular representations of development

Figure 9.1 Ships, Empire Marketing Board.
(Source: Library and Archives Canada/Department of Industry, Trade and Commerce)

manifest in the EMB posters sought to promote a project of caring for distant others while simultaneously using visual imagery to re-order relations between producers and consumers in ways that are not too dissimilar to fair trade campaigns today. Additionally, images from Fair Trade adverts are replete with notions of an interconnected world, invoke racialised imagery, and demonstrate, albeit in a very different social and historical context, the industriousness of formerly colonised producers.

Through an analysis of the EMB campaign, this chapter examines how it shaped the British public's ideas about progress, humanity, and development and their relationship to the Empire overseas in much the same way as the Fair Trade campaign today influences ideas about global connections and humanity, and reconfigures relations between consumers and producers. The primary aim of the British Government's EMB was to increase sales of Empire-grown and Empire-made goods throughout the British Empire. The posters were designed and exhibited to boost a dwindling economy of Empire at the time (see Figure 9.2 below) but also, importantly, to demonstrate the humanitarianism upon which the Empire had supposedly been built (Horton, 2010a). They were arranged on large hoardings in public spaces and thoroughfares across towns and cities throughout Britain, sent to over 25,000 schools, and posted in football stadiums. The billboard displays, which were changed every few weeks, revealed to the British public the

Figure 9.2 Highways of Empire: Buy Empire goods from home and overseas, Empire Marketing Board.

(Source: Library and Archives Canada/Department of Industry, Trade and Commerce)

places and people of the Empire and, importantly, advertised their role and responsibility in its ongoing success.

The establishment of the EMB at this specific and significant moment demonstrates the multiple, varied, and changing nature of colonialism over time and in different spatial contexts (see Lester, 2006). Indeed, the posters' content, design and display challenge the idea of a unified colonial project and identity and provide examples of how changing constellations of networks and reconfigurations of people, ideas and things shaped "Britain's changing place in, and involvement with, the rest of the world" (Ogborn, 2008: 7). At the time that the EMB was established, oppositional identities of home and overseas, and coloniser and colonised were shifting. The posters show how the British colonial government wanted British citizens to identify with the Empire in the later days of colonialism. They articulate an ambivalence between diverse colonial projects shaped simultaneously around ideas of the white man's burden, the economic needs of a dwindling Empire, and civilising missions, in which the colonised are 'out there' yet also part of a collective project toward the establishment of a common wealth of people across the Empire. As public, visual representations during latter-day British imperial rule, they were also a medium through which ideas and forms of humanitarianism toward, and development of, the colonies could be articulated. Although the EMB posters were primarily about enabling the British public to recognise their role as consumers and instil in them a preference for Empire-grown and -produced goods, they also had an important function in demonstrating their role in helping the colonies to develop through establishing an ethos of care for distant others. To this end, the EMB posters presented production processes in the colonies as non-industrial, backward, and inefficient, necessitating and legitimising the purportedly modern, progressive, and humanitarian interventions by the metropole. This is evident in the analysis of the posters below.

This chapter draws upon a collection of 222 of the posters in the Manchester Art Gallery that were donated by EMB in 1933 in response to the gallery's reputation for collecting industrial art. While there has been some recent research on the purpose of the campaign, much less has been written on the posters as visual representations of development ideas (see Auerbach, 2002). This chapter begins by briefly exploring understandings of (visual) representations and their meanings in the context of Empire before detailing the establishment and aims of the EMB and specifically its poster campaign. This is followed by an analysis of the posters to reveal the ways in which they articulated popular representations of development through depictions of people and places of the Empire overseas and through a visual language of care, interdependence and a common humanity. The concluding remarks focus on the extent to which these kinds of popular images pervade contemporary representations in, and understandings of, development today.

Popular representations and Empire

Not all forms of representation can be considered 'popular'. Fiske (1994: 129) suggests that "if the cultural resource does not offer points of pertinence through which the experience of everyday life can be made to resonate with it, then it will not be popular". Thus, for public communication to be popular, it has to speak to the quotidian. However, in the context of mass media, which Herman and Chomsky (1994: 1) argue serves "as a system for communicating messages and symbols to the general populace ... to amuse, entertain and inform", there is also the function of inculcating "individuals with the values, beliefs and codes of behaviour that will integrate them into the institutional structure of the larger society". Thus, popular and public representations have the power to reshape national life and public relations (Anthony, 2011). It is this reshaping that underpinned the objectives and ideology of the public and popular EMB poster campaign. Indeed, the desired economic effects of the campaign would not have been achieved unless the posters had been able to shift consumer behaviour and demonstrated to the British public their links to the Empire overseas.

It is widely acknowledged that different representational forms have varied impacts. Although the principal ways in which popular ideas about the Empire and colonies were diffused was through literature (see Jackson and Tompkins, 2011), some argue that the visual offered "a sensual immediacy" that could not "be rivaled by print media" (Mirzoeff, 2002: 9). Indeed, knowledge about other people and places was often acquired through visual encounters, and various images and illustrations of the colonies produced what McClintock (1995) refers to as "commodity racism". That is, cultural representations and signifiers that reproduce racist imaginaries. This commodification is evident in marketing and advertising campaigns, of which the EMB poster campaign provides a specific and exceptional example.

The EMB posters were forms of advertising that produced particular kinds of commodity culture built on visual images. Particularly useful for this study on representations of development through the marketing of Empire produce is the idea that the commodity image can be used not only to project culture but also to create cultural difference. Moreover, since "every commodity reproduces the ideology of the system that produced it" (Fiske, 1994: 14), this commodification of culture may fix and naturalise inequalities between and within cultures and societies. Thus, advertising does not just sell things but also creates structures of meaning. In the context of Empire, advertising, as a powerful mode of social reading (Wicke, 1988), became a medium capable of enforcing and enlarging Britain's power in the colonial world (Richards, 1990: 127). Moreover, visual colonialism extended into the everyday lives of people as advertising took "scenes of empire into every corner of the home stamping images of colonial conquest on soap boxes, matchboxes, biscuit tins, whiskey bottle, tea tins and chocolate bars" (McClintock, 1995: 209).

Representations are also always about power (Hall, 1997), and in visual and textual colonialist image-making, notions of moral, technical, and political superiority were highly prevalent, articulated through the reproduction of racialised images, stereotyping and caricature (see Stam and Spence, 1983). Despite this power, however, it is important to remember that a public message "does not have a life of its own" (MacKenzie, 1995: xvii) and that both the producer and the consumer of a particular representation are implicated in its transmission and assimilation. Thus, the meanings and uses of cultural resources are multiple and varied, and the whole array of text, content, context, meanings, reception, consumption and audience that produce "spatial circuits of value and meaning, producers, circulators, consumers and regulators" (Pike, 2011: 207) need to be considered. Given the geographically extensive, spatially diverse and very public nature of representations of colonised people that were exhibited in Britain during the late nineteenth and early twentieth centuries, there were inevitably a wide range of diverse meanings and interpretations that emerged. It cannot be assumed that everyone involved in the production of the posters, or those who viewed them, felt the same, or whether they expressed "a general opinion or an idiosyncratic view" (Lewis, 2004: chapter 2, online PhD thesis). Furthermore, representations evident in messages, advertising, mass media, and other forms of public communication can only be deciphered "in terms of the meanings of their own age" (Mackenzie, 1995: xvii) and, therefore, we must be ever aware of the problem of "reading back of contemporary attitudes and prejudices onto historical periods" (MacKenzie, 1995: 214). Notwithstanding this cautionary note and while acknowledging that understandings of the past are inevitably an act of the present (Driver, 1992: 36), historical research has, importantly, located imperial themes in contemporary popular culture, and the EMB posters were "a set of cultural technologies" (Bennett, 1988: 78) that commodified and marketed Empire to an increasingly consumer conscious, and globally aware, British public.

Promoting trade and development: the EMB campaign

The EMB was set up in 1926 by the Colonial Secretary Leopold (Leo) Amery and directed by Stephen Tallents. Although it also supported scientific research and economic analysis, its principal aim was to promote and market Empire products in Britain and thereby persuade British consumers to 'Buy Empire Goods' (see Figure 9.2).

It was hoped that the EMB would stimulate trade and satisfy the demands of the colonies and dominions for greater access to the British market for their agricultural and industrial goods. The EMB represented the British government's first peacetime propaganda campaign and emerged out of the Conservative government's response to intense pressure for reform of the tariff system following the 1924 elections. They advocated non-tariff preference as a way of addressing conflicts between those promoting freed trade, protectionism and preferences. In this attempt to promote "imperial preference without tariffs", the EMB spent £1.1 million between 1926 and 1932 (Meredith, 1987: 30). However, the EMB was short-lived, abolished in 1933 when a system of imperial preference replaced free trade following the signing of trade agreements on the common wealth Tariff Preference by Britain and its 'empire nations' in Ottawa in 1932 (Cronin, 200: 132–133).

In order to publicise and promote Empire trade, the EMB organised poster campaigns, exhibitions, 'Empire Shopping Weeks', Empire shops, lectures, radio talks, a library, advertisements in the national and local press and shop window displays. The most well known was the film unit, led by John Grierson, who is credited with developing the modern documentary film, that produced over 100 films. All forms of publicity were designed to showcase either specific imperial goods or the virtues of an individual nation – with the related goals of boosting sales and developing a product-based imperial consciousness (Cronin, 2004: 133). Overall, the main objective was to increase British consumption of Empire foodstuffs and raw materials with the corollary that Empire purchasing would create increased demand for the manufactured products of the UK and thereby stimulate employment at home. This dual message integrated with the idea that consuming Empire aids the building of Empire, is evident in Figure 9.3.

The most important and visible work of the EMB was its poster publicity campaign, which commissioned and displayed approximately over 800 posters between 1926 and 1933. Most posters were designed to be shown in a series of five individual sheets with one overarching text banner (Horton, 2010a).

These texts provided details of the country being promoted and/or messages that would encourage imperial trade. The posters were extensively displayed, and by 1933 frames were placed at 1,800 different sites in 450 British towns. So extensive was the geography of the campaign that Constantine (1986a) argued that

Figure 9.3 The rice fields of India, and the tea gardens of Ceylon, Empire Marketing Board. (Source: Library and Archives Canada/Department of Industry, Trade and Commerce)

no British consumer could have been unaware of it. In order to ensure the popularity and marketing success of the poster campaign, the EMB committee solicited the help of London's major design houses, important artists as well as designers.[2] As such, the EMB "became a major patron of commercial art" (Constantine, 1986a: 7), relying on a range of personnel including those from media, public relations, and the advertising industry.

Although the primary goal of the campaign was to advertise Empire goods, the EMB also explicitly stated its purpose as selling the *idea* of Empire (Self, 1994: 157). An important aspect of this was its role in educating the British public about the geographical spread, benefits, successes and interconnectedness of Empire. Dismayed by the lack of public knowledge about the British Empire, Tallents "devised a publicity campaign that would provide didactic instruction on what the British Empire was and why it was important to people in Britain" (Horton, 2010a: 3). This significant educational function meant that many advertisements promoting a particular product from the Empire included information about the good or the colony from which it comes (see Figure 9.3), and to ensure that the message could be easily understood, the EMB considered it advisable to include only a few statistics (Horton, 2010a: 3). The EMB, therefore, had the primary function of promoting trade, but this was strongly connected to an educational role and, as such, the "campaign became like a series of geography lessons, a patriotic pageant and an economic spectacle all rolled into one" (Horton, 2010a: 4).

This attempt to 'bring the Empire alive' was based on creating new commercial, scientific, and cultural bonds between the UK and its colonies. What is significant here is that the EMB, while initiated out of a desire to promote trade, simultaneously created and reflected a changing consciousness among the British public about the role and purpose of Empire. It articulated a shift from Empire as domination "to convey the message that the British Empire constituted a single family of diverse yet united peoples" (Meredith, 1999: 217). Tallents and the EMB worked towards this modernising of Britain's image. In depicting the interconnectedness of the economic interests of the metropole and colonies and invoking the metaphor of a single family, the posters attempted to establish links between different parts of the Empire not only through the economies of production and consumption but also through the development of other mutual interests. The family analogy and implied interconnections were evident in posters that urged 'Keep Trade in the Family' and 'Remember your Cousins' (MacKenzie, 1986: 217), and in November and December 1927 the following poem featured alongside the posters:

Let the Empire
Load the Christmas tree
From Christmas to Christmas
May Empire trade increase
The produce of the Home Country
Crowns the Christmas feast
A merry Christmas
The Empire is one large family
God bless us every one
A good resolution
In all your 1928 shopping
Say 'Empire, please!'
(quoted in Merchant, 2004: 5)

The posters were produced at a significant moment in Britain's imperial history, when the metropole and its colonies were witnessing a transition that eventually culminated in independence for many colonies and the setting up of the common wealth. From the 1920s, it was this process that the EMB sought to explain, reflect and to some extent, promote. This meant not just selling the Empire to the British but also selling the British to the peoples of the Empire, and it was the promotion of the idea of a family in which Britain was equivalent to parents, the Dominions were brothers and sisters, and the Colonies were children

Figure 9.4 Growing markets for our goods, Empire Marketing Board.
(Source: Library and Archives Canada/Department of Industry, Trade and Commerce)

that strived to accomplish this (Horton, 2010b). Together with the metaphor of the Empire family, linking consumers to a geography of production produced various geographical attachments and entanglements (Pike, 2011; Miller, 2002), and the image of Empire projected to the British people was one of "complementary economies" (Meredith, 1987: 31, see Figure 9.4 above).

Despite this language of a common wealth and interdependence, the posters continued to reify a hierarchical imperial system and reproduce paternalist and unequal relationships between coloniser and colonised. Thus, although in some ways the EMB posters illustrate the formation of the common wealth, in other ways they reflected older imperial ideas and prejudices (Horton, 2010b: 12). Mackenzie (1984: 2) suggests that the EMB campaign occurred within the broader context of imperialist attitudes in Britain and demonstrated that "jingoism was an omnipresent" cultural facet of everyday British life. Thus, the posters at the same time as informing the British public about colonised places and encouraging the notion of an Empire family, created "for the British a worldview which was central to their perceptions of themselves" as globally powerful. Indeed, the Empire was the very source of the nation's strength, status, unity and pride, and at a popular level this was reflected in the EMB posters. As marketing displays, despite their appeal primarily to middle-class women who had the economic power to effect changes in their domestic consumption patterns, with their overarching depiction of Britain as a benevolent imperial power, the posters acted as a focus for the convergence between classes, genders, and elite and popular culture. Indeed, the only appeal from the EMB to the working classes would have been to instil imperialistic beliefs as they had limited purchasing power. Furthermore, one of the less stated reasons for launching the EMB was the belief that imperialism provided an ideological counter to socialism for the working class, since the project touted imperialism as a solution to the economic problems in Britain (see Mackenzie, 1984). In this way, as Constantine (1986a) wrote "art had been harnessed to a political purpose, and by this means the legitimacy of the Empire had perhaps been revitalised for another generation" (quoted in Horton, 2010a: 38).

The impact and influence of the EMB campaign is difficult to gauge. With no market research at the time, it was difficult to evaluate the extent to which the advertising efforts of the EMB were successful in turning metropolitan homes into sites of imperial consumption (Merchant, 2004: 4) by changing the consumption patterns of the British masses to make purchasing decisions based on where goods came from rather than on price (Cecil, 2006: 2). Generally, however, the economic effects of the campaign were likely to have been modest (Constantine, 1986b: 219–224). At the same time, it is likely that the EMB as a popular and public campaign enjoyed some success in implanting its ideological message about Empire. Through the posters, a vision for the Empire was integrated into the everyday spaces of people's lives and imaginations. The poster campaign had multiple purposes: to promote greater trade between Britain and its colonies, identifying the interconnectedness of Britain and the Empire overseas and increasing understanding of the relationship between producers and consumers. It served to instil national pride in Britain as an imperial power while also educating Britons as to the importance of Empire and their role in sustaining it. However, these posters reflected a further important tangent. Amery and Tallents were keen to depict a more modern version of Empire, one that explicitly invoked a language of care and responsibility towards imperial subjects. Consequently, many posters intertwined the promotion of economic trade with ideas about development, humanitarianism and a 'civilising mission'. These new relations were defined and visually manifest in the EMB posters. As public exhibits and symbols of Empire, the posters conveyed notions of development albeit through images that embedded the superiority of Britain and the British. The following section explores in more detail how messages conveying this responsibility towards the development of others were visually depicted and expressed.

Promoting common wealth and a civilising mission

Ideologies such as those underpinning the EMB that connect people across vast spaces have often shaped notions of caring for distant others (Trentmann, 2007), and an important component of the poster campaign was indeed to encourage the British public to recognise their responsibility towards people in their Empire overseas (Horton, 2010a: 40). As such, in the EMB posters, films and writings,

"British people were represented as both father-like and mother-like, teaching their colonial family about progress and industry as well as supporting and nurturing its welfare and growth" (Horton, 2010b: 45). For Amery (1953: 352), chairman of EMB, it was this development of the colonies that represented "a most wonderful piece of work upon which we are engaged. I think it is the most direct and practical contribution that we, the White peoples of the Empire, can make to the general welfare of mankind". The posters were infused with notions of a common humanity, care for distant others, and forms of economic and social development that reflected progressive strands based on socially liberal and welfarist ideas that were gaining ground in metropolitan thought in the late colonial period. Keen to shift the image of Empire away from associations with subjugation, violence and conflict, the EMB used their posters to depict the sorts of opportunities the Empire could offer its subjects.

In order to re-imagine Empire as "a force for justice and progress", Amery (1953, quoted in Self, 1994: 156) expounded the idea of an integrated common wealth. This was further developed by Tallents, who, following the demise of the EMB, drew a parallel between the EMB and the UNESCO, noting that the Board had come to think of the British Empire primarily as a cooperative concern (see Horton, 2010a: 137). Grierson (1931), head of the EMB film unit, similarly suggested that the EMB was like the League of Nations. Utilising public relations techniques – the untitled poster from the Advance Empire Trade series is powerfully used for the cover of Scott Anthony's (2011) book *Public Relations and the Making of Modern Britain* – and propaganda, the posters' underlying message was to "move Britain's view of empire away from notions of domination" (Horton, 2010a: 114) and in so doing re-model the British Empire as a benevolent, progressive mission towards a 'common wealth' of people.

These popular representations of development were based on a belief that Britain was a pioneering nation that had built for itself an advanced human culture and a model of civilisation (Hobsbawm, 1999). Progress and modernity were important aspects of British colonial identity at home and overseas, and the posters reflected the moral responsibility of helping colonies develop their societies to achieve the kinds of progress exemplified by Britain. Based on a belief in this superiority of British culture and economy, the EMB placed great emphasis on what it believed was Britain's role as the Empire's enabler. Referring to the achievements of the EMB's development work abroad, Tallents commented that, "every colonial civil servant knows how much could and should be done in helping backward peoples to learn new and more scientific ways of rearing their children, tilling their soil and improving their health" (cited in Horton, 2010a: 137). Key themes of development, religion, art and economics suffused their campaign and provided causes onto which the British consumer could project their liberal values.

These visual representations asked the consumer for generosity and support in the maintenance of its humanitarian endeavours and to take pride in their benevolent intentions (Horton, 2010a). The role of the metropole in helping the colonies to develop are evident through a range of visual strategies but most obviously through depictions of a white man educating, supporting, guiding and bringing

Figure 9.5 Empire tobacco from Northern Rhodesia and Nyasaland from the 'Colonial Progress brings Home Prosperity' series, Empire Marketing Board.

(Source: The National Archives, Kew)

modernity and technology to the colonies. This is particularly striking in the disturbing racialised imagery of the larger-than-life white man imparting wisdom to the black child while overseeing agricultural processes in the 'Colonial Progress Brings Home Prosperity' series poster (see Figure 9.5 above).

More specific examples and evidence of how Britain could help develop the colonies is evident in two linked posters – African Transport Old Style and African Transport New Style – that formed a part of the 'Colonial Progress Brings Home Prosperity' series. The first (Figure 9.6), showing Africans transporting goods on their backs across the countryside is followed by another (Figure 9.7) in

Figure 9.6 East African Transport – old style from 'Colonial Progress Brings Home Prosperity', Empire Marketing Board.

(Source: The National Archives, Kew)

Figure 9.7 East African Transport – new style from 'Colonial Progress Brings Home Prosperity', Empire Marketing Board.

(Source: The National Archives, Kew)

which progress has been brought by the white man, who supervises Africans transporting goods in large canoes with a bridge and trucks, symbols of modernity and technology, evident in the background. These posters demonstrated a 'civilising mission' of the British colonialists as well as articulated a rationale for further British intervention in East Africa (Margolin, 1997). Interestingly, the gendered nature of progress is also apparent in these posters in which African women and children are shown to be engaged in more traditional forms of transport, while it is African men who benefit from the knowledge and techniques of Western development.

Depicting the rightness and beneficial nature of Empire, these posters also allude to the need for Britain to help people in the colonies learn new ways of exploiting their natural resources.

What is evident in many of the posters is an acknowledgement that colonised people are hard-working. Their problem, then, is not an unwillingness to work, but ignorance and a lack of the necessary skills, expertise, and technology to develop. Depictions of the industriousness of colonial workers (see Figure 9.8) and the portrayal of production processes as slow and inefficient (see Figure 9.9) appealed to the need to share Britain's modern, industrial expertise and served to justify further imperial intervention.

The metaphor, discussed above, in which the Empire is depicted as a family so as to encourage the British public to buy goods in support of their colonial 'kith and kin' was also an important component of the development focus of the EMB

Figure 9.8 Colombo, Ceylon from the 'Our Trade with the East', Empire Marketing Board.

(Source: Library and Archives Canada/Department of Industry, Trade and Commerce)

Figure 9.9 A teak forest of Burma, Empire Marketing Board.
(Source: Library and Archives Canada/Department of Industry, Trade and Commerce)

campaign. In this large extended Empire family, married British women in the metropole were the imperial housewives whose shopping practices bound the familial Empire together (Merchant, 2004: 1, see Figure 9.10).

The Board's slogan 'Empire Buyers are Empire Builders' designated these women 'Empire builders', suggesting that when housewives cared for their nuclear families by purchasing and preparing Empire foods, they also helped to build and sustain the extended family of the British Empire (Merchant, 2004: 3). Although the parents are in charge, they also have responsibilities towards their children, and the posters encourage the British consumer to play the part of the good parent by buying goods from the colonies and so help their colonial children to grow. Furthermore, they were family and their welfare needed to be protected, and thus notions of care and trusteeship were central to ideas of development. These visual depictions of the progressive benefits of the colonial project as well as familial dependency connected people in ways that emphasised the "progressive rather than aggressive mission of colonialism" (Horton, 2010a: 124).

However, Meredith (1987) contends that the EMB's creation of a more humanitarian imperial project in the minds of the metropolitan public relied on "circulating false images of imperialism and of the British Empire, and by inaccurately comparing the empire to a family" (Meredith, 1987: 32). Indeed, mapping the aesthetics of the Victorian family onto this large Empire family produced

Figure 9.10 The good shopper, Empire Marketing Board.
(Source: Library and Archives Canada/Department of Industry, Trade and Commerce)

paternalistic relations between coloniser and colonised that were deeply hierarchical since caring was never considered a relationship between equals
(Trentmann, 2007). At best this inequality was represented as benevolence and
paternalism, at worst the posters articulated deeply racist stereotypes that reflected
the colonial government's racialised approach to colonial development. For
example, as is conspicuous in some of the posters, "unity amongst men also
required hierarchy of labour" (Horton, 2010a: 41).

In this and other posters, the juxtaposing of different racialised figures "supported the period's models of racial hierarchy and naturalised a belief in white
supremacy" (Horton, 2010b: 174). Posters from the East African Transport series

provide examples of the dehumanised imperial subjects whose physical features are often "hidden or exaggerated beyond individual recognition" whereas "white citizens were represented with distinct personal features as well as good posture, strength and delicacy" (Horton, 2010b: 17).

As was also noticeable in imperial displays at the Great Exhibition in 1851, "subject peoples were represented as occupying the lowest levels of manufacturing civilization. Reduced to displays of 'primitive' handicrafts and the like, they were represented as cultures without momentum except for that benignly bestowed on them from without through the improving mission of imperialist powers" (Bennett, 1988: 95). In all of the posters set in the Empire overseas, industry is never present; instead, images are of growing raw materials or producing agricultural goods, invoking the idea that the colonies represent the rural, traditional countryside positioned in relation to the metropole's industrial, dynamic, and forward-looking city (Figure 9.11). This is clearly apparent in the content and the different artistic styles of some of the posters in which the "colonies are represented in bright and impressionistic style", whereas the metropole is depicted with clarity and sharpness (see Horton, 2010a: 140).

These racialised imageries, although not always overt, were no less powerful or damaging. However, Mackenzie (1984: 118) questions the extent to which the

Library and Archives Canada / Bibliothèque et Archives Canada
www.collectionscanada.gc.ca

Figure 9.11 Making electrical machinery 1928, Empire Marketing Board.

(Source: Library and Archives Canada/Department of Industry, Trade and Commerce)

posters actually created and manipulated popular racialised opinions since by the time they were produced "many of the popular attitudes towards Empire were [already] deeply embedded". Thus, rather than creating the racial character of popular imperialism, perhaps the posters were merely reflecting it (Mackenzie, 1984). The Buy Empire Goods campaign (or indeed the Fair Trade movement more recently), was not therefore neutral but a means by which political traditions could be reworked and mobilised and through which value systems that favour particular identities and relationships reasserted (Trentmann, 2007: 1086).

As popular representations of the development of the colonies, the posters often portrayed ambiguous messages that changed over time. One of the last series of posters presents a quite radical shift in popular representations of imperial relations and development. The promotion of trade within the Empire was given a boost in 1932 when at an Imperial Economic Conference held in Ottawa 'Imperial Preference' was introduced. In the light of this, the EMB was closed down in 1933 as there was no longer a need to actively promote and advertise empire trade. The 'Advance Empire Trade' series (see Figure 9.12a and b) provides provocative and striking imagery of the future common wealth displaying a common and shared vision of progress, enlightenment and development that disrupts many of the previous images discussed above. Here, symbolically, a multiracial group, together, look up towards what appears to be a light symbolising a collective and unified future project of progress.

Understanding popular representations in development today

Popular representations of development are evident in the visual illustrations of Empire created through the posters of the EMB, established in the mid-1920s, a time when attempts were being made by the British government to recast the Empire as a modern interdependent and interconnected whole. This was, in part, articulated through the projection of a humanitarian project to encourage an ethos of care among the British public, one that was wrapped around particular notions of superiority, modernity, and progress. As forms of advertising that promoted a product together with ideas of development, the EMB "took its place at the vanguard of Britain's new commodity culture and its civilising mission" (McClintock, 1995: 208). Yet, the ambivalent moralities of trade, consumption, and development, underpinned by a racialised discourse, inevitably compromised the extent to which moral communities of care could be created and sustained across distance and whether the promotion of markets could include ideas of development such as "welfare, solidarity and public health" (Trentmann, 2007: 1079–1085). Although the posters did present ideas about the role of the British public in developing the colonies, "the colonies were prevented from developing their own economies by a combination of the effects of the open door tariff policy imposed by Britain, of a prohibition of assistance to industries which might compete with British exports and of a policy of trusteeship which portrayed the native at best as a child, at worst as a barbarian" (Meredith, 1987: 36).

Overall, therefore, the posters did promote ideas of development and interconnectedness but only in the context of ensuring and sustaining economic benefits to

(a)

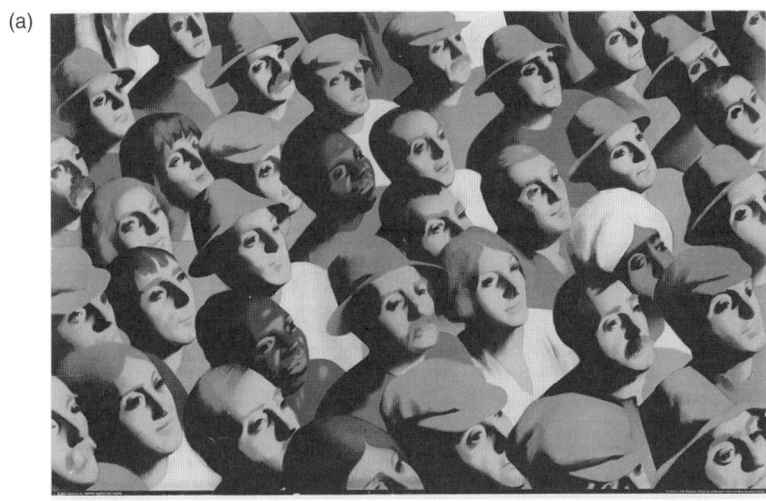

Library and Archives Canada / Bibliothèque et Archives Canada
www.collectionscanada.gc.ca

(b)

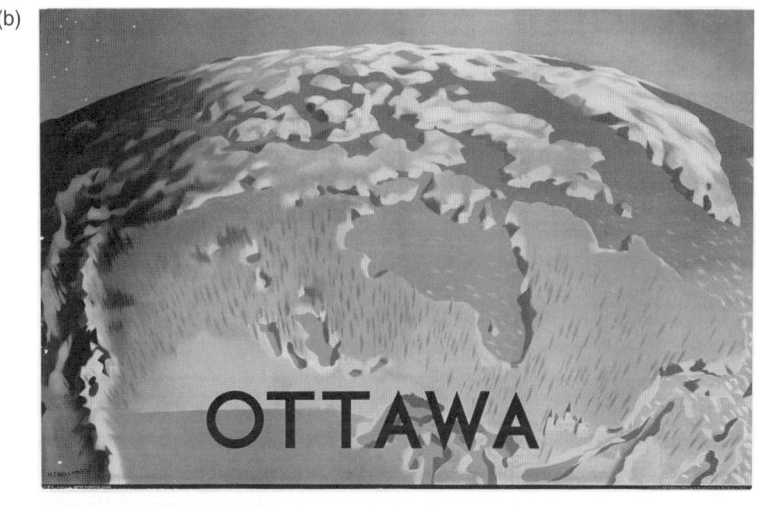

Library and Archives Canada / Bibliothèque et Archives Canada
www.collectionscanada.gc.ca

Figure 9.12a and b The Advance Empire Trade Series, Empire Marketing Board.
(Source: Library and Archives Canada/Department of Industry, Trade and Commerce)

the metropole. Indeed, as Cecil Rhodes once put it, "imperialism was philanthropy plus a 5 per cent dividend on investment" (quoted in Lawlor, 2000: 63). Although modelling overseas development on Britain's technological and scientific advancement did instigate some humanitarian support, it also confirmed the cultural and economic superiority of Britain. The EMB posters reified racial hierarchies through visual images of modern, benevolent colonial whites depicted alongside inferior, yet industrious, colonised others. In debating the purpose and value of exhibiting these posters today, the Manchester Art Gallery acknowledged that "the EMB's sentiments in some ways illustrate the formation of the common wealth, but in other ways they reflect many older imperial ideas and prejudices" (Horton, 2010b: 12).

MacKenzie (1995: xvii), however, reminds us that we must be wary of "moral condemnation befogging intellectual clarity and at times negating the essential characteristics of the critical faculty" whereby we condemn an entire epoch "out of hand as though historical ages themselves can be divided into 'goodies' and 'baddies'". Although racialised images and hierarchies of knowledge and power were reproduced in highly visible public representations, an attempt was made, however fraught, to promote a spirit of a common humanity across the Empire, most conspicuously evident in the 'Ottawa' posters. So, while it is important to explore the legacy of these representations today, this cannot be done outside of an understanding of the historical, economic and cultural context in which they were produced. Additionally, critiquing contemporary representations in, and of, development by identifying their roots in a colonial past has often led to contrived historical comparisons that have run the risk of not only misrepresenting the past but also distorting the present.

With these cautionary notes in mind, however, it remains important to engage with historical material, explore the legacy of present-day ideas, counter the persistence of negative images and reveal how they reproduce hierarchies over time. Postcolonial critiques have revealed the colonial legacy of contemporary development institutions, discourses, and practices (Power, 2003; Kothari, 2006; McEwan, 2009; Duffield and Hewitt, 2009). These studies, illuminating the relevance of Empire and colonialism to contemporary perceptions of development, have interrogated hegemonic understandings of geography, history, subjectivities and progress, demonstrating how these emerged out of colonial projects and the multiple ways in which they continue to be played out in the present (Havinden and Meredith, 1993; Chakrabarty, 2000; Slater and Bell, 2002; Lambert and Lester, 2006). Besides attempting to develop these postcolonial critiques, through an analysis of how ideas about development were understood and framed through popular, public and visual displays, this chapter has also contributed to recent calls to move beyond the privileging of scholarly texts and "conventional notions about the nature of knowledge, narrative authority and representational form" (Lewis, Rodgers, and Woolcock, 2008: 198) within the development context.

As media though which ideas about development are presented, visual images are perhaps the most popular, arresting and influential. 'The Buy Empire Goods' campaign bridged the furthest spatial, economic and emotional distances of the global food system at the time. It aimed to build a community by fostering connections between the metropole and its colonies, and this "caring at a distance" demonstrates just how "problematic it is to think along the simple divide between the 'local' and the 'global' and between 'family' and 'stranger'" (Trentmann, 2007: 1084, 1085). It is at this level that the past can be considered in some senses to have something to offer the contemporary moment of development. Analysis of EMB publicity shows how the British government wanted its metropolitan citizens to understand the relationship between Britain and the Empire, and this was manifest in promoting the importance of progress and development for all

(Merchant, 2004: 1). Despite stereotypical representations of the Empire over-seas, deeper analysis of the posters can therefore offer food for thought to the advertising and marketing campaigns of international development charities and NGOs today that are saturated with images, some of which are provocative and challenging, but many of which continue to reproduce essentialised representa-tions of formerly colonised people and places.

Notes

1 I would like to thank Dr. Melanie Horton at Manchester Metropolitan University and Ruth Shrigley, Principal Manager of Collections Access at Manchester Art Gallery for their support and for sharing their knowledge about the EMB posters.
2 Including, for example, MacDonald Gill, who produced the London underground map (Cronin, 2004: 134).

References

Amery, L. S. (1953) *My Political Life*. London: Hutchinson.
Anthony, S. (2011) *Public Relations and the Making of Modern Britain*. Manchester: Manchester University Press.
Auerbach, J. (2002) "Art, advertising, and the legacy of empire". *Journal of Popular Culture*, 35(4): 1–23.
Bennett, T. (1988) "The exhibitionary complex". *New Formations*, 4: 73–102.
Cecil, C. (2006) "The Influence of Social Conditions on Empire Marketing Board Propaganda, 1926–1933". University Honours Thesis, West Virginia University. Available at: http://wvuscholar.wvu.edu:8881//exlibris/dtl/d3_1/apache_media/L2V4b GlicmlzL2R0bC9kM18xL2FwYWNoZV9tZWRpYS8xNTY3NQ==.pdf. (accessed 4 December 2012).
Chakrabarty, D. (2000) *Provincialising Europe: Postcolonial Thought and Historical Difference*. Princeton: Princeton University Press.
Constantine S. (1986a) *Buy and Build: The Advertising Posters of the Empire Marketing Board*. London: HMSO.
Constantine, S. (1986b) "'Bringing the empire alive': The Empire Marketing Board and Imperial propaganda, 1926–33". In J. M. MacKenzie (ed.), *Imperialism and Popular Culture*. Manchester: Manchester University Press, pp. 192–231.
Cronin, M. (2004) "Selling Irish Bacon: The Empire Marketing Board and artists of the Free State". *Eire-Ireland*, 39(3&4): 132–143.
Driver, F. (1992) "Geography's empire: Histories of geographical knowledge". *Environment and Planning D: Society and Space*, 10(1): 23–40.
Duffield, M., and V. Hewitt, (eds.) (2009) *Empire, Development and Colonialism: The Past in the Present*. Woodbrige & Rochester: James Currey.
Fiske, J. (1994) *Understanding Popular Culture*. London: Routledge.
Goodman, M. (2010) "The mirror of consumption: Celebritization, developmental con-sumption and the shifting cultural politics of fair trade". *Geoforum*, 41(1): 104–116.
Grierson, J. (1931) Annual Report on the Activities of the Empire Marketing Board Film Unit Mimeo. Available at: http://www.is.stir.ac.uk/libraries/collections/spcoll/media/ownwordsemb.php (accessed 04 December 2012).
Hall, S. (1997) *Representation: Cultural Representations and Signifying Practices*. London: Sage.

Havinden, M., and D. Meredith (1993) *Colonialism and Development: Britain and its Tropical Colonies 1850–1960*. London: Routledge.

Herman, E., and N. Chomsky (1994) *Manufacturing Consent: The Political Economy of the Mass Media*. London: Vintage.

Hobsbawm, E. (1999) The Age of Empire, 1875–1914. London: Abacus.

Horton, M. (2010a) "Propaganda, Pride and Prejudice: Revisiting the Empire Marketing Board Posters at Manchester City Galleries". PhD thesis, Department of History, Manchester Metropolitan University, Manchester, UK.

Horton, M. (2010b) *Empire Marketing Board Posters (Manchester Art Gallery)*. London: Scala Publishers.

Jackson, A., and D. Tompkins (2011) *Illustrating Empire: A Visual History of British Imperialism*. Oxford: Bodleian Library.

Kothari, U. (2006) "Spatial imaginaries and practices: Experiences of colonial officers and development professionals". *Singapore Journal of Tropical Geography*, 27(3): 235–253.

Lambert, D., and A. Lester (2006) *Colonial Lives across the British Empire: Imperial Careering in the Long Nineteenth Century*. Cambridge: Cambridge University Press.

Lawlor, E. (2000) *Murder on the Verandah: Love and Betrayal in British Malaya*. London: Flamingo.

Lester, A. (2006) "Imperial circuits and networks: Geographies of the British empire". *History Compass*, 4(1): 124–141.

Lewis, R. M. (2004) "The Planning, Design and Reception of British Home Front Propaganda Posters of the Second World War". PhD thesis, School of Social Sciences, University of Southampton (Winchester University College). Available at: http:// ww2poster.co.uk/phd-research/phd-the-planning-design-and-reception-of-british-home-front-propaganda-posters-of-the-second-world-war-creative-commons-drbexl/ (accessed 7 February 2013).

Lewis, D., D. Rodgers, and M. Woolcock. (2008) "The fiction of development: Literary representation as a source of authoritative knowledge". *Journal of Development Studies*, 44(2): 198–216.

MacKenzie, J. (1984) *Propaganda and Empire. The Manipulation of British Public Opinion, 1880–1960*. Manchester: Manchester University Press.

MacKenzie, J. (ed.). (1986) *Imperialism and Popular Culture*. Manchester: Manchester University Press.

MacKenzie, J. (1995) *Orientalism: History, Theory and the Arts*. Manchester: Manchester University Press.

Mackenzie, John M. (1999) *The popular culture of empire in Britain*. In: The Oxford history of the British Empire. The twentieth century. Oxford University Press, Oxford, pp. 212–231

Margolin, V. (1997) "Review of graphic design: Reproduction and representation since 1800". *Eye*, 25(7): 72–77.

McClintock, A. (1995) *Imperial Leather: Race, Gender and Sexuality in the Colonial Contest*. New York: Routledge.

McEwan, C. (2009) *Postcolonialism and Development*. London: Routledge.

Merchant, E. (2004) "The imperial housewife and the familial empire: The Empire Marketing Board's Family Analogy, 1926–1933". Paper presented at the *"Gender in the Archive"* Graduate Student Workshop, University of Michigan, April 2005. Available at: http://sitemaker.umich.edu/eklanche/files/emb.pdf (accessed 06 December 2012).

Meredith, D. (1987) "Imperial images: The Empire Marketing Board, 1926–32". *History Today*, 37(1): 30–36.

Miller, D. (2002) "The unintended political economy". In P. Du Gay and M. Pryke (eds.), *Cultural Economy: Cultural Analysis and Commercial Life*. London and Thousand Oaks: Sage, pp. 166–84.

Mirzoeff, N. (ed.) (2002) *Visual Culture Reader*. London: Routledge.

Ogborn, M. (2008) *Global Lives: Britain and the World 1550–1800*. Cambridge: Cambridge University Press.

Pike, A. (2011) "Placing brands and branding: A socio-spatial biography of Newcastle Brown Ale". *Transactions*, 36(2): 206–222.

Power, M. (2003) *Rethinking Development Geographies*. London: Routledge.

Richards, T. (1990) *The Commodity Culture of Victorian England: Advertising and Spectacle, 1851–1914*. Stanford: Stanford University Press.

Self, R. (1994) "Treasury control and the Empire Marketing Board: The rise and fall of non-tariff preference in Britain, 1924–1933". *Twentieth Century British History*, 5(2): 153–182.

Slater, D., and M. Bell (2002) "Aid and the geopolitics of the postcolonial: Critical reflections on New Labour's overseas development strategy". *Development and Change*, 33(2): 335–360.

Stam, R., and L. Spence. (1983) "Colonialism, racism and representation". *Screen*, 24(2): 2–20.

Trentmann, F. (2007) "Before fair trade: Empire free trade and the moral economies of food in the modern world". *Environment and Planning D: Society and Space*, 25(6): 1079–1102.

Wicke, J. A. (1988) *Advertising Fictions: Literature, Advertisement, and Social Reading*. New York: Columbia University Press.

10 Band Aid reconsidered

Sentimental cultures and populist humanitarianism

Cheryl Lousley[1]

The pop star charity spectacles of the 1980s remain a touchstone in debates about media representation, humanitarianism and public engagement in development education. Media, communication and development studies scholars argue that the charity representations of Band Aid and Live Aid, in relying on the pitiful image of the racialized 'famine child', shaped popular British stereotypes about Africa and development for a generation, creating persisting impressions of Africans as needy, and white development and aid workers as their caring saviours.[2] This neocolonialist critique is complemented by what Chouliaraki (2012: 4) terms the "commodification argument", which points to how the socio-ecological complexities of humanitarian emergencies and development processes are reduced to simplistic marketing slogans and sentimental narratives of individual generosity, whereby "suffering turns into a fleeting spectacle without moral content". And yet the period is also remembered as "the golden age of humanitarianism" in recent memoirs, television commemorations and legacy events that strive to recapture its populist energy, most notably the 2005 Live 8 concerts that targeted the meeting of the economically dominant Group of Eight national leaders.[3] For example, in his memoir, Oxfam relief manager Tony Vaux (2001: 43) recalls the electrifying experience in Britain during the Ethiopian famine of 1984 when "humanitarianism quickly became a popular cause and the status of aid workers rose high. People in towns and villages all over the UK organized fund-raising events. The whole world joined in simultaneous pop concerts to express their compassion. Money poured into aid agencies as never before". This vision of a 'whole world' participating in compassionate display explains the utopian aspiration that Band Aid still represents; as Edkins (2000: 122) writes, "in supporting Band Aid and Live Aid, even when they knew that this type of aid was problematic, people were participating in the production of the social fantasy, the new humanitarian international community".

These lines of discussion – both the condemnatory and the celebratory – take Band Aid and Live Aid as shorthand metonyms for a range of famine relief and fund-raising initiatives undertaken by a wide array of social actors, largely though not exclusively in the Global North. Their populist politics remain intriguing precisely because they merged humanitarian moral sentiment with the marketing strategies of a globalizing music industry and the audience reach of globally networked national television broadcasting. A critical fixation on the culture industry and its representations of suffering, however, tends to reify celebrity, media and spectacle as self-evidently powerful. Taking my methodological cue from British, American and postcolonial feminist literary studies, I suggest this populist humanitarianism be approached as more than a mass-produced set of representations *about* development but, rather, as *participatory popular cultures* enmeshed in performances of feeling and social practices of community- and nation-building, commodity exchange and international development. I situate the pop music charity spectacles of the 1980s within a broad culture of sentimentality through which participants felt they were cultivating an imagined global community through their circulation of narratives, money and commodities.

To describe the 1980s popular culture surrounding distant humanitarian giving as a 'sentimental' culture is not to condemn it; rather, it serves to name a set of recognized conventions that can be studied in order to understand the specificity of their particular practices, meanings and effects. From a literary perspective, to name a cultural formation 'sentimental' is not the end of the analysis – as if sentimental were simply a pejorative – but its beginning. My literary-historical approach, which attends closely to specific narrative conventions and their social contexts, enables me to draw on the extensive feminist literary criticism on sentimental narratives and cultures and their deep imbrication, from the nineteenth century onward, with commodity culture and social reform movements, including abolitionism, child protection, animal welfare, temperance and humanitarian relief. By following this feminist line of analysis, I call attention to three defining characteristics of 1980s populist humanitarianism that have as yet received little attention: first, its articulation through the terms and objects of domesticity and love; second, its mobilization through social practices of gift exchange that imagine a global 'sentimental economy'[4] organized around love; and third, its feminized position as proximate to but outside recognized sites of political power and influence. I conclude by suggesting that this feminist reading – which emphasizes a minoritarian standpoint without declaring it innocent – is helpful for grasping the relationship between this populist humanitarianism and reigning political discourses and political economies of humanitarianism and development. Indeed, the recoil against sentimentality – the way it is taken as a pejorative, as false emotion, or emotion without knowledge, and as condescending pity – can itself be placed within an analysis of the gendering of acceptable discourses on humanitarianism and development.

On sentimentality and sentimental cultures

Scholars have found sentimentality difficult to discuss without falling into a polarized and gendered debate between an almost visceral condemnation of emotionalism, superficiality and mass culture, on one side, and celebration of the power of sympathetic identification to overcome social divisions, on the other. Within the humanitarianism literature, this divide usually appears as the tension between pity and solidarity: whether the spectator is moved because he or she is able to help one who is helpless ('feeling for'), or whether a campaign fosters empathetic identification with another, in whose cause one joins in solidarity ('feeling with'). The equality of 'feeling with' is generally advocated as a correction to the infantilizing passivity ascribed to Africans when represented as helpless victims and the implicit colonialist hierarchy pity reinforces (Robertson, 2010: 75–76). The sentimental "politics of pity", as Boltanski (1999: 3), following Hannah Arendt, describes it, is further criticized on five main grounds: first, as a politics based on emotion rather than reason, thereby occluding debate about the most rational distribution of limited resources; second, as a form of emotional self-indulgence, which provides more pleasure for the benefactor than help for the one who suffers; third, for relying, almost sadistically, on making a spectacle of suffering, now magnified by mass visual media and celebrity, in order to motivate compassion for a silenced other; fourth, for placing suffering in the moral register of voluntary charity rather than in the political register of solidarity, rights and justice; and fifth, for a de-contextualized, individualizing framework that fails to address – and that indeed, might even obscure – the structural inequities that create impoverished conditions.

However, Boltanski (1999: 103) argues that these same criticisms have been levelled since the rise of English sentimental culture in the eighteenth century. Rather than undermining sentimentality, for Boltanski they confirm the specific political contributions of sentimental rhetoric in its combination of a humanizing identification across distance (social and/or physical), personal introspection and responsibility, and social action. The culture of sentiment, as Bell (2000: 11) details, is what underlies the development of "modern 'affective individuality'", the creation of a private realm of feeling through which both romantic love and an individualized ethical responsibility might be conceived. Bell (2000: 17) argues that "the central problems of sentimentalism concerned precisely the sources of the ethical"; Stern (1997) shows how the sympathetic imagination is crucial for democratic solidarity. Wilson and Brown (2009: 19) thus urge scholars and professionals to be "more attentive to the emotive power of humanitarian narratives", arguing that "laws, state and international humanitarian institutions, and the cold light of reasoned justification are not sufficient to explain why movements spring to life to end some instances of suffering and not others".

Philosopher Richard Rorty (1993: 134) also concedes that the Western culture of human rights is based primarily on the telling of "sad and sentimental stories" rather than the foundational tenets of rationality and moral obligation that philosophers tend to foreground, and thus urges a deliberate strategy of sentimental education to cultivate and sustain a commitment to human rights. Political commitments to rights and justice may flounder without a sentimental education that helps forge ethical subjectivity and nurtures the moral imagination (Nussbaum, 1992; see Slaughter, 2007 for a more nuanced assessment). Chouliaraki (2010: 107), in tracing the shifts in contemporary humanitarian communication from a politics of pity to positive imagery to ironic, 'post-emotional' representations, similarly notes that universalist commitments to empathy and justice and to public action on ethical principles are lost in a textually self-referential aesthetic.

Literary and cultural studies scholarship takes a slightly different approach to these debates by emphasizing the historically specific operations of particular rhetorical conventions, their social contexts and their roles in identity distinctions. Sentimentality is a narrative and dramatic mode based on the cultivation and performance of sympathetic identification, but which is not as monolithic as the standard 'pity versus solidarity' debate would have it. There is no single, ahistorical form of 'sentimentalism', but rather sets of historically specific and contested conventions of feeling, or affective formations, that have meaning within particular social groups (Howard, 1999; Bell, 2000). These modes are neither static nor given, but socially produced and circulated. The danger of using vague terms such as compassion is that this can obscure how performances and experiences of feeling are historical, as if 'we' naturally know what compassion is, can recognize it, and judge its sincerity without cultural training. The very 'failure' of Anglophone publics to perform what development professionals consider to be appropriate displays of development compassion, because falling into pity or 'compassion fatigue', shows how feelings are indeed contested cultural formations.[5]

Sentimentality is described as a cultural formation because it functions in realms beyond textuality, especially as an interiorized practice of sensibility (Bell, 2000). The extension of sentiment from the reading experience to personal introspection and social interaction is foundational to the mode: a sentimental narrative models for the audience the sympathetic response it strives to elicit (sophisticated readers tend to celebrate their ability to read and resist this manipulative power of the sentimental narrative). The extra-textual dimension of sentimentality as a social relation and practice has led critics in recent years to speak of 'sentimental cultures', in which the mode is mobilized hegemonically across a wide range of genres, media and social sites, especially, since the mid-nineteenth century, benevolent institutions and commodity markets (Samuels, 1992; Merish, 2000; Bell, 2000). Cultural theorist Lauren Berlant (1997; 2008) argues that sentimentality has been the dominant cultural mode in the contemporary United States since the 1980s; although rarely found in literary texts, sentimentalism is pervasive in broad-based consumer marketing, popular film and television, and political discourse. For Berlant (2008: 6), the role of the commodity market in circulating sentimental scenes, stories and objects is particularly significant for grasping its pedagogical role in interpellating audiences into an imagined sentimental community of like-feeling participants, what she terms an 'intimate public', through the texts and images that pass among them. Thinking about the circulation of feeling through commodities is a helpful way to approach audiences not as autonomous individuals (or a duped mass) but rather as social networks, cultivated in proper modes of feeling and imagining a common readership through the texts they read. Berlant's (2008) analysis bridges, in a way I aim to emulate, the neocolonialist commodification and humanist arguments about sentimentalism by emphasizing how sympathetic identification and humanization are historically transacted through commodity markets.

Sentimental love: from the home to the world

Berlant (2008) situates her reading of contemporary American sentimental discourse within the commodity realm of 'women's culture' – the novels, magazines,
films and television serials of romance, melodrama and sentimentality written and
produced for conventionally feminized women (even if also, at times, written and
consumed by men) – and its articulation as a *feminine* rhetoric, drawing and reinforcing an association between women, domesticity and private feeling. The
prominence of male musicians in the charity pop responses to the 1984 Ethiopian
emergency has obscured the way in which their rhetoric was also situated within
this feminine realm of private feeling and domestic life (as has its deployment
by Ronald Reagan and subsequent conservative male politicians in the United
States – see Berlant, 1997, 2004). The feminization of sentiment is associated with
the Victorian consolidation of the middle class and the ideology of a gendered
separation of spheres that normatively designated commerce as profane, and the
home as moral, sanctified by the emotional rather than physical labour of women
(Tompkins, 1986; Davidson and Hatcher, 2002). In this context, what made a place
a home, and the inhabitants a family, was a woman engaged in attending to their
emotional needs. As Armstrong (1987: 41) describes, "according to the middle-
class ideal of love ... the female relinquishes political control to the male in order
to acquire exclusive authority over domestic life, emotions, taste, and morality".

Crucially, this domain of domestic love and sympathetic morality becomes not
only the basis for sharply delineated gendered expectations, but also the legitimiz-
ing basis from which bourgeois women engaged in *public* demands and activities
(Davidson and Hatcher, 2002; Sánchez-Eppler, 2005). Feminist and postcolonial
scholarship has shown how Anglo-bourgeois women crafted gender, racial and
class identities, consumer practices and political projects around their affective
labour, which was often rhetorically contrasted with commercial and physical
forms of work to denote its moral tenor. Bourgeois women's public, philanthropic
interventions in the lives of racialized or working class others, through child protection, native schooling, hygiene instruction, Christian missions, urban renewal
and colonial administration, could be justified in terms of bringing familial love
and domestic security to others within the 'imperial family' (Samuels, 1992;
Kaplan, 2002). Rhetorically, to make a claim on the world from the position of the
moral woman or girl child – both as figures seemingly outside official channels of
power – is to do so in the name of love, never the self or self-interest; to value love
is to enter a world that places this 'self-less' woman or girl at its centre. Although
rhetorically distinguished from the spheres of commerce and politics, sentimentality is a mode of negotiating access to social power and goods through claims of
love, innocence, or powerlessness; concomitantly, the socially privileged and
powerful can breach (or disavow) social hierarchies and separate spheres by
showing love and sympathy for the innocent or powerless (Davidson and Hatcher,
2002; Kaplan, 2002; Sanchez-Éppler, 2005).

Domestic scenes and household objects figure prominently in the stories of
giving that circulate through the memoirs, journalism and souvenir publications

surrounding the 1984 Ethiopian emergency. Predictable and repetitious in their sentimental conventions, these stories are significant for how they make demonstrations of love the underlying purpose of participation in famine relief. The usual story is about a common, ordinary person who gives in an extraordinary way; indeed, the story will emphasize the commonness of the giver. The giver will be someone you – the audience for the story – have never heard of before, likely from a place on the social margins, associated with poverty, or youth, or a region distant from the cultural capital, or some other form of powerlessness and want. Their giving is extraordinary because it is disproportionate to their capacity to give. They give too much, in the sense that it is more than is reasonable given their own needs, and this excessiveness is a sign of the sincerity, depth, and spontaneity of their compassion. A related narrative, almost always told in conjunction with the first, is that of the exceptional person – the political leader, the pop star, the jaded journalist – moved, just like everybody else, to 'common tears' when confronted with the scene of suffering.

British journalist Peter Gill (1986: 95) describes some of these acts of giving in his book *A Year in the Death of Africa*. They appear as compassionate acts by way of sentimental conventions of innocence, relative powerlessness and domesticity as idealized haven for love and kindness:

> A couple in Scotland auctioned the contents of their home for the Ethiopian famine appeal after seeing the television pictures. They kept a table, some chairs and a bed for themselves, until the person who had bought their dresser charitably returned it to them. As an example of American compassion, Vice-President Bush pointed to a little girl called Sandra Nathan from Brooksville, Florida, who had given her life savings to the charity CARE. Sandra was six and her savings were $5. A group of Vietnamese boat people in a Hong Kong transit camp collected 6,125 Hong Kong dollars – about £600 – for the local Ethiopian famine relief fund.

This oscillation between middle-class giving and giving by the poor also appears in the list of anecdotes of international giving in *Red Tears*, the memoir of the Ethiopian Relief and Rehabilitation Commissioner Dawit Wolde Giorgis (1989: 203), who writes, of Canadian donations: "In Guelph, Ontario, Fred Benson handed over his 107-acre farm to a Mennonite relief agency to be auctioned off. $250,000 of the money went to famine relief. Eskimos from Fort Smith village in the Northwest Territories organized a show with proceeds going to famine relief". In his 2004 memoir, Michael Buerk, the BBC journalist who, with East African photographer Mohamed Amin, catapulted the famine story into international media attention in October 1984, offers a series of similar sentimental anecdotes of domestic giving. He tells of "an unemployed man" who "sent his benefit cheque – £54, 'all I have,' for Ethiopia's starving" and of "Julius Harper, a ten-year-old in London, [who] raised £96 busking with his recorder in Camden Market" (Buerk, 2004: 297–298). He describes two children, Karen and Russell Eley, "ordinary people, living ordinary lives in an ordinary street", who "went into the living room of their house on the Orrell Park Estate in Liverpool and found their mother crying in front of the television" (Buerk, 2004: 290), watching his report from the famine camp in Korem, Ethiopia. The children then started a fund-raising campaign by walking a wagon through their neighborhood gathering donations for famine relief.

These stories of the gifts of common people are complemented by tales of the tears of powerful men, repeating the long-standing convention of a masculine display of weeping to establish an event as exceptional, and the state as principled (see Ellison, 1999; Chapman and Hendler, 1999). Buerk (2004) writes that Prime Minister Bob Hawke of Australia cried on viewing the television report, as did the BBC technicians and programme editors who, before viewing the footage, had insisted only three to four minutes could be broadcast, so familiar and clichéd were television reports of starvation. Across the Atlantic, the news editors at NBC had declined to pick up the BBC feed for similar reasons, but the European desk sent it through anyway. Buerk (2004) quotes Paul Greenberg, executive director of NBC, recounting that when it was broadcast in the newsroom, "All the side talk, the gossip, the scuttlebutt about the presidential election, just stopped. Tears came to your eyes and you felt you had just been hit in the stomach" (295). That such tears are to be understood as an exceptional eruption of domestic feeling in a normally affectless, masculine public sphere is highlighted in a Canadian Broadcasting Corporation report on Stephen Lewis's inaugural speech to the United Nations on 6 November 1984: "Ambassador Stephen Lewis today rewrote the speech the bureaucrats gave him and made it personal. He told the United Nations he and his family broke down and cried over the TV footage from Ethiopia". A short video excerpt of his speech shows Lewis, later the UN Special Envoy on HIV/AIDS in Africa, saying, "I cannot remember in my entire adult life scenes of such unendurable human desolation. It was heartbreaking. There is no doubt in my mind that Canadians sat and wept as we did and would wish to respond with compassion, generosity, and fervor".[6] Lewis positions his crying body and the nation as common points of transit from home to world: from private, familial love to cosmopolitan love and the "moral community" of humanity as a whole (see Nussbaum, 1996: 7).

The common-person-who-gives and the elite-person-who-cries are frequent tropes because sentimental stories become more compelling the more they highlight and then transcend difference and distance – a differentiation that is usually multiplied through the presence of an intermediary figure and repeated chains of witness, testimony and audience. (For example, there are already four intermediaries from the news anchor, who introduces Lewis, who describes his family, who watch a news report.) Media and development studies critiques of sentimental representations tend to focus on the social distance between the giver and receiver of sympathy, reading humanitarianism in terms of the moral question of 'distant suffering' and questioning whether the giver gains more in social prestige than the indebted recipient (Boltanski, 1999: xv; Moeller, 1999; Chouliaraki, 2006). However, as important, in terms of the structure of the narrative, is the social distance of the neutral intermediaries, who witness, testify and/or give despite having no pecuniary, familial or other vested interest. Slaughter (2009: 94, 100) shows that sentimental humanitarian narratives create an "affective identification with the humanitarian aid worker [that] is metonymical, constructed through a chain of substitutions that ultimately links the reader with [Red Cross founder] Dunant", who is the eminently neutral third-party because an "accidental tourist" to the scene of war. The "third actor", Slaughter (2009: 102) suggests, "introduces the figure of the humanitarian into the intersubjective, two-dimensional drama" of war and suffering. The dramatic presence of the innocent, or non-implicated, third party serves to demonstrate that voluntary intervention in the drama is a self-less or moral rather than self-interested act. Sentimental stories 'surprise' because they encourage us first to expect behaviour and feelings to accord with social position, then show an individual that exceeds the expectation in order to demonstrate that social divisions can be overcome, as the sentimental saying goes, by the 'goodness of the individual heart'. It is the momentary, surprising overcoming of a presumed distance or incapacity that is touching. (That the lofty and the masculine cry, while the lowly give is part of this formula.)

A sentimental economy

The term *sentimental economy* comes from the feminist scholarship on Harriet Beecher Stowe's nineteenth century American sentimental novel *Uncle Tom's Cabin*, which is as ambivalently tainted as Band Aid for its pitiful representations of black slaves yet pivotal popular-cultural role in abolitionism. Stowe scholars use 'sentimental economy' to describe the ways in which the novel replaces the slave economy of debt and exploitation with an imagined national economy managed by prudent, good-hearted people bound by sympathetic love, and the concomitant circulation of the novel, *as itself a commodity*, among a community of sentimental readers, who by sharing this text in common can imagine themselves part of an imagined community of like-feeling fellow citizens (Merish, 2000: 149; Tompkins, 1986). I propose that the donated objects, and even the Band Aid record, be read in this similarly doubled way: as circulating commodities that both gather and imagine a community connected by exchange in global love.

The point of the stories of giving and crying that circulate through the print and television journalism, the memoirs and the souvenirs is to reveal and perpetuate a tremendous affective investment in famine relief and, through it, the utopian aspiration to a world driven by love (not the otherwise dominant 'cold' calculus of geopolitics and financial profit). Most of the sentimental stories of gift giving do not feature money (unless the givers are very poor) but, rather, the giving of personal possessions, from the household china to the farm to the child's allowance. In each story, the amount of money raised is less important than an indication of personal investment, which is always relative to who the person is, usually presented as an act of personal sacrifice: in essence, a giving not of money but of the self. In symbolic inversion of the market economy, the 'sentimental economy' renders Sandra Nathan's $5 equivalent to Fred Benson's $250,000 and to Stephen Lewis's tears by valuing love over money. The money they give is but a sign of the emotional labour they undertake. The money is a means, not an end; a conduit for the giving of the self to another, which is how we might define love. Labour in the more traditional sense is also prominent in many print media stories, such as factory workers who worked for free and through the night producing aid biscuits and Band Aid records, striking ITV television technicians who broke their strike so that an Ethiopian famine programme could be broadcast, and postal workers who delivered for free 6 million appeal envelopes.[7] These, too, are narratives of sacrifice, undertaken, as the slippage between biscuits, records and mail shows, to keep the giving going, the *love* circulating.

To suggest that the Band Aid record commercialized what was, in some original moment, purely about spontaneous, genuine compassion implies a distinction between the tainted realm of the commercial and the moral purity of the humanitarian that sentimentalism itself both constructs and blurs. In these sentimental narratives, the commercial domain as a locus for individual financial success and productivity is evoked both as the normal state of affairs that domestic feeling interrupts and re-organizes *and* for its leveling potential, where the high meet the common, and the common can act together. In his early memoir, Band Aid and Live Aid organizer Bob Geldof (1986: 223) tells this sentimental story about the charity record: "A butcher in Plymouth rang me to ask if you needed special permission to sell records. When I said no, he got rid of all the meat from his window and filled it with the record. The Queen's grocer, Fortnum and Mason, phoned to ask for two boxes to sell in their restaurant; by the end they had sold thousands there". Here, the tropes of the common-person-who-gives and the elite-person-who-cries are transformed into the lowly and lofty both setting aside their own commercial interests in order to participate in a social exchange of altruism. Rhetorically, their acts become altruistic through the narrative contrast with their commercial settings. The Band Aid record, in turn, loses its commodity status in the paired anecdotes; it appears instead as a sacrosanct object of benevolence that *displaces* commodities and commodity exchange.

This circulation of famine relief stories, money and commodities replicates the way objects such as wedding rings, photo albums and personal gifts are exchanged, collected and valued as signs of familial love (even if once commodities), functioning to remember but also to create, through enactment and repetitions, affective attachments. Indeed, the giving of these intimate domestic objects is highlighted in the liner notes to the souvenir DVD of the Live Aid concert, produced and released in 2004, 20 years after the original event. Written by Paul Vallely, also co-writer of Geldof's memoir, and other famine and relief souvenir books, the notes memorialize Live Aid by situating it within the sphere of familial love: "Old couples sent in their wedding rings. One newly wed couple sold their new home and sent in the money … It was a moment, through our tears, of utter clarity of purpose" (*Live Aid*, 2004). Wedding-related stories of giving also appeared in the print media of the time, such as the report of "A newly married woman [who] said that she and her husband would not be sending Christmas presents this year, so that they could give the £100 they would save to Ethiopian refugees" (Cross and Webster 1984). These stories are touching precisely because they symbolically breach and transcend an underscored divide between private, domestic love and a cold, unfeeling world. Whereas Lewis broadens the family to incorporate the nation, whom he presumes "wept as we did", each in their own household, the DVD liner notes move directly from domestic feeling to 'the whole world': "Most of the really special moments in our lives are intensely personal – falling in love, getting married, the birth of child. ... But on a few rare moments in history something happens which is so powerful that we share it with the whole world" (*Live Aid*, 2004).

Although the worldly extension of domestic love appears unmediated in this ecstatic statement, the crucial mediator is the commodity market itself. In a sentimental economy, commodities are appropriated by consumers for personal meaning and, *as such*, are *re-circulated* in the public realm through commodity exchange, now signifying affective investment, not monetary exchange value (Merish, 2000; Sánchez-Eppler, 2005). Commodities become the means for sentimental action precisely because people are bonding not around particular political claims, but through the combination of preexisting collectivities (such as families, neighbourhoods, workplaces, and national television) and a commodity market that seems to *cut across social divisions* of class and nation, allowing both love and goods to travel among strangers. The passing of goods in an affective chain of commodity exchange (furniture to money to grain, or money to record to money to blankets) and the simultaneous circulation of the stories across a wide range of media forms and social sites (not only personal letters, newsletters, television, radio and print, but also the factory floor, the classroom and the neighbourhood street) builds a sense of community around a confirmation and validation of common values and feelings: that others too have been touched in this same way, that others, too, feel something must be done. Berlant (2008: 5) explains that "when this kind of 'culture of circulation' takes hold, participants in the intimate public feel as though it expresses what is common among them, a subjective likeness that seems to emanate from their history and their ongoing attachments and actions". Each story and each exchange adds to the feeling that one is part of a contagious chain of sympathy – what Geldof (1986: 313) termed "a new constituency of feeling" – that seems to cross class lines, national borders and even prison walls.

At its most inspirational, this wave of sympathy seems to augur a day when the whole world might operate on mutual recognition and concern; a fulfilment of the symbolic inversion achieved when the compassionate crying that bonds a family together carries the day at the United Nations. In being moved by the narrated acts of giving, the audience comes to participate in this fantasy of cross-class and cross-nation sympathy whereby the domestic economy of love is not contained within a home or by the antagonisms of politics and commerce but becomes the model for global sympathy and cooperation, performatively enacted in the displacement of the usual commercial fare by the moralized commodity, the Band Aid record, and in the displacement of rock star egos by their super-group co-operations. The power of the sentimental lies in this capacity to suture the self, the family, the nation and the world; rather than being a temporary exception to ordinary sentiments, the donations are instead a reimagining of the politically divided world in terms of the moral space of a feminized household.

A global gift economy

Thinking of commodities within this populist humanitarianism as travelling objects that signify personalization and get exchanged shift the analysis from a narrative of commodification, which finds a contamination or commercialization of authentic humanitarian sentiment, to a more nuanced study of social practices and cultural meanings. Read as charity donations, the exchanges of goods and money for famine relief tend to be considered singular, terminal, one-way acts. But the classical analysis of gift giving in anthropology begins with the argument that gifts are not discrete or terminal; their value does not lie in *use* but in their role in creating and confirming social relations (Mauss, 2002). Gifts travel. So, too, do the stories of gift-giving, and so it is worth lingering on the *circuitous routes* that both the gifts and stories take in this populist humanitarianism, passing through an extended chain of intermediary hands for whom this process of gift giving is intended to be meaningful.

There are well-established lines of development studies criticism that high-light the stereotyped representations behind the humanitarian donation, or the unequal parties and conditionalities of humanitarian and development 'gifts', which symbolically and financially enrich the benefactor at the expense of the recipient (see Stirrat and Henkel, 1997; Hattori, 2003; Kapoor, 2008). Kapoor (2008: 85), for instance, shows how food bags are branded with national flags to produce an image of the "generous nation" through its humanitarian gift giving and development aid, while imposing social obligation and debt on recipients. Here I supplement these arguments by proposing that the circuitous sentimental economy in which relief donations and narratives of gift-giving travel is significant in itself for symbolically offering a mechanism by which the "humanitarian international community" might be imagined and achieved (Edkins, 2000: 122): a global gift economy, wherein geopolitical alliances and financial interests are supplanted by an open, barrier-free affective economy of love and cooperation.

This sentimental logic is evident in a particularly significant non-governmental brand: the slogan, 'With Love from Band Aid', which was imprinted on the ship bows, vehicle doors, bags of grain and Oxfam biscuits sent to Ethiopia and Sudan in 1985 with the funds raised by Band Aid record sales. As a focal point and dis-tinguishing mark, it figures prominently in the television reports of Band Aid's relief contribution.[8] Phrased like a Christmas gift tag (and following Band Aid's Christmas-themed and -timed song), this declaration of love can appear empty and trite from the standpoint of critical distance: a generic slogan by affluent celebrities stamped on mass-produced commodities. It seems to exemplify the hollowness of commodity culture, converting genuine feeling into banal senti-ment. However, recalling that a criticism of commerce is already part of the domestic rhetoric of sentimentality, we can see how Band Aid acts to mitigate the apparent vulgarity of expressing love through money by *personalizing* commodity exchange through the formal conventions of the gift tag.

Godbout (2000) argues that the personalization involved in gift giving provides the trust on which the apparently depersonalized contracts of the market economy can flourish; in turn, the affective value of modern gifts is signified through negotiation with market value. Giving a gift with a high price but generic function can depersonalize the act of gift-giving, while making by hand even a poorly crafted object can intensify the personal relationship. A gift is more personalized the more it disavows its commodity status (such as the hand-written note in the store-purchased card); it should especially disavow reciprocation, standing as if a singular gesture of goodwill, and not associated with any self- or group-interest. As Derrida (1994) has argued, the rhetorical autonomy of the gift, pushed to its logical limit, can make gift giving appear potentially subversive. To be received and acknowledged as a *gift*, the gift must appear to lie outside politics and business, even as it facilitates political, economic and other social relationships. In its very distinction from commodity exchange, sentimental exchange becomes the quintessential alibi for capitalism, making use of commodity chains to travel while displacing an object's commodity status in the act of possession and donation. To adopt Barthes's (2000) formulation, the gift-commodity is both full of personalized meaning (to have sentimental value) and emptied of it (in order to be exchanged).

In the case of Band Aid gifts sent 'with love', both the addressee and addresser are vague and impersonal. The adoption of the formal conventions of gift giving in the slogan makes a gesture toward personalization, while remaining broadly inclusive for both givers and receivers. Anyone who bought a record or listened to the Band Aid single or helped at some point in the production chain could read themselves into the name stamped with love; indeed, they are confirmed as *givers* rather than *consumers* in this moment. And this love is going out to Ethiopians and other Africans, intimately seen on the domestic screen yet strangers, and who, *racialized as strangers*, signify the spectators' openness to loving the whole world. Humbled by the adoption of the punning name Band Aid, which emphasizes the inadequacy of the gift and giver at the very moment of giving, the pop music charity effort cloaked in love what would otherwise remain a merely insufficient monetary transaction. The inadequacy of the effort – a mere 'band aid' that but touches the surface of the wound – is underscored precisely to make the affective dimension appear more significant than the monetary (as with the other sentimental stories of giving).[9] As personified commodities themselves, the pop stars participating in Band Aid and Live Aid were what Schickel (2000) describes as "intimate strangers": familiar household names that also transcend the domestic. The celebrities' personal mediation of the intimate and transcendent enabled the branded records, ships, trucks and grain to travel as personalized offerings of love to distant strangers. The pop music charity efforts thus offered a spectacular endorsement of a sentimental fantasy whereby an intimate economy of love would supplant, by personalizing, the indifferent or uncaring commercial economy of money. Juxtaposition of a global gift economy with a real world fraught with violence and inequality is what gives this social fantasy its ongoing potency.

A populist brand of humanitarianism

The universality imagined in the 'whole world' vision of Live Aid sentiment has long been criticized as a hubristic exercise in the Western imagination (Robbins, 1999). But its overreaching claim to the world has a rhetorical significance *within* Western democracies as a populist narrative that audaciously claims to represent the 'common people' located outside the state and conventional pathways to power (Laclau, 2005). Berlant (2008: 3) describes mass sentimental cultures as "juxtapolitical" rather than "oppositional" to foreground how they operate as an "intimate sphere" situated beside a political sphere which they de-centre and delegitimize because "the political is deemed an elsewhere managed by elites who are interested in reproducing the conditions of their objective superiority, not in the well-being of ordinary people or life-worlds".

The like-feeling community offers a space of inclusion and validation for groups that feel not just excluded from wielding social and political power, but that political power is itself immoral: "intimate spheres *feel* like ethical places based on the sense of capacious emotional continuity they circulate, which seems to derive from an ongoing potential for relief from the hard, cold world" (Berlant, 2008: 6–7, italics in original). The paradoxical way in which wealthy celebrities, such as Geldof or Bono, are taken as voices of the common people comes from this shared feminized position – in their case as performers in the cultural and intimate spheres – as proximate to, but outside, recognized sites of political power and influence. This juxtapolitical position was repeatedly mobilized by Geldof through a symbolic stance of opposition to the political, charity and development *establishment*, delineating a populist, post-political brand of humanitarianism as an alternative.

Geldof was an appealing figure because of his willingness to publicly criticize political leaders in the register of an everyday, 'no-nonsense' language accessible to all (Hall and Jacques, 1986). His face-to-face stand-off with Margaret Thatcher, captured by British news media, re-broadcast in commemorative programmes, and cited by these programmes' interviewees in their reflections on Geldof, showed him as the common man cutting through the evasive language of politicians to put principles first.[10] Television reports and interviews showed Geldof as a scruffy youth 'talking back' to Ethiopian leader Colonel Menigistu and other African heads of state, as well as the European Parliament. Describing himself going to Washington like James Stewart in *Mr. Smith Goes to Washington*, Geldof (1986: 402) writes, "I had put on my green and white flecked tweed type suit with my inevitable yellow-green baseball boots. I thought I was dressed to kill, they thought I looked outrageous. Afterwards kids would say I hadn't let them down by compromising the way I looked when I talked to the government". Rather than offer an alternative *political* vision, Band Aid and Live Aid, like the outpouring of individual donations themselves, offered a sentimental alternative *to politics*, shaming the politicians (regardless of nation or affiliation) for their incapacity to act. The gathering and uniting of the people – the demos – was asserted against the 'politicians' as 'the enemy' (Laclau, 2005).

Live Aid adopted the symbolism of political revolt, representing the powerless (the demos) up against the powerful (the politicians), but without ever losing its high ground because not aiming to ever assume power (holding instead to the position that love not power will change the world). As Lori Merish (2000: 3) describes, "Sentimental narratives present a deeply conservative, paranoid view of power: power is figured as dangerous and intrusive, its effects uncertain and perhaps uncontrollable (power can hurt); satisfaction and ethical value lie in the voluntary, unregulated, deeply felt exchanges of interpersonal life". When this sense of virtue rests on its separation from political life in the protected heart of the domestic, private and cultural spheres, it "paradoxically denigrates the political and claims superiority to it" at the very moment that it enters political debate (Berlant, 2008: 34). When sentimentality contributes to popular dismissal of the realm of the political as tainted and corrupt in comparison with the virtues of private life, a space ironically opens for the populist celebrity as moral actor. Band Aid and Live Aid could be articulated in universalist terms because they were positioned within a popular culture that appealed to youth across classes (see Hall and Jacques, 1986), but also because situated outside politics, which involves standing for one class or ideology against others.

Chantal Mouffe (2000) suggests the evacuation of the political (as the space set aside for contestation) in the name of consensus is one of the ways in which neoliberalism threatens democratic institutions. Political consensus and unity – whether in the name of equality, national unity or economic fundamentalism – can be privileged only at the expense of the antagonisms that give liberal democracy its legitimacy as a space for political freedom and possibility (see also Rancière, 2006). Literary scholars have also noted how sentimentalism has been used in the rhetoric of Anglo neoliberalism, facilitating policies to dismantle welfare states and liberalize economies by way of a moralized language of voluntarist care (Woodward, 2004; Slaughter, 2009; Berlant, 2004). One sign of the intersection of sentimentality and neoliberalism in the populist humanitarianism of 1980s famine relief is how, even though nation-states were the primary financial donors and political targets of public demands for increased aid, the commemorated sentimental anecdotes of giving discussed above consistently de-emphasize the role and power of the state. Not only is the African state rendered as absent or negligent in the representation of Africa as needy and starving, the Western state, too, is rendered impotent. The tears of Australian Prime Minister Bob Hawke and Canadian ambassador Stephen Lewis put a domestic household in the place of national and international bodies of governance. Even the reference to Vice-President Bush functions to deflect from the political to the personal realm, implying that a child who gives carries more significance than what a president or vice-president might do. (The audience for the story knows this is not true; it is moving because it offers the fantasy that it might one day *be true*.)

Concomitantly, in acting despite what was presented as the bureaucratic lethargy and Cold War ideology of the British state, Geldof ironically epitomized the entrepreneurial spirit Margaret Thatcher was seeking to generate in a fiscally liberalized Britain. Band Aid, as embodied by Geldof, appeared to exemplify the free speech and action possible in entrepreneurial initiatives, especially by way of contrast with the professionalized aid agencies that had to maintain diplomatic relations with the states in which they worked. The Band Aid Trust, in turn, based its brand appeal on spending no money on administration and on being antagonistic towards government in general, whether British, European or African. This populist antagonism toward government could be also seen as contributing to the reconfiguration of development around what Mbembe (2001) calls the rise of "private indirect government" because of its role in shifting accountability for public power within a state territory to fiscal accountability to actors outside the state (see also Ferguson 2006). Transnational non-governmental organizations carry the aura of moral sanctity when they embody, to repeat Merish (2000: 3), "deeply felt" and "voluntary" acts of assistance. However, as de Waal (1997) has argued, they are primarily accountable to external, not national or local regulations and donors, and the more that such agencies take on, as private contractors, roles that might otherwise be deemed duties and obligations of the state (such as provision of health, education and environmental services), they can serve to weaken rather than strengthen state hegemony.

Conclusions

Recognizing that sentimental attachments are actively cultivated through displays of emotional labour and acts of exchange helps clarify the prominent role of celebrity, commodity culture and capitalism in humanitarian movements and popular support for development. The coinciding circulation of stories, money and commodities shows how a giving public and a consumer market are produced in tandem: the famine appeals built on preexisting commercial and non-commercial modes of circulation and identification, which were extended and reshaped along new imaginaries through the globalizing currents of transnational media distribution, celebrity and aid and development agencies. The acts of giving generated capital that enabled each of these types of actors to expand their operations, and added value to their brands by their association with relief. Rather than draw a sharp line between crass capitalism and consumerism on one hand and humanitarianism on the other, it is more useful to see how the good feelings of giving, buying and exchange were produced through one another.

The political economies of communication and development have shifted considerably in the decades since Band Aid (see Barnett, 2011), as have the representational strategies of humanitarian campaigns (see Littler, 2008; Chouliaraki, 2010). Nevertheless, a better understanding of the complex interplay of spectacle, capital and affect in the constitution of public sentiments is still important for grappling with global inequalities, distant suffering and social change. Further study of the sentimental culture in which Band Aid emerged can illuminate how it helped legitimize the privatization of aid and development, and set the stage for the more sophisticated development branding exercises that followed, such as

Product Red, a global cause-based marketing strategy fronted by the pop star Bono (see Richey and Ponte, 2011), or why some of these, such as the Make Poverty History campaign of 2006, fail to re-create the populist energy of Band Aid and Live Aid (Sireau, 2009). The lesson to take from my feminist reading of the sentimental culture surrounding Band Aid is that the success of these initiatives is not merely owing to duped audiences mesmerized by spectacle, but to how the commodity market offers ways of participating in good-feeling social action. Rather than simple effects of the amorphous power of mass media, Band Aid and Live Aid worked by suturing localized kinship and social networks with television's intimate mass communities and the personalization of commodity culture in the service of a depoliticized dream of world harmony.

Notes

1 This research was generously supported by a Social Sciences and Humanities Research Council of Canada Postdoctoral Fellowship and a Carson Fellowship at the Rachel Carson Center, Munich, Germany. These funding bodies played no role in research design, analysis, or writing. I would like to thank the Canadian Broadcasting Corporation and the British Film Institute for providing archival access to materials discussed here, and Dr. Graham Huggan, University of Leeds, and Dr. Daniel Brockington, University of Manchester, for their intellectual support and guidance on this project.

2 See van der Gaag and Nash (1987), Benthall (1993), de Waal (1997), VSO (2002) and Kapoor (2008).

3 This phrase is from Vaux (2001): 43. This culture of memorabilia is extensive, and I only touch on some examples here. The BBC produced commemorative broadcasts on the 1st, 10th, 15th, 20th and 25th anniversaries. Other British television networks have also produced "return to Ethiopia" programmes, featuring the journalists who covered aspects of the original story. Memoirs have been published by expatriate doctors and nurses who worked in feeding camps, as well as by journalists and others involved in relief or media. See Gopal (2006) for a discussion of the coordinated marketing memorabilia produced alongside Live 8.

4 As I discuss below, the term *sentimental economy* comes from feminist scholarship on Harriet Beecher Stowe's sentimental novel *Uncle Tom's Cabin*.

5 See VSO (2002); Moeller (1999) on compassion fatigue.

6 'UN Lewis', *The National* (1984). [TV programme] Canadian Broadcasting Corporation, 6 November 1984 (22:16).

7 These stories of sacrificial labour appear in the memoirs (see Geldof, 1986) and television and print media (see David Cross, "British Emergency Food Aid for Ethiopia Famine", *The Times*, 25 Oct 1984, page 1, and Joseph Berger, "Offers of Aid for Stricken Ethiopia Are Pouring Into Relief Agencies", *The New York Times*, 28 Oct 1984, p. 1).

8 Vehicles, grain bags and other aid objects with the 'With Love from Band Aid' slogan are featured in these UK television programmes: "Food and Trucks and Rock 'n' Roll" (disc 4 of *Live Aid*, 2004), "And Tonight Thank God It's Them Instead of You: A Tube Special Report" (*The Tube,* Channel Four, 27 Dec 1985), "Band-aid Relief" (*News At Ten, ITV Late Evening News*, ITV, 26 April 1985 20:00); and "The Band Aid Story" (Channel Four, 19 December 2004).

9 Geldof (1986: 223) describes the concept in just these terms: "I thought it was brilliant – apart from the obvious pun on the word band, there was an extra dimension. What we were doing and what we would raise would be so small in the context of the problem that it would be like putting a tiny plaster on a wound that required twelve stitches".

10 Television clips and reminiscences of Geldof's stand-off with Margaret Thatcher are featured in "The Band Aid Story" (Channel Four, 19 December 2004).

References

Armstrong, N. (1987) *Desire and Domestic Fiction: A Political History of the Novel*. New York: Oxford University Press.

Barnett, M. (2011) *Empire of Humanity: A History of Humanitarianism*. Ithaca: Cornell University Press.

Barthes, R. (2000) *Mythologies*. London: Vintage.

Bell, M. (2000) *Sentimentalism, Ethics and the Culture of Feeling*. New York: Palgrave.

Benthall, J. (1993) *Disasters, Relief and the Media*. London: I.B. Tauris.

Berlant, L. (2008) *The Female Complaint: The Unfinished Business of Sentimentality in American Culture*. Durham: Duke University Press.

Berlant, L. (2004) "Compassion (and withholding)". In L. Berlant (ed.), *Compassion: The Culture and Politics of an Emotion*. New York: Routledge, pp. 1–13.

Berlant, L. (1997) *The Queen of America Goes to Washington City: Essays on Sex and Citizenship*. Durham: Duke University Press.

Boltanski, L. (1999) *Distant Suffering: Morality, Media and Politics*. Cambridge: Cambridge University Press.

Buerk, M. (2004) *The Road Taken*. London: Hutchinson.

Chapman, M., and G. Hendler (1999). *Sentimental Men: Masculinity and the Politics of Affect in American Culture*. Berkeley: University of California Press.

Chouliaraki, L. (2012) "The theatricality of humanitarianism: A critique of celebrity advocacy". *Communication and Critical/Cultural Studies*, 9(1): 1–21.

Chouliaraki, L. (2010) "Post-humanitarianism". *International Journal of Cultural Studies*, 13(2): 107–126.

Chouliaraki, L. (2006) *The Spectatorship of Suffering*. London: Sage.

Cross, D. (1984) "EEC offers £19m aid for victims of famine". *The Times*, 27 October, p. 1b.

Cross, D., and P. Webster (1984) "Ethiopia flies food to famine areas". *The Times*, 26 October, p. 1e.

Davidson, C., and J. Hatcher (2002) "Introduction". In C. Davidson and J. Hatcher (eds.), *No More Separate Spheres!: A Next Wave American Studies Reader*. Durham: Duke University Press.

Derrida, J. (1994) *Given Time: Counterfeit Money*. Chicago: University of Chicago Press.

de Waal, A. (1997) *Famine Crimes: Politics and the Disaster Relief Industry in Africa*. Oxford: Oxford University Press.

Edkins, J. (2000) *Whose Hunger? Concepts of Famine, Practices of Aid*. Minneapolis: University of Minnesota Press.

Ellison, J. K. (1999) *Cato's Tears and the Making of Anglo-American Emotion*. Chicago: University of Chicago Press.

Ferguson, J. (2006) *Global Shadows: Africa in the Neoliberal World Order*. Durham: Duke University Press.

Geldof, B. (1986) *Is That It?* New York: Weidenfeld & Nicolson.

Gill, P. (1986) *A Year in the Death of Africa: Politics, Bureaucracy and the Famine*. London: Grafton.

Giorgis, D. W. (1989) *Red Tears: War, Famine, Revolution in Ethiopia*. Trenton: Red Sea Press.

Godbout, J. T. (2000) *The World of the Gift*. Montreal-Kingston: McGill-Queen's Press.

Gopal, P. (2006) "The 'moral empire': Africa, globalisation and the politics of conscience". *New Formations*, 59: 81–97.

Hall, S., and M. Jacques (1986) "People aid: A new politics sweeps the land". *Marxism Today*, July: 10–14.

Hattori, T. (2003) "Giving as a mechanism of consent: International aid organizations and the ethical hegemony of capitalism". *International Relations*, 17(2): 153–173.

Howard, J. (1999) "What is sentimentality?". *American Literary History*, 11(1): 63–81.

Kaplan, A. (2002) "Manifest domesticity". In C. Davidson and J. Hatcher (eds.), *No More Separate Spheres!: A Next Wave American Studies Reader*. Durham: Duke University Press, pp. 183–207.

Kapoor, I. (2008) *The Postcolonial Politics of Development*. New York: Routledge.

Laclau, E. (2005) *On Populist Reason*. London: Verso.

Littler, J. (2008) "'I feel your pain': Cosmopolitan charity and the public fashioning of the celebrity soul". *Social Semiotics*, 18(2): 237–251.

Live Aid (2004) [DVD]. Toronto: Warner Music Canada.

Mauss, M. (2002) *The Gift: The Form and Reason for Exchange in Archaic Societies*. London: Routledge.

Mbembe, A. (2001) *On the Postcolony*. Berkeley: University of California Press.

Merish, L. (2000) *Sentimental Materialism: Gender, Commodity Culture, and Nineteenth-Century American Literature*. Durham: Duke University Press.

Moeller, S. D. (1999) *Compassion Fatigue: How the Media Sell Disease, Famine, War and Death*. New York: Routledge.

Mouffe, C. (2000) *The Democratic Paradox*. London: Verso.

Nussbaum, M. (1992) *Love's Knowledge: Essays on Philosophy and Literature*. Oxford: Oxford University Press.

Nussbaum, M. (1996) *For Love of Country: Debating the Limits of Patriotism*. Boston: Beacon Press.

Rancière, J. (2006) *Hatred of Democracy*. London: Verso.

Richey, L. A., and S. Ponte (2011) *Brand Aid: Shopping Well to Save the World*. Minneapolis: University of Minnesota Press.

Robbins, B. (1999) *Feeling Global: Internationalism in Distress*. New York: New York University Press.

Robertson, A. (2010) *Mediated Cosmopolitanism: The World of Television News*. London: Polity.

Rorty, R. (1993) "Human rights, rationality, and sentimentality". In S. Shute and S. L. Hurley (eds.), *On Human Rights: The Oxford Amnesty Lectures*. New York: Basic Books, pp. 111–134.

Samuels, S. (ed.) (1992) *The Culture of Sentiment: Race, Gender, and Sentimentality in Nineteenth-Century America*. New York: Oxford University Press.

Sánchez-Eppler, K. (2005) *Dependent States: The Child's Part in Nineteenth-Century American Culture*. Chicago: University of Chicago Press.

Schickel, R. (2000) *Intimate Strangers*. Chicago: Gideon.

Sireau, N. (2009) *Make Poverty History: Political Communication in Action*. Basingstoke: Palgrave Macmillan.

Slaughter, J. R. (2007) *Human Rights, Inc.: The World Novel, Narrative Form, and International Law*. Ashland: Fordham University Press.

Slaughter, J. R. (2009) "Humanitarian reading". In R. A. Wilson and R. D. Brown (eds.), *Humanitarianism and Suffering: The Mobilization of Empathy*. Cambridge: Cambridge University Press, pp. 88–107.

Stern, J. A. (1997) *The Plight of Feeling: Sympathy and Dissent in the Early American Novel*. Chicago: University of Chicago Press.

Stirrat, R. L., and H. Henkel (1997) "The development gift: The problem of reciprocity in the NGO World". *The Annals of the American Academy of Political and Social Science*, 554(1): 66–80.

Tompkins, J. P. (1986) *Sensational Designs: The Cultural Work of American Fiction, 1790–1860*. New York: Oxford University Press.

van der Gaag, N., and C. Nash (1987) *Images of Africa: UK Report*. Oxford: Oxfam.

Vaux, T. (2001) *The Selfish Altruist: Relief Work in Famine and War*. London: Earthscan.

VSO (2002) *The Live Aid Legacy: The Developing World through British Eyes—A Research Report*. London: VSO.

Wilson, R. A., and R. D. Brown (eds.) (2009) *Humanitarianism and Suffering: The Mobilization of Empathy*. Cambridge: Cambridge University Press.

Woodward, K. (2004) "Calculating compassion". In L. Berlant (ed.), *Compassion: The Culture and Politics of an Emotion*. New York: Routledge, pp. 59–86.

Part VI

New media

11 Blogs + Twitter = Change?

Discursive reproduction of global governance and the limits of social media

Tobias Denskus and Daniel E. Esser¹

Introduction

No other popular medium in recorded history has penetrated public life as rapidly as Internet-based social media. Research on the impact of their use has, however, focused mainly on crisis contexts (see, for example, Farrell and Drezner, 2008; Maratea, 2008; Etling *et al.*, 2010), including especially the 'Arab Spring' (see, for example, Breuer, 2012; Howard and Parks, 2012; Shirky, 2011; Aday *et al.*, 2010). Only one study so far has investigated their effects on economic policy-making (McKenzie and Özler, 2011). In light of this empirical dearth, we seek to demonstrate that incorporating analyses of social media content into research on international development policy formulation is a promising avenue for under-standing the reproduction of elite-driven practices of global governance more generally. At the same time, our chapter also provides an opportunity to critically appraise recent assertions that social media has contributed to the formation and sustenance of a global civil society (Thörn, 2007). By focusing on social media coverage of the 2010 United Nations High-Level Plenary Meeting of the General Assembly on the Millennium Development Goals (MDG Summit) in New York City, we present an empirical case and explore its ramifications for the reproduction of exclusive networks in global policymaking.

At the center of global conferences, whether the United Nations Conference on Environment and Development in Rio de Janeiro (Earth Summit) in 1992 or the 2010 MDG Summit, lies a shared interest among national governments to define common ground with respect to pressing global challenges and to confirm political priorities and potential financial commitments to address them. By magnifying the emergence and sustenance of issues around which global social movements galvanise and act, such global conferences also forge collective processes that constitute significant learning experiences for their international participants, organisations and networks. In other words, conferences are not only diplomatic focal points but also serve as vehicles through which epistemic communities create shared discourses and thus maintain their identity and cohesion. Whereas resolutions from the 1992 Earth Summit were disseminated via television, fax and telephone, global conferences today use the Internet as their major strategic communication platform to facilitate instantaneous information flows.

Although Internet access in many countries is not universally available, opportunities for conference outsiders to stay abreast of the latest developments during such events are better than ever before.

A central question, however, is whether communication, in the context of global conferences, is limited to conference organisers and participants transmitting information to passive receivers. The ascent of social media during recent years has made it possible to create and utilise virtual spaces of participatory communication that can, theoretically at least, reinforce or redefine the discourses emanating from global conferences. Especially in light of the 2010–2011 Arab Spring and its use of social media, we must ask whether social media can produce similar momentum at critical junctures of global policy emergence. In order to examine this potential, we first posit the MDG Summit as both a virtual and physical research site. We then provide an overview of the literature on the ritualistic quality of global conferences and explain how we approached the analysis of content generated by two different types of social media. We investigate our research question by examining a sample of 108 blog entries published on 34 different blogs, as well as 3,007 real-time tweets linked both substantively and temporally to the summit. We discuss our findings along three analytical dimensions and, in conclusion, relate our specific observations on the content of social media coverage of the MDG Summit to the larger debate on the discursive reproduction of global policy frameworks in the context of international development policy and practice.

The 2010 MDG summit: the success of 'exceptionally boring meetings'

The 2010 MDG Summit took place during 20–22 September 2010 in New York City. High-level round-table discussions addressed critical global development challenges such as poverty, hunger, gender equality, health, education, sustainable development, the special needs of the most vulnerable, and the establishment of lasting partnerships (United Nations, 2010a). In addition to discussions in the UN General Assembly, over 80 so-called partnership events were held, and several key stakeholders seized the opportunity to announce strategic initiatives aimed at achieving the objectives set forth in the MDGs (United Nations, 2010b). UN Secretary-General Ban Ki-Moon unveiled a $40 billion strategy for improving the health of women and children (United Nations, 2010c), and the meeting's officially proclaimed achievements also included affirming the General Assembly's commitment to the target completion date of 2015 as well as securing pledges of financial support for each of the eight MDGs (United Nations, 2010d). Remarks by participating heads of state generally praised the progress made toward achieving the MDGs, acknowledged areas still requiring improvement, enumerated aspects of their country's contributions to the effort and, in some cases, also offered muted criticism of select issues.

United States President Barack Obama, for example, outlined his administration's policy on development and connected progress on the MDGs to the fulfilment of the Universal Declaration of Human Rights (US State Department, 2010). British Deputy Prime Minister Nick Clegg advanced the case that international development was squarely in the interests of the United Kingdom, and pointed to the Summit as an opportunity for donor and recipient nations to establish clear understandings of their partnerships (DfID, 2010). The Russian Foreign Minister Sergey Lavrov highlighted the UN's unique position for coordinating the international push to eliminate poverty and noted his country's increasing efforts to contribute to that goal (United Nations, 2010e). Somewhat in contrast to the majority of official statements and in parallel to emphasising achievements of his own country, India's Minister of External Affairs, Somanahalli M. Krishna, also recognised the setbacks in progress on the MDGs and welcomed Secretary-General Ki-Moon's initiative to address the 'forgotten MDGs' related to women and children's health (United Nations, 2010f). The Chinese representative, Premier of the State Council Wen Jiabao, stressed China's achievements in lifting its own population out of poverty and the degree to which this trend had contributed toward achieving the first MDG (United Nations, 2010g). Similarly, the Brazilian Minister for Social Development Marcia Lopez emphasised her own country's role in South–South partnerships while stressing the need for honouring and increasing financial commitments if the target date of 2015 is to remain a possibility (United Nations, 2010h).

Other public figures and media stars were highly visible during the event as well. Melinda French Gates, co-chair of the Bill and Melinda Gates Foundation, addressed the UN General Assembly and encouraged those present not to look at the progress toward the MDGs in terms of total success or total failure. She urged delegates not to allow impatience in pursuing the MDGs to overpower the optimism implicit in these goals, citing advances already made and new commitments launched during the summit (Paulson, 2010). An active commentator from the Global South, Queen Rania of Jordan used the summit to promote education, one of the key issues the MDGs cover (Abdulla, 2010). Jeffrey Sachs, professor at Columbia University and one of the most fervent promoters of the MDGs, described the summit as an opportunity to cut through the noise of everyday affairs and to focus on the challenges of development (Guest, 2010). While acknowledging the difficulties of establishing effective funding streams and coping with fractured, individual donor agendas, he argued that the MDG Summit and its associated reporting mechanisms had succeeded in keeping crucial development challenges on the global agenda. Finally, quipping that the summit had been "three or four long days of exceptionally boring meetings" (Arsenault, 2010), singer Bob Geldof also emphasised that it had succeeded in taking stock of the progress of the MDGs up to that point and had outlined further steps for advancing the causes represented within them.

Global conferences as discursive rituals

Reflecting on global conferences, Long (2004: 25) has argued that such mega-events have become part of the process of "knowledge production", "dissemination" and "transformation" in global politics, multilateral organisations and constructivist analysis of international relations (see also Bøås and McNeill, 2004). Global conferences are thus part of the discursive development repertoire that includes meetings and consultancy missions (Bøås and McNeill, 2004; Mosse, 2005), the outputs of these undertakings such as consultancy reports or evaluations (Harper, 1998; Mosse and Lewis, 2005), as well as the work- and lifestyles and *habitus* of international development personnel (Mosse, 2011; Fechter and Hindman, 2011). Chabbott's (1998: 214) observations from the 1990 World Conference on Education for All (EFA), although stemming from the pre-digital era, can still be considered a blueprint for understanding global summits on international development:

> [EFA] in some ways mimicked a recipe already established in other sectors by earlier world conferences. EFA organizers used the [UN] Declaration of Universal Human Rights and other existing declarations as a basis for drafting a declaration and plan of actions couched in terms of human rights so often repeated that no nation-state could resist the invitation to accept by acclamation. The recipe provided for a series of follow-up meetings and conferences to reiterate goals, publicize progress – or lack of it – thus applying normative pressure to nation states and organizations.

Unsurprising in light of these observed dynamics, the UN officially regards global conferences as important tools to 'shape our global future' (United Nations, 1998; see also Schechter, 2001). Little's (1995: 286) conclusion from ethnographic research at the 1992 Earth Summit captures this centrality when he characterises them as "an increasingly important part of the modern world [which] have diverse meanings and impacts". At the same time, Little (ibid.) also points to their role "as forums for the creation of a new political cosmology and the mystification of crude power politics". Both aspects are elaborated on further by Lechner and Boli (2005). Echoing Rothenbuhler's (1998: 27) definition of rituals as "the voluntary performance of appropriately patterned behavior to symbolically effect or participate in the serious life", as well as Bauman's (1989: 262) conceptualisation of performance as "an aesthetically marked and heightened mode of communication, framed in a special way and put on display to an audience", Lechner and Boli (2005: 102) describe global conferences as

> a secular ritual by periodically focusing world attention on selected topics through events in a particular format that lead to the affirmation and promulgation of knowledge and principles guiding global action. As part of a larger whole, they have helped to make culture that transcends regional traditions. Enshrining certain ideas and symbols as 'totems' of world society, they have contributed to defining a global reality.

The genealogy of the MDGs is a telling vignette illustrating the ritual power of global conferences. Jan Vandemoortele (2007: 23), a long-time staff member of the United Nations Development Programme (UNDP) and one of their key intellectual architects, has argued that "the MDGs were not developed from scratch; they resulted from an incremental, and sometimes piecemeal, process of generating a political consensus on the major elements of the development agenda – mostly through a series of world summits and international conferences in the 1990s". Based on expert interviews with senior international bureaucrats, Hulme and Fukuda-Parr (2009), however, paint an entirely different picture, one that focuses on global conferences' performative role. Instead of forging a negotiated political consensus, Hulme and Fukuda-Parr (2009: 16) outline a process driven by a few senior policymakers who dominated the agenda-setting process:

> The process to develop the 'final' MDG list [...] was undertaken by an ad hoc group, headed by the UN Secretariat's Michael Doyle. [...] Key figures in this ad hoc group were not the leaders of the official UN statistical world, whose efforts could be lauded and then set aside. Instead, they were the World Bank's Eric Swanson, OECD-DAC's Brian Hammond, and UNDP's Jan Vandemoortele. All had worked together on the IDG monitoring document, *2000: A Better World For All,* published in June 2000. As Swanson reflected, this group had developed a sense of solidarity and camaraderie, having previously put together a successful public communication document – glossy and with eye-catching diagrams – that was a departure from the standard, bureaucratic reports they had all produced for many years.

These insights into the real world of policymaking are an important reminder that an analytic focus on the content of global conferences would risk obfuscating their real function, namely, to manufacture consent through ritualistic enactment. Moreover, although most of those present remain excluded from actual policymaking, they nonetheless perform important roles. Little (1995: 286) observed this during the Earth Summit:

> By writing only about the event as conceived of and presented by the United Nations, observers are implicitly accepting the official version that this is "the event" worthy of scrutiny, while the numerous other (non)events should best be ignored or forgotten. Such a limited treatment of the process also tends to highlight the 'show' or performative side of the process.

Taking such insights into consideration in relation to social media coverage of current global conferences, we must ask whether social media perform similar affirmative, discourse-reinforcing roles or, either alternatively or concurrently, create virtual spaces of agency in which these discourses can be scrutinised. Data generated by social media in the context of one of the major development conferences of the recent past can help us answer this question.

Social media content as data

Blogs are chronologically arranged posts to web pages, usually focusing on a single subject, and updated by an individual or organisation. Twitter Inc. is an online service provider for microblogging. Similar to blogging in that it allows an individual ('tweeter') to share thoughts or interesting news stories, it is called 'microblogging' because it limits users to 140 characters per message. Individuals with a Twitter account can create messages called 'tweets'. When a tweet is sent, it reaches the sender's 'followers', meaning anyone who has agreed to receive the sender's tweets by way of a free subscription to the sender's account. A network of followers, therefore, could be as small as a few friends or as large as the more than 11 million followers receiving pop music star Lady Gaga's tweets (Twitaholic, 2011). In June 2011, Twitter reported that its users were sending 200 million tweets per day (Twitter, 2011). In addition to sending personal status updates, Twitter also allows users to assign labels to particular content called 'hashtags', as well as to 'retweet' messages sent by others. Hashtags allow Twitter users to label the subject of their message by adding the # symbol to a specific keyword of their choosing, such as #MDG. 'Retweeting' is similar to forwarding an e-mail; it gives users the ability to retransmit information, ideas or breaking news to their followers. Retweeting is a tool often used to generate social action and to disseminate information to a network of individuals quickly (see Boyd, Golder and Lotan, 2010). This connectivity of individuals by linking networks has the ability to spread information within minutes or even seconds, a phenomenon that lies at the heart of global social networking.

In order to capture social media coverage of the MDG Summit, we began the content search in a convenient sample of 24 blogs that we considered frequent producers of commentary on global development issues. As most blogs have lists of hyperlinks to other 'favourite' blogs, 10 new blogs were added to this list during the process, thus enlarging our sample to 34 blogs. We then followed snowballing sampling strategy for blog research, mindful that this approach may not guarantee a representative sample (Li and Walejko, 2008). However, snowballing in social media analysis, "avoids the problems associated with methods that rely on the categorization of groups", according to Browne (2005: 49). Consistent with post-positivist approaches to ensuring empirical validity – see, for example, Creswell and Miller (2000: 124) – we also circulated our complete list of blogs covered among fellow bloggers and received affirmative feedback with respect to its scope. We then ran basic keyword searches for entries posted in each blog between 15 July and 15 November 2010. Search terms included 'Millennium Summit', 'MDG Summit', 'Millennium Development Summit', 'MDG' and 'UN Summit NEAR MDG' (the latter being a Boolean search term). After collecting all relevant entries, we used the qualitative analysis software NVivo to create discursive nodes in order to capture the context in which specific terms were used frequently. The results are outlined and visualised further below.

We approached the Twitter component by identifying appropriate search engines for harvesting archived tweets. This initial search rendered only one suitable search engine (www.topsy.com) because it was able to move beyond real-time analysis, allowing for a collection of messages sent several months prior. Search engines such as www.google.com had recently discontinued their Twitter search capabilities for public users, while subscription software such as www. discovertext.com only permits collection as far back as 30 days. Inquiries with the

Library of Congress (LoC) in Washington, D.C., helped clarify that these restrictions were likely owing to Twitter Inc.'s decision to donate its tweets archive to LoC. LoC began indexing the data in 2011 and has recently begun to release some of the data for public use, but not timely enough for us to use these data as the basis for this study. We therefore relied on data provided by www.topsy.com. We performed searches using the hashtag #MDG for each hour of the three days during which the summit took place, starting at 9 a.m. on 20 September 2010 and concluding at 8 p.m. on 22 September 2010, generating a total of 3,007 hits: 1,162 on the first day, 843 on the second and 1,002 on the third.

Some limitations affecting the tweet research component could not be avoided. For the hours between 1 p.m. and 2 p.m., 2 p.m. to 3 p.m., and 5 p.m. to 6 p.m. EST on each of the three days, the searches on www.topsy.com yielded a total of 10 pages each. Since hour windows are the shortest possible time frame and the maximum number of pages that can be accessed for each search was 10, there was no method of verification accessible to us that could prove whether the search would have yielded more hits than those that could be viewed on the 10 pages generated by the software. However, since our complete Twitter dataset consists of tweets collected during 59 separate hours, we are confident that the effect of potential imprecision during nine of these 59 slots on our overall sample is small.

Results

Blogging analysis

Our review of 34 blogs rendered a total of 108 relevant blog entries written by a total of 29 bloggers: 16 are men, 13 are women and 4 are collaborative entries. One blog lists no author, which is not uncommon in the development blogosphere. The number of relevant entries per blog ranges from 1 to 14. Bloggers with established ties to the global development industry dominate the upper half of the frequency ranking. Table 11.1 provides an overview of this distribution and the blogs most relevant to the MDG Summit.

Mark Leon Goldberg and Alanna Shaikh are affiliated with the independent UN news website, UN Dispatch. Duncan Green was the Head of Research for Oxfam International. Tom Paulson is a radio host at Seattle's KPLU. Lawrence Haddad is the Director of the Institute of Development Studies at the University of Sussex. Laura Freschi either blogged independently or together with William Easterly out of the Development Research Institute at New York University. Linda Raftree works for PLAN USA.[2]

We conducted a content analysis in NVivo in order to identify salient themes and issues. The analysis was based on both manual and computer coding. Keywords such as 'aid', 'future', 'gender', 'measurability' and 'South' were first coded as simple nodes, based on keyword searches, and later linked to other simple nodes, thus creating so-called tree nodes, which act as umbrella terms or categories. Figure 11.1 depicts the six tree nodes ('measurability', 'gender', 'government', 'MDGs', 'aid' and 'attitude'). Textual proximity in the dataset defined

Table 11.1 Overview of the most relevant blogs (number of entries relevant to the 2010 MDG Summit)

Blogger	No. of entries	Collaborative entries	URL
Mark Leon Goldberg	14		www.undispatch.com
Tom Paulson	13		http://humanosphere.kplu.org
Duncan Green	10	2, with Matt Davies and Sam Bickersteth	www.oxfamblogs.org
Lawrence Haddad	7	1, with Andy Sumner	www.developmenthorizons.com
Alanna Shaikh	7		www.unidispatch.com; http://endtheneglect.org; http://bloodandmilk.org
Linda Raftree	7	1, with William Easterly	http://lindaraftree.wordpress.com
Laura Freschi	5		http://aidwatchers.org

the parenting relationship in which each tree node is a parent to keywords with which it is closely associated. Three additional keywords ('future', 'Africa' and 'Sachs') also appeared frequently and were therefore listed as well, but they stood in no clear association with other nodes. They were thus categorised separately, bearing the potential of becoming tree nodes in their own right at a deeper level of analysis.

'Aid' was frequently linked to calls for increased 'donor' attention (51 times) or 'funding' (43), the fulfilment of the promise for 'change' (72) on US President Obama's part (63), to the 'UK' (46), as well as to former US President William J. Clinton's (37) and philanthropist Bill Gates's efforts (42) to raise awareness and increase donations toward the MDGs. As depicted in Figure 11.1, the tree node 'attitude' serves as a category label that acts as a tree node linked to simple nodes through word searches performed by proxy. Bloggers' 'attitude' was dominated by a general sense that the MDGs were far from being fulfilled in addition to calls for a change in international strategy through increased 'accountability' (58) and 'transparency' (37). The MDGs are considered a 'promise' (32) that has 'failed' (19) to be realised, therefore necessitating reinvigorated 'commitment' (24). The keyword 'future' appeared 28 times in the dataset and also acts as a tree node for terms that reflect a concern for the direction in which donors, the private sector, and American and British governments will be taking their efforts toward meeting the MDGs. 'Gender' occurred 28 times and could be linked to two other frequently used terms, namely, 'children' (108) and 'women' (89). The dominant focus on women and children was highlighted in contrast to the node 'men', which only occurred five times in the dataset.

The MDGs themselves were linked closely to 'poverty' (456), 'health' (211), 'education' (108), 'hunger' (43) and 'water' (25). With regard to health, the simple nodes under this umbrella were 'AIDS' (18), 'HIV' (16) and 'malaria'

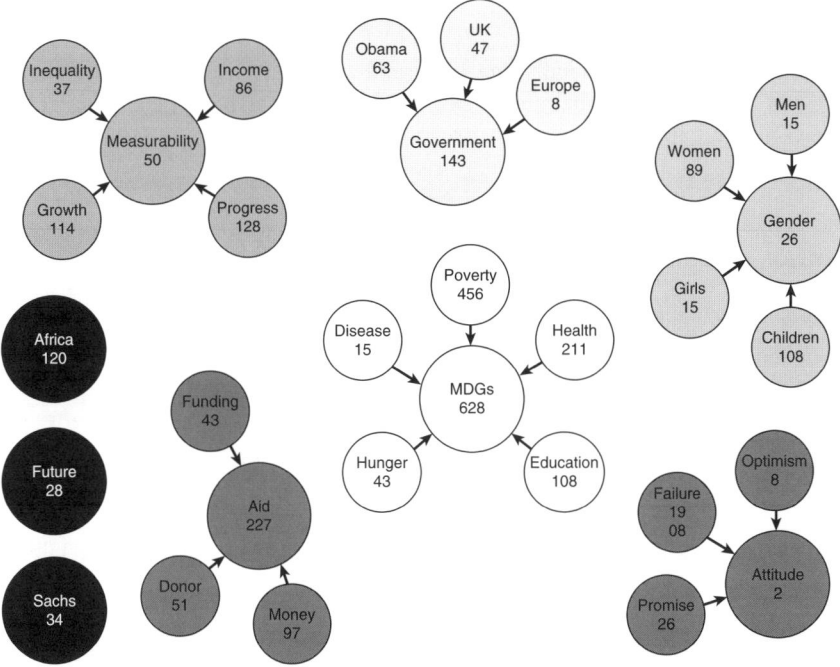

Figure 11.1 Tree nodes of blog content on the 2010 MDG Summit (108 blog entries).

(16), indicating the diseases that have received the greatest amount of political attention and resources during the past decade despite the fact that other causes of ill health are not only more lethal on a global scale, but also can be more effectively treated (see Esser, 2009). Another tree node representing a key issue in relevant blog entries was 'measurability' (50), associated most commonly with 'progress' (128), 'growth' (114) and 'income' (86). Bloggers also mentioned measurability in the context of 'impact' (57), 'outcomes' (35) and 'results' (29). Finally, the geographic foci that emerged clearly linked the MDGs to locations in the Global 'South' (20). However, 'Africa' as a stand-alone term occurred 120 times in the dataset, eclipsing all other developing regions. Indeed, specific names of African countries such as 'Ethiopia' (18), 'Tanzania' (11), 'Ghana' (10) and 'Congo' (4) were each associated more often with the summit than references to the entire Latin American region.

Tweet analysis

Our content analysis of the 3,007 tweets indicated that key issues raised in the tweets related to education, children, maternal health, world leaders, the reduction of Canada's development aid, speeches by the Prime Ministers of the UK and

Australia, the World Bank, the G20, hunger, TEDxChange, former US President Clinton, China, Bolivian President Evo Morales, print media websites (in particular, the UK newspapers *The Guardian* and *Financial Times*), and links to UN strategy reports as well to individual blogs and video clips. Judging by the Twitter account name, the overwhelming majority of tweeters active in the context of the MDG Summit appeared to be either organisations' communication units or individuals directly affiliated with such organisations. These prominently included accounts registered by international NGOs, for instance @AmnestyOnline, @Oxfam or @savethechildren. The most active individual tweeter – Adrian Lovett at Save the Children – sent 22 tweets during the three-day event. The two second-most active non-organisational accounts dropped off significantly compared to Lovett's activity: UNDP Administrator Helen Clark and Michael Shapcott, a Canadian academic, each sent four related messages. Table 11.2 provides an overview of the most active non-organisational Twitter accounts relating to the 2010 MDG Summit.

Although some of the bloggers are also mentioned in the tweets, traditional media as featured more prominently reference points, including, for example, Jeffrey Sachs's op-ed in the *Financial Times* blog (Sachs, 2010). Given the 140-character limit, quotations by government representatives and prominent public

Table 11.2 Top non-organisational Twitter messages during the 2010 MDG Summit

---

Adrianlovett (22)

---

http://t.co/PUhaiH5http://youtu.be/5H2Nlq49V2cNthabiseng TshabalalaMy #mdg blog 1: just off plane http://bit.ly/cMzKRzEx UK PM Gordon Brown says he is 'angry but inspired' about children out of schoolMe and Nthabiseng Tshabalala at the #1goal event today http://twitpic.com/2qe9laDutch aid minister says the top 3 answers to education crisis are "teachers, teachers, teachers"RT @benhewittindia: India to be "shining example" on MDGs - but not on mothers and children: http://toi.in/c3i9bqAussie ex-PM Kevin rudd says education is critical to reducing child mortality4 hrs to our big moment in Grand Central. Will we reach 3m people?1goal event underway. World bank promising to shift $750m into schools. It's a start...

VIDEO "We're going to do our bit" UK minister tells Sian http://t.co/c3oSfUPTeam Save the Children cooking up a little idea for tomorrow when leaders agree their child health strategy - watch this spaceMe and Claire Danes: could we get any closer? http://twitpic.com/2qglr8

Save the Children is making its own commitment to saving children's lives. We will invest $2bn - with your helpThe big strategy on health is out. Big commitments and this only happened because millions called for action. Now for deliveryVIDEO Now this is good. Who is that masked man delivering a tasty message to world leaders? http://bit.ly/d4mRpEThank you @mummytips for helping us make our lovely energy bars http://twitpic.com/2qx49hWatch UN strategy launch in 1hr from now - http://bit.ly/9BSbBJ (choose channel 4). This wouldn't be happening without you!Here's the UN announcement of the Global Strategy for Women just out http://bit.ly/b4aJg6VIDEO See my attempts to hand out energy bars at UN Summit. Msg to leaders: RUN DON'T WALK http://bit.ly/aEc7kwWen, Meles and now Stoltenberg speaking at UN mother and child health event.

---

helenclark-undp (4)

I'm @ the #MDGSummit, with the Global Leaders Council for Reproductive Health. Did you know that 1 #MDG concerns maternal health?

I'm @ the #MDGSummit making opening remarks at the Spanish #MDG Achievement Fund #SocialJustice.Where there is strong leadership, an absence of conflict, sufficient capacity & funding for development, there will be #MDG progress

Just discussed #MDG progress in Latin America with President of Bolivia Evo Morales

Michael-shapcott (4)

OECD reports Canada well below both UN target and int'l avg on official development assistance http://bit.ly/baoKV3Does Canada deserve a seat at UN Security Council, considering our shrinking international development profile? http://bit.ly/bzyppaShocking #MDG facts on Canada: Aid spending down, UK spends 50% more per person than Cda, military gets 4x more http://bit.ly/aoSaTsRT [2] @Oxfam: Day 1@ #MDG #UNSummit: Millennium Development Goals: Will world leaders stand up, or hit snooze button?

Asteris (3)

RT @guardiannews UN: Corporate lobbying is blocking food reforms http://bit.ly/chjo2N #MDGRT @texasinafrica What's missing in this week's #MDG conversations http://bit.ly/aSRYqt "western thinking abt development is elite-driven"RT @AmnestyOnline #MDG Summit: World leaders fail to uphold rights of the poorest http://bit.ly/dzUoAt Summits aren't enough, @UN

Cfpdx (3)

@QueenRania: "We have 1 goal --to give childen [sic] w/ no voice & no hope the chance to realize their 1 goal – to go to school." #saveMDG #mdg

Melinda Gates: Recession pressured global efforts | Beyond Binary - CNET News #TED xChange #MDG http://post.ly/yoi7From Clinton Global Initiative to the U.N. Summit, philanthropy goes into overdrive this week - #CGI2010 #MDG... http://ff.im/qRoj2

Jeffdsachs (3)

RT @EndOfPoverty: Did you know you can watch the #MDG Summit live via webcast? http://bit.ly/bjdKsc

RT @anujkp: #MDG Jeffrey Sachs' blog on FT re: #Bhutan PM's address in UN GA. http://bit.ly/bthi7N

FT blog: China's performance at the UN summit is extraordinary... #MDGSummit #UNweekDML #MDG http://bit.ly/dwF7gl

Milieunet (3)

UNEP Report: Green Economy can Reduce Poverty and Help Meet Millennium Development Goals http://bit.ly/9rQ6MI #MDG

Stand Up Against Poverty 2010 http://bit.ly/bSD8lMTEDxChange 2010: Melinda French Gates about the Millennium Development Goals http://bit.ly/dlpt2K

mjw-alexander (3)

Lots of excitement at France's announcement at the #mdg summit that they will focus on a financial transaction tax for the G20First day of #mdg summit and @actionaid ceo is speaking about women and hunger. Lets hope world leaders listenGreat @guardian blog following the #mdg summit live at http://tinyurl.com/2cbnrvk

---

[1] Number in brackets denotes total count of tweets sent during the event by this Twitter user

[2] RT = retweeted by this Twitter user

figures were (re)tweeted frequently, for instance "Dutch aid minister says the top three answers to education crisis are 'teachers, teachers, teachers'" (@adrianlovett) or "@QueenRania: We have 1 goal – to give children [sic] w/ no voice & no hope the chance to realize their 1 goal – to go to school" (RT by @cfpdx). Such informational or motivational tweets were complemented – although to a lesser extent – by what one might call 'vanity tweets', which mainly cite the names of government officials or other public figures, arguably as a signal that the tweeter considers himself or herself to be part of the epistemic community of international development. The latter observation also underlines the main difference between the results of our blog analysis and our subsequent analysis of tweets; Twitter is used almost entirely as a broadcasting tool. Overall, tweets were used primarily by members of the epistemic community to share third party content rather than to establish an online presence or a distinctive digital identity for individuals or organisations.

Discussion

Social media as 'ideas space', as Oxfam blogger Duncan Green has called the blogosphere (2011), had rather little to add to traditional notions of epistemic communities in the context of the 2010 MDG Summit. Social media involvement during the summit mainly came as event updates, not as a catalyst of changes with respect to how the event was portrayed, discussed or criticised. It also seems doubtful that social media contributed in ways indicated by earlier research on epistemic communities and their gatherings. Networking or self-marketing (Weller, Dröge and Puschmann, 2011), the normalisation of new terms (Reinhardt et al., 2009) and impact of online information flows on 'offline' physical professional spaces (Ebner and Reinhardt 2009) appear inapplicable to the context of global conferences. With reference to Rothenbuhler's (1998) ritual theory framework, we therefore argue that traditional, pre-digital conference rituals are still very much alive in the digital age. Three important aspects of this claim are highlighted in the following.

Rituals and physicality

Even though virtual space is potentially without borders, the analysis of blogs and Twitter suggests that there is still a strong physical community element that played a role during the summit. Many of the bloggers and some of the institutional Twitter users were located in New York City during the event and arranged 'meet-ups'/'tweet-ups'. For instance, in her blog entry from 18 September 2010, New York University Professor Karen Grepin mentions an event organised in New York City on 21 September 2010 defined as a 'Meet-up of tweeters working on international development, ICT4Development and related areas who are in NYC on 21 September' (Grepin, 2010). The link also provides a list of all attending tweeters. While social media thus accompanied the actual event in New York City, the MDG Summit remained a de facto 'invited space', which potentially also explains why there were only a few contributions from outside the 'Northern' development community. This underscores how powerful the ritual space of world conferences still is and that, in this regard, little has changed since the Earth Summit 20 years ago.

Rituals and discourses

The Twitter content analysed in this study suggests that the theme of the summit was widely considered incontestable,[3] which may explain why few individuals not affiliated with development organisations tweeted on the event. Still, while one might be tempted to dismiss the summit on this basis, this stance would miss an important point highlighted by Rothenbuhler (1998: 15):

> Many critics of ritual make the mistake of expecting rites and ceremonies to be indicative. Judged that way, many of them are obviously false – they do not accurately describe the world in which they occur. But viewed as time-outs from the usual constraints of practical affairs, they are occasions for imaging how things could be or evaluating how they ought to be.

The summit and the MDGs more generally, therefore, lend themselves to discursive analysis. Global performances such as summits exercise a particular 'disciplinary power', which creates and reinforces boundaries of international relations practices that are delineated linguistically in order to privilege certain interpretations over others (George, 1994; Teivainen, 2007). Such performances are "about placing individual subjects in regimented/regulated systems and locales" (Debrix, 2003: 16). The MDG Summit drew affluent and mobile visitors to the city and 'made' them participate in side events and share information on presentations by public figures with an interest in international development. It did so not through coercion but by creating opportunities for reliving learned practices (Lang, 2003). "Ritualized agents do not see themselves as projecting schemes", as Bell (1992: 206) reminds us, "they see themselves only acting in a socially instinctive response to how things are". Five years before the official MDG deadline, the summit did not aim to introduce new ideas or terms that needed to be discussed in the epistemic community or create a marketplace for individual experts, organisations or academics to present 'new' work. Anchored in traditions, the summit also did not present an opportunity that encouraged contestation or support.

Rituals and practice

Performing the MDG Summit to strengthen the MDGs as a "vehicle that presently dominates global discussions about poverty eradication" (Hulme and Fukuda-Parr, 2009: 30) appeared to be successful, at least according to official statements by international politicians and diplomats. As our Twitter analysis shows, *TedX* events were one of the most noted forms of communication outside the official performance, but these events were essentially performed within the accepted conventions of critical engagement (more broadly, they have been criticised for perpetuating an "apolitical, techno-optimist" culture of development – see Foremski, 2012). Even critical blog posts appear at best to have been virtual extensions of what Rothenbuhler (1998: 45) has described as "ritually structured conflict" in "anti-institutional events": "Sit-ins, protest marches, burning effigies, verbal threats, chanting and so on, are all performances patterned to symbolically effect the serious life".

Conclusion

Global conferences as central components of contemporary global governance are ritualised spaces in which global culture is reproduced by virtue of individual as well as institutional performances. Our research on site-specific processes in the digital age confirms that emerging international development policies continue being framed 'offline', with very limited input provided through social media. For those concerned about a democratic deficit in international policymaking (e.g. Thörn, 2007), our findings are therefore sobering. The hope that social media might make a significant contribution toward global democratic participation in agenda setting (Dahl, 1989; Held, 1995) was not fulfilled by social media content generated during the MDG Summit. While the epistemic community framing international development policies today is larger, and communication about it is faster and in theory also more open, this process continues to be shaped by what Mosse (2005: 22) has termed "professionalist" dynamics. In his embedded research in development organisations, he detected "a professional *habitus* [which] automatically transferred the actuality of events into the preconceived categories of legitimate meaning and ideal process: 'decisions taken democratically by the committees', relationships denuded of power/interest, the power free flow of information, or the absence of pressure on staff to meet targets". While the use of social media in development projects may indeed catalyse positive change in specific settings – see Schimmelpfennig (2011) – global dynamics of how international development is conceived and defined do not seem to be affected by social media to any significant degree. In essence, then, although members of this epistemic community actively take part in the ontological dynamic, the community itself remains as exclusive as ever. Or, in blogger Laura Seay's tweeted words: "So ends a day of listening to rich people talk about ways to help poor people they'd never dream of letting in the door."

Notes

1 This chapter is an elaboration of the article "Social Media and Global Development Rituals: A Content Analysis of Blogs and Tweets on the 2010 MDG Summit", *Third World Quarterly*, vol. 34, no. 3 (2013). We thank the editors of this volume for their valuable feedback and guidance. We also gratefully acknowledge advice on current developments in Twitter research offered by Melissa Hire at the US Library of Congress and Tom Emerson at topsy.com. The School of International Service's Dean's Office offered generous financial support. Cora Lacatus and Eric Eggleston provided excellent research assistance, and Emily Edgecombe and Jed Byers helped copyedit the manuscript. All remaining errors are our own.

2 Blogger Laura Seay (http://texasinafrica.blogspot.com) also stood out because she was frequently referred to in other blogs, mainly because her blog lists many entries related to the summit, something that implicitly highlights the importance of 'curating' a virtual archive in the blogosphere.

3 A recent UN Foundation report notes that 89% of Americans surveyed were not familiar with the MDGs; however, when provided with a brief explanation of each, 87% of those surveyed said they believe the United States should be very or somewhat involved in trying to achieve the MDGs. These figures are, in part, a reflection of the level to which those surveyed could recall hearing about international events and associating humanitarian involvement with the UN, according to the researchers. The survey by WorldPublicOpinion.org showed a smaller but significant number of Americans (75%) is willing to pay the estimated individual cost of fully funding the goals (see United Nations Foundation, 'United Nations approval rating rises to 60% in new opinion poll', 2010, available at: http://www.unfoundation.org/news-and-media/press-releases/2010/united-nations-approval-rating-rises-to-60-percent.html [accessed 21 June 2012]; World Public Opinion. org, 'Publics in developed countries ready to contribute funds necessary to cut hunger in half by 2015', 2008, available at: http://www.worldpublicopinion.org/pipa/articles/bt developmentaidra/554.php?lb=btda&pnt=554&nid=&id [accessed 22 June 2012]).

References

Abdulla, R. (2010) "Queen Rania Speaks at the MDG Summit in New York". Available at: http://www.queenrania.jo/media/speeches/queen-rania-speaks-mdg-summit-new-york (accessed 21 September 2012).

Aday, S., H. Farrell, M. Lynch, J. Sides, J. Kelly, and E. Zuckerman (2010) *Blogs and Bullets. New Media in Contentious Politics*. Washington, DC: United States Institute of Peace.

Arsenault, K. (2010) "September 2010 MDG Summit: 13 Minutes You Just can't Miss". *One* [blog], 18 November. Available at: http://one.org/blog/category/september-2010-mdg-summit/?aux=36 (accessed 21 September 2012).

Bauman, R. (1989) "Performance". In E. Barnouw (ed.), *International Encyclopedia of Communications*, vol. 3. New York: Oxford University Press, pp. 262–266.

Bell, C. (1992) *Ritual Theory, Ritual Practice.* Oxford: Oxford University Press.

Bøås, M., and D. McNeill (eds.) (2004) *Global Institutions and Development Framing the World?*. London: Routledge.

Boyd, D., S. Golder, and G. Lotan (2010) "Tweet, tweet, retweet: Conversational aspects of retweeting on Twitter", paper presented to the *43rd Hawai'i International Conference on System Sciences (HICSS-43),* Kauai, 5–8 January, available at: http://www.danah. org/papers/TweetTweetRetweet.pdf (accessed 6 February 2013).

Breuer A. (2012) *The Role of Social Media in Mobilizing Political Protest: Evidence from the Tunisian Revolution*. Bonn: German Development Institute.

Browne, K. (2005) "Snowball sampling: Using social networks to research non-heterosexual women". *International Journal of Social Research Methodology*, 8(1): 47–60.

Chabbott, C. (1998) "Constructing educational consensus: International development professionals and the world conference on education for all". *International Journal of Educational Development*, 18(3): 207–218.

Creswell J., and D. Miller (2000) "Determining validity in qualitative inquiry". *Theory into Practice* 39(3): 124–130.

McKenzie, D., and B. Özler (2011) "The Impact of Economics Blogs". *Development Impact* [blog], 5 August. Available at: http://blogs.worldbank.org/impactevaluations/node/621 (accessed 21 June 2012).

Dahl, R. (1989) *Democracy and Its Critics*. New Haven: Yale University Press.

Debrix, F. (2003) "Language, nonfoundationalism, international relations". In F. Debrix (ed.), *Language, Agency, and Politics in a Constructed World*. London: M. E. Sharpe, pp. 3–25.

DfID (2010) "Speech by Deputy Prime Minister Nick Clegg at the United Nations Millennium Development Goals Summit". Available at: http://www.dfid.gov.uk/Media-Room/News-Stories/2010/Deputy-Prime-Minister-Nick-Cleggs-speech-to-the-UN-General-Assembly/ (accessed 21 September 2012).

Esser, D. E. (2009) "More money, less cure: why global health assistance needs restructuring". *Ethics and International Affairs*, 23(3): 225–234.

Etling, B., J. Kelly, R. Faris, and J. Palfrey (2010) "Mapping the arabic blogosphere: Politics and dissent online". *New Media and Society*, 12(8): 1225–1243.

Farrell, H. and D. Drezner (2008) "The power and politics of blogs". *Public Choice*, 134(1–2): 15–30.

Fechter, A. and H. Hindman (2011) *Inside the Everyday Lives of Development Workers: The Challenges and Futures of Aidland*. Sterling: Kumarian Press.

Foremski, T. (2012) "The 'Golden Arches' of TED and the rise of the techno-humanists". *ZDNet* [blog], available at http://www.zdnet.com/the-golden-arches-of-ted-and-the-rise-of-the-techno-humanists-7000002076/ (accessed 21 September 2012).

George, J. (1994) *Discourses of Global Politics: A Critical (Re)Introduction to International Relations*. Boulder, CO: Lynne Rienner.

Green, D. (2011) "Is the Blogging Bubble about to Burst?". *From Poverty to Power* [blog], 15 June. Available at: http://www.oxfamblogs.org/fp2p/?p=5790 (accessed 21 September 2012).

Grepin, K. (2010) "One More Reason Why Living in New York City is Amazing". *Karen Grepin's Global Health Blog [blog]*, 18 September. Available at: http://karengrepin.com/2010/09/one-more-reason-why-living-in-new-york.html (accessed 21 September 2012).

Guest, P. (2010) "MDG Interview: Jeffrey Sachs". *This is Africa* [blog], 22 September. Available at: http://web.thisisafricaonline.com/2010/09/22/mdg-interview-jeffrey-sachs/ (accessed 21 September 2012).

Harper, R. (1998) *Inside the IMF: An Ethnography of Documents, Technology and Organisational Action*. London: Academic Press.

Held, D. (1995) *Democracy and the Global Order: From the Modern State to Cosmopolitan Governance*. Cambridge: Polity Press.

Howard, P. N., and M. R. Parks. (2012) "Social media and political change: Capacity, constraint, and consequence". *Journal of Communication*, 62(2): 359-362.

Hulme, D., and S. Fukuda-Parr (2009) "International Norm Dynamics and 'the End of Poverty': Understanding the Millennium Development Goals (MDGs)". BWPI Working Paper 96. Manchester: Brooks World Poverty Institute.

Lang, A. (2003) "Conflicting narratives, Conflicting moralities: The United Nations and the failure of humanitarian intervention". In F. Debrix (ed.), *Language, Agency, and Politics in a Constructed World*. London: M. E. Sharpe, pp. 171–195.

Lechner, F., and J. Boli (2005) "Constructing world culture". In F. Lechner and J. Boli (eds.), *World Culture: Origins and Consequences*. Oxford: Blackwell, pp. 81–108.

Li, D., and G. Walejko (2008) "Splogs and abandoned blogs: The perils of sampling bloggers and their blogs". *Information, Communication and Society,* 11(2): 279–296.

Little, P. (1995) "Ritual, power and ethnography at the Rio Earth Summit". *Critique of Anthropology*, 15(3): 265–288.

Long, N. (2004) "Contesting policy ideas from below". In M. Bøås, and D. McNeill (eds.), *Global Institutions and Development Framing the World?*. London: Routledge, pp. 24–40.

Maratea, R. (2008) "The e-rise and fall of social problems: The blogosphere as a public arena". *Social Problems*, 55(1): 139–160.

Mosse, D. (2005) *Cultivating Development: An Ethnography of Aid Policy and Practice.* London: Pluto Press.

Mosse, D. (2011) "Introduction: The anthropology of expertise and professionals in international development". In D. Mosse (ed.), *Adventures in Aidland: The Anthropology of Professional International Development.* Oxford: Berghahn Books, pp. 1–31.

Mosse, D., and D. Lewis (2005) *The Aid Effect: Giving and Governing in International Development.* London: Pluto Press.

Paulson, T. (2010) "Melinda Gates Impatiently Optimistic at the UN Anti-Poverty Summit". *Humanosphere* [blog], 24 September, Available at: http://humanosphere.kplu. org/2010/09/melinda-gates-impatiently-optimistic-at-the-un-anti-poverty-summit/ (accessed 24 June 2012).

Reinhardt, W., Ebner, E., Beham, G. and Costa, C. (2009) "How people are using Twitter during conferences". In: V. Hornung-Prähauser & M. Luckmann (eds.), Creativity and Innovation Competencies on the Web, Proceeding of 5th EduMedia Conference. Salzburg: Salzburg Research, pp. 145–156.

Rothenbuhler, E. (1998) *Ritual Communication: From Everyday Conversation to Mediated Ceremony.* London: Sage.

Sachs, J. D. (2010"China's Performance at the UN Summit is Extraordinary". Beyondbricks [blog], 22 September. Available at: http://blogs.ft.com/beyond-brics/2010/09/22/jeffrey-sachs-extraordinary-china/#axzz1Re6UbSGe (accessed 24 June 2012).

Schechter, M. (2001) United Nations-Sponsored World Conferences: Focus on Impact and Follow-up. Tokyo: UNU Press.

Schimmelpfennig, S. (2011) "Tracking the World Vision/NFL shirt donation controversy". *Good Intentions Are Not Enough* [blog], 12 February. Available at: http://goodintents. org/aid-debates/world-vision-nfl-controversy (accessed 24 June 2012).

Shirky, C. (2011) "The political power of social media technology, the public sphere, and political change". *Foreign Affairs*, 90(1): 28–42.

Teivainen, T. (2007) "The political and its absence in the World Social Forum: implications for democracy". *Development Dialogue*, 49: 69–79.

Thörn, H. (2007) "Global civil society and de-/democratisation: AIDS politics, anti-apartheid and the World Social Forum". *Development Dialogue*, 49: 159–169.

Twitaholic (2011) "Top 100 Twitterholics based on Number of Followers". Available at: http://twitaholic.com/ (accessed 24 June 2012).

Twitter (2011) "200 Million Tweets Per Day". *Twitter Blog* [blog], 30 June. Available at: http://blog.twitter.com/2011/06/200-million-tweets-per-day.html (accessed 24 June 2012).

United Nations (1998) *United Nations Global Conferences: What Have They Accomplished?*. New York: UN Department of Public Information.

United Nations (2010a) "Programme". Available at: http://www.un.org/en/mdg/ summit2010/programme.shtml (accessed 24 June 2012).

United Nations (2010b) "High-Level Plenary Meeting on the Millennium Development Goals: A Compilation of Partnership Events and Action Commitments". Available at: http://www.un.org/en/mdg/summit2010/pdf/HLPM%202010_CRP_ Side%20events. pdf (accessed 24 June 2012).

United Nations (2010c) "UN Summit Concludes with Adoption of Global Action Plan to Achieve Development Goals by 2015". Available at: http://www.un.org/ millennium-goals/pdf/Closing%20press%20release%20FINAL-FINAL%20Rev3.pdf (accessed 24 June 2012).

United Nations (2010d) "Keeping the Promise: United to Achieve the Millennium Development Goals. United Nations General Assembly", A/RES/65/1. Available at: http://www.un.org/en/mdg/summit2010/pdf/outcome_documentN1051260.pdf (accessed 24 June 2012).

United Nations (2010e) "Statement by H.E. Mr. Sergey Lavrov, Minister of Foreign Affairs of the Russian Federation". Available at: http://www.un.org/en/mdg/summit2010/debate/RU_en.pdf (accessed 24 June 2012).

United Nations (2010f) "Statement by H.E. Mr. S. M. Krishna Minister of External Affairs of India". Available at: http://www.un.org/en/mdg/summit2010/debate/IN_en.pdf (accessed 24 June 2012).

United Nations (2010g) "Towards the Attainment of the Millennium Development Goals: Statement by H. E. Wen Jiabao, Premier of the State Council of the People's Republic of China". Available at: http://www.un.org/en/mdg/summit2010/debate/CN_en.pdf (accessed 24 June 2012).

United Nations (2010h) "Statement by HE Marcia Helena Carvalho Lopes, Minister for Social Development and the Fight against AIDS". Available at: http://www.un.org/en/mdg/summit2010/debate/BR_en.pdf (accessed 24 June 2012).

US State Department (2010) "Remarks by President Barack Obama at the Millennium Development Goals Summit". Available at: http://usun.state.gov/briefing/state-ments/2010/ 147593.htm (accessed 24 June 2012).

Vandemoortele, J. (2007) "Can the MDGs foster a new partnership for pro-poor policies?". In J. Brinkerhoff, S. Smith, and H. Teegen (eds.), *NGOs and the Millennium Development Goals: Citizen Action to Reduce Poverty.* London: Palgrave Macmillan, pp. 23–48.

Weller, K., Dröge, E., and Puschmann, C. (2011) "Citation analysis in Twitter: approaches for defining and measuring information flows within tweets during scientific confer-ences". In: M. Rowe, M. Stankovic, A. Dadzie & M. Hardey (eds.), Making sense of microposts (#MSM2011). Crete: Workshop at Extended Semantic Web Conference (ESWC 2011), pp. 1–12.

12 FollowMe.IntDev.Com

International development in the blogosphere

Ryann Manning[1]

Blogs cover many of the same issues as both newspapers and journals, but with an eye toward what they mean for practitioners and policymakers. You'll get stories from the field, scathing critiques of the latest development fads, and heated debates on everything from microfinance to conflict minerals. The blogosphere is the one place where geography is no barrier to the conversation. Academics, journalists, donors, Washington think tank-ers, UN or NGO staff — they all bounce ideas around here.

Dave Algoso (2010)

It's a brilliant intellectual community, this little slice of the world that is our visible college... But I am greedy. I want more. I would like a larger college, an invisible college, of more people to talk to, pointing me to more interesting things. People whose views and opinions I can react to, and who will react to my reasoned and well-thought-out opinions, and to my unreasoned and off-the-cuff ones as well ... With the arrival of Web logging, I have been able to add such people to those I bump into – in a virtual sense – every week.

J. Bradford DeLong (2006: 8)

Recent years have seen an explosion of Internet-based communication and publishing forums, ranging from Facebook and Twitter to more traditional websites.[2] These have dramatically lowered the barriers to producing and distributing content, and people can now easily share information, experiences, perspectives, artwork, and almost anything else with their fellow Internet users around the world. Some decry this proliferation of online publishing as chaotic, overwhelming, rife with minutiae, and lacking in standards. Others claim it heralds the emergence of a more democratic, inclusive world of free speech, public debate, open exchange of knowledge, and global collaboration.

This chapter will consider these divergent claims with regard to one popular form of online publishing, the blog or weblog, and specifically those blogs concerned with issues of global poverty and international development.[3] Today's students and practitioners of development, and members of the public, can choose from a vast array of development-related blogs, ranging from travelogues and personal accounts by field workers to in-depth analysis by development experts.[4] But who are these bloggers, and who reads their blogs? What topics do they discuss? What are the norms and culture of the development blogosphere, and how are these established and enforced? Does the blogosphere contribute to more open sharing of knowledge and help democratise development discourse, or simply provide a new platform for already dominant perspectives, or some combination of both?

After briefly outlining my theoretical framework and methodology, I will provide an overview of the blogosphere and some preliminary ideas of what makes blogs different from other forms of publication and discussion, followed by a case study of one debate that exploded across many development blogs in April–May 2010. I analyse this conversation to better understand who is included and excluded from the blogosphere, what forms of expertise are valued, what status differentials are evident, and what norms and practices are at work. My goals are to shed light on the blogosphere as an alternative forum for discussion and debate, to contribute to theory on public spheres and knowledge communities, and to help the development community better understand what the emergence of a vibrant blogosphere means for them.

Theoretical framework

The blogosphere can be conceptualised as both a public sphere in which people gather to debate issues of public interest (Habermas, 1989, 1991; Barlow, 2008); and as a community of experts or 'invisible college' for creating and verifying knowledge and expertise (Knorr-Cetina, 1999, 2007; DeLong, 2006; Wagner, 2008; Fourcade, 2009).[5] These two conceptions are not incompatible, but they do point to a tension between open, inclusive exchange on the one hand, and expert-centric discourse on the other.

A public sphere may be physical or virtual (Barlow 2008; Calhoun, 2004), or it may be enacted through social interaction, therefore "exist[ing] *only between* people, and com[ing] into being when people speak public-spiritedly" (Eliasoph, 1998: 16). According to Habermas's original conception, a public sphere must be inclusive, must disregard status, and must "problematiz[e] … areas that until then had not been questioned" (1991: 36). Critics have challenged both the legitimacy and efficacy of real-world public spheres, arguing that numerous obstacles prevent people from participating fully and on equal footing, or limit the influence of public opinion on political action (Fraser, 2007).

Some argue that the public sphere has become, in our modern era, 'transnational' or 'global', which further complicates its legitimacy and efficacy (Fraser, 2007). When issues are global, who must take part for a conversation to be considered inclusive? What does it mean for inclusiveness and parity of participation when skills and resources for engaging in an online public sphere vary dramatically (DiMaggio *et al.*, 2004)? Does the digital nature of an Internet-based public sphere, including the blogosphere, serve to meaningfully expand participation, or does it merely reflect and reinforce various status differences and, as some have claimed, "empower transnational elites, who possess the material and symbolic prerequisites for global networking" (Fraser, 2007: 56)?

The blogosphere can also be conceived of as an invisible college (DeLong, 2006; Wagner, 2008): a community of people who have, or seek, knowledge. As described in the second of the epigraphs that open this chapter, this "invisible" community may be broader and more extensive than our immediate visible community (DeLong, 2006). The invisible college also reflects and embodies a particular type of culture – what Knorr-Cetina (1999, 2005) calls an "epistemic culture" – for creating knowledge, and for observing, verifying, or validating the knowledge that others create.[6] It is a network of ties among people with various types of expertise, reflecting relationships of collaboration and exchange (Wagner, 2008), and it may shape what experts define as important or legitimate, or what we believe qualifies someone as an expert (Fourcade, 2009).

Methods

This chapter draws on data from two phases of qualitative research: first, an inductive, exploratory study of the international development blogosphere and relevant literature, from which I derived research questions for the second phase, a case study of one unusually vibrant conversation involving numerous blogs.

Overview study

I began following development blogs in September 2010, and did so more systematically from February to May 2011 (Appendix A).[7] To identify a sample, I asked development professionals which blogs they read, if any, and I visited the blogs they suggested as well as blogs linked to in posts or on blogrolls.[8] I used blog rankings and search engines, such as Technorati and Wikio, to search for additional development-related blogs. I focused on influential and widely read blogs: those frequently cited or linked to by other bloggers, or mentioned by development professionals.[9] I also selected blogs that reflected the diversity of the international development blogosphere in terms of content and authorship, and I specifically sought blogs written by Africans.[10] I limited the sample to English language blogs and to those which discuss, often among other topics, African countries or issues. This excluded many vibrant blog communities around the world, but helped provide a more manageable scope of analysis with clear relevance to development practice.

I then identified and analysed blog-mediated conversations (Efimova and de Moor, 2005) involving blogs in this sample, selecting conversations that were particularly contentious, or that discussed blogging or involved negotiation over blog norms and etiquette. Sampled conversations included a debate over publishing first-hand accounts of violent conflict; discussions of professional motivation in international development and of the practice and influence of blogging; and controversies over gift-in-kind aid programs. For conversations involving a large number of blogs, I used search engines to find additional blogs that took part but were not otherwise identified through links. I stopped collecting data on a particular conversation when I had exhausted all relevant links, including trackbacks, or I had reached theoretical saturation (Corbin and Strauss, 2008: 263).

In total, I read hundreds of blog posts from 48 blogs (see Appendix A) and used QSR NVivo qualitative analysis software to code a sample of 87 separate posts, along with their associated comments (sometimes dozens per post), on 28 of these blogs. I also pulled basic information about the blog and bloggers from these 28 sampled blogs, and coded in detail the more permanent elements (such as the 'About Me' sections and blogrolls) of a subset of eight diverse and influential blogs.[11]

Case study

After exploratory analysis of all 28 blogs, I iterated between literature and data in developing the following analytic questions:

- How inclusive is the international development blogosphere as a public sphere (Habermas, 1991; Fraser, 2007)? Who contributes to blogs, who follows blogs, and who does not?
- Does the blogosphere "disregard status" (Habermas, 1991: 36)? If not, what status differentials are evident, and how do those affect the interactions that take place?
- If the blogosphere is an invisible college in which experts create, observe, and verify knowledge (Knorr-Cetina, 2007), what kind of expertise is valued and how do people signal or evaluate expertise?
- What are the norms and practices of discourse on the blogosphere – what Eliasoph called "civil practices", "political manners", and "etiquette" in public discourse (1998: 10, 21)? How are these established and enforced?

I address these questions with a case study based on 17 posts from 11 separate blogs, and supplementary sources, in which blogosphere participants debate a controversial gift-in-kind initiative. This case study represents a uniquely vibrant, wide-ranging, and influential conversation among the many that I sampled.[12] It was chosen as an 'extreme' case – see Gerring, (2007: 101–105) – in order to explore the mechanisms and characteristics of blog-mediated conversations, and because it offers insights on many of the theoretical questions of interest.

An introduction to the international development blogosphere

The blogosphere is in many ways a microcosm of the Internet as a whole: vast, eclectic, and in constant motion. This diversity and dynamism make it difficult to generalise about blogs, but the following sections provide an overview of common (though not universal) characteristics that distinguish blogs from other publication and discussion forums, as well as some observations on who participates in the blogosphere.

What is a blog?

One common feature of blogs is the presence of the author. Bloggers typically place themselves at the centre of what they create, leading some to say blogs are "narcissistic" (Papacharissi, 2010: 146) or rely too heavily on the personality of the blogger, "the messenger rather than the message" (as quoted in Hendel, 2009: 14). One study of a random sample of blogs (Papacharissi, 2007) found that the majority more closely resemble online diaries (Hookway, 2008) than citizen journalism. Even blogs that are predominantly focused on news, research, or other public-interest topics also frequently incorporate personal elements, including photos, humour, emotion, and biographical details, as in the examples in Table 12.1.

Another distinguishing characteristic of blogs is their dynamism (Barlow, 2008; Nayar, 2010). Because recent posts are listed first and most prominently, blogs look different from one visit to another. Active bloggers may post more than once each day – for instance, Blattman, Okafur, and the AidWatch bloggers averaged 46, 32, and 39 posts per month respectively in 2010 – and the most dynamic blogs also tend to be the most popular (Barlow, 2008: 75). As one scholar of cyber culture explains, "If there is a logic and 'spirit' for blogs, it would be that of *perpetual change*" (Nayar, 2010: 90). This frequent updating and near-instantaneous publication means that blogs sometimes have the most up-to-the-minute information about an emerging situation, and often discuss news stories, research findings, and other topics much sooner than print publications or even other online sources. One study frames this as a "first-mover advantage" (Farrell and Drezner, 2008: 17). Table 12.2 includes comments on the value of blog dynamism as well as vivid real-time accounts posted by bloggers covering the April 2011 crisis in Ivory Coast.

Blogs are also known for their interactivity and interconnectedness, as seen in conversations and co-production that take place among bloggers and their readers and across blogs and other websites (Herring *et al.*, 2005; Barlow, 2008; Farrell and Drezner, 2008; Walker, 2006). Empirical studies have shown that interconnected blogs are only a small subset of the blogosphere (Herring *et al.*, 2005), but others have demonstrated that readership is heavily skewed towards well-connected, influential 'A-list' blogs (Farrell and Drezner, 2008). Because readers are likely to discover a blog through links or search engines, these interconnected blogs are more typical of the experience of blog *readers*, even though they may not be representative of the total population of *blogs*. That said, it is also possible that the networks of development blogs resemble those of US political blogs, which Adamic and Glance (2005) found were clustered into internally dense but distinct networks separated by ideology. To the extent that these tightly linked networks of blogs repeat the same information or perspectives, the result can be "an echo chamber of mutual confirmation" (Kreutz 2009: 30).

The interconnectedness of blogs is created primarily through hyperlinks, embedded in posts or listed on blog sidebars. Links enrich the experience of readers by leading them to new sources of information or to interest-based online communities. Links are also an important tool for bloggers to collectively create,

Table 12.1 Presence of blogger

Blog characteristic	Illustration	
Presence of author		
About me	"I have worked in the field of international aid, relief and development since the early 1990s ... At different times I have been stranded, mugged, shot at, deathly ill, upgraded, dissed, pampered, promoted, in the vicinity of bomb blasts, detained, reprimanded, micro-managed, empowered, and ignored".	J n.d.(a)
	"The best jobs I ever held were (a) rock-climbing instructor, and (b) music store salesman. (I have become considerably less cool since that time) ... My work ethic and habits derive from two years cooking chicken at a vaguely militant KFC outlet. After a manager resembling Hulk Hogan forces you to clean grease traps, you can handle pretty much anything".	Blattman n.d. (a)
Personal accounts	"Grief and loss are an intrinsic part of this expat life... Everyone suffers, even those that stay behind, the ones that surround you and watch you turn your back and walk away mid sentence, while you walk through the little foot path you've put together over that abyss ... holding one child on each arm, praying to god that you'll be strong enough to get everyone safe to the other side".	Angelica 2011
	"So The Wife and I were blessed with a baby girl yesterday. A bundle of joy, six and a half pounds of loveliness, we couldn't be more elated. We'll have the outdooring (naming ceremony) in due course. Like all new parents, it's all about change, lots of change to our life, and an abundance of love".	Ofosu-Amaah 2011
Raw emotion	"I suffer in my flesh to see mutilated bodies on the pavement ... I suffer in my flesh to realize that a life is worth nothing but a bullet ... I scream, I scream my pain, and hear my body twitch as it is jolted by the sight of this waste, of this enormous human misery ... I can no longer hold back the tears at the thought that the history of violence on the continent still has a long way to go, worse, it is now commonplace and natural ..."	Njamkepo 2011
	"As all our readers know, Kate and I ordinarily rely on humor to help us face the unthinkable horrors with which our professions bring us into casual contact. However, there are times when laughter deserts me ... I am so thankful, every day, that I was lucky enough to have been born in a place where I can take the safety and survival of myself and my loved ones for granted".	Taub 2011

Table 12.2 Dynamism of blogs

Blog characteristic	Illustration	
Dynamism		
Frequent posting	"Web2.0 lore has it that frequency drives traffic, especially cross-linking, and eclectic helps. My favourite bloggers post very regularly but don't feel the need to do more than add a link and a comment to a good quote or source, or post a picture".	Cranston 2009
	"Duncan Green currently blogs five times per week. The majority of the FP2P readers (81%) think that this amount is 'about right'".	Zdravkovic 2010
Early source of news	"I'm not really all that smart, I just read a lot of blogs and discuss them a lot on Twitter … I'll still come out looking like a genius for knowing what's going to hit the *New York Times* 2–3 days ahead of when you read it and forward it to me asking me if I've seen it!"	Raftree 2010c
	"Thanks for the great blogs and feeds guys. I get a fairly large portion of my news through the two of you … I know, scary isn't it!"	Bengtsson 2011
Real-time accounts	"We have heard sustained gunfire since 5 am yesterday … Our water has been cut, and our power is intermittent … I hope that this insanity ends soon". A few hours later: "Things are escalating rapidly … It is nearly 10:30 pm right now, and we are under curfew … I just want to get information out there that things are getting real bad".	Seay 2011a
	"I'm hearing that it's the wild west in at least two neighborhoods. Killings in a factory outside Abidjan, widespread looting, some of which can be found on YouTube, and many deaths. On the ground reports are hard to come by, and are not making it into mainstream news reports".	Urbanregor 2011

elaborate upon, and evaluate ideas and information, and are the connections that facilitate cross-blog conversations. Linking to another blogger can signify respect or give credit for content, and it also helps circulate traffic. Some bloggers go beyond cross-linking and engage in guest-blogging or collaborate on a group blog, as shown in Table 12.3.

Co-production also takes place through the interactions among bloggers and their readers in blogs' comments sections (Walker, 2006). As shown in Table 12.3, readers provide feedback, pose questions, and express opinions. Bloggers read and respond to these comments, and may pose questions to readers, invite

Table 12.3 Interactivity and interconnectedness of blogs

Blog characteristic	Illustration	
Co-production		
Guest bloggers	William Easterly's *Aid Watch* blog involved 8 guest bloggers from 4 April to 19 May 2011, including representatives of academic and research institutions and a few practitioner-bloggers.	Easterly et al 2011
	Blogger J. at *Tales from the Hood* has guest-blogged on *Hand Relief International, On Motherhood & Sanity, Shotgun Shack,* and *Good Intentions Are Not Enough.*	J n.d.(b)
Group blogs	One of the most famous and influential blogs on the blogosphere, T*he Huffington Post*, has more than 9,000 bloggers.	Wikipedia 2011a
	International blog *Global Voices* is "a community of more than 300 bloggers and translators around the world who work together to bring you reports from blogs and citizen media everywhere".	Anonymous 2010b
Reader-generated content	"I got a great comment … on my last post …: '*Do you know of any good blogs from local aid workers? … It'd be great to read something from a different perspective …*' He's right of course". The blogger continued with a full post on the topic, and 31 commenters added links to "local" blogs.	Raftree 2010d
Comments and conversation		
Praise for blog	"I'm one of those silent subscribers on the end of your RSS feed. From NZ. Your post motivated me to drop you a note as a small gesture of support for the value I get from your blog".	Quinn 2009
	"This is Sam Grant from Ulaanbaatar, Mongolia.... I really enjoy your blog and consider it great form of ongoing education".	Grant 2009
Request for more	"I found your comment about aid workers as 'translators' intriguing. Can you elaborate on this idea?"	Dotter 2011
	"I agree with Rachel. I'd be interested to hear and think more about this concept".	Cothran 2011
	"@Rachael & @Tanya I've been thinking about this concept since watching the founder of Global Voices, Ethan Zuckerman's TED talk …"	Lentfer 2011b

(Continued)

Reader opinions	"[Starts by quoting original post:] 'In Africa, we have lost the meaning of life, the desire to live is gone.' (Certainly not true, these are phases that we must go through. Look at Europe today an[d] imagine how bloody European history was … Don't think there is a quick fix for Africa)".	Cadmun 2011
	"Changing the puppets in the French puppet show in Africa for their own interest has been an old unwritten French policy. The problem with many of us Africans, who cry foul to neocolonialism, is that we are just like the proverbial slave whose yoke of slavery was removed, but went back to his master to say he did not feel secured without the yoke".	Sam 2011

input, or incorporate reader-generated content into future posts. Bloggers also read and comment on other blogs, and lively discussions among bloggers and readers sometimes emerge over the norms of blogging or the content or tone of particular posts, as show in Table 12.4. Interactivity and co-production on the blogosphere can be seen as characteristic of both a public sphere and invisible college: of interaction around issues of public interest, and efforts to create, observe, verify, or validate knowledge.

Who blogs and for whom?

Blogs, like other Internet forums, are widely believed to open participation to a larger, more diverse group of people, but this claim is highly contested. In any case, there is little question that blogging has exploded in popularity and scope. By one count, there were in April 2011 more than 160 million blogs on the Internet, not including micro-blogging services such as Twitter, with tens of thousands more blogs added each day.[13] There are blogs on every imaginable topic, from motherhood to celebrity gossip to obscure intellectual pursuits, but the most popular topics are politics, technology, culture, and daily life (Technorati, 2011).

International development bloggers range from well-known experts (e.g., William Easterly) to unknown amateurs and those who blog anonymously (such as J at 'Tales from the Hood'). Some blog in an official capacity, whereas others explicitly state that their blogs are not connected to their employers. As Algoso argues in the first epigraph that opens this chapter, however, blogging crosses geographic barriers (Algoso, 2010); bloggers represent nearly all countries, regions, and demographic groups, and they blog in dozens of languages (Kumar et al., 2004; China Internet Network Information Center, 2007). Of the 28 blogs sampled for this chapter, 8 are affiliated with an organization, while 6 involve 2 or more bloggers. Among those bloggers who provide such information, 4 are Africans and 17 are from Western countries; and 14 are men and 9 women.[14] Blogs also differ in status and influence (Marlow, 2004; Song et al., 2007; Murphy, 2010d; McKenzie and Ozler, 2011), and a blog's level of influence can

Table 12.4 Interactivity and interconnectedness of blogs (cont.)

Blog characteristic	Illustration	
Conversations about norms		
Critique of tone	"I wonder whether you are being too harsh on the student commentator".	JB 2011
	"I agree with JB. I think you were hard on the kid. It's like this. If you see an infant crawling on the ground, can you really chastise that infant for not knowing how to walk?"	Cook 2011
	"@JB … I agree with you: while that students' comment was supremely unenlightened, perhaps I should have been harsh on her/his teacher instead?"	J 2011b
	"As the student commenter in question, I think perhaps my comment was poorly worded and misunderstood."	ert 2011
Debate over posting real-time accounts	"Escalating fears and violence thrive in low information environments. Explosive rumor is the greatest ally. The killing becomes self-fulfilling. I'm only suggesting that bloggers and commenters don't become part of the problem". (Discussing Seay 2011a, quoted in Table 12.3.)	Blattman 2011c
	"Absolutely agree, but there's a difference between rumor and an on-the -ground report from a reliable and knowledgeable source, no? I didn't post those e-mails lightly; the decision to do so involved a lot of discussion with the source and a lot of thought on my part. Of course it's only one story... but shouldn't that information be out there, especially when it's consistent with reports from reputable organizations[?] …"	Seay 2011b
	"Laura, I do agree with you that you had a responsibility to post what you heard. And I also agree that what you posted is not rumor … My only point was to make sure that other voices were heard as well".	Canavera 2011
	"I'm not suggesting one shouldn't report what's happening on the ground, especially first-hand accounts. I would draw a distinction between the first hand accounts and … posts that begin 'I don't know about if this will be technically a genocide?' My question would be whether these are … speculative and inflammatory".	Blattman 2011c
	"I agree with Laura in that the information should be out there, but also that it should be taken at face value (meaning one report, most likely biased, and highly localized)".	Bengtsson 2011

both be affected by (Farrell and Drezner, 2008) and affect (McKenzie and Ozler, 2011) the offline status of its readers. One prominent subgenre of the development blogosphere is economics blogs; a recent study of found that these blogs had a strong positive effect on dissemination of information and on the bloggers' reputation among economists, and, in some circumstances, could change readers' attitudes about the topics they covered (McKenzie and Ozler, 2011).

Many bloggers embed tracking software that collects basic information about who visits their blogs, but may not publicise this data. Of the 28 blogs analysed for this chapter, only 4 include links to readership numbers.[15] These 4 averaged between 2,252 (ClustrMaps, 2011a) and 21,453 (ClustrMaps, 2011b) visits per month in the last year.[16] Visits came from dozens if not hundreds of countries around the world, but US-based IP addresses were the most common on all 4 blogs (between 38% and 49% of visits) followed by those in the UK (ClustrMaps, 2011a, c). Even Dibussi Tande of 'Scribbles from the Den', an African blogger, received 41% of his visits from US-based IP addresses (ClustrMaps, 2011d).

In principle, free blog-hosting software and user-friendly templates allow anyone with basic Internet literacy and connectivity to begin blogging in moments, but in reality, various barriers to participation serve to significantly limit the blogosphere's inclusiveness. These barriers often (though not always) correlate with socioeconomic status, and they include the cost or difficulty of connecting to the Internet, differing levels of Internet literacy, and comfort with the blogosphere's norms and practices (Ashley *et al.*, 2009; Calhoun, 2004; DiMaggio *et al.*, 2004; Barlow, 2008; Hargittai and Hinnanti, 2008; Raftree, 2010b). Even people with high-quality Internet access and who are reasonably Internet-savvy may find the blogosphere bewildering (Barlow, 2008).

The One Million Shirts controversy

From time to time, the blogosphere explodes with passion, outrage, or heated debate around a single issue. In April 2010, a young American entrepreneur launched a new philanthropic endeavour: to collect one million donated T-shirts and send them to Africa (Anfeld, 2010). On 27 April, the initiative was reported on Mashable, an extremely popular technology blog (Elliott, 2010). A hashtag, #1millionshirts, was created on Twitter, and hundreds if not thousands of people weighed in.[17] Although the majority responded positively (Sadler, 2010c), there was resounding and often scathing criticism from the international development and African diaspora communities.[18] One prominent development blogger dubbed it 'one of the worst advocacy ideas of the year' (J., as quoted in Easterly, 2010), and an African blogger called it the "1 millionth stupid idea by wannabe do gooders" (Ruge, 2010a).

As the debate caught fire, dozens if not hundreds of development professionals, African residents, and others commented online or via Twitter. The initiative's founder responded in tweets, online videos, and comments on his and other blogs. On 30 April, just three days after the project first caught widespread public attention, the founder and several others participated in an open round-table discussion via Skype and teleconference, in order to discuss how the project might be improved (Murphy, 2010a). On 12 May, TIME covered the debate (Wadham, 2010). Over the next three months, in response to critics, One Million Shirts revised its project, invited a few blogger-critics to serve as advisors, and eventually closed down entirely (Sadler, 2010d, e).

During the most frenetic days, several participants called the debate revolutionary and a new paradigm for transparency and participation in development, thus echoing an argument made by some activists and observers of the blogosphere (Kreutz, 2009). As one blogger – initially one of the loudest critics and later one of those invited to help advise the initiative – wrote on 2 May:

> For the first time … social media, philanthropy, development, accountability, logistics, common sense, top-down solutions, and recipient voices all collided in spectacular fashion. Right out in the open. A project was launched, summarily bashed, killed and redirected in the span of 70 hours... The conversation that started with a single tweet, turned into an avalanche of blogs ripe with disdain from the aid corner for yet another ill-conceived top-down, Western-driven project. The conversation migrated from 140 characters of quibbles into full analytical blog posts, rants, and well-reasoned open letters.
>
> (Ruge 2010a)

Similarly, an expert on technology for development at UNICEF blogged that "this is how real-time information will inform the future of development work" (Fabian, 2010).

Revolutionary or not, this was certainly a uniquely influential moment for the international development blogosphere, when a discussion online not only caught the attention of professionals and lay people around the world, but directly affected practice. This offers an extreme case in which the unique characteristics of the blogosphere, and its potential impact, are laid bare. What does it suggest about the blogosphere as an alternative representation of international development? Does the blogosphere resemble a public sphere, a knowledge community, neither, or both? Who was included and excluded from the debate? How did participants signal their own expertise or evaluate the expertise of others, and how did that expertise and other factors affect participants' status within the debate? What norms and practices of the development blogosphere were visible in this process?

'Who speaks for whom':[19] inclusion, exclusion, and the missing million recipients

It is difficult to determine exact numbers, but the debate over One Million Shirts certainly involved a larger and more diverse group of people than would usually be consulted about a new project. Bloggers posted at least 62 separate posts, many of which drew dozens of comments, and One Million Shirts posted at least four in response (Schimmelpfennig, 2010a). Even more people participated via Twitter. The debate involved many development professionals, though perhaps an atypical subset (Barder, 2010; Thorpe, 2010b). The debate also involved a number of African citizens, on the continent and in the diaspora, and others living in or with some connection to African countries (African T-Shirt Company, 2010; Loomnie, 2010; Ruge, 2010a, b; Murphy, 2010a; Beye, 2011). One African blogger wrote that "for the first time, the voices of individual Africans were heard" (Ruge, 2010a). Moreover, most of the individuals involved in the debate – including many of the prominent bloggers – would not have had such an influential voice outside of the blogosphere.[20] By locating their conversation on the blogosphere, participants shifted the boundaries of debate, and redefined (at least for a moment) the criteria for determining who gets to be included.

On the other hand, participation by people from different backgrounds and nationalities, including a few of African descent, does not necessarily make the debate inclusive (Raftree, 2010b; Loomnie, 2010). The African citizens who participated, for instance, were an elite group: they read and wrote in English, had access to the Internet or Twitter, and were sufficiently savvy and connected to hear about the debate, understand its parameters, and feel confident to engage. Many were members of the African diaspora living in the United States or Europe. As mentioned earlier, significant barriers to online participation still exist, even more so in poor communities in the developing world (Calhoun, 2004; DiMaggio *et al.*, 2004; Barlow, 2008; Hargittai and Hinnanti, 2008; Raftree, 2010b). Technical jargon and programmatic complexity can also make it difficult for non-professionals to participate in debates over development. (Indeed, the One Million Shirts debate may have caught fire in part because it was relatively straightforward to understand.)

Notably absent from this debate, moreover, were any of the actual individuals meant to benefit from the initiative. One blogger called this the "elephant in the room" (Raftree, 2010b), and she and others asked what might have been different had the project's beneficiaries – many of whom would probably have gladly accepted the donated shirts – been involved in the conversation (Loomnie, 2010; Beye, 2011). This highlights an important paradox: development professionals may aspire to give beneficiaries a say in the design and implementation of projects, but they have to reconcile this with the fact that beneficiaries' preferences may sometimes contradict proven 'best practices' (Raftree, 2010b; Thorpe, 2010c). As the popular anonymous blogger J. (2010d) asked, "How and on what bases do we decide when to privilege the voice of aid recipients over the experience of aid providers, and vice versa?"

Thus, the specific controversy over One Million Shirts evolved into a broader discussion of whether opening development projects to public scrutiny online may require those who currently hold power in the industry to relinquish some control, and how blogs and social media might fundamentally change the nature of transparency, accountability, and participation in international development – in other words, how they might create a more inclusive public sphere (Morealtitude, 2010; @booksquirm, 2010). The dynamics of the conversation demonstrate, however, that this reshuffling of traditional relationships did *not* result in a flattening of hierarchy; instead, the participants adopted new criteria for assessing status and expertise.

Who listens to whom: expertise and status in a virtual debate

Despite the claims of some that the blogosphere is inherently inclusive and democratic, this case reveals that certain forms of expertise do matter in online conversations and that participants who are perceived as experts enjoy higher status. In fact, the relative openness of the blogosphere – the very characteristics that make it more inclusive of a variety of voices – may heighten the importance of signalling expertise. Because anyone may take part, participants must devise ways to distinguish among the multitude of perspectives and choose which viewpoints to weigh more strongly. Specifically, two types of expertise were valued most by participants in the One Million Shirts debate, as shown in the examples in Table 12.5: expertise gleaned through experience in the field of development, and expertise based on African identity or close familiarity. (Other types of expertise we might expect to matter, such as formal credentials, were less important.)[21] Participants took pains to signal one or both of these types of expertise and explicitly referenced the expertise of others as evidence of the validity of their arguments. The One Million Shirts founder, in contrast, was portrayed as naïve and ignorant because he lacked any experience in development or in Africa (Wadham, 2010).

Some people involved in the conversation argued that the views of Africans and development experts (a minority of participants) should outweigh the views of the majority of participants who lacked this expertise. The One Million Shirts founder, for instance, pointed to the fact that more people responded positively to his project than criticised it, and then asked, "Does the 80/20 rule apply here? Would you just say that all of the people saying good things don't know what they're talking about? And because someone has a blog and has been somewhere or done something in Africa at one time, they are right?" (Sadler, 2010c). Becky (2010) and several other commenters argued that the answer was 'Yes':

> Those 20 people … probably DO mean a whole lot more than those 600 people commending you … That's because those 20 people aren't just people with blogs who've 'done something in Africa at one time'. They're people who have dedicated their lives to aid work, to learning what works and what doesn't in international development, and they're people who ARE African, and can tell you first-hand what is needed in their individual communities.

From this perspective, the vaunted egalitarianism of blogs seems illusory, and the blogosphere comes to resemble more a knowledge community limited to experts than a Habermasian public sphere that "disregard[s] status" (Habermas, 1991: 36).

Sarcasm, outrage, and constructive criticism: norms and practices on display and under debate

The One Million Shirts debate not only reveals some of the norms and practices of the international development blogosphere, but also how these are established,

Table 12.5 Signals of and references to expertise

Type of expertise	Illustration	
Development experience		
	"For someone that has worked in international development assistance for a good part of my life (US AID, Peace Corps, PVO and PVO umbrella groups) ..."	Weeks 2010
	"I'm not an expert on T-shirt distribution in Africa but I do have 16 years experience working in international development, and my current work involves identifying and sharing good and bad practices in aid".	Thorpe 2010a
	"I spent four years in Thailand working on the tsunami recovery and for over two of those I ran an organization that tracked all the aid coming into the country. I speak Thai fluently and regularly spoke with the entire gamut of society ..."	Schimmelpfennig 2011
	"It's worth noting ... that the tirade of criticism that the [One Million Shirts] idea has generated has come from a core group of aid and development practitioners who between them probably have more than two centuries of professional aid experience. In other words, people who know what they're talking about".	Morealtitude 2010
African identity or familiarity		
	"The following is based on personal experience and study, which, in the grand scheme of things, is nothing compared to the experts out there – most importantly, the Africans who receive aid and then the professionals and academics who keep the industry on its toes".	Anstis 2010a
	"As an African who grew up in Africa and lived in the context, I can attest to that".	Beye 2011
	"As an African, I beg the 1 Mil Shirts campaign dies a slow death".	Ruge 2010a
	"Just a shout-out from one of the MANY T-shirt businesses in Africa saying we'd love an invite to the call (organized by Mobile Active)".	African T-Shirt Company 2010
	"I was working with the Anglican Church in Lubumbashi, DRC ... in the mid-1990s, when World Vision distributed boxes of clothing to churches in the town".	Scott 2010

negotiated, and enforced. In particular, two sets of norms were explicitly discussed: a widely shared norm privileging transparent and open public discussion, and contested norms that define the appropriate tone or style for blogging. Together, these examples demonstrate how participants in the blogosphere work to "create and enforce manners for political conversation" (Eliasoph, 1998: 10).

When criticism of his initiative first emerged, the One Million Shirts founder responded by asking people to take the discussion offline (Sadler, 2010b; Shaikh, 2010). This challenged one of the core norms of the blogging community: that discussions of public interest should take place in public, visible to anyone who might want to observe or take part. Bloggers rejected the founder's request that they e-mail or call him directly, insisting the debate continue online. Their reasoning is explicitly normative: "I am not calling. I am writing this blog post, because I think public discussion is important" (Shaikh, 2010), or "the conversations and debates about what is 'good aid' and what isn't need to happen out in the open: not via personal e-mail or direct phone call" (J, 2010b; also see Easterly, 2010). The bloggers successfully enforced this norm, and the conversation took place in full public view.

The One Million Shirts debate also revealed a degree of contestation among blogosphere participants over the appropriate tone and style of discourse. Some bloggers assumed a moderate, respectful approach (Anstis, 2010), whereas others were sarcastic and downright snarky in their criticism (for instance, J, 2010b; Easterly, 2010; and Ruge, 2010a, b).[22] Several bloggers and commenters, including the One Million Shirts founder, objected to the harsh commentary (Sadler, 2010c, d) and some bloggers wrote posts defending their snarky tone (Seay, 2010; J, 2010c; Schimmelpfennig, 2010b). Table 12.6 includes examples from both sides of the argument.

Sarcasm, biting criticism, and irreverent humour are common stylistic features of blog-based communication, not only in the debate over One Million Shirts but more broadly (Hendel, 2009; Murphy, 2010c). Indeed, one scholar argues that "the modern conception of snark" is an outgrowth of the Internet itself (Hendel, 2009: 6). Snark is credited with driving traffic to the most popular blogs (Hendel, 2009), and may help explain the explosive spread of the One Million Shirts debate. As one commenter said, "snarky, cutting, funny blog posts get read and disseminated and drive points home quicker, sharper, than hand holding and head patting would" (Rachel, 2010). Though attacked by some as unnecessarily nasty or aggressive (e.g., Denby, 2009), snark has also been defended as "a clarion call of frustrated outrage" (Sternbergh, 2009). Such outrage may play a role in the development bloggers' snarkiness; as Laura Seay (2010) wrote, "sometimes you have to laugh to keep from crying at how bad an aid idea is, how poorly thought-out a government decision was, or how horrible a situation innocent people have to endure".

A snarky tone is thus part of what distinguishes blogs from other representations of development, but its use represents a trade-off. As one study of snark in news items found, readers considered snarky items more engaging, entertaining, and humorous, but less credible and less desirable (Hendel, 2009). Snarky posts may capture attention and express the intensity of bloggers' opinions, but they

Table 12.6 Debating style and tone

Point of view	Illustration	
Criticising snark		
	"Judging by the response Sadler got from a group of foreign aid bloggers, you'd think he wanted to toss squirrels into wood chippers or steal lunch boxes from fourth-graders".	Wadham 2010
	"Why does everyone have to beat someone down? Why does everyone have to laugh and be sarcastic when someone, who is new to this world, is trying to help?"	Sadler 2010d
	"I feel as though the dissenting points are right, but why knock someone down a peg when you can make the choice to lift them up?"	Dave 2010
	"I'd like to believe that humility and respect … should be a central tenet for engagement in development … Coming out of the gate and calling someone a moron is only going to make them defensive and less likely to listen".	Stefanotti 2010
In defence of snark		
	"You need a thick skin to work in international aid. If you can't handle some snark, you probably can't handle all the misery your project will put you through as it gets going".	Shaikh, as quoted by Seay 2010
	"Snark is a communications tool like any other, used judiciously. It gets the point across. It gets attention".	Anonymous 2010a
	"Sometimes the hard things have to be said. Sometimes – often, actually – those to whom the hard things need to be said simply do not want to hear them … Very often just saying the unpopular thing, no matter how nice you are about it, makes you 'snarky'".	J 2010c
	"Despite all my time and effort spent calmly and reasonably educating donors and impromptu aid workers about in-kind donations, none of this has had the impact that a few snarky tweets and a blog post from Tales from the Hood has had on the public dialog. What I failed to do in 13 months of calm and reasonable dialog, J. managed to do in one day".	Schimmelpfennig 2010b

also risk undermining the credibility of the argument and turning off some readers. As a result, there is no consensus in the development blogging community on
whether and when a snarky tone is appropriate or effective. Instead, bloggers and
their readers debate the norms of style and etiquette – as they debate most issues
– out loud and in the open.

Conclusion

The blogosphere has emerged as a vibrant new forum for creating and disseminat-
ing knowledge and for debating the practice of development. It differs in important ways from other arenas in which development is discussed: it has the potential,
in at least some circumstances, to involve a larger and more diverse array of
voices; it is more interactive and dynamic; and it is more flexible in content, tone,
and style. It also has important limitations regarding its inclusiveness, the parity
of participation, and its effectiveness in influencing policy and practice. Proponents
of Internet-based forums, including blogs, have high hopes that they will be great
levellers, allowing more people to participate in public discourse and on a more
equal footing, and facilitating collaboration and exchange of knowledge across
national, cultural, and even linguistic boundaries. Others have suggested that the
blogosphere merely provides a new venue for elite dominance.

The case study presented in this chapter suggests that both positions are right.
For now, the blogosphere is open to broad participation but privileges certain
forms of expertise, and it remains dominated by a sophisticated and wired global
elite. During the One Million Shirts debate, the international development blogosphere behaved like both a public sphere and an invisible college.

On the one hand, the blogosphere provided space for people to come together
to "deal with matters of general interest" (Habermas, 1989: 231) and to "speak
public-spiritedly" (Eliasoph, 1998: 10). As Fraser (2007) predicted, however, the
transnational nature of this public sphere complicated its legitimacy and efficacy.
The blog-based debate over One Million Shirts included a large number and variety of voices, but it also unintentionally excluded any of the actual beneficiaries.
In principle, the debate was open and transparent, and bloggers firmly defended
this norm, but in reality most participants were members of a sophisticated global
elite. Despite claims that it heralded a new paradigm (Fabian, 2010; Ruge, 2010a),
the debate seemed instead to privilege existing status markers, particularly professional experience. The fact that African identity was also seen as a valued source
of expertise could prove more revolutionary to traditional hierarchies, but the
relative paucity of African voices in this case – and the absence of the project's
intended beneficiaries – left that potential largely untested. In the end, the debate
proved effective in changing the practices of one organisation, but many others
continue to engage in similar gift-in-kind schemes.[23]

On the other hand, the participants in One Million Shirts acted in some ways
as members of an invisible college. One blogger and expert in both development
and information technology, for instance, described the One Million Shirts conversation not only as public debate, but also an exercise in creating and synthesiz-
ing knowledge:

A development concept has been aired. It has been discussed. Literature has been created around it. Sources cited. Histories referenced. A community built. Real-time input, from 'the field' has just become an actor in 'aid/charity/development'. Voices from places which otherwise would never be represented spoke. People in 'the place' ('Africa') where the 'aid' was going got to weigh in. Experts who had not met each other were able to share experience, synthesize and create new literature on giving, aid, and development theory (Fabian 2010).

When seen from this perspective, the slice of the blogosphere sampled here may ultimately be best understood as an elite, knowledge-based public sphere: inclusive of a wide array of voices, but with many populations excluded; addressing issues of public interest, but in a way that privileges certain forms of expertise; inviting input from anyone who wishes to engage, but also acting to verify and reject those ideas that the high-status participants deem substandard. The norms that emerge also reflect this hybrid between a public sphere and invisible college: discussions are interactive and occur openly, as in a public sphere, but viewpoints are given differing weights according to the perceived expertise of their proponents.

Appendix A

Table 12.7 lists the blogs I followed while preparing this chapter and all blogs sampled for the analysis. Most are concerned with international development, but a few cover other topics. This list should not be considered comprehensive or representative, nor should it be seen as an endorsement.

Table 12.7 "Blogroll"

Blog name	URL
...My Heart's in Accra	http://www.ethanzuckerman.com/blog/
A View from the Cave	http://www.aviewfromthecave.com/
Admitting Failure	http://www.admittingfailure.com/
Aid Thoughts	http://aidthoughts.org/
Aid Watch	http://aidwatchers.com/
AidBlogs	http://aidblogs.org/
Black Looks	http://www.blacklooks.org/
Blood and Milk	http://bloodandmilk.org/
Can? We? Save? Africa?	https://savingafrica.wordpress.com/
Chris Blattman	http://chrisblattman.com/
Crooked Timber	http://crookedtimber.org/
Dani Rodrik's weblog	http://rodrik.typepad.com/dani_rodriks_weblog/
Find What Works	https://findwhatworks.wordpress.com/
From Poverty to Power	http://www.oxfamblogs.org/fp2p/
Global Voices in English » Development	http://globalvoicesonline.org/-/topics/development/
Good Intentions Are not Enough	http://goodintents.org/

(*continued*)

Table 12.7 (continued)

Blog name	URL
Hauser Center, Humanitarian & Development NGOs	http://hausercenter.org/iha/
How Matters	http://www.how-matters.org/
Huffington Post	http://www.huffingtonpost.com/
Jimmy Kainja	http://jimmykainja.co.uk/
Koranteng's Toli	http://koranteng.blogspot.com/
la vidaid loca	https://lavidaidloca.wordpress.com/
Mashable	http://mashable.com/
MobileActive	http://www.mobileactive.org/
Nicholas D. Kristof	http://kristof.blogs.nytimes.com/
On Motherhood and Sanity	http://onmotherhoodandsanity.blogspot.com/
One Million Shirts	http://1millionshirts.org/blog/
Orgtheory.net	https://orgtheory.wordpress.com/
Owen abroad	http://www.owen.org/
Pambazuka News: Blogging Africa	http://www.pambazuka.org/en/category/blog/
Pop!Tech	http://poptech.org/blog/
Project Diaspora	http://projectdiaspora.org/blog/
Scarlett Lion	http://www.scarlettlion.com/
Scatterplot	https://scatter.wordpress.com/
Scribbles from the Den	http://www.dibussi.com/
Siena Anstis	http://siena-anstis.com/
Stratosphere International Community Education	http://stratosphereinternational.ca/#blog
Tales from the Hood	http://talesfromethehood.com/
Texas in Africa	http://texasinafrica.blogspot.com/
The Rising Continent	http://therisingcontinent.wordpress.com/
Three Avocadoes	http://www.nonprofitcoffee.com/
Timbuktu Chronicles	http://timbuktuchronicles.blogspot.com/
Wait … What?	http://lindaraftree.wordpress.com/
Wanderlust	http://morealtitude.wordpress.com/
We (Heart) Failure	http://weheartfailure.com/
Whydev.org	http://www.whydev.org/
World Society, Institutional Theory, and Globalization	https://worldpolity.wordpress.com/
Wronging Rights	http://wrongingrights.blogspot.com/

Notes

1 Many thanks for their helpful comments and suggestions to the editors of this volume and an anonymous reviewer, and to Jason Beckfield, Christopher Marquis, Kathleen McGinn (who first suggested the idea of an elite public sphere), and Kristin Perkins of Harvard University. Fault for any remaining flaws is, of course, mine alone.

2 Facebook and Twitter are Web-based social networking services in which users create and share content.

3 A 'blog' (or 'weblog') is an online diary with regular posts 'arranged in reverse chronological order and archived' (Papacharissi, 2010: 145). 'Bloggers' create and contribute to blogs, and the 'blogosphere' is the ecosystem of blogs.

4 Many of these blogs could be categorised as 'aid blogs', focused on the policy and practice of international development assistance, but the development blogosphere is

much broader. My sample includes, for instance, blogs like Global Voices, with citizen journalism from a variety of developing countries, and Timbuktu Chronicles, which covers technology and entrepreneurship in Africa. See below and Appendix A for more information on the full sample and sampling strategy.

5 Some scholars disagree and describe the Internet (including blogs) as a private sphere (Papacharissi, 2010).

6 A few development bloggers have themselves referred to the blogosphere as an epistemic community (e.g., Algoso, 2011).

7 As mentioned above, many but not all of these blogs focus on international aid or development assistance; others cover development-related issues and/or developing countries but are not 'aid blogs'. Any preponderance of aid blogs in my sample is not by design, but is a reflection of which blogs are read by development professionals, and which blogs those link to.

8 The development professionals included former colleagues and personal and professional contacts, and individuals interviewed for a separate study. A blogroll is a list of other blogs that are recommended by a blogger.

9 I could not sample on readership statistics because very few blogs publicise readership statistics, and there is no agreed 'A-List' for international development blogs.

10 I included blogs that are more technical and others that are more personal; blogs written by unknown figures and others written by well-known experts; and blogs with critical or alternative voices, as well as those with more mainstream perspectives.

11 These include three of the most well-known development blogs (two of which won Aid Blog Awards in 2010); two popular African bloggers (one a winner of the 2008 Black Weblog Awards), and three other active practitioner-bloggers. Of the nine bloggers on these eight blogs, three are women, four are men, two of the men are African, and one is anonymous. The blogs are ... *My Heart's in Accra, AidWatch, Blood and Milk, Chris Blattman, Good Intentions Are Not Enough, Scribbles from the Den, Tales from the Hood,* and *Timbuktu Chronicles.*

12 I discovered later that this conversation was selected by aid bloggers and readers as 'Best Debate' in the 2010 Aid Blog Awards (Murphy, 2010b, d).

13 These statistics come from *BlogPulse,* an "automated trend discovery system for blogs" run by the Nielson company. On 18 April 2011 at 10 a.m., *BlogPulse* identified 160,103,053 blogs, with 80,306 new blogs and more than 1 million posts indexed in the last 24 hours (*BlogPulse,* 2011).

14 Information about bloggers came from their 'About Me' or similar sections, or from other publicly available online profiles. In cases where blogs had two bloggers, I included demographic information for both (if available). For larger group blogs, I included information only about the bloggers whose posts were included in the sample.

15 As of 15 June 2011, these were *Tales from the Hood, Wait ... What?, Scribbles from the Den,* and ... *My Heart's in Accra.* All use ClustrMaps, which provides statistics and readers' geographic locations (ClustrMaps, 2011a, b, c, d). A few other bloggers provided statistics but with little background on the data (Green, 2009; Blattman, n.d. b).

16 These are visits, not unique visitors.

17 Hashtags are words or phrases prefaced by a hash symbol. They are used to track mentions of a particular topic (Messina, 2010). According to one blogger, there were more than 1,500 tweets on the topic by the afternoon of April 28, plus posts by many widely-read development bloggers (Fabian, 2010).

18 Critics called the initiative wasteful and potentially harmful, and objected to aspects of its messaging. They cited the negative impact of free shirts on local businesses; the cost of shipping; the portrayal of Africa and Africans as desperate and undifferentiated; and the use of photos of unnamed shirtless Africans, including many children. Many argued that clothing was rarely (if ever) a priority for impoverished communities.

19 This phrase comes from Loomnie (2010).

20 Some of the bloggers are seasoned professionals working as managers, technical experts, or consultants (e.g., Barder, n.d.; Shaikh, n.d.). However, according to their public profiles, few held positions with the most powerful development organisations, and few are particularly prominent (offline) industry experts. A notable exception is William Easterly. (Some of the other prominent bloggers in my sample, including Chris Blattman and Duncan Green, did not engage in the One Million Shirts conversation). Of course, as McKenzie and Ozler (2011) have shown, the act of blogging may improve bloggers' offline reputations.

21 A few cited academic expertise, but this was less common (Joe, 2010; Loomnie, 2010).

22 The term 'snarky' is frequently used on the blogosphere to mean snide, sarcastic, and sharply critical, or as a recent study defined it, as having "attributes of wit, aggression, informality, irony, and critique" (Hendel, 2009: 1).

23 Bloggers discussed several gift-in-kind initiatives in the year following the One Million Shirts debate, most prominently World Vision's distribution of Superbowl T-shirts (Freschi, 2011). These initiatives are sometimes dubbed #SWEDOW ('Stuff We Don't Want'), a term coined by a blogger (J, 2010a).

References

@booksquirm (2010) "Comment". On Raftree (2010b).

Adamic, L. A., and N. Glance (2005), "The political blogosphere and the 2004 US election: Divided they blog". *Proceedings of the 3rd International Workshop on Link Discovery.* Chicago: ACM, pp. 36–43.

African T-Shirt Company (2010) "Comment", 29 April. On Fabian (2010).

Algoso, D. (2010) "A Grad Student's Guide to the International Development Blogosphere". *Find What Works* [blog], 30 November. Available at: https://findwhatworks.wordpress. com/2010/11/29/a-grad-students-guide-to-the-international-development-blogosphere/ (accessed 18 April 2011).

Algoso, D. (2011) "Would You Hire Me If I Disagreed with You? What If I Did It Publicly?". *Find What Works* [blog], 3 March. Available at: http://findwhatworks. wordpress.com/2011/03/04/would-you-hire-me-if-i-disagreed-with-you-what-if-i-did-it-publicly/ (accessed 17 October 2011).

Anfeld, S. (2010"We've Got a Press Release!".*1 Million T-Shirts* [blog], Available at: http://1millionshirts.org/blog/weve-got-a-press-release/#content (accessed 11 May 2011).

Angelica (2011) "On Nostalgia—Moving on". *On Motherhood & Sanity* [blog], 13 June. Available at: http://onmotherhoodandsanity.blogspot.com/2011/06/dreaming-of-child-hood-photo-post.html (accessed 30 June 2011).

Anonymous (2010a) "Comment", 30 April. On Seay (2010).

Anonymous (2010b) "About". *GlobalVoices* [blog], 11 November. Available at: http:// globalvoicesonline.org/about/ (accessed 21 April 2011).

Anstis, S. (2010) "An Open Letter to 1 Million Shirts". *Siena Anstis* [blog], 28 April. Available at: http://siena-anstis.com/2010/04/an-open-letter-to-1millionshirts/ (accessed 09 May 2011).

Ashley, H., J. Corbett, D. Jones, B. Garside, and G. Rambaldi (2009) "Change at hand: Web 2.0 for development". In J. Corbett, B. Garside, G. Rambaldi, and H. Ashley (eds.), *Change at Hand: Web 2.0 for Development.* London: International Institute for Environment and Development and Technical Centre for Agricultural and Rural Cooperation, pp. 28–33, available at: http://pubs.iied.org/pdfs/14563IIED.pdf (accessed 10 November 2012).

Barder, O. (n.d.) "Owen's CV". *Owen Abroad* [blog], available at: http://www.owen.org/ about/cv (accessed 9 November 2012).

Barder, O. (2010) "Aid Projects and the Wisdom of Crowds". *Owen Abroad* [blog], 29 April. Available at: http://www.owen.org/blog/3286 (accessed 9 May 2011).

Barlow, A. (2008) *Blogging America: The New Public Sphere*. Westport: Praeger Publishers.

Becky (2010) "Comment", 28 April. On Anstis (2010).

Bengtsson, V. (2011) "Comment", 2 April. On Blattman (2011b).

Beye, H. (2011) "Comment", 8 February. On Schimmelpfennig (2010a).

Blattman, C. (n. d. a) "About Me". *Chris Blattman* [blog]. Available at: http://chrisblattman.com/about/biosketch/ (accessed 10 April 2011).

Blattman, C. (n. d. b) "Official Bio". *Chris Blattman* [blog]. Available at: http://chrisblattman.com/about/official-bio/ (accessed 10 April 2011).

Blattman, C. (2011a) *Chris Blattman* [blog]. Available at: http://chrisblattman.com/.

Blattman, C. (2011b) "Mass Killing in Abidjan?". *Chris Blattman* [blog], 1 April. Available at: http://chrisblattman.com/2011/04/01/mass-killing-in-abidjan/ (accessed 10 April 2011).

Blattman, C. (2011c) "Comments", 2 April. On Blattman (2011b).

Blattman, C. (2011d) "Introducing Our Baby Girl, Amara Blattman Annan!". *Chris Blattman* [blog], 5 April. Available at: http://chrisblattman.com/2011/04/05/introducing-our-baby-girl-amara-blattman-annan/ (accessed 10 April 2011).

BlogPulse (2011) "BlogPulse Stats". Available at: http://www.blogpulse.com/ (accessed 18 April 2011).

Cadmun (2011) "Comment", 13 April. On Njamkepo (2011).

Calhoun, C. (2004) "Information technology and the international public sphere". In D. Schuler and P. Day (eds.), *Shaping the Network Society: The New Role of Civil Society in Cyberspace,* Cambridge: MIT Press, pp. 229–251.

Canavera, M. (2011) "Comment", 2 April. On Blattman (2011b).

China Internet Network Information Center (2007) "CNNIC Releases 2007 Survey Report on China Weblog Market Number of Blog Writers Reaches 47 million Equalling One Fourth of Total Netizens". Available at: http://www.cnnic.net.cn/html/Dir/2007/12/27/4954.htm (accessed 13 July 2011).

ClustrMaps (2011a) *Clickable Map of All Visitors: lindaraftree.wordpress.com.* Available at: http://www3.clustrmaps.com/counter/maps.php?url=http://lindaraftree.wordpress.com (accessed 15 June 2011).

ClustrMaps (2011b) *Visitors to ethanzuckerman.com/blog.* Available at: http://clustrmaps.com/counter/maps.php?url=http://ethanzuckerman.com/blog (accessed 15 June 2011).

ClustrMaps (2011c), *Visitors to talesfromethehood.wordpress.com.* Available at: http://www3.clustrmaps.com/counter/maps.php?url=http://talesfromethehood.wordpress.com (accessed 15 June 2011).

ClustrMaps (2011d) *Visitors to www.dibussi.com.* Available at: http://clustrmaps.com/counter/maps.php?url=http://www.dibussi.com (accessed 15 June 2011).

Corbin, J. M., and A. Strauss (2008) *Basics of Qualitative Research*, 3rd ed. Thousand Oaks: Sage Publications.

Cothran, T. (2011) "Comment", 31 March. On Lentfer (2011a).

Cranston, P. (2009) "Comment", 16 February. On Green (2009).

Dave. (2010) "Comment", 28 April. On Anstis (2010).

DeLong, J. B. (2006) "The invisible college". *Chronicle of Higher Education, 52:* 47–60.

Denby, D. (2009) *Snark: It's Mean, It's Personal, and It's Ruining Our Conversation.* New York: Simon and Schuster.

DiMaggio, P., E. Hargittai, C. Celeste, and S. Shafer (2004) "Digital inequality: From unequal access to differentiated use". In K. Neckerman (ed.), *Social Inequality*. New York: Russell Sage Foundation, pp. 355–400.

Dotter, R. (2011) "Comment", 30 March. On Lentfer (2011a).

Easterly, W. (2010) "Nobody Wants Your Old T-Shirts". *AidWatch* [blog], 27 April. Available at: http://aidwatchers.com/2010/04/nobody-wants-your-old-t-shirts/ (accessed 9 May 2011).

Easterly, W., and L. Freschi (2011) "Author Archives: Guest Blogger". *Aid Watch* [blog]. Available at: http://aidwatchers.com/author/guest/ (accessed 3 June 2011).

Efimova, L., and A. de Moor (2005) 'Beyond personal webpublishing: An exploratory study of conversational blogging practices', paper presented to the *38th Hawaii International Conference on System Sciences (HICSS-38)*, Hawaii, 3–6 January. Available at: https://doc.novay.nl/dsweb/Get/Version-22432/HICSS05_Efimova_deMoor. pdf (accessed 6 February 2013).

Eliasoph, N. (1998) *Avoiding Politics: How Americans produce Apathy in Everyday Life*. Cambridge: Cambridge University Press.

Eliasoph, N., and P. Lichterman (2003) "Culture in interaction". *American Journal of Sociology*, 108(4): 735–794.

Elliott, A. (2010) "1MillionShirts Leverages Social Media to Help Clothe Africa". *Mashable* [blog], 27 April. Available at: http://mashable.com/2010/04/27/1millionshirts-wants-tees/ (accessed 11 May 2011).

ert (2011) "Comment", 14 March. On J (2011a).

Fabian, C. (2010) "1 Million Tweetshirts—How to Fail Fast and With Scrutiny". *MobileActive* [blog], 28 April. Available at: http://www.mobileactive.org/1-million-tweetshirts-how-fail-fast-and-scrutiny (accessed 9 May 2011).

Farrell, H., and D. W. Drezner (2008) "The power and politics of blogs". *Public Choice*, 134(1–2): 15–30.

Fourcade, M. (2009) *Economists and Societies: Discipline and Profession in the United States, Britain, and France, 1890s to 1990s*. Princeton: Princeton University Press.

Fraser, N. (2007) "Transnationalizing the public sphere: On the legitimacy and efficacy of public opinion in a post-Westphalian world". In S. Benhabib, I. Shapiro, and D. Petranovi (eds.), *Identities, Affiliations, and Allegiances*. Cambridge: Cambridge University Press, pp. 45–66.

Freschi, L. (2011) "In Zambia, Pittsburgh Won the Super Bowl: Why is World Vision Perpetuating Discredited T-Shirt Aid?". *AidWatch* [blog], 14 February. Available at: http://aidwatchers.com/2011/02/in-zambia-pittsburgh-won/ (accessed 9 May 2011).

Gerring, J. (2007) *Case Study Research: Principles and Practices*. New York: Cambridge University Press.

Grant, S. (2009) "Comment", 17 February. On Green (2009).

Green, D. (n.d.) "About This Blog". *From Poverty to Power* [blog]. Available at: http://www.oxfamblogs.org/fp2p/ (accessed 30 April 2011).

Green, D. (2009) "Who reads this blog? Analysis of the first hundred posts". *From Poverty to Power* [blog], 16 February. Available at: http://www.oxfamblogs.org/fp2p/?p=155 (accessed 30 April 2011).

Habermas, J. (1989) "The public sphere". In S. Seidman (ed.), *Jurgen Habermas on Society and Politics: A Reader*. Boston: Beacon Press, pp. 231–236.

Habermas, J. (1991) *The Structural Transformation of the Public Sphere*. Cambridge: MIT Press.

Hargittai, E., and A. Hinnant (2008) "Digital inequality: Differences in young adults' Use of the Internet". *Communication Research*, 35(5): 602–621.

Hendel, J. (2009) "A Study of Snark in News Media". Master's Thesis. Department of Journalisam, University of Missouri. Available at: https://mospace.umsystem.edu/xmlui/handle/10355/5350 (accessed 6 February 2013).

Herring, S. C., I. Kouper, J. C. Paolillo, L. A. Scheidt, M. Tyworth, P. Welsch, E. Wright, and N. Yu (2005) "Conversations in the Blogosphere: An Analysis 'From the Bottom Up'", paper presented at the *38th Hawaii International Conference on System Sciences (HICSS-38)*, Hawaii, 3–6 January.

Hookway, N. (2008) "'Entering the blogosphere': Some strategies for using blogs in social research". *Qualitative Research,* 8(1): 91–113.

J (n. d. a) "About". *Tales from the Hood* [blog]. Available at: http://talesfromthehood. com/about-2/ (accessed 24 May 2011).

J (n. d. b) "Curriculum Vitae". *Tales from the Hood* [blog]. Available at: http://talesfro-methehood.com/curriculum-vitae/ (accessed 24 May 2011).

J (2010a) "#SWEDOW". Tales from the Hood [blog], 20 April. Available at: http://tales-fromethehood.com/2010/04/20/swedow/ (accessed 9 May 2011).

J (2010b) "1,000,000 Shirts". *Tales from the Hood* [blog], 27 April. Available at: http:// talesfromethehood.com/201004/27/1-million-shirts/ (accessed 9 May 2011).

J (2010c) "Not Ready to Make Nice". *Tales from the Hood* [blog], 28 April. Available at: http://talesfromethehood.com/2010/04/28/not-ready-to-make-nice/ (accessed 9 May 2011).

J (2010d) "Comment", 2 May. On Raftree (2010b).

J (2011a) "Dear Students—1: Motivation". *Tales from the Hood* [blog], 13 March. Available at: http://talesfromethehood.com/2011/03/13/dear-students-1/ (accessed 1 May 2011).

J (2011b) "Comment", 14 March. On J (2011a).

J (2011c) "Dear Students—2: Sacrifice". *Tales from the Hood* [blog], 20 March. Available at: http://talesfromethehood.com/2011/03/20/dear-students-2/ (accessed 1 May 2011).

Joe (2010) "Comment", 3 May. On Raftree (2010b).

Knorr-Cetina, K. (1999) *Epistemic Cultures: How the Sciences Make Knowledge.* Cambridge: Harvard University Press.

Knorr-Cetina, K. (2007) "Culture in global knowledge societies: Knowledge cultures and epistemic cultures". In M. D. Jacobs and N. W. Hanrahan (eds.), *The Blackwell Companion to the Sociology of Culture.* Oxford: Blackwell, pp. 65–79.

Kreutz, C. (2009) "Exploring the potentials of blogging for development". In J. Corbett, B. Garside, G. Rambaldi, and H. Ashley (eds.), *Change at Hand: Web 2.0 for Development.* London: International Institute for Environment and Development and Technical Centre for Agricultural and Rural Cooperation, pp. 28–33. Available at: http://pubs.iied.org/ pdfs/14563IIED.pdf (accessed 10 November 2012).

Kumar, R., J. Novak, P. Raghavan, and A. Tomkins (2004) "Structure and evolution of blogspace". *Communications of the ACM,* 47(12): 35–39.

Lentfer, J. (2011a) "If I had only known…". *How Matters* [blog], 30 March. Available at: accessed 1 May 2011 (http://www.how-matters.org/2011/03/30/if-i-had-only-known/).

Lentfer, J. (2011b) "Comment", 31 March. On Lentfer (2011a).

Loomnie (2010) "Comment", 3 May. On Raftree (2010b).

Luo, X. R., J. Zhang, and C. Marquis (2011) *Accounting to the Public: Internet Activism and Corporate Social Responsiveness in Emerging Markets*, unpublished mimeo.

Marlow, C. (2004) "Audience, Structure and Authority in the Weblog Community". Paper presented to the International Communication Association Conference, New Orleans, 27–31 May. Available at: http://rockngo.org/wp-content/uploads/mt/archives/ICA2004. pdf (accessed 6 February 2013).

McKenzie, D., and B. Ozler (2011) "The Impact of Economics Blogs". World Bank Policy Research Working Paper no. 5783, Washington, DC: The World Bank. Available at: http://blogs.worldbank.org/impactevaluations/working-paper-the-impact-of-econom-ics-blogs (accessed 21 September 2011).

Messina, C. (2010) "Hashtags". Wiki article, 3 June. Available at: http://twitter.pbworks.com/w/page/1779812/Hashtags (accessed 13 May 2011).

Morealtitude (2010) "Afrika Can Haz T-Shirtz? (or How New Media can Value-Add to the Aid Industry)". *Wanderlust* [blog], 29 April. Available at: http://morealtitude.wordpress.com/2010/04/29/afrika-can-haz-t-shirtz/ (accessed 9 May 2011).

Murphy, T. (2010a) "#1millionshirts Phone Conf Running Blog". *View From The Cave* [blog], 30 April. Available at: http://www.aviewfromthecave.com/2010/04/1millionshirts-phone-conf-running-blog.html (accessed 9 May 2011).

Murphy, T. (2010b) "The ABBAs: Best Aid Debate for Going 'On and On and On'". *A View From The Cave* [blog], 20 December. Available at: http://www.aviewfromthecave.com/2010/12/abbas-best-aid-debate-for-going-on-and_20.html (accessed 15 June 2011).

Murphy, T. (2010c) "The ABBAs: The Name of the Game is Snark". *A View From The Cave* [blog], 21 December. Available at: http://www.aviewfromthecave.com/2010/12/abbas-name-of-game-is-snark.html (accessed 15 June 2011).

Murphy, T. (2010d) "The ABBAs Wrap Up". *A View From The Cave* [blog], 24 December. Available at: http://www.aviewfromthecave.com/2010/12/abbas-wrap-up.html (accessed 15 June 2011).

Nayar, P. K. (2010) *An Introduction to New Media and Cybercultures*. Chichester: Wiley-Blackwell.

Njamkepo, G. (2011) "Cote D'Ivoire—Weeping With Every Tear in My Body". *Scribbles from the Den* [blog], 12 April. Available at: http://www.dibussi.com/2011/04/cote-divoire-weeping-with-every-tear-in-my-body.html (accessed 8 May 2011).

Ofosu-Amaah, K. (2011) "Parenthood". *Koranteng's Toli* [blog], 8 March. Available at: http://koranteng.blogspot.com/2011/03/parenthood.html (accessed 24 May 2011).

Okafur, E. (2011) *Timbuktu Chronicles* [blog]. Available at: http://timbuktuchronicles.blogspot.com/.

Papacharissi, Z. A. (2007) "Audiences as Media Producers: Content Analysis of 260 Blogs". In M. Tremayne (ed.), *Blogging, Citizenship and the Future of Media*. New York: Routledge, pp. 21–38.

Papacharissi, Z. A. (2010) *A Private Sphere: Democracy in a Digital Age*. Cambridge: Polity Press.

Quinn, D. (2009) "Comment", 16 February. On Green (2009).

Rachel (2010) "Comment", 29 April. On Seay (2010).

Raftree, L. (2010a) "Comment", 29 April. On Anstis (2010).

Raftree, L. (2010b) "The Elephant in the Room". *Wait... What?* [blog], 2 May. Available at: http://lindaraftree.wordpress.com/2010/05/02/the-elephant-in-the-room/ (accessed 9 May 2011).

Raftree, L. (2010c) "Why Aid and Development Workers Should Be Reading Blogs". *Wait...What?* [blog], 30 November. Available at: http://lindaraftree.wordpress.com/2010/11/30/why-aid-and-development-workers-should-be-reading-blogs/ (accessed 30 April 2011).

Raftree, L. (2010d) "Where are the Local Aid and Development Worker Blogs?". *Wait... What?* [blog], 9 December. Available at: https://lindaraftree.wordpress.com/2010/12/09/where-are-the-local-aid-and-development-worker-blogs/ (accessed 30 April 2011).

Ruge, T. (2010a) "FOUND: The 1 Millionth Stupid Idea by Wannabe Do Gooders". *Project Diaspora* [blog], 28 April. Available at: http://projectdiaspora.org/2010/04/28/found-the-1-millionth-stupid-idea-by-do-gooders/ (accessed 9 May 2011).

Ruge, T. (2010b) "And You Will Hear Our Voices". *PopTech* [blog], 2 May. Available at: http://poptech.org/blog/and_you_will_hear_our_voices (accessed 9 May 2011).

Sadler, J. (2010a) "What Happens with the T-Shirts in Africa?". *1 Million T-Shirts* [blog], 19 April. Available at: http://1millionshirts.org/blog/what-happens-with-the-t-shirts-in-africa/ (accessed 11 May 2011).

Sadler, J. (2010b) "Comment", 27 April. On Sadler (2010a).

Sadler, J. (2010c) "Comments", 28 April. On Anstis (2010).

Sadler, J. (2010d) "Listening, Learning and Shifting Focus". *1 Million T-Shirts* [blog], 3 May. Available at: http://1millionshirts.org/blog/listening-learning-and-shifting-focus/ (accessed 9 May 2011).

Sadler, J. (2010e) "A Hard Blog Post to Write… 1 Million Shirts". *1 Million T-Shirts* [blog], 28 July. Available at: http://1millionshirts.org/blog/a-hard-blog-post-to-write-1millionshirts/ (accessed 11 May 2011).

Sam (2011) "Comment", 20 April. On Njamkepo (2011).

Schimmelpfennig, S. (2010a) "What Aid Workers Think of the 1 Million Shirts Campaign". *Good Intentions Are Not Enough* [blog], 28 April. Available at: http://goodintents.org/aid-debates/1-million-shirts-campaign (accessed 9 May 2011).

Schimmelpfennig, S. (2010b) "Why do Aid Bloggers Get Snarky". *Good Intentions Are Not Enough* [blog], 29 April. Available at: http://goodintents.org/in-kind-donations/aid-bloggers-get-snarky (accessed 11 May 2011).

Schimmelpfennig, S. (2011) "Comment", 8 February. On Schimmelpfennig (2010a).

Schofer, E., and W. Longhofer (2006) 'The Structural Sources of Associational Life', unpublished mimeo.

Schofer, E., F. O. Ramirez, and J. W. Meyer (2000) "The effects of science on national economic development, 1970 to 1990". *American Sociological Review*, 65(6): 866–887.

Schussman, A., and J. Earl (2004) "From barricades to firewalls? Strategic voting and social movement leadership in the Internet age". *Sociological Inquiry*, 74(4): 439–463.

Scott, C. (2010), "Comment", 30 April. On Morealtitude (2010).

Seay, L. (2010) "Snark Isn't a Bad Thing". *Texas in Africa* [blog], 29 April. Available at: http://texasinafrica.blogspot.com/2010/04/snark-isnt-bad-thing.html (accessed 11 May 2011).

Seay, L. (2011a) "From Abidjan". *Texas in Africa* [blog], 1 April. Available at: http://texasinafrica.blogspot.com/2011/04/from-abidjan.html (accessed 12 April 2011).

Seay, L. (2011b) "Comment", 2 April. On Blattman (2011b).

Shaikh, A. (n.d.) "Alanna Shaikh: Resume". *Alanna Shaikh* [web page]. Available at: http://www.alannashaikh.com/?page_id=2 (accessed 9 November 2012).

Shaikh, A. (2010) "Say No to Old Clothes". *Blood and Milk* [blog], 28 April. Available at: http://bloodandmilk.org/2010/04/28/say-no-to-old-clothes/ (accessed 9 May 2011).

Song, X., Y. Chi, K. Hino, and B. Tseng (2007) "Identifying opinion leaders in the blogosphere". In *Proceedings of the Sixteenth ACM Conference on Information and Knowledge Management*. New York: ACM, pp. 971–974.

Stefanotti, J. (2010) "Comment", 29 April. On Seay (2010).

Sternbergh, A. (2008) "Snark Attack". *New York,* 28 December. Available at: http://nymag.com/arts/books/reviews/53159/ (accessed 10 November 2012).

Taub, A. (2011) "This Is Not Good: From Abidjan". *Wronging Rights* [blog], 1 April. Available at: http://wrongingrights.blogspot.com/2011/04/this-is-not-good-from-abidjan.html (accessed 12 April 2011).

Technorati (2011) "Top 100 Blogs". Available at: http://technorati.com/blogs/top100/ (accessed 18 April and 11 May 2011).

Thorpe, I. (2010a) "Comment", 28 April. On Schimmelpfennig (2010a).

Thorpe, I. (2010b) "Comment", 29 April. On Barder (2010).

Thorpe, I. (2010c) "Comment", 3 May. On Raftree (2010b).

Urbanregor (2011) "Comment", 1 April. On Blattman (2011b).

Wadham, N. (2010) "Bad Charity? (All I Got Was This Lousy T-Shirt!)". *TIME*, 12 May. Available at: http://www.time.com/time/world/article/0,8599,1987628,00.html (accessed 9 May 2011).

Wagner, C. S. (2008) *The New Invisible College: Science for Development*. Washington, DC: Brookings Institution Press.

Walker, D. M. (2006) "Blog commenting: A new political information space". *Proceedings of the American Society for Information Science and Technology,* 43(1): 1–10.

Wall, M. (2005) "'Blogs of war': Weblogs as news". *Journalism,* 6(2): 153–172.

Weeks, J. (2010) "Comment", 2 May. On Ruge (2010b).

Yang, G., and C. Calhoun (2007) "Media, civil society, and the rise of a green public sphere in China". *China Information,* 21(2): 211–236.

Zdravkovic, A. (2010) 'From Poverty to Power (FP2P) Blog Evaluation". Oxford: Oxfam, available at: http://www.oxfamblogs.org/fp2p/wp-content/uploads/FP2P-blog-evaluation.ppt (accessed 30 April 2011).

Part VII

Conclusion

13 Conclusion

Popular representations of development – taking stock, moving forward

David Lewis, Dennis Rodgers and Michael Woolcock

The central theme of this book has been that distinctive and useful insights into the phenomenon of development can be gleaned by going beyond the source material most familiar to academics and practitioners – namely, research monographs, journal articles and policy reports – to include contributions from popular culture. We hope to have shown that novels, films, television and (most recently) social media, if viewed with a correspondingly critical eye, can convey a rich understanding of how development processes are encountered, experienced and explained by different actors and in turn embraced, endured or rejected by them. It bears repeating that we are not, of course, arguing that traditional empirical analyses – to which all three of us have actively contributed throughout our careers – should be discarded, or that policy responses to (say) poverty rates can be discerned with equal validity through national household surveys and postmodernist paintings. To borrow from the language of economics, popular culture is not a substitute for but a complement to orthodox social science, in the sense that it provides a different but potentially fruitful epistemological entry point for engaging with complex phenomena (such as 'development') that encompass all aspects of human life.

At the same time, we also hope that this volume has shown how popular representations of development can often convey powerful truths in subtle and wide-ranging ways that no regression table or ethnographic account can possibly achieve. For this reason alone, it is clearly imperative to engage with popular representations, and to consider them seriously. The broad themes emerging from this volume have been addressed in the Introduction. In this concluding chapter, we seek to identify particular issues that together we believe could constitute an initial future research agenda for the widening community of scholars, practitioners and artists interested in engaging with – or, better yet, actively producing – popular representations of development.

We do not claim to be the first to raise these particular concerns; they have been addressed with varying degrees of frequency by others, and doubtless there are already specific contributions to them of which we are unaware. Moreover, these issues are merely indicative, since a number of other equally valid topics could readily be proposed. They do, however, seem to us to be areas that might yield especially fruitful insights, and which are important not just for scholars and practitioners but for the broader communities of citizens who, directly or indirectly, find themselves encountering the vicissitudes of 'development' and wanting – or being asked or required – to make a tangible response. The topics we focus on are the following:

1. How popular representations of development can successfully compete or even supersede social scientific representations from the perspective of both conceptual and empirical representation.
2. The political economy of popular representations of development, including the differences between 'independent' versus 'mainstream' media, and the way that popular media productions shape debates.
3. The extent to which popular representations of development provide *alternative* critiques that allows for the articulation of views that would be unacceptable – even dangerous or libelous – if expressed in more orthodox mediums.

We address each of these issues in turn below, before then concluding with some thoughts about the more general question of how one might implement supportable strategies for fruitfully integrating the insights of 'orthodox' and 'popular' representations of development into policy research.

An agenda for future engagement with popular representations of development

(1) Popular representations of development versus social scientific representations

Can popular representations actually contribute to, or even extend and challenge, formal scholarship? Coming from a social science perspective, as we do, this is obviously an important consideration, even if notions of authenticity and validity are obviously variable both within and between disciplines (and more broadly, as we mention in chapter 2). In this regard, however, it is interesting to note the historian Philip Zelikow's recent commentary on the 2012 Steven Spielberg film *Lincoln*, which he argues provides a novel answer to a question that has long vexed students of the 16th US presidency, an answer that is not to be found in any of the academic texts on which the film's script was ostensibly based. The puzzle is why Lincoln pushed so hard in January 1865 for the passage of the 13th Amendment to the US Constitution – which would abolish slavery – when he had just won a national election and by waiting only a few months longer would have had an even larger majority in Congress and thus face a stronger likelihood that the highly controversial amendment would pass. The film's novel answer is that Lincoln was worried the civil war could end at any moment, and with it the provisional powers that laws passed in wartime against slavery – in particular, the Emancipation Act – afforded. These laws would lapse in peacetime, meaning that a different sequence of legal manoeuvers would have to be put in motion to end slavery, which would in turn be far more difficult to devise and to control politically, and would thus face a correspondingly uncertain fate.

Zelikow further argues that the film's producers were in a position to present this novel and (to his mind) persuasive answer as a serious one – that is, not merely a convenient contrivance for dramatic (and thus commercial) effect – because of their deep commitment to understanding their subject matter. "Because filmmakers can often devote far more resources to research than scholars can, because the sheer process of a painstaking reconstruction of a past world can itself yield insights about it, it has always been possible that filmmakers might add to our collective historical understanding, rather than either popularizing or debasing it. In Mr. Spielberg's *Lincoln*, that possibility is happily realized".[1] Likewise, as the field of popular representations of development matures, we hope one of its emergent features will be its capacity to extend and challenge academic and policy research on a regular basis.[2]

More generally, popular representations of development are often better at demonstrating and exploring the salience of key social scientific concepts. Take Karl Marx's (1979: 108) famous observation that people "make their own history, but they do not make it just as they please; they do not make it under circumstances chosen by themselves, but under circumstances directly encountered, given and transmitted from the past". This distinction between agency and structure – between individual choices and broader processes shaping what constitutes the array of choices themselves and the normative basis on which decisions (if any) are made – is one of the foundations of social science, but also one whose salience is not self-evident. Introductory (and advanced) social science texts can explore this distinction in great verbal detail, but it is perhaps most powerfully conveyed through popular mediums, which enable multiple lives, layers and even realities – and the interplay between them – to be captured simultaneously. Novels (e.g., John Steinbeck's *The Grapes of Wrath*, Umberto Eco's *The Name of the Rose*, William Boyd's *Any Human Heart*), films (e.g., *Hotel Rwanda*, *The Constant Gardener*, *The Matrix*) and television programmes (e.g., *The Wire*, *Game of Thrones*, *Deadwood*) are deftly able to capture the contingencies of life, the broad factors that shape the domain of individual decisions, of what is even think-able, say-able and do-able at any given time and place.[3]

Similarly, other important concepts such as counterfactuals – what would have happened to a particular person or peoples but for the interjection of a particular event (see Lebow, 2010; Morgan and Winship, 2007) – can be more powerfully demonstrated in popular mediums than in social scientific texts. Films such as *It's a Wonderful Life*, *Closing Doors* and *Run Lola Run*, for example, graphically portray the different fates that await a protagonist when one seemingly minor event (such as making or not making a train) takes place. Science fiction is a particularly instructive medium in this regard, with 'alternative history' one of the genre's oldest literary traditions; novels such as William Gibson and Bruce Sterling's *The Difference Engine*, Orson Scott Card's *Pastwatch: The Redemption of Christopher Columbus* or S. M. Stirling's *The Peshawar Lancers* offer elaborate and detailed visions of different development paths, respectively in nineteenth century Britain, fifteenth century Americas and twenty-first century India.

Understanding counterfactuals is very important in programme evaluation, since it is important to be able to distinguish between the effect of the programme (if any) and other processes going on at the same time; if one is assessing the impact of a job training programme, for example, it is important to qualify one's conclusions on the basis of whether the broader economy is booming or in recession. But in programme evaluation, and academic social science more generally, the counterfactual is unobservable – the same people cannot both participate and not participate in a development project – so it must be imputed or inferred (e.g., by establishing a 'control' group). Popular mediums face no such 'real-world' restriction, and are thus able to perfectly (literally) identify what would have happened. These are but two examples among many of how complex concepts in social science are fruitfully conveyed and explored in popular mediums, and which demonstrate how a dialogue between them can be mutual beneficial.

Many of the contributions to this volume highlight how popular representations of development are able to provide distinctive and instructive insights, in part because they have the luxury of being able to ignore the strictures of representing the messiness of 'actually existing reality' and are instead able to present more universal ideal-types. Sometimes, however, this benefit derives from the nature of the subject matter itself. Take, for example, the ambiguities of successful development – for example, empowering marginalised groups, enhancing the quality and accessibility of justice institutions, and expanding health care and education for all. The pressures emanating from successful development are especially salient when they evince challenges to prevailing forms of authority, identity and expectations; this is an issue that is arguably underexplored in the social sciences, but is frequently addressed in popular mediums.

Consider, for example, the numerous Indian films and television soap operas in which young women begin to assert their independence as a result of their education and heightened awareness of rights, often embodied in the pursuit of 'love marriages' and professional careers, only to elicit the wrath of their more 'traditional' fathers, bosses, mothers-in-law and community leaders, who may or may not eventually come around.[4] Aggregated to the societal level, such tensions, left unchecked, can become violent, as is currently evident in the context of the 'Arab Spring'. Although empirical social science might be able to assess (albeit crudely) this dynamic at the aggregate level (e.g., Acemoglu and Robinson, 2009), this has rarely been the case at an individual level, and popular mediums can far more deftly capture the complicated, contentious and multivalent ways in which constituent elements of modernity – social equality, the rule of law, heightened individualism, the primacy of professional norms over familial/communal obligations – unfold out of lockstep with one another, thereby generating both inner personal tensions and outward societal 'anomie'/'alienation' (e.g., Naguib Mahfouz's *Adrift on the Nile*).[5] At the same time, too often such schisms and the conflicts they generate are interpreted as 'failed' development when in fact they are often a direct consequence of *successful* development (Barron, Diprose and Woolcock, 2011). Certainly, as a long line of social theorists from Marx to Merton and beyond have argued, political revolutions are more likely when economic conditions are *improving*, not declining.[6] Although often pointed out, the dynamics underlying these complex processes have not always been clearly conveyed by social scientific works. On the other hand, the best popular representations of development – whether novels or films, as we highlight in our chapters in this volume on the 'fiction of development' and the 'projection of development' – often explore them in careful and compelling ways.

(2) The political economy of popular representations of development

In general terms, it is common to hear assertions to the effect that 'small-scale', 'independent', 'budget' or 'alternative' media are less craven to elite economic interests than 'mainstream' outlets, and that this makes a difference to their coverage of issues such as immigration, poverty, exclusion, justice or the efficacy of foreign aid. But is small really beautiful in this respect? Although the relationship between big news conglomerates and particular individuals and groups is well known – for example, News Corp and Rupert Murdoch – the political economy of the supposedly 'independent' press is more opaque. Similarly, why would low-cost, 'niche' films be better able to "speak truth to power"? Are they not also captured by either their own commercial imperatives (with fewer margins for error) or the demands for simplicity that effective advocacy often requires? Another potentially instructive related avenue for analysis concerns the 'mainstream' media's coverage of key development issues vis-à-vis that of the expanding number of niche outlets made possible via the Internet. Some of the chapters in this volume begin to explore these concerns, but much remains to be done. It is likely that this will be a controversial area of investigation, open to abuse and appropriation by different interest groups, as recent – and often heated – debates concerning the right to information and open vs. closed Internet access have demonstrated.

Another important political economy question concerns the way that popular media productions shape – by design or default, helpfully or harmfully – the contours of cultural difference, social critique and political debate. In particular, what are the pitfalls of looking at popular representations of development when the measure of their legitimacy becomes their popularity? *Kony 12*, for example, an independent video produced in the United States campaigning for the capture of the leader of the Lord's Resistance Army (a revolutionary group in rural Uganda), was viewed an astonishing 95 million times on YouTube in less than nine months after its release in March 2012: is this a harbinger of things to come in the world of development advocacy? To what extent do such productions confuse or clarify complex realities? What role, if any, can development educators play in helping viewers engage more critically and constructively with such material (see Schomerus, Allen and Vlassenroot, 2012)? *Kony 12*, of course, pales in comparison to PSY's *Gangnam Style*, a music video that has been viewed (at the time of writing) over a *billion* times in less than five months. It has become the most-viewed video in history, and yet is in effect a critique of the social pretensions accompanying economic inequality in South Korea.[7] This level of global 'impact' – or at least exposure – for notionally progressively causes is unprecedented, and yet it is not unambiguously clear how, why or even whether such high-profile coverage drives or reflects change.[8] Even if such productions could be demonstrated to have a positive 'effect', these technologies can presumably be deployed for harmful and divisive purposes. In any event, as the costs of such productions come down, and with them ever-lower barriers to entry for non-professionals, we are surely (for better or worse) on the eve of a vast explosion and 'democratization' of visual representations of development.

In a related manner, it is not clear to what extent social media is actually contributing to more inclusive, effective and accountable politics, whether with regards to development or beyond. The chapters in this volume are relatively sanguine about the extent to which new social technologies are qualitatively shifting the tone and terms of development debates, but in other circles one frequently hears concrete examples of how mobile phones, tweets, etc., are providing a new generation of 'tools' for promoting real-time 'social accountability' (e.g., in the context of the Arab Spring). Under what conditions, then, do social media actually accomplish these more noble and ambitious political objectives? Or are these expectations just unrealistically high, a product of excessive initial enthusiasm? Much remains to be understood about whether and how new social media will alter, or merely consolidate, existing, state-society-business relations.

(3) Popular representations of development as alternative critique

Popular representations of development often allow both 'providers' and/or 'recipients' of development interventions to articulate views – whether critical or supportive – that would be unacceptable (even seditious) in more orthodox mediums. Just as political cartoons can convey ideas regarding the folly (or worse) of a presiding government that would never be tolerated if expressed verbally or in writing, so too can popular representations allow those most affected by development to convey potentially radical sentiments in relatively safety or anonymity. Parables, metaphors, songs, graffiti, plays, allegories and fables have long served this role for oppressed or 'occupied' groups around the world; a good example is the famous sixteenth century Nicaraguan play *El Güegüense*, which pokes fun at the Spanish colonial regime's treatment of the indigenous population. The deployment of such narrative forms to discuss development issues seems to us to be relatively under-explored, yet a potentially interesting avenue for research. It would also be interesting to compare and contrast more 'traditional' instances of such forms of narrative resistance with newer ones such as viral videos or Internet memes.

At the same time, popular representations of development need not only be a tool of the marginalised, and can also be used by those in positions of power wanting to provide a trenchant critique of the enterprise they find themselves overseeing, but without wanting to jeopardise their careers by ignoring standard confidentiality clauses in contractual undertakings. Phil Montgomery, for example, a 25- year veteran of managing large development projects in Asia and Melanesia, found writing a novel, *Two Roads East* (see Montgomery, 2012), the most powerful and insightful (and therapeutic!) medium by which to convey the perennially awkward mix of virtue and vice, wonder and frustration, accomplishment and disappointment, hope and personal sacrifice, that defined his working life on an everyday basis. One can discuss sensitive matters such as widespread corruption and technical incompetence in a novel with a frankness and detail that would undoubtedly lead to suspension if articulated more formally in a traditional public forum (such as a newspaper op-ed or an open letter to a professional association). More generally, an increasing number of public figures are resorting to fiction in order to talk about their life histories, from British writer Salman Rushdie's fictional autobiography (*Joseph Anton*) to former French President Valery Giscard D'Estaing's romantic novel about a purported affair with Princess Diana of Wales (*La Princesse et le Président*).

Conclusion

The above are the types of issues, among many, that traditional empirical analysis does not, and in some important methodological sense cannot, adequately address, at least on their own; as a partial correction, it is our hope that the ideas and insights on display in popular culture can be given their rightful place and accorded the scholarly dignity to which they are entitled. Precisely because 'development' reflects and encompasses all aspects of human endeavor and experience, a more complete rendering of them demands that we take seriously the array of ways by which and through whom they are conveyed by and to others. Development studies and development policy will surely be the richer for doing so.

John Harriss' contribution to this volume shows how combining popular and scholarly approaches to development is both relatively easy to do and very rewarding in teaching. Students appreciate being shown how seemingly arcane conceptual issues such as 'poverty traps' play out in high-profile books and films such as Frank McCourt's *Angela's Ashes*. But how far can such an approach inform research, which is clearly a different enterprise? How can a more mutually beneficial dialogue be sustained between popular and scholarly representation of development in ways that enhance the quality and relevance of our knowledge claims? What are the constraints that we need to overcome – indeed, should we want to overcome them – to make this a reality? These epistemological challenges ultimately speak to perennial tensions within and between different forms of knowledge claiming.

One hopeful and recent example of a potential avenue to explore might be the highly acclaimed book by Katherine Boo (2012), *Behind the Beautiful Forevers: Life, Death, and Hope in a Mumbai Slum*. Although overtly a work of narrative nonfiction, Boo is able to convey for a broad audience a highly visceral sense of the sights, smells, energy, tensions and tragedies of this setting in ways that combines the best aspects of popular and scholarly sensibilities without being recognizably either. Her book draws on three years of investigative reporting and an array of related academic studies, yet eschews the formal discussions of theory and method that scholarly works require in favor of a 'tone' one would usually associate with a novel. The book has been criticised for failing to engage with the 'big question' issues that inevitably frame poverty in India (Breman, 2012), and also for the construction of its characters, whose inner thoughts are presented in an omniscient manner that is problematic, not least because Boo admits to hardly speaking the local slum language. But there is no doubting the power and empathy of the book, which in recent years has probably done more than any other non-fiction book to bring the issue of Indian slum life to the forefront of mainstream concern. For this reason, we can only hope that the praise and prizes her book has received encourages others to pursue similarly innovative (and courageous) 'hybrid' forms of communication.

Notes

1 For further discussion, see Zelikow (2012). In a different domain, Yoshino (2011) uses the plays of Shakespeare as the raw material for a scholarly inquiry into the nature of justice (see also Posner 2009). Similarly, Kern (2004) uses nineteenth and twentieth century novels to provide a detailed cultural history of causal inference.

2 At the same time, Guardian journalist Simon Jenkins (2013) cautions that many "filmmakers happily play fast and loose with the facts", pointing to the way that films such as *Argo* or *Zero Dirty Thirty*, respectively about the 1979 Teheran hostage crisis and the killing of Osama bin Laden, both contain major historical inaccuracies, despite their being captioned 'true stories'. Jenkins suggests that such inaccuracies exist (perhaps legitimately) "to advance a cause" or simplify a narrative, but then goes on to argue that "if 'true story' appears in a film's preamble and is clearly wrong, the film should carry certificate L, for lie", in order that viewers would at least "know where we stood".

3 The usage of Western examples of novels, films, and television here is largely because these are the ones with which we are most familiar; we are acutely conscious of the vast array of excellent contributions of this sort that are non-Western in origin and content (e.g., the films of Satyajit Ray, the novels of Chinua Achebe and Gabriel García Márquez, to name but three).

4 Students in a graduate class taught by one of us (Woolcock) have shown how these dynamics play out in India across class differences, using as source material advertisements for sanitary pads – a looming multi-billion dollar business as India's middle class rapidly expands, but one which demands engagement with an issue heretofore deemed virtually unbroachable in private, let alone public, settings. Advertisements targeting (or invoking) the wealthy, for example, feature young attractive women living on their own in luxurious high-rise apartments, enjoying a seemingly care-free life in which they revel in their financial, social and sexual autonomy (a life whose pleasures are enhanced, it is inferred, because of the women's use of a particular company's pads), whereas advertisements promoted to lower middle-class women feature, for example, a humble domestic scene in which a conservatively dressed young woman is surrounded by vigilant family members, most notably a scowling father, who ponder the merits of the woman's request to be allowed an evening out to socialise with friends. It is clear the only view that really counts is that of the father, who grudgingly allows his daughter her wish upon learning (or being persuaded) that she is getting better grades at school, made possible in part because of her use of pads (see also Stanley's [2012] helpful analysis of intra-family tensions as rendered in contemporary Indian soap operas).

5 In popular culture, these classic social scientific concepts enjoyed a brief implicit moment in the spotlight in the early 1980s with a famous song by the British rock band Dire Straits called 'Industrial Disease'. Indeed, one of the song's many deft lines

is "Sociologists invent words that mean 'industrial disease'". Though we have not explored music in this book, it too can convey powerful themes and resonant emotions in ways scholarly and policy texts cannot hope to do; indeed, it is an ancient and universal medium for doing so.

6 Consider, for example, Alex de Tocqueville (1856: 323–24), who argued that "Nothing short of great political genius can save a sovereign who undertakes to relieve his subjects after a long period of oppression. The evils which were endured with patience so long as they were inevitable seem intolerable as soon as a hope can be entertained of escaping from them. The abuses which are removed seem to lay bare those which remain, and to render the sense of them more acute; the evil has decreased, it is true, but the perception of the evil is more keen ..."

7 Similarly, in the opposite direction, one could also point to the wildly popular television musical show *Glee*, whose stars include those who are overweight, physically disabled and socially awkward, and which unabashedly promotes a message of inclusion and tolerance.

8 Paluck (2009) provides an encouraging assessment of one such effort, in which villagers in Rwanda who listened to a radio broadcast promoting peaceful relations based on mutual respect and understanding subsequently reported having more durably prosocial views towards rival ethnic groups than a 'control' group who did not listen to such a broadcast. Even so, much remains to be learned about (a) the conditions under which popular representations promote, consolidate or erode inter-group relations; (b) which particular topics in development seem more or less amenable to generating durable shifts in public perceptions through their portrayal in popular media; and (c) how this effectiveness varies across different 'scales' or modes of production (e.g., amateur versus budget versus blockbuster films).

References

Acemoglu, D. and J. Robinson (2009) *Economic Origins of Dictatorship and Democracy.* New York: Cambridge University Press.

Barron, P., R. Diprose, and M. Woolcock (2011) *Contesting Development: Participatory Projects and Local Conflict Dynamics in Indonesia.* New Haven: Yale University Press.

Boo, K. (2012) *Behind the Beautiful Forevers: Life, Death, and Hope in a Mumbai Undercity.* New York: Knopf.

Breman, J. (2012). "Life and Death in Annawadi". *New Left Review*, 78: 152–170.

Jenkins, S. (2013). "Should 'true story' films such as Zero Dark Thirty and Argo be rated L for lie?", *The Guardian* "Comment is Free" online commentary, 17 January, available at: http://www.guardian.co.uk/commentisfree/2013/jan/17/zero-dark-thirty-argo (accessed 5 February 2013).

Kern, S. (2004) *A Cultural History of Causality: Science, Murder Novels, and Systems of Thought.* Princeton: Princeton University Press.

Lebow, R. (2010) *Forbidden Fruit: Counterfactuals in International Relations.* Princeton: Princeton University Press.

Marx, K. (1979) *The Eighteenth Brumaire of Louis Bonaparte* in *Karl Marx/Friedrich Engels, Collected Works*, vol. II. New York: International Publishers.

Montgomery, P. (2012) *Two Roads East.* Sydney: Philip Montgomery.

Morgan, S. L., C. Winship (2007) *Counterfactuals and Causal Inference: Methods and Principles for Social Research.* New York: Cambridge University Press.

Paluck, E. L. (2009) "Reducing Intergroup Prejudice and Conflict Using the Media: A Field Experiment in Rwanda". *Journal of Personality and Social Psychology*, 96(3): 574–587.

Posner, R. (2009) *Law and Literature,* 3rd ed. Cambridge: Harvard University Press.

Schomerus, M., T. Allen, K. Vlassenroot (2012) "Kony 12 and the Prospects for Change: Examining the Viral Campaign". *Foreign Affairs*, 13 March.

Stanley, A. (2012) "On Indian TV, 'I Do' Means to Honor and Obey the Mother-in-Law". *New York Times*, 25 December.

de Tocqueville, A. (1856) *The State of Society in France Before the Revolution of 1789.* London: John Murray.

Yoshino, K. (2011) *A Thousand Times More Fair: What Shakespeare's Plays Teach Us About Justice.* New York: HarperCollins.

Zelikow, P. (2012) "Steven Spielberg, Historian". *New York Times* online commentary, 29 November, available at: http://opinionator.blogs.nytimes.com/2012/11/29/steven-spielberg-historian/ (accessed 5 February 2013).

Index